Urban Voices

Urban Voices

Accent Studies in the British Isles

Edited by

Paul Foulkes
*Department of Linguistics and Phonetics,
University of Leeds*

and

Gerard J. Docherty
Department of Speech, University of Newcastle

A member of the Hodder Headline Group
LONDON

First published in Great Britain in 1999 by
Arnold, a member of the Hodder Headline Group
338 Euston Road, London NW1 3BH

http://www.arnoldpublishers.com

Co-published in the United States of America by
Oxford University Press Inc.
198 Madison Avenue, New York, NY 10016

British Library Cataloguing in Publication Data
A catalogue entry for this book is available from the British Library

Library of Congress Cataloging-in-Publication Data
A catalog record for this book is available from the Library of Congress

Production Editor: Julie Delf
Production Controller: Sarah Kett
Cover Design: Andy McColm

ISBN 0 340 70608 2
ISBN 0 340 74105 8 (cassette)
ISBN 0 340 75952 6 (cd)

Typeset by J&L Composition Ltd, Filey, North Yorkshire

What do you think about this book? Or any other Arnold title?
Please send your comments to feedback.arnold@hodder.co.uk

Contents

Acknowledgements

We wish to thank all the contributors for their willingness to present their data in the way we requested, and for submitting on occasions to unforeseen editorial pressures. All contributions were read by at least two referees, and we are grateful to the reviewers of the submissions. We are also grateful to the anonymous reviewers of the original book proposal.

In compiling this book we have benefitted greatly from the continuing advice and encouragement of Jim Milroy, Lesley Milroy, Jane Stuart-Smith, Dominic Watt and Ann Williams.

Thanks also to the following, who all assisted us in some way during the production of this book: Joan Colman, John Esling, Kimberley Farrar, Paula Hall, Barry Heselwood, Mark Jones, Paul Kerswill, Ghada Khattab, Rona Kingsmore, John Kirk, Carmen Llamas, Catherine Macafee, Ronald Macaulay, Mike MacMahon, April McMahon, Berenice Mahoney, Diane Nelson, Joan Rahilly, Euan Reid, Mark Sebba, Tim Shortis, Katie Wales, Victoria Watt, and John Wells.

We are grateful to the International Phonetic Association for permission to reproduce the International Phonetic Alphabet; to John Laver and the Edinburgh University Press for permission to reproduce the Vocal Profile Analysis Protocol in Stuart-Smith's chapter; and to Simon Patterson and London Regional Transport for permission to use *The Great Bear* on the cover.

Map of locations featured in *Urban Voices*

THE INTERNATIONAL PHONETIC ALPHABET (revised to 1993, updated 1996)

CONSONANTS (PULMONIC)

	Bilabial	Labiodental	Dental	Alveolar	Postalveolar	Retroflex	Palatal	Velar	Uvular	Pharyngeal	Glottal
Plosive	p b			t d		ʈ ɖ	c ɟ	k g	q ɢ		ʔ
Nasal	m	ɱ		n		ɳ	ɲ	ŋ	N		
Trill	ʙ			r					R		
Tap or Flap				ɾ		ɽ					
Fricative	ɸ β	f v	θ ð	s z	ʃ ʒ	ʂ ʐ	ç ʝ	x ɣ	χ ʁ	ħ ʕ	h ɦ
Lateral fricative				ɬ ɮ							
Approximant		ʋ		ɹ		ɻ	j	ɰ			
Lateral approximant				l		ɭ	ʎ	L			

Where symbols appear in pairs, the one to the right represents a voiced consonant. Shaded areas denote articulations judged impossible.

CONSONANTS (NON-PULMONIC)

Clicks		Voiced implosives		Ejectives	
ʘ	Bilabial	ɓ	Bilabial	'	Examples:
ǀ	Dental	ɗ	Dental/alveolar	p'	Bilabial
!	(Post)alveolar	ʄ	Palatal	t'	Dental/alveolar
ǂ	Palatoalveolar	ɠ	Velar	k'	Velar
‖	Alveolar lateral	ʛ	Uvular	s'	Alveolar fricative

OTHER SYMBOLS

ʍ Voiceless labial-velar fricative

w Voiced labial-velar approximant

ɥ Voiced labial-palatal approximant

ʜ Voiceless epiglottal fricative

ʢ Voiced epiglottal fricative

ʡ Epiglottal plosive

ɕ ʑ Alveolo-palatal fricatives

ɺ Alveolar lateral flap

ɧ Simultaneous ʃ and x

Affricates and double articulations can be represented by two symbols joined by a tie bar if necessary.

k͡p t͡s

VOWELS

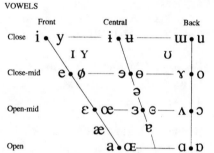

Where symbols appear in pairs, the one to the right represents a rounded vowel.

SUPRASEGMENTALS

ˈ	Primary stress	
ˌ	Secondary stress	ˌfoʊnəˈtɪʃən
ː	Long	eː
ˑ	Half-long	eˑ
˘	Extra-short	ĕ
ǀ	Minor (foot) group	
‖	Major (intonation) group	
.	Syllable break	ɹi.ækt
‿	Linking (absence of a break)	

DIACRITICS

Diacritics may be placed above a symbol with a descender, e.g. ŋ̊

̥	Voiceless	n̥ d̥		̈	Breathy voiced	b̤ a̤		̪	Dental	t̪ d̪
̌	Voiced	s̬ t̬		̰	Creaky voiced	b̰ a̰		̺	Apical	t̺ d̺
ʰ	Aspirated	tʰ dʰ		̼	Linguolabial	t̼ d̼		̻	Laminal	t̻ d̻
̹	More rounded	ɔ̹		ʷ	Labialized	tʷ dʷ		̃	Nasalized	ẽ
̜	Less rounded	ɔ̜		ʲ	Palatalized	tʲ dʲ		ⁿ	Nasal release	dⁿ
̟	Advanced	u̟		ˠ	Velarized	tˠ dˠ		ˡ	Lateral release	dˡ
̠	Retracted	e̠		̴	Pharyngealized	tˤ dˤ		̚	No audible release	d̚
̈	Centralized	ë		̴	Velarized or pharyngealized	ɫ				
̽	Mid-centralized	e̽		̝	Raised	e̝		(ɹ̝ = voiced alveolar fricative)		
̩	Syllabic	n̩		̞	Lowered	e̞		(β̞ = voiced bilabial approximant)		
̯	Non-syllabic	e̯		̘	Advanced Tongue Root	e̘				
˞	Rhoticity	ɚ a˞		̙	Retracted Tongue Root	e̙				

TONES AND WORD ACCENTS

LEVEL			CONTOUR		
e̋ or ˥	Extra high		ě or ᷄	Rising	
é or ˦	High		ê	Falling	
ē or ˧	Mid		e᷄	High rising	
è or ˨	Low		e᷅	Low rising	
ȅ or ˩	Extra low		e᷈	Rising-falling	
↓	Downstep		↗	Global rise	
↑	Upstep		↘	Global fall	

Contributors

Paul Foulkes: Department of Linguistics and Phonetics, University of Leeds, Leeds LS2 9JT, UK (p.foulkes@leeds.ac.uk)

Gerard J. Docherty: Department of Speech, University of Newcastle, Newcastle upon Tyne NE1 7RU, UK (g.j.docherty@ncl.ac.uk)

Deborah Chirrey: Department of English, Edge Hill University College, St Helens Road, Ormskirk, Lancashire L39 4QP, UK (chirreyd@admin.ehche. ac.uk)

Beverley Collins: Faculteit der Letteren, Rijks Universiteit Leiden, PN van Eyckhof 4, Postbus 9515, 2300 RA Leiden, Netherlands (collins@pcmail. leidenuniv.nl)

Nigel Hewlett: Department of Speech and Language Sciences, Queen Margaret University College, Clerwood Terrace, Edinburgh EH12 8TS, UK (n.hewlett@ sls.qmced.ac.uk)

Raymond Hickey: Department of English, University of Essen, Universität-straße 12, D-45117 Essen, Germany (r.hickey@uni-essen.de)

Paul Kerswill: Department of Linguistic Science, University of Reading, Whiteknights, PO Box 218, Reading RG6 6AA, UK (p.e.kerswill@reading. ac.uk)

Kevin McCafferty: Engelsk Institutt, Det humanistiske Fakultet, Universitetet i Tromsø, N-9037 Tromsø, Norway (kevin.mccafferty@hum.uit.no)

Anne Grethe Mathisen: Department of British and American Studies, University of Oslo, PO Box 1003 Blindern, N-0315 Oslo, Norway (a.g.mathisen@iba. uio.no) (fam.mathisen@ah.telia.no)

Inger Mees: Department of English, University of Copenhagen, Njalsgade 80, DK-2300, Denmark (mees@hum.ku.dk/)

Lesley Milroy: Program in Linguistics, University of Michigan, 1087 Frieze Building, Ann Arbor, MI 48109, USA (amilroy@umich.edu)

Mark Newbrook: Department of Linguistics, Monash University, Wellington Road, Clayton, Victoria 3168, Australia (mark.newbrook@arts.monash.edu.au)

James M. Scobbie: Department of Speech and Language Sciences, Queen Margaret University College, Clerwood Terrace, Edinburgh EH12 8TS, UK (j.scobbie@sls. qmced.ac.uk)

Jana Stoddart: KAA FF UP, Krizkovskeho 10, 771 47 Olomouc, Czech Republic (stodda@risc.upol.cz)

Jane Stuart-Smith: Department of English Language, 12 University Gardens, University of Glasgow, Glasgow G12 8QQ, UK (j.stuart-smith@englang.arts.gla.ac.uk)

Laura Tollfree: Department of Linguistics, Monash University, Wellington Road, Clayton, Victoria 3168, Australia (laura.tollfree@arts.monash.edu.au)

Peter Trudgill: Department of English, University of Fribourg, Miséricorde, CH-1700 Fribourg, Switzerland (peter.trudgill@unifr.ch)

Alice Turk: Department of Linguistics, University of Edinburgh, Adam Ferguson Building, George Square, Edinburgh EH8 9LL, UK (turk@ling.ed.ac.uk)

Clive Upton: School of English, University of Leeds, Leeds LS2 9JT, UK (c.s.upton@leeds.ac.uk)

Dominic Watt: Department of Linguistics and Phonetics, University of Leeds, Leeds LS2 9JT, UK (d.j.l.watt@leeds.ac.uk)

J. D. A. Widdowson: National Centre for English Cultural Tradition, University of Sheffield, Sheffield S10 2TN, UK (j.widdowson@sheffield.ac.uk)

Ann Williams: Department of Linguistic Science, University of Reading, Whiteknights, PO Box 218, Reading RG6 6AA, UK (a.williams@reading.ac.uk)

1

Urban Voices – Overview

Paul Foulkes and Gerard J. Docherty

Urban Voices is a collection of specially commissioned chapters written by researchers concerned with accent variation in the English spoken in the British Isles. Contributors include sociolinguists, dialectologists, phoneticians and phonologists.

We have two immediate aims in assembling these chapters. These are (i) to provide a collection of recent research based on empirical studies of accent variation; and (ii) to collect together descriptive data yielded by such studies to stand as a reference resource. Contributors were therefore asked to do two things: first provide a description of the phonetic features of a particular accent, and then discuss methodological and/or theoretical implications of their data.[1]

In this Overview we first outline these two aims in more detail. We then take a brief excursus to address the various labels which have been used to cover the sort of work we have collected here, suggesting that a new term is required in order to encapsulate the diversity of interests represented. Following this, the general structure of the book is described in detail. Finally, we turn to the individual contributions, offering a précis of each of them. This enables us to tackle a third, less direct, aim. A prime motivation for collecting any work together in the way we are doing here is, of course, to *raise* questions as well as answer them. By inviting contributions from a range of academic disciplines, all of which focus on accent variation, we hope to identify some of the strengths, limitations, tensions and gaps in sociolinguistics, dialectology, phonetics and phonology. By doing this we hope to provide a platform for continued research in these fields.

1.1 *Immediate aims*

1.1.1 Empirical research on accent variation

The first aim of this book is to represent a cross-section of recent research carried out on accent variation. No similar collection has appeared since *Sociolinguistic Patterns in British English* (Trudgill ed. 1978). As indicated by its title, the latter is a collection of works by sociolinguists, and in his Introduction to the collection Trudgill identifies the common debt owed by its contributors to the pioneering methodology of Labov and his colleagues. Trudgill goes as far as to call the work represented in the book 'sociolinguistics proper', although it is perhaps more widely regarded as one branch of the broad discipline of socio-linguistics. This branch has been variously labelled **variationist sociolinguistics** or **urban dialectology**, and in 1978 it was still in its relative infancy outside of North America. It has since continued to flourish, and is still characterised by studies where empirical data are exploited to yield answers to linguistic questions: advancing linguistic theory, furthering our understanding of the structure of language, and accounting for the dynamics of variation and change (see further Chambers 1995).

In the intervening two decades a wealth of fieldwork, description and analy-sis has been carried out, and many of the central concerns of such work have remained largely intact. Labov remains inarguably the most prominent player on this stage, as will become clear in many of the chapters in the present volume. However, twenty years is a long time in linguistics. Urban dialectology has been touched by technological advances, new paradigms in adjacent theoretical fields, and perhaps most of all by upheavals in the social structure of the communities under scrutiny. Methods of data collection and analysis have been refined and reassessed, and the findings of such work are being exploited for an increasingly wide range of purposes. And while Labov's work still exerts tremendous influ-ence, research on English in the British Isles has inevitably begun to develop its own character, shaped by its architects, and by the influence of neighbouring academic disciplines and traditions. In order to reflect this diversity of interest we have therefore sought contributions to *Urban Voices* not only from sociolin-guists, but also from linguists of other backgrounds for whom phonological and/or phonetic variation is important.

Although the common focus of this book is on variation within the British Isles, this should not be taken as indicative of parochialism. Rather, the discus-sions raise important general issues in linguistic theory and methodology, for our understanding of speech production and perception, and the mechanisms of linguistic change. Some of these issues are broached in more detail below.

1.1.2   Descriptive resources

Our second principal aim is to draw together descriptive material pertaining to the accents spoken in urban areas of the United Kingdom and Ireland. It should not be overlooked that the data collected in empirical studies form a highly valu-able resource in themselves. Published work emanating from empirical projects tends necessarily to be selective in the data which are presented, since, by design, researchers tend to be setting out to use a subset of their collected data as evi-dence in some particular theoretical debate. Journal articles tend to present data drawn from a micro-study of some or other variable with a view to illustrating, for example, that change is in progress in pronunciation, or that the range of variation can be interpreted as supportive of a particular theoretical or methodological stance. Indeed, all of the offerings in the present volume follow this very path. However, the concentration on a selection of variants (combined of course with the temporal constraints found in the execution of any empirical research project) usually results in large portions of the collected data being unpublished, or only partly analysed, and often even wholly untouched.

While it was impossible to rectify such a situation fully in the course of the two years or so in which this book took shape, we have sought to tap into the collected fieldwork corpora held by the contributors to bring as much descriptive material as possible into the light. We have asked all contributors to present descriptions of the spoken vernacular(s) of their area(s) of research, which are as full and detailed as possible. (Note that we concentrate on aspects of phonetic and phonological variation; see J. & L. Milroy (eds) 1993 for a collection of chapters discussing grammatical variation.)

The accent descriptions follow a standard format which is described in detail below. This process of aggregating descriptions in itself raises numerous interesting and important issues in terms of the aims and methods of work which centres on variation data (which we again address below).

The assembled material will serve as a valuable resource tool, to be used in conjunction with established sources such as Wells (1982). First and foremost this makes a great deal of comparable data accessible for the conventional pursuits exercised by dialectologists, sociolinguists, phonologists and phoneticians. However, beneficiaries of this material will also include those working in the increasing number of fields where a thorough understanding of non-standard spoken vernaculars is vital. These include education (e.g. J. & L. Milroy 1985a; L. Milroy 1987a: 202ff.), speech therapy (e.g. L. Milroy 1987a: 208ff.), forensic phonetics (e.g. Nolan 1991, 1997; Mahoney, Dixon & Cocks forthcoming) and speech technology (e.g. Hoequist & Nolan 1991).

Speech technology is perhaps the most prominent commercial area in which an understanding of variation in speech has been sought. However, a recent upsurge in telephone sales and call centres has led to a much wider commercial interest in the features of accents, and in public attitudes to variation.

Telesales companies have apparently taken great care to locate their call centres in regions where their workers' accents will be favourably perceived. The south of Scotland, the north-east of England, Yorkshire, south Wales, Derby and Merseyside have all recently reaped the benefit of this new line of industry. So far, though, there has been little involvement on the part of linguistic researchers. Instead, companies tend to execute their own research. The Institute for Personnel and Development, for instance, has carried out qualitative interviews with recruitment consultants to assess perceptions of employees' accents (IPD 1996). A few accents seem to have a fairly universal perception, with Birmingham continuing to fare badly. However, the perception of both Received Pronunciation (RP) and 'Cockney' varied widely in the IPD study, while the influx of call centres in 1998 to Merseyside (Jones in *The Independent on Sunday*, 29 November 1998) brings into question the usual stigma attached to Scouse.

The changing and varying perceptions of accents revealed by commercial research suggests that academic linguists have a potentially important role to play in explaining this range of perceptions. However, no wide-scale attitude survey has been carried out since Giles' work in the 1970s (e.g. Giles 1970; although see Newbrook this volume for a local study). It would not be surprising to find that changes in attitudes to variation are linked to the ongoing and widespread changes in both social structure and pronunciation that are described in *Urban Voices*.

1.2   *Accent studies*

Interest in accent variation, as we have already noted, is widespread, and various labels have been assigned to academic pursuits concerning accent variation. The terms **sociophonetics** and **sociophonology** have been used to reflect the relatively recent interest in variation on the part of phoneticians and phonologists. More common than these are **urban dialectology** and **variationist** (or **quantitative) sociolinguistics**. All of these names clearly derive from modifications to the names of other fields, to reflect the origins of such work as a side-branch of longer-established traditions. As such, work on accent variation seems to find itself in peripheral areas of various disciplines. None of the labels we have listed seems to us particularly revealing in capturing the range of empirical and theoretical considerations which are found across the spectrum of work on accents.

We suggest that the lack of a single label inhibits communication between parties interested in accent variation. In this excursus we take a brief look at the names currently used by those researching on accent features. We conclude that a novel term, **accent studies**, might be better suited than any of the existing ones as a means of marking out a unified territory for research on accent variation.

The first pair of current labels, sociophonetics and sociophonology, appear mutually exclusive in their scope, encapsulating as they do the long-standing divide between phonetics (as the study of sounds in their concrete form) and phonology (by contrast the study of 'sounds' as abstract entities in a linguistic system). As such, neither can adequately express the obvious fact that empirical observations of language are almost always interested in both the concrete and the abstract. The procedure of many chapters included in *Urban Voices*, for example, involves collecting concrete/phonetic data, but also exploiting those data to assess their implications for our understanding of the linguistic system. This dual interest is clearly reflected in the chapters by Scobbie, Hewlett & Turk and by Tollfree, who examine some of the implications of phonetic variation for our understanding of phonological representation and organisation. Similarly, the chapters by Watt & Milroy, Hickey, Trudgill, and Docherty & Foulkes assess the implications of phonetic variation for our understanding of how change is initiated and how it filters through the phonological system.

'Urban dialectology' reflects an interest in regional dialects of English that has been apparent since at least the time of Chaucer, and dialectology as a reasonably well-defined scholarly subject has been pursued in Britain for well over a century (see further Chambers & Trudgill 1980). Until relatively recently the defining characteristics of dialectology have been a concentration on geographical variation, with research carried out mainly in rural locations, and with one of its main aims being the recording and preservation of non-standard forms. Much work has targeted older male informants, on the assumption they would be the best guardians of such forms, and interest in lexical variation has been especially prominent. The contribution here by Stoddart, Upton & Widdowson discusses the continuing role of some of these considerations.

The innovative work of Labov brought about an abrupt change of tack in the pursuits of dialectology. Interest turned to urban dwellers (on the basis that the majority of the inhabitants of the USA, as in Britain, live in urban areas), informants were sampled from a range of social groups (defined by socioeconomic class, gender, age, and/or ethnicity), and much more attention became directed towards phonetic and phonological variation (since subtle variation in pronunciation patterns was identified as correlating with these social categories). The name urban dialectology reflects this developing paradigm while keeping sight of its ancestry. Several chapters included in *Urban Voices* can be said to fit into this mould, although various issues are raised concerning methodology (e.g. McCafferty, Hickey, Newbrook), analysis (e.g. Williams & Kerswill, Stuart-Smith), and interpretation of results (e.g. Watt & Milroy, Mees & Collins, Mathisen).

The label 'urban dialectology', however, is also in some respects unsatisfying. One of the first items in the curriculum of a typical undergraduate course in linguistics is the difference between **accent** and **dialect**. The latter is taken to refer to any differences between varieties of the same language, whether at the level of pronunciation, phonology, morphology, syntax, lexis or pragmatics. Accent, by contrast, refers to differences of segmental or suprasegmental pronunciation and/or phonology. With this distinction in mind, almost all work carried out under the rubric urban dialectology can in fact be said to investigate differences of accent rather than dialect, and reference to 'dialectology' would therefore appear slightly imprecise. (Watt 1998 picks up this concern, preferring the term 'accent levelling' to the more usual 'dialect levelling'.)

Labels such as variationist or quantitative sociolinguistics, like urban dialectology, also locate the sort of work we are concerned with in its general academic and historical context. Research in the areas of convergence between language and society has developed at much the same rate as dialectology, beginning perhaps with the anthropological tradition in North America in the early part of the twentieth century. Sociolinguistics itself is now generally considered a remarkably broad field, encompassing not only studies of linguistic variation but also issues such as language planning, conversation analysis, sign language, bilingualism, and pidgin and creole studies (e.g. Wardhaugh 1998; but see Chambers 1995 for a view emphasising variationism; and Cameron 1990 for a critique of Labovian work as part of sociolinguistics *per se*).

It must be reiterated, though, that much of the work collected here has been carried out with an interest outside of the normal remit of sociolinguistics. The fieldwork collection and subsequent analysis of some of the projects reported in this book, for example, have been performed with an eye on matters such as instrumental phonetics (Docherty & Foulkes; Scobbie, Hewlett & Turk), acquisition (Scobbie, Hewlett & Turk) and theoretical phonology (Tollfree). It is also true that the potential beneficiaries of the detailed descriptive work made possible in these studies include linguists working in fields as diverse as education, forensics, commerce, and speech synthesis and recognition, which themselves would not normally be considered part of sociolinguistics.

The maturity of the discipline and its expanding range of participants is reflected in the profile of the contributions to *Urban Voices*. This seems to us to justify the introduction of a new 'hoop' label to mark out a field of enquiry which intersects (at least) dialectology, sociolinguistics, phonetics and phonology. We therefore consider the work collected in *Urban Voices* to exemplify **accent studies**.

Calling for a new label should not be taken as merely a trivial issue of nomenclature. By uniting work in overlapping disciplines under a single banner, accent variation can be seen as a pursuit in its own right, rather than being an issue towards the periphery of numerous separate academic traditions. Accent variation therefore becomes a central issue, accessible to and fed by researchers from various backgrounds.

1.3   Urban Voices – *contributions*

1.3.1   Structure of chapters

The contributions in *Urban Voices* focus on urban accents of England, Wales, Scotland, Northern Ireland and the Republic of Ireland. The order of presentation is more or less geographical.

Eleven chapters concentrate on single locations: Newcastle upon Tyne (Watt & Milroy), Sheffield (Stoddart, Upton & Widdowson), West Wirral (Newbrook), Sandwell (Mathisen), Norwich (Trudgill), South East London (Tollfree), Cardiff (Mees & Collins), Glasgow (Stuart-Smith), Edinburgh (Chirrey), (London)Derry (McCafferty) and Dublin (Hickey). The other three chapters draw upon data from more than one site: Milton Keynes, Reading and Hull (Williams & Kerswill), Edinburgh and Glasgow (Scobbie, Hewlett & Turk), and Derby and Newcastle upon Tyne (Docherty & Foulkes).

To reflect the overriding aims of the book, each chapter has two main parts. After a brief introduction (section 1 of each chapter), there follows a description of the vernacular(s) of the area(s) concerned, concentrating on the phonetic, phonological and suprasegmental features of the accent (section 2). In the remainder of the chapter authors discuss some of the theoretical and/or methodological implications of their data.[2]

The urban centres represented here cover a very wide geographical expanse, but collecting this material together reveals glaring gaps in the canon of areas which have been investigated. Many important sites appear largely unresearched, at least on a large scale and in recent years, such as Manchester, Birmingham, Bristol and Leeds. Some such gaps are being filled (notably via the recently started *Survey of Regional English* – Kerswill, Llamas & Upton forthcoming; Upton & Llamas forthcoming), but we hope *Urban Voices* will inspire research in new locations.

1.3.2 Presentation of descriptive material

Authors follow a standardised format of presentation in order to ensure that the descriptive sections are comparable across chapters.

First, transcriptions of local vowel pronunciation norms are provided, employing the keywords used by Wells (1982) to characterise the lexical sets of English. The keywords themselves are described by Wells (1982: xviii) as 'intended to be unmistakable no matter what accent one says them in', and have become a standard tool within descriptive dialectology. To this set we have added horsES, to represent the vowel typically used in e.g. *-es* plural forms and the *-ed* past tense suffix. All accent descriptions in *Urban Voices* therefore take as a point of departure the following keywords:

KIT	DRESS	TRAP	LOT	STRUT	FOOT	BATH
CLOTH	NURSE	FLEECE	FACE	PALM	THOUGHT	GOAT
GOOSE	PRICE	CHOICE	MOUTH	NEAR	SQUARE	START
NORTH	FORCE	CURE	happy	letteR	horsES	commA

Several authors have also found it necessary to add other keywords where the local phonology demands it (for example where there is evidence of a split in the GOAT set, with pre-L items like GOAL differing in their typical realisations). All keywords are represented in SMALL CAPITALS, following Wells' style of presentation.

The main pronunciations used for all the keywords are summarised in table form (the first main table in each contribution) for easy reference. Comments are then offered on those keywords which display interesting or unexpected features.

In the summary vowel tables a single transcription can be taken as indicating that little or no variation has been identified in the local pronunciation patterns.[3] Thus, for example, Derby KIT tends to have [ɪ] almost without exception.

Where, by contrast, there are cases of substantial variation, all main variants are listed in the table, and comments explaining the distribution of variants are found in the commentary. The most widespread variants are listed before more restricted ones, separated by the symbol > to express the difference in currency. Variants separated by the symbol ~ are taken to have roughly equal currency.[4] Thus, as an illustration, the table entry for Derby GOOSE is ʉː > uː ~ iː. This indicates that the majority pronunciation is [ʉː], but both [uː] and [ɨː] can also be heard. The subsequent commentary points out that the back variant [uː] occurs predominantly before L, and can also be heard in the speech of older informants in other phonological contexts; the unrounded [ɨː] is largely an innovation in younger speech.

Following the vowel material, authors comment on any consonantal features which characterise the accent(s) under discussion. Information on stops is presented first, then on nasals, fricatives and approximants. Finally, brief comments are given, where available, on suprasegmental features such as intonation and rhythm.

In the consonantal discussions we also employ SMALL CAPITALS to represent categories, in keeping with the style used for the vowel keywords. Thus, comments can be found under subheadings such as STOPS, T, H, L and R, and references are made to well-known processes such as H-dropping, R-intrusion and L-vocalisation. In most cases these representations can be considered equivalent to similar labels using phonemic transcriptions such as /t/, /h/ and /l/-vocalisation, although certain relatively trivial differences emerge, such as the use of TH as a cover label for both the dental fricatives, [θ] and [ð]. The issue of phonemicisation is nonetheless an important one in the general discussion of the aims and methods used in the type of research discussed in this book (see further below).

All transcriptions are given using the symbols of the International Phonetic Alphabet in its 1996 format. A copy of the IPA is included on p. xi.

1.3.3   Fieldwork profiles

The actual process of gathering the descriptive material in this way entails certain problems and raises various important issues. First and foremost, only one chapter in this collection (Stuart-Smith's on Glasgow) was based on fieldwork carried out after the initial invitation to contribute. Hickey (for Dublin) and Stoddart, Upton & Widdowson (for Sheffield) formally updated their fieldwork at least in part with this book in mind, while contributors whose data were collected before 1990 (Trudgill for Norwich and Newbrook for West Wirral) have drawn upon recent informal observation and their native speaker intuition in order to assess any ongoing change since their last formal fieldwork. Thus, almost all of the descriptive work presented here has been based on fieldwork carried out for purposes other than *Urban Voices*. In most cases, therefore, authors have imposed a *post hoc* structure onto their existing fieldwork data. This inevitably means that there are inconsistencies across the contributions in terms of fieldwork design and data analysis. Contributions differ, for example, in the number of informants that have been recorded, the overall social profile of the cohorts (with respect to age, class and ethnicity), the time over which the fieldwork was collected, the type(s) of elicitation technique used, the number of analysts, and the type of analysis (auditory, instrumental, and in part intuitive). The authors' own aims in their original research also result in some disparity in the amount of detail given concerning sociolinguistic variation. However, most

Table 1.1 Overall fieldwork profiles

	Total informants	Age range	Collection dates
Newcastle	32	16–67	1994
Derby	35	14–85	1995
Sheffield	25	12–83	1952, 1997
West Wirral	68	11–80	1980
Sandwell	57	16–70	1984
Norwich	77	10–93	1968, 1983
Milton Keynes	134	4–70+	1990–1998
Reading	36	14–70+	1995–1998
Hull	36	14–70+	1995–1998
South East London	90	15–89	1990–1994
Cardiff	86	9–65+	1976–1990
Glasgow	32	13–60	1997
Edinburgh	14	17–73	1995
(London)Derry	107	teens–73	1994–1995
Dublin	140	c. 20–c. 40	1994–1998

of the differences are relatively minor with respect to the descriptive aims of this book. All contributions include data sampled from both males and females and from a wide age range. Almost all of the fieldwork referred to was performed in the mid to late 1990s, and all studies include data from sizeable samples of speakers (see L. Milroy 1987a for a discussion of sampling criteria). Nonetheless, we are concerned that sources should be as explicit and accountable as possible. With this consideration in mind it is imperative that such differences be borne in mind when referring to the data collected here (a point which is also raised by Wells (1982: xv) in respect of his own survey of accents).

Table 1.1 above summarises the general profile of the fieldwork samples described in this book (see the relevant chapters for more detailed information).

1.4 *Themes*

The papers in *Urban Voices* illustrate the diversity of interests which characterise work on variation in the British Isles. In their contributions authors demonstrate an immediate concern with dialectology, sociolinguistics, phonetics, theoretical phonology and historical linguistics. The contributors also number people who have previously addressed variation in the context of, for example, speech disorders, forensic analysis and language acquisition.

The chapters tackle various persistent and recurrent questions in linguistic research. Sometimes these are approached from quite different perspectives in different academic traditions. Bringing together contributors who have differing research interests therefore enables us to reveal some of the tensions across the various traditions in terms of theoretical assumptions, research methods, analysis techniques and data interpretation. It is one of the main aims of this volume to highlight such issues in order to inspire continued research. In the remainder of this Overview we offer a précis of the contributions and the general themes which emerge from the collection.

1.4.1 Linguistic change

Several chapters address one of the longest-standing questions in linguistics – the **causes and effects of language change**. Many studies within urban dialectology have detected age-correlated variation in a community and interpreted it as change in progress. An important question which emerges from such findings is whether change is brought about by pressures **internal** to the linguistic system itself, or whether it is the speakers who can be held responsible, adopting forms found in other varieties. In the latter case, sociolinguists often explain change as the result of **external** influences. (As we shall see later, the term 'external' is used in a slightly different sense in phonology and phonetics.)

The chapter by Trudgill concentrates on this internal/external dichotomy. With reference to his well-known real-time study in Norwich, Trudgill discusses the relative roles of **exogenous** versus **endogenous** factors in ongoing change. The former are changes influenced by spoken varieties external to a community – principally pressures towards dedialectalisation as speakers adopt standard forms in preference to local forms. Endogenous changes, by contrast, are those which appear to have been instigated by system-internal factors applying within a single community. Trudgill suggests that both types are present in ongoing changes in Norwich, and thus argues against the claims of J. Milroy (1992).

Meanwhile, Hickey's study of changes in Dublin English leads him to conclude that some changes escape adequate explanation in terms of the usual internal/external dichotomy. Hickey argues that some changes appear to be brought about not by contact with external varieties or by systemic pressures, but by social factors *within* a community. A similar conclusion might be drawn from the data discussed by Docherty & Foulkes. In Derby and Newcastle, fine-grained phonetic variation correlates with speakers' social characteristics, but no clear motivations for the variation can be seen by observing either external varieties or system-internal pressures.

1.4.2 External influence: standard versus non-standard

When assessing external motivations for change, it has often been pointed out that changes tend to be modelled on other varieties. In British studies the standard form of the language has more often than not been identified as the main external model (see e.g. the review by Milroy, Milroy & Hartley 1994). The contribution here by Trudgill exemplifies this pattern, identifying most (but not all) changes as moves towards the standard form. Similarly, Newbrook's main interest is in West Wirral speakers' usage of local versus non-local forms in different speaking styles, and their attitudes to the variant forms available to them. He finds that informants generally – but not always – rate RP forms as more prestigious than marked local variants.

Conversely, it has also been pointed out that RP has little cachet for many speakers, particularly those outside England (L. Milroy 1987b: 105ff.; Watt & Milroy, Hickey, Tollfree this volume). Stuart-Smith (this volume) goes as far as to comment that RP is often regarded with 'hostility' in Glasgow.

Several recent studies have in fact shown indications that *non-standard* varieties are coming to exercise more and more influence on variation and change. Trudgill's Norwich data collected in 1983, for instance, reveal new changes such as H-dropping, TH-fronting, and an increasing use of labial forms of R. All of these appear to be modelled not on RP but on non-standard varieties. Other chapters included in the present volume find similar evidence for the sudden appearance of non-standard variants in the speech of a community. Most of the recurrent changes recorded by our contributors appear to stem from non-standard varieties as they are spoken in the south-east of England. Plenty of evidence is therefore marshalled to support Wells' (1982: 301) speculation that London's 'working-class accent is today the most influential source of phonological innovation in England and perhaps in the whole of the English-speaking world'. TH-fronting (the use of [f] and [v] instead of [θ] and [ð]) and labial forms of R are also noted in Milton Keynes, Reading, Hull, Newcastle and Derby. These particular changes are mainly in evidence within England, but there are also some signs of infiltration into both Cardiff English and also Scottish varieties (TH-fronting appears in Glasgow, for example).

Glottal(ised) forms of voiceless stops, meanwhile, have become so ubiquitous as to generate regular (and almost always unfavourable) comment in the media. These are recorded in a wide variety of the locations included here, and form the main substance of discussion in the chapters by Mees & Collins, Mathisen, and Docherty & Foulkes. Glottals, too, are often cited as originating in non-standard speech in the south-east of England, although they also have a long independent history in Scotland (e.g. Andrésen 1968; Milroy, Milroy & Hartley 1994), and there is in fact some evidence that they have been present in RP for longer than has usually been credited (Collins & Mees 1996).

The source for these recent and widespread changes has often been cited as Estuary English (Rosewarne 1984, 1994; see also John Wells' website: http://www.phon.ucl.ac.uk/home/wells/estu.htm). This term is used, particularly in the media, to describe a variety intermediate between RP and Cockney. As Watt & Milroy suggest, Estuary English itself is probably a **levelled** form (see below), rather than a unitary, well-defined variety. All of its features can be located on a sociolinguistic and geographical continuum between RP and Cockney, and are spreading not because Estuary English is a coherent and identifiable influence, but because the features represent neither the standard nor the extreme non-standard poles of the continuum.

The emergence of influential non-standard varieties raises important issues concerning the ongoing status of the standard as a reference point for speakers, the social and geographical networks which facilitate influence and contact between varieties, and the nature of the contact which is required for influence to take place. What is certainly clear is that we can no longer assume that speakers of non-standard varieties automatically orient themselves towards the standard: variation and ongoing change may potentially be influenced by a range of external varieties. Given the changing status of RP, we might perhaps reassess the continuing role of RP as an educational norm, particularly with regard to the teaching of English as a foreign language.

The standard variety furthermore plays a prominent role in most descriptive dialectological work. However, this too is not without its drawbacks. When describing a regional accent or non-standard dialect, it is usual to refer to the standard form, at least implicitly, to enable readers unfamiliar with the variety being described to understand its features. This is particularly true when it comes to describing, and transcribing, vowel variants and the phonological categories they represent. Doing this, though, can create potentially misleading impressions. Vowels on the whole carry more responsibility than consonants in determining differences between accents. They are also harder to describe in phonetic terms, given the nature of vowel articulation in a continuous phonetic space, and the well-known problems of the IPA cardinal vowel system (see Butcher 1982).

An important task in sociolinguistic work, though, is to identify the phonologically relevant vowel categories underneath the myriad phonetic variants. Wells' (1982) keywords represent as good an attempt at this task as is currently available: examining many varieties of English we can usually identify a maximum of 24 lexical sets. The vowels of these 24 sets take many physical forms, but the lexical membership of the 24 sets is relatively stable across accents. This means, however, that finding a suitable IPA symbol to represent the phonological category is a less obvious procedure than it is in the case of consonants like, say, /m/ or /s/, where the surface phonetic variation is less marked. An analyst faces a far from straightforward task in selecting a single symbolic label to represent a vowel category from the very wide potential range of options. It is for this reason, to reiterate, that we have elected in *Urban Voices* to use Wells' keywords as a descriptive base rather than phonemic notations.

The usual solution to this problem, at least as far as English is concerned, is to use the symbols which most nearly capture the phonetic qualities of the standard accent. It is commonplace, for instance, to see /u/ representing the GOOSE set, /æ/ for TRAP, and /ʌ/ for STRUT, all of which closely match the spoken qualities of RP. We would not suggest for a second that Derby English or any other form would be a better choice, or that there is an implicit prescriptivism in selecting standard forms as convenient reference labels. However, this taken-for-granted methodological procedure may result in misleading predictions about phonological categorisation and patterning. For example, /u/, by dint of its labelling, is invariably treated as a phonologically back, rounded, vowel, and as such should pattern with other back or rounded vowels. We might argue, though, that this is not transparently the case for speakers of accents who, for example, pronounce GOOSE with [ʊu] or [ɨː]. For these speakers we may ask whether the phonological representation of this vowel ought to link it explicitly with other diphthongs or central vowels. The objection might be raised that the actual label used is arbitrary, and that for all speakers there is just the one vowel category irrespective of the varying phonetic forms used. But in this case a transcription like /u/ is clearly more abstract than one like /m/. The latter not only adequately represents the phonological category, it also reflects very closely the phonetic forms used for that category, and also provides a transparent guide to the phonological links the category enjoys with other nasals and bilabials. /u/, on the other hand, cannot be said to perform the latter two tasks with equal efficacy.

The predilection for using vowel symbols reminiscent of the standard spoken form should not, of course, be interpreted literally as a suggestion that a single variety underlies all others, or that one accent can be seen to derive from another. But our ideas about language structure do become coloured by practices such as this. A simple but telling example of this is provided by Lass (1989). Lass points out that there is a received wisdom that English does not have phonologically front rounded vowels. This makes English unlike most of the other members of the Germanic family of languages. There are numerous non-standard varieties of English, however, where *phonetically* front rounded vowels appear. Examples include [y] in GOOSE in parts of Scotland (Lass 1989: 183ff.), and [ø] in Newcastle NURSE (Lass 1989: 190; see also Watt & Milroy this volume). Had it been in RP that such pronunciations occurred, we would probably have become quite used to thinking of English as fitting the majority pattern of Germanic languages in having, say, /y/ and /ø/. The apparent blip in the typological pattern is the result of the social history of the English language, and the dominance of a standard variety where such vowels do not occur phonetically.

1.4.3 Levelling

It is clear that ongoing changes are not all characterised by convergence towards the standard form, leading many researchers to talk of a process of **dialect levelling** (or, since it is usually pronunciation differences at stake, **accent levelling**). Such a position is argued in the chapters by Watt & Milroy and Williams & Kerswill. Levelling is defined by Williams & Kerswill as 'a process whereby differences between regional varieties are reduced, features which make varieties distinctive disappear, and new features emerge and are adopted by speakers over a wide geographical area', and its history is traced briefly by Watt & Milroy. Levelling differs from standardisation (or dedialectalisation) in that speakers do not automatically abandon their local forms in preference for the standard. Rather, there appears to be a tension between speakers' desire to continue signalling loyalty to their local community by using local speech norms, and a concurrent urge to appear outward-looking or more cosmopolitan. Watt (1998: 7), by way of illustration, summarises the motivation behind ongoing changes in the Newcastle vowel system in terms of younger speakers aiming to 'dispel the "cloth cap and clogs" image', and to 'sound like northerners, but *modern* northerners'. Speakers can achieve these aims by avoiding variants which they perceive to be particularly indicative of their local roots, while at the same time adopting some features which are perceived to be non-local. It seems to be important, too, that the incoming features do not signal any other particularly well-defined variety, because of the potential signalling of disloyalty to local norms. This is especially true where the standard accent is concerned, due to its connotations of conformity or 'snobbishness' (see e.g. Hickey this volume).

1.4.4   Changes in social structure and behaviour

The rise in linguistic levelling appears to be linked to large-scale modifications in social and demographic structure. Recent years have seen major changes in the social fabric of Britain (as they have elsewhere), with relatively large increases in geographical and social mobility reflecting the fragmentation of traditional close-knit local communities (Giddens 1997: 258ff.; see further the discussions by Watt & Milroy and Williams & Kerswill). To reflect shifts in social class structure and to accommodate the increasing *embourgeoisement* of the country, the UK Office for National Statistics has recently seen fit to redraft its demographic classification system (ONS/ESRC 1998). Meanwhile, increasing geographical mobility, both long-term (as people move away from city centres) and short-term (for work and leisure), has led to an increase in contact between speakers of different vernaculars, which in turn seems to have facilitated a convergence of linguistic forms.

Increasing mobility enables individuals to expand their social networks (Milroy & Milroy 1985b). This therefore leads to a proliferation of **weak ties**, and as has been shown before, it is largely through these weak ties that linguistic innovations can enter a community (e.g. J. Milroy 1992). In keeping with network strength as an explanation for change, it is no surprise that in several communities (notably Newcastle and Cardiff) it is the middle class – where there is normally a greater array of weak ties – which is leading in the adoption of many levelling changes.

There are, however, numerous working-class communities where levelling changes are firmly established, and yet where the network structure is still relatively close-knit compared with the local middle class (e.g. Hull, Derby and Glasgow; this was also the pattern found in Middlesbrough by Llamas 1998). It is usually assumed that externally motivated changes require face-to-face contact in order to be successfully implemented (e.g. Trudgill 1986: 54), but findings such as those in Hull and Glasgow, where levelling changes are taking place *without* much interpersonal contact, demand further explanation.

One possible explanation which has often been mooted (e.g. Viereck 1968: 65), but rarely taken very seriously by linguistic researchers, concerns the linguistic effects of the spoken media.

Regional features are becoming more commonplace, for example, in the medium of pop songs (notably with e.g. Pulp, Oasis, Blur, All Saints and Catatonia). Such features appear to be easily mimicked by fans. Similarly, even very young children find it quite simple to repeat external regional variants that they have heard on the television, or via speaking toys (where North American accents are commonplace).

Television and radio clearly do play a part in disseminating new vocabulary, although their role in promoting long-term pronunciation variants is less clear. It has been suggested that prolonged exposure to particular varieties on television and radio at least helps to consolidate those changes which are being implemented through personal contact. Trudgill (1988: 44), for instance, describes this effect of media exposure as a 'softening-up process produced by the engendering of favourable attitudes'.

It may be, though, that television will come to play a greater role in the near future. As Williams & Kerswill point out, there has in recent years been a great upsurge in television directed at the youth market, in which non-standard registers and accents (particularly southern varieties) are *de rigueur*. At the same time, the most popular television shows are soaps and dramas set in lower-class urban locations (*Coronation Street* in Manchester, *EastEnders* in London). Numerous media articles have played on the role exercised by television in disseminating, or at least preserving, regional features (e.g. Bathurst in *The Observer Review*, 24 March 1996; O'Leary in *The Times*, 16 March 1998; Wainwright in *The Guardian*, 16 March 1998). But few academic studies have seriously attempted to assess this influence, as noted for example by Cruttenden (1997: 130) with reference to claims that Australian soaps play a role in the spread of high rising intonation (e.g. by Bathurst in *The Observer Review*, 24 March 1996).

What is also true is that television now plays a much more prominent role in everyday life than it ever has before. Almost all households in the UK possess a television, and a recent survey shows the average person over 16 years of age spends almost half their leisure time watching television or listening to the radio (19 hours out of 42; Giddens 1997: 368). Giddens (1997: 368) makes the telling claim that '[i]f current trends in TV watching continue, by the age of eighteen the average child born today will have spent more time watching television than in any other activity except sleep'. If such a claim is borne out, many children will come to spend more time exposed to non-local varieties than to their local vernacular. The possible effects of such exposure on acquired speech patterns remain to be formally tested, but are certainly worth considering in the context of continuing changes over the next few years.

1.4.5   Social profiles of speakers

Several of the chapters in this book focus on the relationship between linguistic variation and change and the social characteristics of speakers. Although much work in urban dialectology has isolated **social class** as the most important social factor underlying changes in progress, many recent studies in

Britain have identified **gender** as prior to class (reviewed by e.g. Milroy, Milroy & Hartley 1994). The contributions here by Watt & Milroy, Mees & Collins, and Mathisen all concentrate on the role of gender in ongoing changes. Some of their findings support the established view that females in western industrialised societies tend to use fewer non-standard variants than males (see Labov 1990; Chambers 1995: 102–3 for a summary of such a view). However, there is evidence that the dichotomy between standard and non-standard is being superseded by an orientation on the part of speakers to **non-local** versus **local** forms. Females have repeatedly been shown to use fewer local forms than males, i.e. those variants which particularly characterise the speech of a given locality. This does not mean that females necessarily orient themselves towards the standard more than males, but rather that they are more susceptible to influences from any kind of non-local forms. In the current climate, where non-standard varieties are becoming more and more influential, it follows that females are more likely to be the harbingers of incoming variants, even if they are non-standard in origin.

The Cardiff research described by Mees & Collins offers a very clear indication of the effect on speech patterns of a speaker's personal orientation to her locality. Mees & Collins focus on a real-time study of four Cardiff women. Two of these women express ambitious career plans and a strong desire to improve their socio-economic circumstances. Their use of non-local glottal variants has increased dramatically during the real-time study, which can be interpreted as a sign of weak orientation to the local community.

McCafferty, meanwhile, examines a social characteristic rarely included in variationist studies in these islands, **ethnicity**, with reference to the speech patterns of Protestants and Catholics in (London)Derry. He finds that features of variation and change differ across the two groups, but the differences are not straightforwardly aligned with common perceptions of ethnic differences in Northern Ireland. Protestants are not oriented towards British speech forms, nor are Catholics towards Southern Irish ones. Furthermore, McCafferty's data show little to support assumptions that divisions are strongest among the working classes.

More generally, McCafferty's study highlights the lack of interest in the phonetics and phonology of ethnic subcommunities, in particular those of immigrant origin (notwithstanding Wells 1973). Another major change in recent years in the demographic profile of Great Britain has been the growth in the ethnic minority population. The 1991 census indicates that 5.5% of the population are immigrants or descendants of immigrants (Giddens 1997: 211), but this figure is far exceeded in several places. An example of this is Bradford, where over 50% of the residents in some suburbs are of Pakistani origin (Bradford Education 1996). Research is currently under way on changes in British Panjabi (Stuart-Smith & Cortina-Borja 1996; Heselwood & McChrystal 1998), but the lack of published work on the phonetics and phonology of the *English* spoken in ethnic subcommunities remains conspicuous.

1.4.6 Individual speech patterns

Another field of research which has made little impact so far on sociolinguistic or phonological work concerns variation at the level of the **individual** speaker. A good deal is known about variation related to geographical and social differences between speakers, as well as differences in the speech of individuals which are triggered by phonological context or by speaking style. But several studies by phoneticians have also shown that different individuals may adopt markedly different articulatory strategies in the production of the 'same' sounds (e.g. Lindau 1975; Pandeli 1993). Understanding the scope and nature of individual variability may have wide-ranging implications for our understanding of issues at the core of variationist sociolinguistics and phonology, such as how linguistic innovations occur, and what the structure of phonological units is. It is also, of course, of vital importance to forensic work, where identifying individual features is a prime concern.

Equally, instrumental phonetic work has overwhelmingly concentrated on data gathered from just a few individuals. In part this is due to practical constraints. Commonly used techniques are often expensive and/or invasive (such as electropalatography, fibroscopy or electromyography), with the result that researchers are often forced to investigate their own speech, or that of a small number of subjects. One disadvantage of such practice, though, is that the findings may potentially be unrepresentative of the speech community at large. Acoustic studies, such as that reported here by Docherty & Foulkes (and see also e.g. Holst & Nolan 1995), are better placed to use larger samples. However, this is still comparatively rare. Phonetic work is rarely touched by considerations common in sociolinguistic work, such as in terms of sampling and representativeness (see further Docherty forthcoming). More generally, as Laver (1994: 55) remarks, accent features have not particularly concerned phoneticians (with the obvious exception of Wells 1982).

1.4.7 Variation and change – phonetic and phonological perspectives

While the questions of linguistic variation and change are central to sociolinguistic work, they have not enjoyed quite such a prominent position in phonetics, or in phonology (but for notable counter-examples see Harris 1985; Kiparsky 1988; and papers in Hinskens, Van Hout & Wetzels eds 1997). However, those phoneticians interested in variation and change have, like sociolinguists, tended to seek external explanations for observed patterns. (The term 'external' tends to be used with a wider definition than in sociolinguistics, referring to any factor which is not system-internal.) Phonological theorists, on the other hand, have nonetheless often sought to accommodate what is known about some aspects of variation and change into their models, and have on the whole produced what are in effect system-internal predictions to account for them.

The most influential phonetic work on sound change has been produced by

Ohala (e.g. 1974, 1983, 1989), who takes the view that all changes are induced by the natural properties of the laws of physics operating on the articulatory and auditory systems. Explanation for the origins of sound changes (in the sense of innovations which may subsequently penetrate the system as a whole) should therefore be sought with reference to, for example, the laws of aerodynamics, the inertia of the vocal organs, or the varying abilities of the perceptual system to respond to different sound frequencies (see also Foulkes 1997c). It follows, therefore, that instrumental phonetic techniques present a potentially useful methodology to identify the origins of change. The chapters here by Docherty & Foulkes, and Scobbie, Hewlett & Turk, both centre on instrumental phonetic research, and the information such techniques can furnish with respect to variation and change.

Acoustic analysis of vowels has become a mainstay of work in the Labovian tradition. Formant analysis in particular has become the default method of analysis in many circles, particularly in North America (where, it must be said, it often appears to be adopted rather uncritically). Formant analysis, however, has been shown to be problematic in many respects (reviewed briefly in the chapter by Docherty & Foulkes; see also Watt 1998).

The contribution here by Scobbie, Hewlett & Turk turns to an instrumental study of a different aspect of vowel quality: duration. They present a survey of previous accounts of the Scottish Vowel Length Rule (SVLR), of which few have used instrumental analysis or large speech samples. Citing preliminary data from their ongoing study of Glasgow and Edinburgh speakers, as well as partial reanalyses of previous studies, Scobbie, Hewlett & Turk draw into question several widely held assumptions about the SVLR.

The chapter by Docherty & Foulkes turns to instrumental analysis of consonantal variables, concentrating on variants of T in Newcastle and Derby English. Few previous sociolinguistic studies have cited acoustic data drawn from studies of consonants rather than vowels. While this chapter is novel in this respect, similar work on suprasegmental aspects of particular accents is another heavily under-represented area. There is, however, some ongoing work which seeks to fill this gap: see Grabe, Nolan & Farrar (forthcoming) and Farrar, Grabe & Nolan (forthcoming).

Stuart-Smith, meanwhile, tackles another aspect of speech production which has hitherto played only a small role in sociolinguistic or phonological work. With reference to her Glasgow corpus, she presents the first detailed analysis of voice quality as it correlates with a speaker's sociolinguistic characteristics.

Tollfree's chapter provides a brief introduction to two highly divergent contemporary theoretical models of phonology. One model, Articulatory Phonology, envisages variation and change as essentially externally motivated facts. The other, Government Phonology, provides a mechanism to represent the causes of change within its system of representation and organisation, and thus offers a view which predicts them to be internally motivated.

Articulatory Phonology takes **gestures** as its phonological primes. Gestures are said to be cognitive representations which generate articulatory trajectories over space and time, and thus closely mirror the detailed activities of a small set of semi-independent articulators. There is no segmental level of representation. This is an innovation found in various current models of phonology, and which marks a radically different approach from models which are more directly derivatives of phoneme theory. Thus, for example, the phonological specification underlying the articulation of [b] would include a gesture to generate lip closure and opening, which partly overlaps another gesture to generate vocal fold vibration; but these gestures are not organised into a higher-level segmental structure. Variation is countenanced as arising from changes to the magnitude of execution of a gesture, and/or modifications to the degree of temporal overlap among gestures. Such modifications are said to result from the temporal and physical constraints found in natural speech rather than through system-internal factors. Systemic change may eventually ensue, however, if a new generation learns a qualitatively different gestural configuration for a particular lexical item. Although Articulatory Phonology is not beyond criticism in several respects (as shown by Tollfree; see also McMahon, Foulkes & Tollfree 1994), the degree of resolution it permits in modelling articulatory variation makes it a highly attractive model with which to investigate the variation typically found in sociolinguistic work.

The second model outlined by Tollfree in many ways represents current phonological theory at another extreme. Government Phonology is deemed by its proponents to be a purely cognitive model. It is therefore ontologically (and, for some of its practitioners, methodologically) wholly divorced from phonetic material. All variation, and thus ultimately change, is said to be motivated by structural properties of the phonological system. Variants at the phonetic level are deemed to reflect discrete changes in the phonological structure of a segment – phonological primes may only be added or deleted from a segment's specification. Such changes are said to be induced by an asymmetry in the syntagmatic relationships between segments, according to their positions in syllable structure.

Ultimately, neither Articulatory Phonology nor Government Phonology can fully predict the variation found by Tollfree in London ʟ realisations. Taken together, however, the two models serve to illustrate the gulf which has grown between phonology as an academic discipline, and the conception of a speaker's phonology in its usual implicit form in the sociolinguistic literature. On the one hand we see key differences across disciplines in the conception of what 'phonology' is and does. On the other, we see a marked difference in the perceived role of variation in adding to our understanding of a speaker's phonological knowledge. We address these issues in the next section.

1.4.8 phonology and Phonology

One of the most important issues which differentiates the conception of phonology across the various disciplines is that of the segment or phoneme. In many branches of theoretical phonology, segmental representations have either been done away with altogether, or are regarded as epiphenomenal. They have also been questioned within phonetics and psycholinguistics (see e.g. Lindblom 1986b; Ohala 1992; Nolan 1992; Cutler 1992). Segmental representations remain, however, fundamental to sociolinguistic work, particularly with regard to the representation of linguistic change.

In part this focus on segmental representation is the child of practical necessity. Auditory analysis of data samples is much the fastest and easiest method, and transcriptions using alphabetic symbols are the most viable result of this process. It would be hard to imagine how analysis by ear alone could produce a workable transcription using only phonological primitives of the type countenanced by, say, Articulatory Phonology (although see Kelly & Local 1989 for analysis using Firthian prosodic phonology). It has been pointed out many times before, though, that segmental representations may have more to do with the categories a listener (or analyst) operates with than with the processing used by the speakers themselves in their cognitive phonological planning (e.g. Kerswill & Wright 1990). Segmental representations may indeed therefore match quite closely with categories important for *listeners*, for example in on-line lexical access. However, a segmental transcription may be quite some way removed from an adequate model of *speaker*-based activities, such as the phonological-level planning of an utterance, or long-term lexical storage. It has furthermore been shown that segmental awareness is weaker amongst people who are illiterate, and speakers of languages which do not use alphabetic writing systems (see Bertelson & de Gelder 1991 for an overview). In turn this suggests that segmental processing may be in part mediated by orthographic knowledge.

Although many of these points may be acknowledged by sociolinguists, their import is rarely addressed. However, recall the aims of variationist work, as summarised by Trudgill (1978: 11) in a discussion of the work of Labov:

> [Labov's] main objective . . . has not been to learn more about a particular society, nor to examine correlations between linguistic and social phenomena for their own sake. Rather, he has been concerned to learn more about language, and to investigate topics such as the mechanism of linguistic change; the nature of linguistic variability; and the structure of linguistic systems.

By failing to pay attention to developments in theoretical phonology, there is a danger that variationist work is falling short of fulfilling these aims. Initial analysis of data in segmental terms is probably a methodological necessity. However, allowing empirical analysis to grind to a halt at the level of phonemic representation does a disservice to the goal of yielding information about speakers' phonological knowledge and processing. These may require reference to smaller units, or units of a non-segmental and/or non-linear nature. Some recent work, e.g. by Nagy & Reynolds (1997), offers an attempt to resolve this impasse by exploiting data from sociolinguistic studies to assess claims in current theoretical models.

Much harder to shake may be the received wisdom on how linguistic change is transmitted through phonological systems. Labovian work on vowel systems is founded on the paradigmatic relationships between phonemic units. The system itself is said to induce changes, for example to avoid potential mergers between units (see especially Labov 1994: ch. 11). It is not yet clear what implications for such hypotheses may ensue if the segmental level were abandoned altogether, as has happened in some branches of phonology.

From the illustrations provided by Tollfree, we see not only that phonological theory has progressed a long way beyond simple phonemic representation, but also that variation data do not figure highly on the agenda for much phonological work. For many phonologists one crucial research goal is to identify universal aspects of phonological structure and organisation. Following a tradition harking back to the structuralists (and perhaps to the ancient Greeks – see Chambers 1995: 227), phonologists tend to be concerned with issues such as the cognitive representation of paradigmatic distinctions, and the methods by which languages convey distinct messages through different sound combinations. Since the goal is to understand universal characteristics like these, it follows that the highly diverse phonetic forms which speakers use to convey those essential contrasts are largely irrelevant. Variation in phonetic form is therefore often seen to be a problem, a source of 'noise' obscuring from view the phonological structures assumed to be invariant across speakers. (In some quarters this view is taken to yet another level of abstraction: even the surface variation found in different *languages* may be regarded as of only subsidiary interest compared with the fundamentals of linguistic systems.)

But once again, a failure to address the fundamental fact of variability in speech may hinder progress in phonology. Phonological knowledge must enable listeners to cope with variability in the speech of others, and (arguably) plays a part in producing variable phonetic output on the part of the speaker. Understanding the nature and role of variability would therefore appear to be a highly productive route towards constructing an adequate model of phonological knowledge.

1.4.9 Variation as 'noise'

The conception of variation as dysfunctional is, of course, widespread outside sociolinguistics. In some recent phonetic and psycholinguistic research, however, variation has been awarded a central place.

Lindblom (e.g. 1986b, 1990), for example, has argued that phonetic variation may be actively manipulated by speakers to serve communicative functions:

> speech motor control is not organized to generate strictly invariant and clearly segmented acoustic correlates of speech units. Rather, speakers have the freedom to vary, that is to elaborate (overarticulate) or simplify (underarticulate) their speech under the control of communicative and situational constraints. My account suggests the following hypothesis: Phonetic variation originates from the circumstance that the units of speech need to be realized in physically explicit form only to the extent that they are

tacitly presupposed by the talker to be inferred by the listener's active perceptual mechanisms . . . The purpose of the variation is optimization. As the communicative and social-situational demands show short-term time variations, speech is accordingly adapted sometimes to production goals (simplification), sometimes to listener-oriented goals (elaboration). (Lindblom 1986b: 499)

To illustrate this we can cite examples of assimilation between segments, such as *stone gate* being produced [stoʊŋ ɡeɪt]. Assimilations like this are often viewed as a hindrance to the listener's task of phonemic identification, since the phonetic velar nasal is ambiguous – it could signal either the phonological category /n/ or the category /ŋ/. Such a view of course takes a heavily functional view of perception, assuming that contrasts present at the level of the system ought to be present in the phonetic form in order for communication to be maximally efficient.

By contrast, in Lindblom's model, speakers are argued to exploit variation as part of their communicative plan. It is therefore not necessarily dysfunctional or accidental, but a fundamental property of the phonological system. For Lindblom, it may indeed be true that in certain communicative situations an assimilation leads to communicative problems (as when talking to a non-native speaker, for example). But in other situations the assimilation may have a positive value. For example, where rapid communication is important, and the speaker can assume the listener's linguistic experiences to be similar to her own, the assimilated [ŋ] may enable the listener's perceptual system to gain faster access to the upcoming velar stop in *gate*. The redundancy inherent in the system will usually guarantee that the word *stone* has been identified by the time the nasal is articulated (it is not necessarily the case that lexical access has to be achieved by decoding the whole set of phonological units underlying the phonetic string). Variation is not therefore automatically viewed as a mask which poses problems for listeners as they attempt to identify an invariant unit underlying different phonetic forms.

In a similar vein, Pisoni (1997) has argued that many long-standing assumptions and research methods have in some respects *impaired* our understanding of how, for example, the perceptual system works (see also the thorough discussion of Pisoni's work in relation to the vowel formant plot method by Watt 1998: 42ff.). By treating variation as a nuisance, and seeking experimental ways to access the assumed invariant properties of the perceptual system, the fundamental properties of the speech perception system are often overlooked:

> speech perception is extremely robust and adaptive over a wide range of environmental conditions that introduce large physical changes and transformations in the acoustic signal. For example, normal hearing listeners can adapt easily to changes in speakers, dialects, speaking rate, and speaking style, as well as a wide variety of acoustic transformations . . . without any noticeable difference in performance. (Pisoni 1997: 9)

Pisoni (p. 10) continues to suggest that 'the human perception and memory systems appear to encode and retain very fine details of the perceptual event'.

Translated into phonological vocabulary, this might imply that a speaker's knowledge of phonology is not a minimalist means of producing a set of contrasts. Rather, our phonological knowledge may at least *include* very detailed holistic representations based on our experiences as speakers and listeners (see Ladefoged 1972 and Linell 1979 for similar proposals). Knowledge of categories and recurrent sound patterns may be deduced from this detailed information. Crucially, though, experience of variability would serve a fundamentally positive role in a speaker's phonological processing: speakers will be better equipped to comprehend new voices and novel utterances if they have a wider experience of variation. (See Nathan, Wells & Donlan 1998 for a similar view with reference to phonological acquisition.)

The detailed understanding of variation furnished by sociolinguists therefore appears highly valuable for a research programme of this sort, although direct connections are still few and far between.

1.4.10 Theory and data – the wider role of variation and empirical work

Many of the considerations raised over the last few pages lead us to a more general question concerning the role of variation and empirical data at large, both within and outside of linguistics.

Work in the established academic disciplines of phonology and phonetics have often differed in many respects from dialectology and sociolinguistics with regard to their methodological and theoretical assumptions, and the perceived role of variability. However, empirical research and an understanding of variation are becoming increasingly important for them. It is generally accepted that linguistic theory and observation of linguistic data go hand-in-hand, and neither can exist independently (e.g. Dixon 1997: 133–4; Docherty *et al.* 1997: 278–82). No linguistic investigation can proceed without reference to concrete data of some sort, no matter how informal or intuitive the collection method used. Equally, an analyst necessarily and unavoidably brings to bear certain theoretical assumptions to any analysis of data. Work within the sociolinguistic tradition has always emphasised the principle of **accountability**, i.e. the explicit reporting of how data have been assembled, analysed, presented and interpreted. This represents the minimally expected good practice in almost every other discipline which has an empirical content. It allows other researchers to assess the observations which have been used to inform theory, and therefore permits alternative analyses and interpretations as well as replication of results. Much work in linguistics, however, has not followed this practice, thereby leaving the reliability and generality of data and analysis inscrutable to others.

Beyond the academic sphere, variation in speech has long been a subject of interest and debate for the layman as well as the linguist (see the thorough discussion by Chambers 1995: 208ff.). It plays a key role in our everyday perception of ourselves and our interlocutors. It may affect our success in communication, and our job prospects. It remains a key issue in educational policy, and is increasingly exploited by commercial interests with a view to improving sales and marketing techniques. Understanding variation is crucial in new technologies, where machines need to be trained to comprehend and replicate the natural variability of human speech. Successful diagnosis and remedy of speech disorders is enhanced by a detailed knowledge of personal, regional and social variation, as is the increasingly important legal practice of forensic speech analysis.

We hope that *Urban Voices* promotes further research into variation of all types, and a continuing cross-fertilisation of ideas and practices.

Notes

1 We appreciate the help given to us by Bethan Davies, Ghada Khattab, Diane Nelson, Jane Stuart-Smith and Dominic Watt during the writing of this Overview. The opinions expressed in the Overview remain our own, and are not necessarily shared by the aforementioned, or by the other contributors to this book.
2 Three contributions diverge slightly from this format. The descriptive data on Edinburgh are presented separately, in the chapter by Chirrey. Scobbie, Hewlett & Turk present a theoretical discussion based on both Edinburgh and Glasgow data. The chapter by Docherty & Foulkes, which provides the description of Derby speech, draws equally on data from Newcastle in its discursive portion.
3 This may mean that formal research has shown there to be little variation as far as a given vowel is concerned. Alternatively, the vowel may not (yet) have been formally analysed in sufficient detail for such information to have been brought to light. Commentary notes indicate when a vowel has been formally analysed. In empirical work of the kind described in this book, it is usually the case that formal analysis is made of variables which have emerged as interesting through informal observation, intuition, or pilot studies. Vowels and consonants which are not formally analysed are therefore less likely to show sociolinguistic variation, although it is of course by no means impossible that they might.
4 Following the comments in note 3, this may again mean that equal currency has been identified in formal analysis, or that the variants have not been analysed in fine detail. Commentary notes again explain when formal study has taken place.

2

Patterns of variation and change in three Newcastle vowels: is this dialect levelling?

Dominic Watt and Lesley Milroy

2.1 *Introduction*

In this chapter we discuss the results of a variationist analysis of the reflexes of three vowels as they are used in the urban dialect of Tyneside (the conurbation in the north-east of England centring on Newcastle upon Tyne). We focus chiefly on two issues. First, we examine the distribution of variants in relation to the speaker variables of age, social class and gender, commenting also on current variationist interpretations of the effects of these variables on patterns of language use. Second, we attempt to provide a framework which allows us to make sense of changes which the Newcastle vowel system is evidently undergoing.

The chain shift model, as described by Labov (1994), is currently highly influential. Such a model attempts to specify universal constraints on change in vowel systems. Further, vowel systems (or parts of vowel systems) are said to undergo a co-ordinated set of changes, such that movement of one element triggers a change in an adjacent vowel, which in turn displaces its neighbour, and so on. This is the framework used for describing the Northern Cities Shift, a set of vowel changes affecting a number of cities in the United States which lie north of Philadelphia and westward of eastern New England. Although there is no doubt that American vowels are currently undergoing change, it is not clear that the changes are co-ordinated as the chain shift model suggests (see further Gordon 1997). It appeared to us as we examined our data that the Newcastle vowel system was indeed also undergoing change. As we shall see, some changes also involve co-ordinated movements of more than one vowel. However, a chain shift model does not capture the evident patterns, namely that variants characteristic of a larger area than the Tyneside region appear to be spreading at the expense of extremely localised variants. This is the phenomenon known as *dialect levelling*, which appears to account for our data better than the chain shift model. Before describing the details of our data and analytic procedures, we look a little more closely at how this concept has been used by sociolinguists and what a dialect levelling model of change might look like.

2.1.1   Dialect levelling

The concept of dialect levelling, referring to the eradication of socially or locally marked variants which follows social or geographical mobility and resultant dialect contact, was developed in the European dialectological literature (see for example Wrede 1919; Haag 1929/30). It turns up frequently in the general linguistic literature without much accompanying analysis of the dynamics of levelling (see for example Thomason & Kaufman 1988: 30). Sociolinguists such as Trudgill (1986), Kerswill (1996b) and Britain (1997a) have begun to deconstruct the traditional notion of levelling (and the related *koineisation*; see Siegel 1985) as they consider changes precipitated by dialect contact. One view of levelling is that it is a linguistic reflex of the large-scale disruption, endemic in the modern world, of those close-knit, localised networks which can be shown to maintain highly systematic and complex sets of socially structured linguistic norms (L. Milroy 1987b). Auer & Hinskens (1996: 4) point out that in the developed countries of Europe these processes, arising from industrialisation, urbanisation, mobility and increased ease of communication at regional, national and international levels, have brought about dialect contact to an extent hitherto unknown. To this list of precipitating factors we might add the more recent phenomenon of *counterurbanisation*, or the movement of urban populations into surrounding rural areas (Cross 1990; Dorling 1995; for details of counterurbanisation in the Tyneside region see Barke & Buswell 1992). It seems reasonable to assume that these dynamics have operated earlier and more intensively in North America, as discussed by Chambers (1995: 57–66) within a broad social network framework.

The question is whether we can develop a sociolinguistically sophisticated, explicit and generalizable account of change within a dialect levelling framework. We have suggested already that changes in social network structure are a crucial factor, and the role of weak, uniplex ties in facilitating change is consistent with this suggestion (Milroy & Milroy 1985b; J. Milroy 1992). But we also need to attend to the dynamics of key extralinguistic variables such as gender, age and class which have repeatedly been shown to be instrumental in mapping the social trajectory of change. In the following sections we shall first present relevant background information on the three vowels discussed. Next, we set out the results of our analysis of reflexes of these vowels in a working-class and a middle-class Newcastle community. Finally, we examine some implications of this work for our understanding of language change. We turn initially, however, to a description of Newcastle English, dealing first with the vowel system, and secondly with information concerning the consonantal and prosodic features of the variety.

2.2   *Descriptive material*

The descriptive section of this chapter is based on data drawn from the 26-hour corpus collected as part of the project *Phonological Variation and Change in*

Table 2.1 Design of Newcastle fieldwork sample

Working class (WC)				Middle class (MC)			
Younger (15–27)		Older (45–67)		Younger (15–27)		Older (45–67)	
Male	Female	Male	Female	Male	Female	Male	Female
4	4	4	4	4	4	4	4

Contemporary Spoken British English (henceforth *PVC*; ESRC grant no. R000234892; Milroy, Milroy & Docherty 1997). In Newcastle upon Tyne recordings of 32 speakers were made following a social network model (Milroy & Milroy 1985b), divided to sample the community along parameters of age, gender and broadly defined socio-economic class. (A parallel sample was collected in Derby – see Docherty & Foulkes this volume.) The 32 informants were thus selected according to the design in Table 2.1.

Fieldwork in Newcastle upon Tyne centred on the electoral wards of Woolsington (for WC informants) and Westerhope (for MC). To obtain naturalistic speech samples, informants were recorded in conversational exchange in self-selected dyads for around 45 minutes. The fieldworker on the whole played a minimal role, often remaining out of sight of the speakers. All informants then read a word-list of around 200 items.[1]

2.2.1   Vowels

Table 2.2 Newcastle vowels – summary

KIT	ɪ	FLEECE	iː > ei ~ ɪi	NEAR	iɐ ~ iə
DRESS	ɛ	FACE	eː ~ ɛː ~ ɪə > eɪ	SQUARE	ɛː ~ eː
TRAP	a	PALM	ɑː ~ ɒː	START	ɑː ~ ɒː
LOT	ɒ	THOUGHT	ɔː > ɑː	NORTH	ɔː > ɑː
STRUT	ʊ	GOAT	oː > ʊə ~ θː	FORCE	ɔː > ɑː
FOOT	ʊ	GOOSE	uː ~ ɵʊ	CURE	jʊɐ ~ jʊə
BATH	a	PRICE	ɛi ~ ai	happY	i
CLOTH	ɒ	CHOICE	ɔɪ	lettᴇʀ	ɐ ~ ə
NURSE	øː ~ ɜː > ɔː	MOUTH	aʊ > ɛʉ ~ uː	horses	ə
				commᴀ	ɐ ~ ə ~ a

Comments

TRAP/BATH

Wells (1982: 375) reports a long variant [aː] before voiced consonants as in *lad*, *band*; this is rather uncommon in contemporary Newcastle English. [ɑː] is found in *master, plaster, disaster* (Beal 1985).

STRUT/FOOT
May be heard as [ə] among middle-class speakers, particularly females.

NURSE
The traditional [ɔ:] is now scarce. This variant is reported to be a consequence of 'burr retraction' (backing of vowels before [ʁ]; see Beal 1985: 42; Påhlsson 1972). Central pronunciations around [ɜ:] are most frequent. Use of a front rounded variant [ø:] is on the increase, particularly among young women. *Learn, German* and *jersey* may be heard, though rarely, with [ɑ:] among male speakers.

FLEECE
Alternates between [i:] and [ei] ~ [ɪi]: the diphthongal form is confined to morphologically open syllables, thus [si:z] *seize* but [seiz] *sees*.

FACE
Predominantly [e:], which varies somewhat in height: [ɛ:] is used a good deal by female speakers (thus [mɛ:t] *mate* but [mɛt] *met*). [ɪə] is very common among male speakers; [æi] may occasionally be heard in *eight, game*, etc. A southern/midland-type closing diphthong [eɪ] is rare, but becoming more common among MC speakers, particularly females, and most often in formal styles.

PALM/START
Among older and WC speakers chiefly [ɒ:], reported to be a consequence of 'burr retraction' (see comments on NURSE). [ɑ:] is increasingly frequent.

THOUGHT/FORCE/NORTH
Generally [ɔ:], though [a:] is sporadic in WC pronunciations of *walk, talk, bald, all, wall, fall, call, ball, war*, etc.

GOAT
Mostly [o:]; [ʊə] is used with great frequency among older and WC men. The central variant [ɵ:] is common among older WC and young MC men, but avoided altogether by females. [oʊ] is infrequent but is favoured by younger MC speakers, especially women. Archaic pronunciations of *know, snow, old, cold* etc. take [a:] (as per some THOUGHT/NORTH/FORCE items). [aʊ] is used by some WC men in *old, gold, soldier, shoulder*.

GOOSE
As with FLEECE, an alternation can be heard between [u:] and [ɵʊ] in morphologically open and checked pairs such as [brɵʊz] *brews* and [bru:z] *bruise*. Some older speakers of Tyneside English have [i:] in *do*.

PRICE
A similar alternation to the Scottish Vowel Length Rule obtains among words of the PRICE set (J. Milroy 1995; see also Scobbie, Hewlett & Turk this volume):

raised [ɛi] is found before voiceless stops and fricatives, [ai] elsewhere, thus [nɛif] *knife* but [naivz] *knives*. Male speakers, particularly older and/or WC ones, may sometimes use [iː] in *night* and *right*.

MOUTH
Chiefly [aʊ], but frequently closer to [ɛʉ] among women. The traditional [uː] of *down, town, house, out*, etc. is now confined almost exclusively to the speech of WC males (with the exception of the widespread *Toon* to refer to the city of Newcastle and its football team).

happY
Close and often long [iː]; may exceed stressed vowel in duration (see Local 1990).

lettER/commA
Often very open [ɐ] among older and/or WC speakers; [ə] more generally heard for MC speakers.

2.2.2 Consonants

T
Newcastle has a highly complex set of T variant patterns, structured in relation to sociolinguistic, phonological, syntactic and discourse-level constraints (see Docherty, Foulkes, Milroy, Milroy & Walshaw 1997). In pre-pausal positions a fully released or spirantised [t] is invariably used (see the discussion in Docherty & Foulkes this volume), although [ʔ] is making some inroads into sentence tags in this context. In intervocalic position at least five variants occur commonly across the PVC whole sample: [ɹ ṯ t ʔ t͡ʔ] (see Table 2.3).
    The first variant reflects the 'T-to-R rule' (Wells 1982: 370) and occurs only in

Table 2.3 Percentage realisations of T in word-final pre-vowel position, Newcastle speakers (N = number of tokens analysed)

Variant →	ɹ	ṯ	t	t͡ʔ	ʔ	N
Older WC females	40	18	27	12	2	404
Older WC males	15	35	7	42	2	178
Young WC females	21	39	5	20	13	402
Young WC males	3	59	4	23	12	230
Older MC females	12	27	39	20	2	366
Older MC males	6	32	5	53	4	398
Young MC females	2	42	5	17	34	383
Young MC males	1	46	4	27	23	305

a restricted set of common verbs (e.g. *get*, *let*, *put*) and non-lexical words (e.g. *but, not, what, that*). The [ɪ] variant is also marked sociolinguistically, occurring most often in the speech of older females, and hardly at all in younger speech (with the exception of the young WC females, where two of the four individuals were responsible for all the tokens noted in the relevant cell of Table 2.3). Glottal stops are virtually categorical for all speakers before syllabic ʟ (e.g. *bottle*). In pre-vocalic positions [ʔ] is rarely found in the speech of older informants, but is becoming more frequent in younger (particularly MC female) speech, which we interpret as another sign of levelling. The variants transcribed [t͡ʔ] are usually described as 'glottal reinforced', and are discussed in detail by Docherty & Foulkes (this volume). They occur in intersonorant position (e.g. *hatter, winter, alter*), and are in the main more characteristic of male speech, being particularly avoided by females in word-list reading.

P, K

Glottal reinforced variants akin to those described for ᴛ occur in intersonorant contexts, with evidence that ᴘ is subject to reinforcement more frequently than either ᴛ or ᴋ (see Table 2.4; Docherty *et al.* 1997: 300–1). The reinforced forms are again less prominent in female speech.

TH, F

The labiodental forms [f, v] for /θ, ð/ can be found in younger, particularly WC, speech but are still relatively scarce. Some speakers produce glottal reinforced variants of /f/ and /θ/ as well as those already described for stops, e.g. in *Kathy* [ka͡ʔθi] and *sulphur* [sʊl͡ʔfɐ]. It is not clear how widespread such variants are across speakers or the lexicon.

H

Tyneside is one of few urban areas in Britain where [h] is usually pronounced. The only exceptions appear to be unstressed function words (*him, her* etc.).

R

Usually [ɹ], but [r] can be found, usually in intervocalic position. A labiodental or bilabial approximant [ʋ] ~ [β] is increasing in young speech (Foulkes &

Table 2.4 Percentage use of glottal reinforced variants for ᴘ, ᴛ, ᴋ in word-medial position

	% Glottal reinforced tokens			N tokens analysed		
	P	T	K	P	T	K
Male	87	82	82	*337*	*952*	*404*
Female	58	42	37	*328*	*1,098*	*345*

Docherty in press). The 'Northumbrian burr' [ʁ] is nowadays very rare and almost wholly restricted to rural areas.

Tyneside English is non-rhotic. Linking and intrusive R are relatively rare in comparison with other accents in England, and both display significant socio-linguistic patterning. Linking R is used in around 80% of cases by older MC speakers, but drops to *c.* 40% for the young WC. Intrusive R occurs at a rate of around 20% in WC speech, and is virtually absent in unmonitored MC speech. However, there are signs that MC speakers in particular display a wholly unexpected style-shifting, using significantly more intrusive R in word-list readings (see further Foulkes 1997a, b).

L

Usually clear (non-velarised) in all positions.

2.2.3 Suprasegmentals

Tyneside English is distinguished by the fact that it typically has rising intonation in declarative utterances (Cruttenden 1997: 133; see also Local, Kelly & Wells 1986).

2.3 *Levelling of phonetic variation in three Tyneside vowels*

Levelling of localised variants in Tyneside English appears to have been going on for at least forty years. Viereck's studies of the Gateshead dialect (1966, 1968), the fieldwork for which was carried out in the late 1950s, suggest that changes in the direction of 'Standard English' (i.e. RP) had already precipitated the loss of certain traditional Tyneside forms. Viereck's prognostication of the fate of the variety is gloomy:

> Some dialectal features seem to be more stable and less likely to succumb to Standard English in the near future. Others, however, will no doubt soon be completely replaced, especially since the area under investigation is urban and consequently the pressure of the standard language rather great, so that the traditional dialect is bound to become increasingly mixed. Further, the fluctuation of the population must be reckoned with as well as sociological factors, all of which contribute to a dilution of traditional dialects. [. . .] the time will soon come when historically developed, genuine dialect phonemes are no longer heard. [. . .] All this, we feel, increases the urgency of studying archaic, traditional dialect before these features disappear completely. (Viereck 1968: 76)

Viereck attributes the levelling process to 'various influences which undermine its traditional character', namely 'education, [. . .] mass media – radio, television and film – and to the whole linguistic climate of a large commercial centre' (1968: 65). The last of these includes Gateshead's 'change of population' brought about by 'a great number of people [who] have poured into this area from other parts of the country' (1968: 65). It is, Viereck believes, 'extremely important for the proper understanding of Gateshead, as well as any other urban dialect, to study its traditional local features, or the survivals of them, before it is too late' (1968: 65–6).

Viereck's (1968) study concentrates exclusively on vowels: it is apparently the loss of traditional features of the vowel system that concerns him most. The present chapter similarly concentrates on aspects of variation and change in the Tyneside vowels, focusing on those within the FACE, GOAT and NURSE sets. These vowels exhibit gross phonetic differences which, in the case of FACE and GOAT, are characterised principally by diphthongisation, while in words of the NURSE set a range of phonetic variants spanning the vowel space from front to back can be heard. Among the latter there exists a marked distinction between 'peripheral' and 'central' variants. At least as far as FACE and GOAT are concerned, the range of variants can readily be analysed as discontinuous, in that it is comparatively easy to categorise tokens as either 'diphthongal' or 'monophthongal' using auditory analysis. Tokens of NURSE, on the other hand, though scattered across the vowel space in a continuous fashion, appear to cluster around certain points in the space, with the result that we can with reasonable ease distinguish three variant categories associated with each cluster. We begin with a discussion of the FACE and GOAT classes.

2.3.1   FACE and GOAT

The FACE and GOAT vowels are often said to behave as 'mirror images' of one another: indeed, the tendency toward front–back symmetry in vowel systems is said to be universal (Liljencrants & Lindblom 1972; Crothers 1978; Lindblom 1986a; Schwartz, Boë, Vallée & Abry 1997) and as such underlies much of the research carried out into aspects of variation and change in vowel systems, including, as we have seen, Labov's (1994) work on American vowel systems. The similarities between these vowel classes in terms of their phonetic exponents can be taken as evidence of this symmetrical relationship. The 'default' (or at any rate most common) variants of both vowels in Tyneside English (henceforth TE) are long, peripheral monophthongs [eː] and [oː] of the type heard frequently in a large area of England north of a line extending from Grimsby in the east to Liverpool in the west, dipping south of Sheffield (see Trudgill 1990: 61). Both FACE and GOAT can be realised also by centring diphthongal variants [ɪə] and [ʊə], where a near-peripheral nucleus is followed by an ingliding central vowel. Finally, both word-classes have closing diphthongal variants – approximately [eɪ] and [oʊ] – somewhat similar to those found in midland and southern varieties of British English, though these 'pan-English' variants appear relatively infrequently in our data.

This symmetrical relationship is, of course, something of an idealisation of the real situation. An audibly very conspicuous difference between the FACE and

GOAT classes concerns the fronting of GOAT to a quality we symbolise [ɵː], for which there is no parallel case in the FACE class. The use of this variant is in fact one of the most widely stereotyped features of TE. According to Orton, Sanderson & Widdowson (1978), similar variants of GOAT are restricted to the extreme north-east corner of rural England, and in cities to the Tyneside urban area. The articulatory properties of this variant are rather unclear and its acoustic properties difficult to determine, though Viereck (1966, 1968), Wells (1982) and Lass (1989: 190) all symbolise it [ɵː]; for our purposes [ɵː] will suffice to represent a variant of GOAT which is clearly different from [oː], [ʊə] and [oʊ]. The different territorial spreads of these variants (ranging from the extremely localised through the generally northern to the pan-English) are relevant to a discussion of change in terms of a dialect levelling framework.

2.3.2 NURSE

As noted above, the range of phonetic exponents of this vowel in TE is very broad, and we shall distinguish here three variant types. First, the literature typically makes reference to a retracted variant, transcribed [ɔː] (Jones 1911; Viereck 1966, 1968; Påhlsson 1972; Wells 1982; Lass 1983; Beal 1985; Hughes & Trudgill 1996).[2] Its use is analysed either as neutralisation of the phonetic distinction between words of the THOUGHT/NORTH/FORCE set like *short* and (some pronunciations of) *shirt*, or as full merger, where all members of the NURSE class are categorically realised with the retracted [ɔː]. In the latter case, we would expect *short* and *shirt*, *bird* and *board*, *fur* and *four*, etc., to be homophonous. This, apparently, is the view of Tyneside dialect dictionary compilers such as Todd (1987) or Dobson (1987); Dobson glosses the entry *Gizashort* as *A small whisky*, or *May I have a shirt?* (Dobson 1987: 28) and renders NURSE words like *germs*, *bird* and *first* using <-or->, as in *jorms*, *bord*, *forst*.

A central variant of the NURSE vowel, which has a geographically wider distribution in contemporary northern English than the retracted, 'merged' variant described above, is also heard in Tyneside a great deal more frequently. This can be labelled [ɜː], although the range of non-peripheral qualities of this vowel in TE is wider than the IPA symbol suggests. Since this variant is quite distinct from realisations of the THOUGHT/NORTH/FORCE set, we may infer that the merger postulated with such confidence in earlier descriptions of TE was either not categorical for all Tyneside speakers, or was falsely reported (for discussions of comparable problems with putative mergers elsewhere see Milroy & Harris 1980; Labov 1994: 311–90; Faber & Di Paolo 1995).

A third variant of NURSE is also evident in the data: this is a fully fronted and rounded variant. Like Wells (1982: 375) we symbolise it [øː].[3] As such, its quality is similar to that reported for varieties of Southern Hemisphere English (for discussions of such pronunciations in South African and New Zealand English, see Wells 1982: 607–8; Lass 1989, 1990).

To summarise: we can divide the vowel continuum into three sections with respect to variable realisations of the NURSE vowel, yielding a retracted variant

Table 2.5 Variants of FACE, GOAT and
NURSE in Tyneside English

FACE	GOAT	NURSE
eː	oː	ɜː
ɪə	ʊə	ɔː
eɪ	oʊ	øː
	θː	

similar or identical in quality to the vowel of NORTH in this dialect, [ɔː], a front
rounded variant [øː], and a central variant [ɜː]. Since [ɜː] resembles the corresponding vowel in neighbouring varieties, and is moreover the commonest contemporary variant of NURSE in TE, it can be considered the 'default' or
'unmarked' variant. The ten variants of the three variables investigated in this
study are listed in Table 2.5.

The motivation for attempting to handle patterns of variation and change in
these vowels in terms of a dialect levelling framework is at this point fairly clear.
Although the specifically local variants of all three vowels are extremely salient
because of their perceptual distance from less localised variants, these latter
variants are more commonly used by speakers of TE. In order to specify the
social trajectory of the levelling process – the order and manner in which it is
implemented by different sectors of the population – we turn now to examine
the distribution of local versus supra-local variants of FACE, GOAT and NURSE
with respect to the social variables of gender, age and social class.

2.3.3   Data

The data used for this study were drawn from the *PVC* conversational material.
A minimum of 40 (stressed) tokens of each variable per speaker was aimed for.
This was somewhat problematic in the case of NURSE, which shows up relatively
rarely, and most frequently in unstressed syllables (*her, were*, etc.). When the figures for each speaker subgroup are aggregated, however, distinctive patterns
readily emerge despite differences in sample size between individual speakers.
All tokens of the three vowel variables were transcribed using IPA notation, and
grouped according to the variant categories set out in Table 2.5.[4]

2.3.4   Quantitative analysis

(a) FACE

Figure 2.1 shows as rounded percentages the distribution of variants of FACE on
the basis of the aggregated scores for each speaker group (the actual scores are
given in the Appendix).

A number of clear patterns can be discerned in Figure 2.1. Firstly, the prefer-

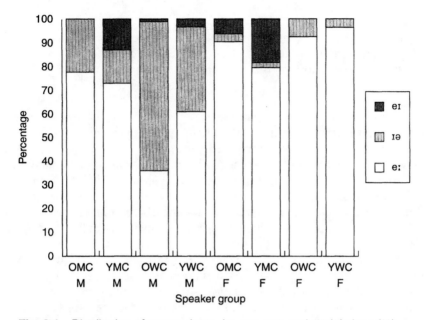

Fig. 2.1 Distribution of FACE variants, by sex, age and social class (%)
(O = older, Y = young; MC = middle class, WC = working class; M =
male, F = female)

ence for the unmarked variant [eː] is overwhelming for all groups except the
older WC males. For this group, the general pattern is reversed, with speakers
using almost twice as many tokens of [ɪə] as of [eː]. Use of [ɪə] becomes less frequent as a function of age (the younger WC male group uses it just 36% of the
time as opposed to the older WC male group's 63%), and of class (with [ɪə]
accounting for 22% and 14% of the older MC male and younger MC male
samples respectively). Gender, however, is the variable which divides the speakers most sharply, as female speakers use centring diphthong variants very rarely.
Statistical analysis confirms the primacy of gender in accounting for the distribution shown in Figure 2.1; log linear models indicate that the effect of speaker
sex on its own is very highly significant ($p < 0.0001$), as are class and age when
gender is taken into account ($p = 0.0001$ gender + class; $p = 0.0076$ gender +
age + class).[5]

The frequency distribution of tokens of the closing diphthong [eɪ] is also
interesting with respect to the effects of gender, class and age. Although this
variant occurs infrequently, its use is chiefly confined to the speech of young MC
males and females (12% and 18% respectively of all FACE variants in the speech
of these groups). An even smaller proportion of [eɪ] – just 6% – shows up in the
older MC female sample. However, this variant is used much more idiosyncratically by individual speakers than the others. Recall that historically it is not a
Tyneside or even a northern variant, but is characteristic of the English south

and midlands; of the total of 30 tokens of [eɪ] in the young MC female sample, 29 are accounted for by a single speaker, while in the young MC male sample, all 18 tokens are accounted for by a single speaker (see below for similar patterns with respect to realisations of the GOAT vowel).

(b) GOAT

Again, a number of very clear patterns emerge from this distribution (Figure 2.2), some of which are parallel to the FACE patterns reviewed above. Very evident is the preference for the unmarked variant [oː] by all groups except the WC males; OWC males use the variants [oː], [ʊə] and [əː] in approximately equal proportions. These figures confirm the preference among OWC males for more traditional localised variants. As noted with respect to the FACE variant, it is the gender variable which primarily accounts for the distribution shown in Figure 2.2; the centring diphthong variant [ʊə] is used chiefly by men, while female speakers avoid this variant almost entirely. Only six tokens of [ʊə] were recorded from a total sample of 754 GOAT tokens for the female speaker groups. Male speakers, on the other hand, use this variant rather more frequently; it represents some 16% of their total sample. Its distribution amongst male speakers is, moreover, associated with the age and social class of the speaker, as is evident from Table 2.6.

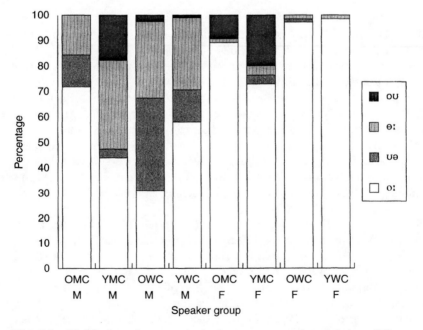

Fig. 2.2   Distribution of GOAT variants, by sex, age and social class (%)

Table 2.6   Use of [ʊə] by male speakers
by age and class, as a percentage of total
GOAT tokens (N = 710)

OMC	YMC	OWC	YWC
12	3	36	12

As might be expected, the OWC males use this 'old-fashioned' variant (Wells 1982; Lass 1989: 188) more frequently than other groups, with [ʊə] accounting for over one third of their GOAT tokens. The young WC and older MC groups both use [ʊə] much less but in equal proportions, while the young MC group avoid it almost entirely. This variant is thus strongly associated with older WC males. The strongest effect is for class, sex and age taken into account together ($p = 0.0025$; class + sex only: $p = 0.0042$).

A similar pattern of distribution is found for the fronted GOAT variant [ɵ:]. This variant is also avoided almost completely by female speakers, and represents less than 1% of the GOAT tokens for three of the four female groups. For the fourth group (YMC) it accounts for just 4%. The effect of gender is therefore very highly significant here ($p < 0.0001$). Amongst male speakers, on the other hand, the pattern of distribution set out in Table 2.6 is similar to that for [ɵ:] in Table 2.7, except that the YMC speakers also use this conservative fronted variant to a greater extent than do the OWC. When we look at the results of statistical modelling which emerge from this complex distribution, we find that the class effect is only marginally significant at the 5% level even when sex is included in the analysis ($p = 0.0442$) and that the influence of speaker age is less marked still.[6] This tendency for well-educated young men to use an apparently localised variant is reminiscent of the distribution of fronted /ay/ and /aw/ variants described by Labov (1963) on Martha's Vineyard, and is explained as a symbolic affirmation of local identity.[7]

To conclude this review of the distribution of GOAT variants, we comment briefly on the distribution of the [oʊ] variant. As noted in section 2.3.1, this closing diphthong is historically associated with the south of England and with high

Table 2.7 Use of [ɵ:] by male speakers by age and class, as a percentage of total GOAT tokens (N = 710)

OMC	YMC	OWC	YWC
15	35	30	28

prestige supra-local speech patterns. Of all the male groups, only young MC males use it to any substantial extent (17% of all GOAT tokens, as opposed to 2% and 1% for the older and younger WC groups respectively) while it did not appear at all in the OMC male sample of 175 tokens. The proportion used by YMC males is very similar to that of their female counterparts (19%). Both groups use this relatively rare variant more than OMC women (9%). On the face of it, YMC speakers of both sexes are particularly inclined to adopt what is essentially a non-local but very socially salient variant. However, we need to treat these figures warily, for exactly the reasons noted in our discussion of the parallel FACE variant [eɪ]. Of the 30 [oʊ] tokens recorded for the YMC male group, 18 were used by a single individual and 11 by a second, while the other two speakers in the group did not use this variant at all; of the 34 tokens of [oʊ] recorded for the YMC female group 27 were produced by the same speaker who produced all but one of the tokens of [eɪ] in the FACE sample.

(c) NURSE
We turn finally to consider the distribution of variants of the NURSE vowel. As discussed above, we expect to find a pattern in the data that reflects the observations by Wells (1982), Lass (1983) and others that the traditional, retracted, 'merged' form [ɔː] has lost ground to the less marked central variant [ɜː] in the speech of our Tyneside informants (see also Hughes & Trudgill 1996; Watt 1996, 1998). The data shown in Figure 2.3 support this claim, but reveal an additional complexity.

Tokens of the supra-local (unmarked) central variant [ɜː] represent more than

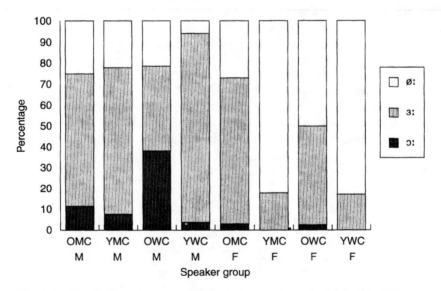

Fig. 2.3   Distribution of NURSE variants, by sex, age and social class (%)

half (52.5%) of all tokens in the sample. The fronted variant [ø:] is also widely used, especially by young women of both social classes, accounting for two fifths of all NURSE tokens. The retracted and highly localised variant [ɔ:], on the other hand, accounts for only a little over 7% of the total sample. Once more, gender is the principal factor underlying these patterns of variation ($p < 0.0001$), with age also having a considerable effect ($p = 0.0159$). The age by sex interaction effect is very highly significant ($p = 0.0011$), arising from the preference for [ø:] among young women generally, which contrasts with the older MC (male and female) and younger MC male preference for [ɜ:].

The distribution of the retracted variant [ɔ:] among male speakers (it is hardly used at all by women) suggests that it is recessive; it is associated chiefly with older WC men where it represents 38% of all NURSE tokens. This substantial figure confirms claims noted earlier that it was once a much more widely distributed Tyneside variant which has since lost ground to less localised forms. Other male groups use it a great deal less: 4% is the figure for the young WC group, and 12% and 8% respectively the figures for the older and younger MC groups.

Turning now to the fronted [ø:] variant of NURSE, a strong preference for this variant by younger female speakers of both classes (over 80%) is evident in Table 2.8. Older WC women use this variant around half the time, while for older MC women it represents just over a quarter of their NURSE tokens. Thus, while women all agree in avoiding the localised variant [ɔ:], the two less localised variants are distributed chiefly according to gender and age.

The patterns of use summarised in Table 2.9 present a sharp contrast with those in Table 2.8. Older MC men use the [ø:] variant at much the same level as older MC women, while younger MC and older WC groups show a clear contrast with the preferences of their respective female counterparts. The young WC group, however, use it very rarely – just over 6% of the time.

Table 2.8 Use of [ø:] by female speakers by age and class, as a percentage of total NURSE tokens (N = 605)

OMC	YMC	OWC	YWC
27	82	50	82

Table 2.9 Use of [ø:] by male speakers by age and class, as a percentage of total NURSE tokens (N = 551)

OMC	YMC	OWC	YWC
25	22	21	6

Note that the young WC male group's figure for the retracted variant [ɔː] is also rather small by comparison with those for other male speaker groups. Thus, these speakers are distinct both from older speakers who characteristically use this variant, and from younger women who favour [øː].

2.4   *Discussion*

In this section we attempt to pull together the chief patterns which have emerged from our analysis of all three vowels, and suggest that a dialect levelling framework best accounts for the patterns of variation which are evident and the patterns of change which can be inferred. The southern and midland closing diphthongal variants of FACE and GOAT vowels (the best candidates for the soubriquet of 'prestige' variants) occur infrequently, and when they do, are used mainly by younger MC speakers of both sexes. They also have a more limited distribution in the speech of older MC females. Given current theories of the role of gender in language change (see below) and the association in the far north of these non-indigenous closing diphthongs with a range of higher status RP-influenced accents, their primary association with speaker age and class rather than gender is noteworthy.

The unmarked northern mainstream monophthongal FACE and GOAT variants [eː] and [oː] are used at high frequencies by women, young speakers and MC speakers. The NURSE vowel is a little more complicated in that two non-traditional supra-local variants emerge. The unrounded variant, preferred by younger men, seems to have a limited supra-local distribution in the north of England. The rounded variant, preferred by younger women, represents a closer approximation to a variant with a wider distribution in the English south and midlands. Thus, in the case of all three vowels, the dramatic gender difference can be generalised as a female preference for unmarked mainstream variants, and an equally strong male preference for strongly localised variants, as shown in Figure 2.4. In the case of NURSE, young men and women use distinctly different supra-local variants. Within the male group, the traditional variants of NURSE, GOAT and FACE are distributed rather consistently. All three decline steeply in frequency through the speaker groups of older working class to younger middle class.[8]

With one or two exceptions to the overall pattern (notably the preference for the [øː] variant of GOAT by young MC males), the shift away from traditional forms of the three vowel variables is most advanced among MC males, particularly the younger group. The young male MC patterns reflect those which are more clearly evident in female speech, which is much more homogeneous with little sign of the age- and class-related patterns so clearly evident in Figure 2.4.

Chambers (1995) reviews the contribution of the variationist studies of the last thirty years to our understanding of social mechanisms of language change

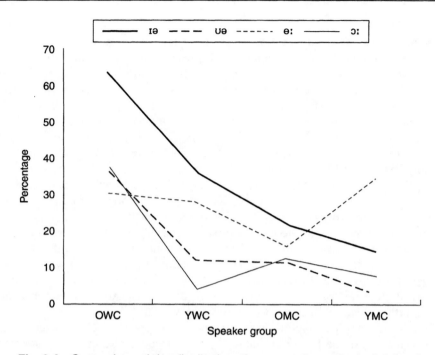

Fig. 2.4   Comparison of the distribution of conservative variants: [ɪə] (FACE), [ʊə], [eː] (GOAT) and [ɔː] (NURSE), male speakers only (%)

in progress. The question is how far the findings reported here are consistent with this substantial body of research.

First, the FACE, GOAT and NURSE vowel reflexes all show symmetrically different patterns of distribution between generations. However, although cross-generational changes in the FACE and GOAT vowels seem to be phonologically co-ordinated, the chief dimension of change is not easily described in phonological terms such as raising, fronting, backing, or as shifting in any co-ordinated way as the Northern Cities Shift in the United States is characterised. The salient pattern of change is a reduction in variability across two generations; localised variants either disappear or are reduced in number and younger speakers prefer mainstream, unmarked variants.

Second, women are greatly in advance of men in preferring the unmarked variant with respect to both GOAT and FACE vowels and the variant with the widest territorial distribution with respect to the NURSE vowel. Figure 2.4 graphically reveals the staggered age and class pattern evident in the slow spread of mainstream variants into male speech concomitant with the recession of highly localised variants. This result is in line with variationist studies which have generally identified women as innovators. The social class contrast mirrors the gender contrast, as we have come to expect in variationist sociolinguistics. Working-class speakers and men are more conservative, and middle-class speakers and women prefer the mainstream unmarked variants.

It is at this point that we depart a little from the conventional wisdom on both class and gender. With the partial exception of the NURSE vowel, the main issue here is that the discourse of 'stigma' and 'prestige' and the social motivations which these terms imply does not illuminatingly describe the patterns of change evident in our data. This is because the FACE and GOAT variants which might be the best candidates for prestige forms, i.e. the closing diphthongs characteristic of RP and southern Englishes, hardly enter into the picture. This is perhaps surprising, given that the isogloss which divides northern mainstream monophthongal from southern diphthongal variants has been moving steadily northward for two hundred years, and has certainly gained ground in author LM's lifetime. For example, as a student in Manchester in the early 1960s LM was aware that GOAT and FACE monophthongal realisations were the norm among young local speakers. However, according to Trudgill (1990: 61) the isogloss which marks the limit of the southern variants now runs north of Liverpool and Manchester. So although at national level this southern mainstream/prestige variant is slowly advancing, at this regional level it is apparently not. Although localised variants in Newcastle are vanishing, the dialect as a whole is not moving towards a nationally prestigious homogenised variety. And it is difficult to know in what sense the monophthongs might be described as 'prestige' variants.

Finally, although variability is apparently being progressively reduced, men and women continue to use available linguistic resources to construct sharply differentiated genderlects. Differentiation by gender is much sharper than differentiation by class and seems in fact to be tantamount to a sociolinguistic priority. We have seen that in both FACE and GOAT cases women converge on the unmarked monophthongal variant, while the men use localised variants very much more frequently. In the somewhat more complex case of the NURSE vowel, younger men and women are converging on *different* supra-local variants.

The pattern of change which emerges here corresponds to a pattern of dialect levelling as discussed in section 2.1: the reduction of variability at the expense of locally marked variants where there is mobility of speakers and dialect contact. In this case the contact is between speakers of different localised dialects as well as those from outside the region who move into cities. The resulting levelled variety corresponds to what is traditionally known as a 'regional standard' (Wolfram 1991). Again, in agreement with a substantial body of earlier variationist work, we can surmise that the social dynamic driving the formation of a levelled dialect is the dissolution of the territorially based close-knit network which is needed to keep localised norms intact. Such dissolutions have accelerated throughout Europe in the post-war years (Auer & Hinskens 1996). Dorling (1995) and Cross (1990) draw attention to the phenomenon of *counterurbanisation* – the movement of city-dwellers seeking homes in the surrounding countryside. Following from urbanisation and its accompanying mobility, this too will have the effect of disrupting long-established local networks. What is of interest here, however, is that the social dynamics that drive levelling – divisions of gender, age and class – seem to be similar to the dynamics driving linguistic change of other kinds.

We noted that the levelled variety diffusing through the Newcastle speech community is by no means pan-English; again (with the partial exception of the NURSE variant preferred by young women) it is localised to the north of England, just as so-called 'Estuary English', a comparable levelled variety which is currently eliciting much prescriptive comment, is localised to the south-east. In both cases the forces driving levelling are probably the same (viz., geographical and social mobility and the movement of city-dwellers into rural areas). Currently, several comparable varieties continue to develop around Britain's major urban areas. Kerswill (1996b) reports on a study of the new dialect developing in Milton Keynes, a town which attracts migrants from all parts of Britain (see also Williams & Kerswill this volume). Yet it is surely misleading to describe these levelled varieties as 'standards' of any kind – even regional standards – although we might describe them as koines (see Britain 1997a for a discussion of this term). This is because standards by definition are institutionally imposed, like the now recessive British prestige accent Received Pronunciation (see further L. Milroy forthcoming)[9] and the essence of a levelled variety is that it develops by quite regular sociolinguistic processes, as we have seen. It is therefore seriously misleading to blur the distinction between levelled varieties and standards or to characterise variants which emerge from the levelling process as prestigious.

In conclusion, let us revisit Labov's (1990) comments on gender, class and language change:

> As the innovators, women in intermediate social classes spontaneously create the differences between themselves and men. In adopting new prestige features more rapidly than men, and in reacting more sharply against the use of stigmatised forms, women are again the chief agents of differentiation. (Labov 1990: 240)

In light of the data presented here, this formulation is surely problematic, although if phrased in terms of local versus supra-local, it would gain in generality. The correct generalisation appears to be that men tend to retain localised forms (which may or may not be stigmatised) and women adopt supra-local forms (which may or may not be prestigious). As before, the association of men with localised forms is not new in sociolinguistics (see again Chambers 1995). Consider further what Labov has to say:

> The mechanism of change is not linked to sex differences in any clear and simple way. Either sex can be the dominant factor. But the number of cases where men are in the lead is relatively small. Furthermore, the male dominated changes are all relatively isolated changes such as the centralisation of /ay/ and /aw/ or the unrounding of /o/. All those cases of chainshifting that we have been able to examine with quantitative means are dominated by women. (Labov 1990: 219)

While we observe in Newcastle a very different pattern of vowel variation and change from that described by Labov (1991 *et passim*), we do find that men use proportionately many more localised variants. A more general adoption of the local/supra-local dichotomy and a more serious examination of processes of dialect levelling in cities will lead in turn to a closer examination of what is meant by 'standard' or 'prestige'. Indeed, in the American context, the term 'standard' appears to refer to a supra-local levelled variety of the kind we have considered here, rather than a class-marked and institutionally imposed reference accent like RP (Wolfram 1991: 210). Similarly, so-called local standards are analogous to those which have emerged in Britain and are currently extending their social and geographical territory. It is likely therefore that the framework presented here will also be helpful in characterising some language changes in American urban contexts.

Appendix

(a) Distribution of FACE variants by age, gender and social class

Group	eː	ɪə	eɪ	Total
OMC M	112	31	0	143
YMC M	106	21	18	145
OMC F	139	4	10	153
YMC F	132	4	30	166
OWC M	63	110	1	174
YWC M	118	69	5	192
OWC F	112	9	0	121
YWC F	147	4	0	151
Total	929	252	64	1,245

(b) Distribution of GOAT variants by age, gender and social class

Group	oː	ʊə	eː	oʊ	Total
OMC M	127	21	27	0	175
YMC M	76	5	59	30	170
OMC F	176	0	2	18	196
YMC F	126	5	6	34	171
OWC M	55	63	53	3	174
YWC M	113	23	53	2	191
OWC F	188	1	1	0	190
YWC F	196	0	1	0	197
Total	1,057	118	202	87	1,464

(c) Distribution of NURSE variants by age, gender and social class

Group	ø:	ɜ:	ɔ:	Total
OMC M	38	98	19	155
YMC M	34	110	12	156
OMC F	40	105	4	149
YMC F	144	30	1	175
OWC M	20	39	36	95
YWC M	9	130	6	145
OWC F	76	72	5	153
YWC F	105	23	0	128
Total	466	607	83	1,156

Notes

1 We are grateful to Penny Oxley for carrying out the Newcastle fieldwork, to Paul Foulkes for supplying the descriptive consonantal information contained in this chapter, and to David Walshaw for his assistance with statistical matters. Thanks are also due to Ann Williams and Paul Kerswill for their helpful comments on drafts of this chapter.

2 O'Connor (1947) uses [oː], though his transcription system substitutes a length distinction for qualitative differences in pairs like [i] ~ [ɪ], [e] ~ [ɛ], etc.

3 This vowel is in fact variably rounded, such that NURSE may be perceptually very close to [eː] or [ɛː] in the speech of some Tyneside speakers: *work* and *first*, for example, may overlap with (monophthongal) realizations of *wake* and *faced*. Compare this with the front unrounded [ɛː] for NURSE in Liverpool English (Knowles 1978: 84; see also Newbrook this volume).

4 The FACE and GOAT vowels were analysed independently by James and Lesley Milroy respectively. Comparisons of percentage scores for the variants [eː] and [ɪə] of FACE and [oː], [ʊə], [əː] and [ou] of GOAT using *Minitab* 10 to generate Pearson product-moment correlation coefficients show an extremely high level of correspondence. For both vowels, the correlation between the two sets of transcriptions was very highly significant (FACE: $r = 0.939$, $p < 0.002$; GOAT: $r = 0.959$, $p < 0.002$).

5 Log linear modelling of the data was carried out using the Numerical Algorithm Group's *GLIM* 3.77 program.

6 Details of the effects of following phonological context upon the distribution of variants of the FACE, GOAT and NURSE variables may be found in Watt (1998); a lack of space here precludes discussion of such effects.

7 Alternatively, it may be that [əː] has been 'reallocated' (Britain 1997a) as a prestige variant because of its similarity to the centralised nucleus of RP [əu]: see Lass' (1989: 188) commentary on a similar proposal in Orton (1933). A central vowel [ɜː] is reported by Williams & Kerswill (this volume) to be a high-status variant of GOAT favoured especially by young Hull women; contemporary Bradford English also features a GOAT variant approximating this quality (Watt & Tillotson 1999).

8 The correlations between each speaker group's paired scores for FACE and GOAT are found to be very highly significant: [eː ~ oː], $r = 0.917$, $p < 0.002$; [ɪə ~ ʊə], $r = 0.964$,

$p < 0.002$; [eɪ ~ oʊ], $r = 0.981$, $p < 0.002$). This can be taken to indicate a symmetrical relationship between these two variables at a phonological level (see Watt 1998).

9　Changes in the status of RP and in relations between urban dialects and institutional spoken standards have been noted in the press for some time: in a recent article entitled *Britain's crumbling ruling class is losing the accent of authority*, for instance, we hear that 'the upper-class young already talk Estuary English, the cockneyfied accent of the South-east' (Neal Ascherson, *Independent on Sunday*, 7 August 1994; see also Wells 1994).

3

Derby and Newcastle: instrumental phonetics and variationist studies

Gerard J. Docherty and Paul Foulkes

3.1 *Introduction*

In this chapter we present a description of the accent of Derby, and discuss the role of instrumental phonetics within the variationist tradition.[1] In the discussion we refer both to these Derby data and also to subsections of the Newcastle data outlined by Watt & Milroy (this volume). The Derby and Newcastle corpora were both collected for the project *Phonological Variation and Change in Contemporary Spoken British English* (Milroy, Milroy & Docherty 1997). The sample design and recording contexts for the Derby corpus are almost identical to those described by Watt & Milroy (this volume) for Newcastle, with minor differences in the ages of informants and the items included in the word-list. The fieldwork profile is given in Table 3.1.

Fieldwork in Derby was carried out using a social network model (Milroy & Milroy 1985b), and centred on the electoral wards of Chaddesden (for WC informants) and Spondon (for MC). Informants were recorded in self-selected dyads, with the fieldworker playing a minimal role and often remaining out of sight. For the purposes of the description given in this chapter we also recorded three further informants, all relatives of the second author, and who at the time were in their early eighties.

Table 3.1 Fieldwork design for Derby corpus

Working Class (WC)				Middle Class (MC)			
Younger (14–27)		Older (45–67)		Younger (15–27)		Older (45–67)	
Male	Female	Male	Female	Male	Female	Male	Female
4	4	4	4	4	4	4	4

3.1.1   Derby and Derby English

Derby is a medium-sized city (population *c.* 215,000 at the 1991 census), 125 miles north of London. It is largely an industrial city, famed originally for production of silk and pottery, and more recently as a major railway centre and the home of Rolls Royce. Its profile and atmosphere have changed noticeably in the last few years since the opening of the University of Derby, which has led to a sudden influx of several thousand young people from a wide catchment area. Derby is the only city in the county of Derbyshire, and is located in the far south of the county. As a result, speech patterns in the city differ markedly in many respects from those found in the county at large.

References to the speech and language of Derby and Derbyshire are few and far between in the literature. The only scholarly sources which focus specifically on the area appear to be Pegge (1896) and Hulme (1941), which are very valuable from a historical perspective. More jocular treatments are given by Wright (1975), and by Scollins & Titford (1976/77) for the town of Ilkeston (which, as anyone in the whole county will tell you, has a dialect *sui generis*). Derby's geographical position nonetheless makes it an interesting proposition for the dialectologist, since it is generally recognised as lying on the cusp of several major dialect areas (cf. Wright 1905: 4; Wells 1982: 350; Hughes & Trudgill 1996: 65). Overall, Derby's salient accent features mark it as a northern variety, as shown by the numerous similarities with the accent of Sheffield (see Stoddart, Upton & Widdowson this volume). However, there are some obvious links with south midlands varieties (e.g. the male variants of the PRICE vowel), and the increasing influence of the south-east on the speech of young city Derbeians is very apparent. These latter remarks are less true of county accents, which blend more gradually into those of neighbouring Yorkshire, Nottinghamshire and Staffordshire.

3.2   *Descriptive material*

3.2.1   Vowels

Table 3.2 Derby vowels – summary

KIT	ɪ	FLEECE	iː ~ ɪi	NEAR	ɪː ~ ɪ(j)ə
DRESS	ɛ	FACE	ɛɪ	SQUARE	ɛː
TRAP	a	PALM	ɑː ~ ɒː	START	ɑː ~ ɒː
LOT	ɒ	THOUGHT	ɔː	NORTH	ɔː
STRUT	ʊ	GOAT	əʉ ~ ou	FORCE	ɔː
FOOT	ʊ	GOAL	ou > əʉ	CURE	jɔː > juːə
BATH	a	GOOSE	ʉː > uː ~ iː	happʏ	iː > ɪ
CLOTH	ɒ	PRICE	aɪ ~ ɑɪ ~ ɒɪ ~ aːː[1]	lettɐ	ə
NURSE	ɔː > iː	CHOICE	ɔɪ	horses	ə > ɪ
		MOUTH	aː > aʊ	commᴀ	ə

Comments

TRAP/BATH
Usually [a], but [ɑː] is used in several lexical items where northern varieties typically have [a], such as *aunt, father, calf* (but not *master*).

LOT/CLOTH
One, none and *tongue* (but not *once*) invariably pattern with this set rather than
STRUT; other items such as *mother, bugger* may follow suit for older speakers
(thus [mɒðə], [bɒɡə]), but generally pattern with STRUT nowadays.

STRUT/FOOT
May appear as [ə] in more self-conscious speech styles, particularly by females.

NURSE
Usually [əː], but there are examples of raised [ɨː] amongst older WC speakers,
considered a West Midlands feature by Wells (1982: 361). Amongst the same
speakers there is also a (probably) lexically restricted [ɛː] in e.g. *her, were, stir*.
Archaic dialect forms with [ɒ] in e.g. *horse, work, first* (thus [ɒs], [wɒk], [fɒst])
may still be found, but are increasingly becoming restricted to rural areas and
the speech of older Derbeians.

FLEECE
Some dialectal remnants of [ɪ] in *week*.

FACE
Predominantly a diphthong [ɛɪ], with reduced monophthongs in a restricted set
of words such as *take, make* ([tɛk, mɛk]) especially amongst older speakers. Day
names vary between this and the FLEECE set, thus e.g. *Monday* may be [mʊndɛɪ],
[mʊndiː], [mʊndɪi], or [mʊndɪ].

PALM/START
Overwhelmingly [ɑː] or slightly rounded [ɒː], but dialectal remnants of [ɛɪ] in
father, rather, half persist in older WC and rural speech.

THOUGHT/FORCE/NORTH
Usually [ɔː], although for old Derbeians one may find examples of an
unrounded vowel after /w/ in e.g. *water* [watə], and rarely [ou] before the historical velar fricative (thus e.g. [θout] for *thought*).

GOAT/GOAL
Older WC males retain back rounded variants of the [ou] / [ɒu] type in all contexts, whereas amongst other speaker groups these forms appear only before /l/.
Southern-type centralised and (partly) unrounded variants [əʉ] / [əɨ] / [ɐʉ] predominate for young speakers and the older MC. Older speakers sometimes use

a monophthong [uː] in the item *go* and [ʊ] in its derivative *going*, but not in word-list readings.

GOOSE
Generally [ʉː] (or slightly diphthongal [ʊʉ]) except before /l/, where [uː] predominates. [uː] may on occasions be found in other contexts for older speakers, and unrounding to [ɨː] is relatively common in young speech. Rare examples of *-ook* words (e.g. *look, cook*) with this vowel rather than the STRUT vowel can still be found among the older WC.

PRICE
[aɪ] accounts for *c.* 60% of MC tokens, but only *c.* 30% of WC ones. WC males generally use a diphthong with a back first element, [ɑɪ] or [ɒɪ]. Females typically use a diphthong with a very long first element and weak offglide [aːˑ']. This gender split is almost absolute, i.e. males virtually never use [aːˑ'], and females very rarely use the backed variants. There are, in addition, rare cases with [ɛɪ] or [iː] in *right, night* etc. which may still occasionally be found amongst older speakers.

MOUTH
The main local variant is a monophthong [aː], which is the norm for all groups. Standard [aʊ]-like diphthongs do occur, however, and are more common in MC speech and more formal styles.

CURE
Overwhelmingly [jɔː], with rare examples of [juːə], mainly amongst older WC males.

happY
Mainly patterns with the FLEECE set, although northern short [ɪ] appears in suffixed forms (thus *happiness* and *countries* are typically [apɪnəs] and [kʊntɹɪz]). The short variant also appears sporadically in older WC speech, and quite generally for the pronouns *me, he, she, we* when unstressed.

horsEs
[ɪ] only appears in comparatively rare cases of style-shifting: [ə] is by far the commonest form.

3.2.2   Consonants

T
[ʔ] is almost categorical for word-final /t/ before a consonant. It is also the majority pronunciation where /t/ occurs pre-pausally, but significantly more so for young speakers (overall 81% versus 61% for the older speakers in our conversational data; $p = 0.015$). The most marked sociolinguistic patterning occurs in pre-vocalic position (e.g. *water, put off*), where glottals occur only 9% of the time for older speakers, in contrast with 60% for younger speakers ($p < 0.001$).

No significant class or gender patterns emerged in our study of glottal variants in Derby.

A particular local characteristic is that glottal stops may also appear in consonant clusters where epenthetic [t] might be expected, e.g. *else*, which may be pronounced [ɛlʔs̠] or [ɛwʔs̠] (and similarly for *golf, self, health* etc.).

The 'T-to-R rule' applies (Wells 1982: 370), yielding e.g. [geɹ aːʔ] for *get out*. The use of [ɹ] here is socially correlated (37 of the 65 tokens in our data were produced by older WC females) and is retreating in the face of advancing glottal variants (only two tokens of [ɹ] were produced by young speakers).

S, Z, T, D

Alveolars are frequently slightly retracted, giving them a distinctly low pitch. /s/ is occasionally voiced when intervocalic, thus *place* [plɛis̠] but *places* [plɛiz̠əz̠], and *us* is always [ʊz] (or [ʊz̠]). Palatalisation is very common before /j/, yielding e.g. [ʃtjʉː] for *stew*.

NG and H

Both are variable, as in most northern and Midlands varieties. The velar nasal alternates most commonly with alveolar [n], but also with stopped [ŋg], and with [ŋk] in *something* and *nothing*.

TH

The labiodental forms [f, v] for /θ, ð/ have made great inroads into younger WC speech, such that all eight young WC speakers made at least variable use of them, and three speakers even used labiodentals categorically in word-list readings. In conversational style the young WC produced 62% labiodentals, in contrast with just 7% by the young MC. No labiodental tokens were produced by older speakers in our data (J. Milroy 1996). /ð/-initial function words such as *the, then, they* do not participate in the alternation with [v]; instead they are likely to be rendered with a dental stop [d̪]. The use of dental stops in these function words is also found in older speech.

R

Usually [ɹ], but [r] is found rarely amongst older speakers, usually in intervocalic position. A labiodental or bilabial approximant [ʋ] ~ [β] is increasingly used by the young, sometimes variably rather than categorically (Foulkes & Docherty in press).

Derby is non-rhotic. Linking R occurs virtually categorically; intrusive R is the norm for all groups, appearing on average in 55% of tokens in the corpus, with no significant sociolinguistic patterning (Foulkes 1997a, b).

L

Derby has the usual clear–dark dichotomy according to syllable position, although as Wells (1982: 370) notes, the auditory difference is often less clear than in the south.

Sequences of /kl, gl/ are often rendered [tl] and [dl], which is auditorily very salient in word-final position (e.g. *pickle, haggle* as [pɪtl], [adl]). This usage in word-final position is, however, almost wholly restricted to older speakers. Renditions of /tl/ and /dl/ with velars are rarer, highly stigmatised, and usually concurrent with ʟ-vocalisation (e.g. *little bottle* as [lɪkuː bɒkuː]). Vocalisation of ʟ is frequent but socially, stylistically, phonetically and phono-logically complex. Vocalised forms are more common in male rather than in female speech, younger rather than older, and WC rather than MC, such that the highest vocalisers are younger WC males (77% in word-list readings). All speakers produce more [l] in word-list readings than in their vernacular. Vocalisation is possible but unlikely where a syllabic lateral follows an alveo-lar (e.g. *battle*), but does not occur in cases of /kl/ → [tl] (thus *pickle* may be [pɪtl] but never *[pɪtuː]). However, vocalisation is the norm in other syllabic contexts (e.g. *haggle* and unmodified *pickle*), as well as in /-l(C)#/ sequences (e.g. *salt, old, dial*).

3.2.3   Suprasegmentals

The rhythm and prosody of Derby speech do not stand out in any way in com-parison with standard southern British English. It is possible, but still rare, to hear young speakers using rising and/or high level intonation patterns in declar-ative utterances (Cruttenden 1995; 1997: 129ff.).

3.3   *Instrumental phonetics and variationist studies*

3.3.1   Introduction

Instrumental phonetic techniques have long been exploited to solve problems in the interconnected fields of language change, phonology and dialectology. Laboratory-based investigations of sound change were being carried out over a century ago (e.g. Rousselot 1891), and have been revived more recently by Ohala (e.g. 1974, 1983, 1989). Applications of phonetic work to theoretical phonology, meanwhile, have been highlighted by the Laboratory Phonology collections (Kingston & Beckman 1990; Docherty & Ladd 1992; Keating 1994; Connell & Arvaniti 1995), and within quantitative sociolinguistics acoustic analysis was pioneered by Labov in 1968, forming the basis for the seminal work of Labov, Yaeger & Steiner (1972).

All of the analyses carried out by Labov *et al.* (1972) focus on vowel for-mant patterns, and this practice has since become widespread. Acoustic analy-sis of vowels normally entails taking measurements of the first and second formants (F1 and F2) around the vowel's midpoint, or at a point where for-mants show their maximum 'inflection' (Labov *et al.* 1972: 29), and stressed vowels are investigated as a priority (Labov 1986: 403). These measurements are then plotted as a reflection of a vowel's height and frontness. Variations across age groups are often interpreted as representative of change in progress. Instrumental analysis is argued to provide a more objective view of the data than auditory analysis alone (Labov 1994: 25), and frequently throws up information beyond the scope of auditory analysis: formant plots, for example, often reveal very subtle differences in vowel quality correlating with one or more social characteristic.

F1-F2 plots do not, however, provide flawless representations of relative vowel quality (Labov *et al.* 1972: 31; Labov 1986; Stevens 1997; Watt 1998). Some vowels, particularly close front ones, carry a great deal of information in the third formant, while vowel duration also plays a significant role in perception (e.g. Peterson & Lehiste 1960; Lindblom 1963). A typical F1-F2 plot does not cater for these parameters. The effect of lip-rounding is also difficult to represent unambiguously. More important, perhaps, are the problems involved in normalising the data obtained from different subjects (e.g. Labov *et al.* 1972: 264; Labov 1986: 415ff.; Holmes 1986; Labov 1994: 56, 68; Pisoni 1997). Put simply, different speakers produce 'the same' vowel with formants of different values. This is most obviously the case when comparing males versus females or children. But there is no inscrutable algorithm for transforming the mathematical differences between speakers, which can therefore render the interpretation of formant measures extremely difficult.

In spite of these various problems, the use of formant plots has become a well-established methodology in variationist research, and as such demonstrates the profitability of uniting instrumental phonetic techniques with sociolinguistic practices. The findings of Labov *et al.* (1972) have inspired a wealth of similar studies, such as recent papers by Clark, Elms & Youssef (1995), Faber & Di Paolo (1995) and Sabino (1996).

Considering the popularity of formant analysis, it is surprising how few phonetic studies in the variationist literature have touched upon variables other than vowels. A rare exception to this pattern is Yaeger-Dror (1997), who cites pitch-track data to support observations on intonation differences in American English.

Consonantal variables, however, appear to have been almost entirely overlooked. This is no doubt in part because it is usually possible to make robust *auditory* discriminations of the variants which typically crop up in consonantal variable studies. The use of the glottal stop for /t/ in English is a case in point: the auditory difference between [t] and [ʔ] is sufficiently stark that any use of instrumental techniques to discriminate between them would appear to be analytical overkill (but see section 3.3.2 below).

Perhaps the principal reason for the neglect of consonants, however, is that major advances in the theoretical literature have overwhelmingly concentrated on vowels. Refinements to *theoretical* proposals have thus sought data of a similar nature, leading to a snowballing proliferation of vowel studies. A clear illustration of this observation is provided by Labov (1994), a work of some 600 pages summarising a wide collection of previous variable studies, on the basis of which general principles of language change are formulated (see section 3.4). Only around 70 pages touch upon consonantal topics, and none of the discussion concerns instrumental data.

In this chapter we present data drawn from acoustic analysis of two consonantal variables: glottal(ised) variants of intervocalic /t/ in Newcastle English, and non-glottalised pre-pausal /t/ in both Newcastle and Derby speech. These data serve not only to fill the gap in the variationist literature. Rather, they suggest that work on variation and change can be enhanced by making use of a more detailed phonetic analysis than is usually the case in consonantal studies. They furthermore yield somewhat different theoretical implications from those of vowel studies, both from a sociolinguistic perspective and also with regard to the phonological modelling of variation and change.

3.3.2   Glottal and glottalised variants of Newcastle /t/

Glottal forms of /t/ have been studied extensively in sociolinguistic work on British English (e.g. Trudgill 1974; Macaulay 1977, 1991; Reid 1978; Newbrook 1986; Mees 1987; Holmes 1995; Mees & Collins this volume; Mathisen this volume). In most localities that have been investigated, auditory analysis has been used to distinguish non-glottalised [t] variants from those involving a glottal articulation, [ʔ] and/or [ʔ͡t].

Newcastle English, however, is characterised by having two distinct types of glottal variant (Watt & Milroy this volume). First, what sounds on auditory analysis to be a plain glottal stop occurs categorically before syllabic /l/ (e.g. in *battle*). The second type of variant presents the auditory impression of a glottal stop reinforcing any of the three voiceless stops /p, t, k/ when they occur between sonorants (e.g. in *happy, set off, bacon*). These variants are usually labelled 'glottalised', and transcriptions suggestive of double articulations have been used, such as [ʔt] (O'Connor 1947) or [tʔ] (Wells 1982: 374). The temporal co-ordination of the laryngeal and supralaryngeal articulation is an issue to which we return below.

The two types of glottal variant in Newcastle English are not only subject to different phonological constraints; they also enter into quite different sociolinguistic patterns (see further Docherty, Foulkes, Milroy, Milroy & Walshaw 1997). [ʔ] is variably substituted for non-initial pre-vocalic /t/ (e.g. in *set off, water*) by younger speakers, especially middle-class females, and as such appears to be a non-local form entering Newcastle English. The glottalised forms, by contrast, are largely the preserve of older males. There is therefore strong evidence that in Newcastle the two types of glottal variant play different sociolinguistic and phonological roles, and thus they demand separate analytic treatment. Because of this complex patterning, we undertook acoustic analysis of Newcastle glottals, at first in order to corroborate our auditory judgements. However, our findings turned out not only to conflict markedly with the received phonetic wisdom, they also reveal sociolinguistic correlation at an unexpectedly subtle level. We deal with each of these points in turn.

3.3.2.1   *Acoustic correlates of glottal variants*

Treatments in the phonetic literature usually describe [ʔ] as sharing the properties of other voiceless stops (e.g. D. Jones 1967b: 77; O'Connor 1973: 26; standard IPA definition). That is, an occlusion is made and held for an appreciable time while air pressure builds up behind the closure, and the vocal cords do not vibrate. Henton, Ladefoged & Maddieson (1992: 77) make the general statement that the closure duration in [ʔ] is at least as long as that found in other stops, and Byrd (1994) finds a mean closure duration of 65ms for the [ʔ] tokens in the TIMIT database.

Figure 3.1 shows a spectrogram of the word *total* spoken by the first author (GJD). The spectrogram illustrates the acoustic features one would expect to be produced by the articulatory activity just described:

- A – onset phase in which the articulators come together. Because the active articulators are the vocal folds, which are of course also responsible for phonation, the voicing pattern in the adjacent vowels is perturbed, yielding a period of creaky voicing (presumably caused by the vocal folds stiffening and/or closing to execute the glottal stop).
- B – the 'stop gap', or occlusion phase in which the articulators are held together. No air passes out of the vocal tract, resulting in no acoustic energy in the spectrographic trace.
- C – release phase in which the articulators part. Airflow restarts, resulting in an acoustic transient (abrupt onset of acoustic energy across a wide frequency range).

Phones transcribed as [t͡ʔ] imply concurrence or overlap of two voiceless stops, predicting in turn that the acoustic correlates of such sounds should also bear close resemblance to those of individual voiceless plosives.

There have, however, been several comments on the complexity of glottal articulations, and variability in the realisation of [ʔ] (Grice & Barry 1991; Pierrehumbert & Talkin 1992; Nolan 1995; Ladefoged & Maddieson 1996). Many of these note that full glottal closure and creaky voicing form a continuum, and suggest that the percept of a glottal stop may be cued purely by a period of creaky voice.

Bearing in mind such claims, we undertook acoustic analysis of a sample of 549 tokens from the Newcastle corpus. From word-list readings we extracted all items spoken by all speakers which on auditory analysis appeared to contain a glottal. Because glottal variants are subject to sociolinguistic skewing, the number of tokens analysed per speaker group varies considerably, as summarised in Table 3.3.

Figure 3.2 illustrates a typical glottal token (in the item *total*), and Figures 3.3

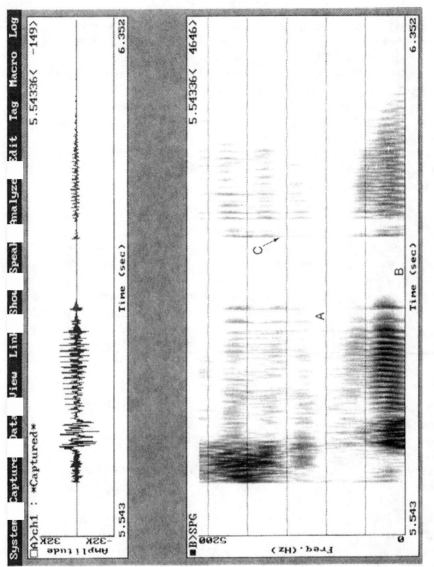

Fig. 3.1 Spectrogram of *total* spoken by author GJD, showing 'canonical' [?]

Table 3.3 Number of tokens analysed acoustically, per speaker group

	Young WC	Older WC	Young MC	Older MC	Total
Males	176	143	79	20	418
Females	111	15	5	0	131

and 3.4 show glottalised forms from the Newcastle data. The glottalised tokens differ from the 'pure' glottal variants in terms of the presence of movement of the second formant in the previous vowel: formant transitions are caused by gestures involving the supralaryngeal vocal organs. 79% of our tokens contained F2 transitions, the exceptional cases sounding clearly like glottal stops.

What is striking, however, is the absence in all three spectrograms of the silent 'stop gap' which is usually characteristic of voiceless stops. Instead, voicing continues throughout the entire consonantal portion, and in each case the auditory percept of a glottal articulation is created simply by an interval of creaky voicing (thus supporting the comments of e.g. Nolan 1995). No less than 70% of our tokens were fully voiced, with only 3% displaying a voiceless period of the sort of duration normally associated with voiceless stops.

It is also apparent that the auditory label 'glottalised' in fact covers two distinct types insofar as their acoustic features are concerned. 'Type 1' glottalisation is illustrated in Figure 3.3, and 'Type 2' glottalisation in Figure 3.4. Type 2 is distinguished in that it contains an acoustic transient (a vertical striation reflecting a release burst, marked by an arrow in Figure 3.4). The transient is indicative of the release of a closure in the vocal tract. Since the vocal cords are clearly continuing to vibrate, this transient must reflect the release of an oral (presumably alveolar) closure, which in turn suggests that the glottal articulation in Figure 3.4 precedes the oral activity. The two types are summarised in Table 3.4.

Type 2 accounts for 26% of our tokens, which is higher than would be expected given claims (e.g. Wells 1982) that the glottal articulation is timed to *follow* the oral articulation in Newcastle English. Upon relistening to our data in the light of this finding, we did not find it at all easy to make consistent auditory discriminations of the two types, which reflects the phonetic subtlety involved in their production.

Our acoustic analysis has therefore exposed interesting information from a

Table 3.4 Summary of acoustic characteristics of
glottalised tokens

	Type 1	Type 2
Transient	no	yes
Temporal order	oral – glottal	glottal – oral

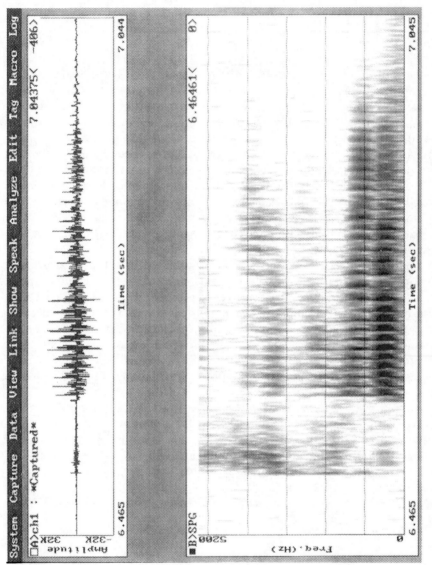

Fig. 3.2 Spectrogram of *total* spoken by young MC Newcastle male

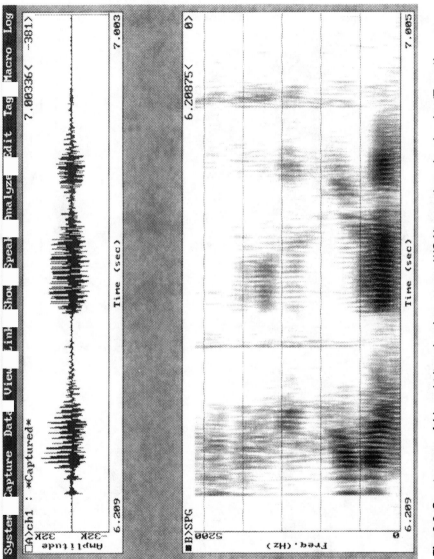

Fig. 3.3 Spectrogram of *I bought it* spoken by younger WC Newcastle male, showing 'Type 1' glottalisation (see text)

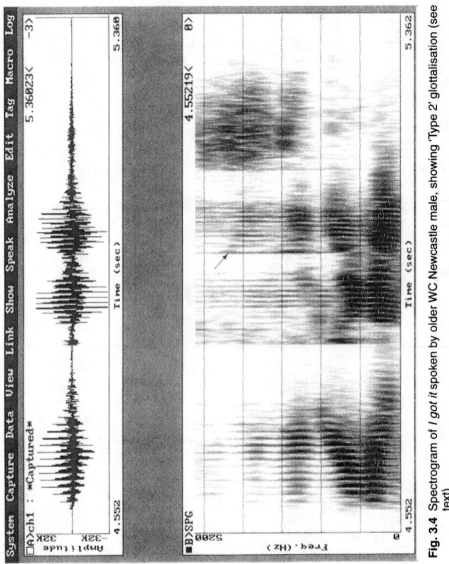

Fig. 3.4 Spectrogram of *I got it* spoken by older WC Newcastle male, showing 'Type 2' glottalisation (see text)

purely descriptive perspective, suggesting that the articulatory basis of glottal variants diverges from the received wisdom.

3.3.2.2 Sociolinguistic patterning of glottalised variants

Variation is expected in any detailed investigation of large amounts of data. With this in mind, it may not be surprising that some of the glottalised tokens display slightly different features from others. However, close examination of the acoustic data shows that Type 2 glottalised tokens do not occur with a random distribution across the corpus, but in fact correlate with particular speaker variables. Figure 3.5 shows the proportion of Type 2 glottals produced by each speaker group.

Notwithstanding the wide diversity in the number of tokens analysed, clear patterns emerge from Figure 3.5. Most notably, Type 2 tokens account for a far higher proportion of the older males' productions than any other group, and there is a very large difference between the older WC males and the corresponding females (47% versus 13%). By contrast, younger speakers from both social classes produce far fewer Type 2 tokens, and there is little difference in the scores for males and females. The great disparity in the number of tokens analysed and the number of informants per cell means that reliable statistical observations are extremely hard to make (further investigation of such patterns from a much larger speaker sample is necessary to confirm these results). However, there is a clear suggestion of skewing in the distribution of Type 2 tokens, with age (and possibly gender) seeming to be a factor in their appearance. We therefore have tentative evidence to suggest that highly subtle acoustic parameters – subtle enough to prevent robust auditory discrimination – enter into sociolinguistic patterns in a manner parallel to that often found in vowel formant studies. Put bluntly, older males appear to be producing glottalised tokens with

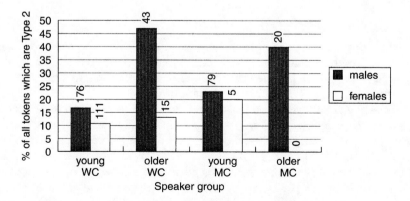

Fig. 3.5 Sociolinguistic distribution of Type 2 glottalised tokens (number above each bar = N tokens analysed)

a different articulatory co-ordination than other members of the speech community: they have a greater tendency to time the oral gesture such that it lags behind the accompanying glottal articulation.

Although this evidence is tentative, we present in the next section another case study which presents a much stronger (if more complex) case to argue that sociolinguistic patterning of consonants takes place at a remarkably subtle level of phonetic implementation.

3.3.3   Pre-pausal 'released' [t] in Newcastle and Derby

This section focuses on non-glottal variants of /t/ in pre-pausal positions in both Newcastle and Derby English. Although glottal variants are widespread in various phonological contexts in Newcastle, they are almost categorically prohibited in pre-pausal position. Tokens before a pause are instead – from an auditory perspective – clearly 'released' voiceless alveolars, i.e. they sound like [t]s as described in standard phonetic texts (e.g. Ladefoged 1993: 8). Whilst this pattern of realisation is clearly related to prosodic structure, it has been argued that the salient non-glottalised release acts as a turn-handover cue in this accent (Local, Kelly & Wells 1986; Docherty *et al.* 1997).

In Derby glottal stops in pre-pausal positions are far more widespread, but in the self-conscious context of word-list readings most speakers produce what sound like 'released' [t]s, just as in Newcastle.

We undertook spectrographic analysis of pre-pausal [t]s from both varieties, taking (where possible) 12 items from each speaker's word-list readings (*sheet, gate* etc.). As with the glottalised variants discussed in section 3.3.2, there is little in the way of robust auditorily discriminable variation within these 'released' stops. However, the acoustic analysis again revealed descriptively unexpected findings (section 3.3.3.1), and also showed correlation between fine-grained phonetic features and social characteristics of the speakers (section 3.3.3.2).

3.3.3.1   *Acoustic correlates of 'released'* [t]

Figure 3.6 illustrates an example of what we term a 'canonical released stop', in that it displays the acoustic features predicted in standard textbook descriptions of voiceless stops. The key elements are the voiceless 'stop gap' and the release burst (see section 3.3.2.1 for further explanation).

The canonical pattern accounted for remarkably few of our tokens – 24% of the 348 Derby examples, and only 9% of the 360 analysed from Newcastle. The majority of tokens displayed unexpected acoustic characteristics, illustrated in Figures 3.7 and 3.8. Figure 3.7 displays a perseveration of voicing throughout the entire stop, and is accompanied by a clear continuation of energy in the frequency ranges of the preceding vowel formants right up to the release burst. Figure 3.8 exemplifies what we term 'extended frication', a period of fricative energy preceding the stop gap, presumably created by a relatively slow tongue

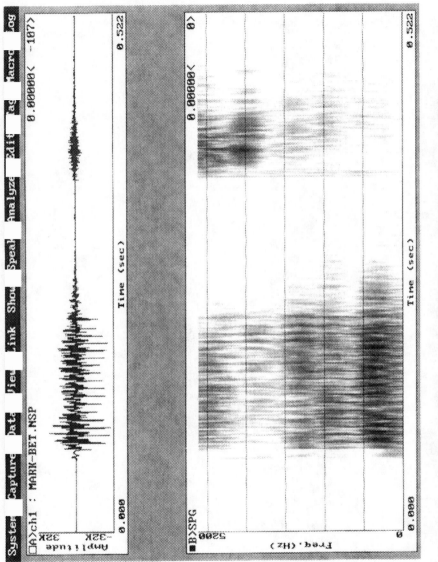

Fig. 3.6 Spectrogram of *bet* spoken by young MC Derby male, showing 'canonical' [t]

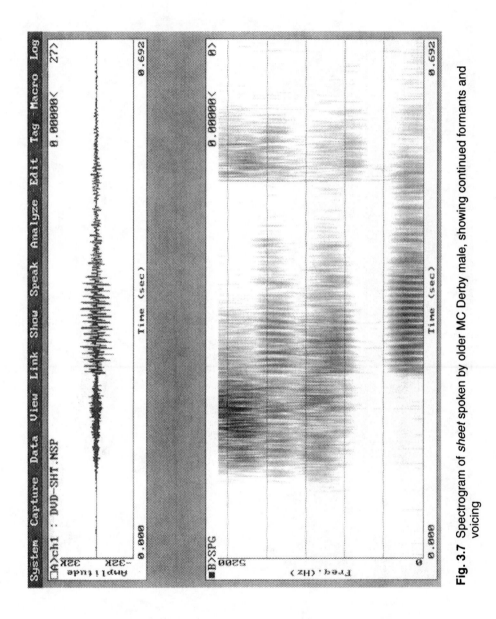

Fig. 3.7 Spectrogram of *sheet* spoken by older MC Derby male, showing continued formants and voicing

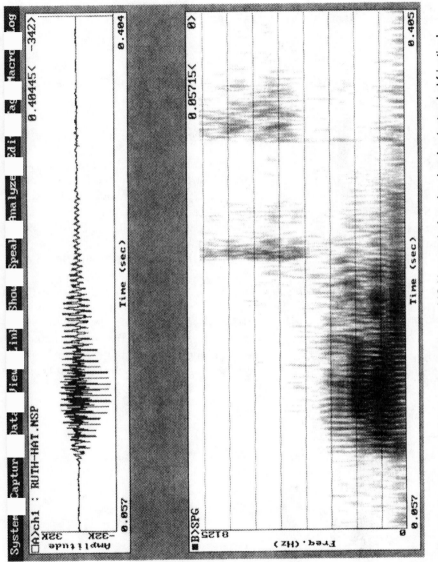

Fig. 3.8 Spectrogram of *hat* spoken by young MC Newcastle female, showing 'extended frication'

Table 3.5 Occurrence of acoustic features (percentage occurrence in parentheses)

	Tokens analysed	Continued formants		Continued voicing		Extended frication	
Derby	348	258	*(74)*	27	*(8)*	0	*(0)*
Newcastle	360	295	*(82)*	157	*(44)*	118	*(33)*

tip closure. The rate of occurrence of these three acoustic features is summarised in Table 3.5.

3.3.3.2   *Sociolinguistic patterning of 'released' features*

The acoustic patterns which comprise the 'released' variants, like those of the glottalised forms discussed in section 3.3.2, are not randomly distributed across the speaker sample. Rather, quantitative analysis strongly suggests that at least some of the features, and combinations of features, are significantly associated with particular subgroups. We cite here three examples.[2] First, the presence of continued voicing (CV) is graphically represented in Figure 3.9.

The CV pattern is clearly found more frequently in Newcastle than Derby, and in Newcastle is significantly more common in male speech. There is little difference according to age, suggesting a stable distribution of the CV pattern.

Extended frication (EF) tokens are displayed in Figure 3.10. EF tokens occur only in Newcastle, and correlate with both age and gender: they are more common in female speech, and are used more frequently by the young. This latter finding is therefore suggestive of a change in progress, in that younger speakers are employing a different articulatory strategy for pre-pausal [t], with females leading the way.

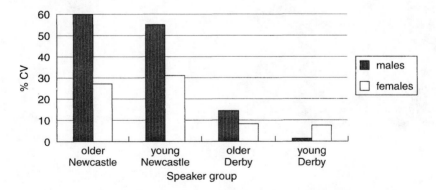

Fig. 3.9 Distribution of tokens with continued voicing (CV) by speaker group

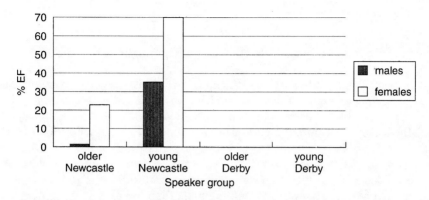

Fig. 3.10 Distribution of tokens with extended frication (EF) by speaker group

Our third example concerns canonical (CL) tokens, defined as the combination of silent stop gap and release burst (and excluding any of the other acoustic features). These tokens are displayed in Figure 3.11.

CL tokens appear to be associated with females of both age groups in both cities. There are also age-based correlations: the CL pattern occurs more frequently for older speakers in Newcastle, but younger speakers in Derby. Thus we have evidence suggestive of a change in progress in both varieties, but operating in different directions. CL tokens are on the increase in Derby, but are decreasing in Newcastle.

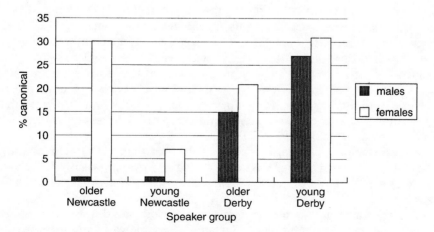

Fig. 3.11 Distribution of canonical tokens by speaker group

3.4   *Discussion and conclusion*

One possible means of accounting for our findings might be that the diverse patterns fall out from a process of 'weakening' of the laryngeal and/or supralaryngeal gestures, with different acoustic manifestations resulting from different degrees of weakening. With pre-pausal [t] in particular, it might be argued that the stops have little information-bearing content, and the articulatory system may therefore be permitted a good deal of variability in the realisation of these stops. (In Lindblom's (1990) terms, they are being produced at the hypo- end of the hyper–hypo continuum.) As we noted earlier, however, it has been argued at least for Newcastle English that the prohibition on glottal forms in this context serves a conversational/pragmatic function as a turn-handover cue (Local *et al.* 1986; Docherty *et al.* 1997). In this sense, then, these stops clearly have a *high* information content.

Moreover, the distribution of the various acoustic patterns is patently not random or in free variation, but structured. Fine-grained phonetic features correlate with speakers' social characteristics, most notably age and gender. The overall pattern of distribution appears analogous to the sort of findings that emerge in consonantal studies where auditory analysis is used, and also in vowel formant analyses. Furthermore, the degree of phonetic subtlety revealed in our findings appears at first glance similar to that found in vowel studies (e.g. Labov 1994). It may therefore be tempting to view and interpret our data in similar terms.

Instrumental data pertaining to vowels have been exploited for the development of hypotheses relating to the actuation and transmission of sound change, most notably by Labov (e.g. 1994). Recurrent trends have been revealed across phonological systems. For example, long vowels have a tendency to rise through the vowel continuum over time, whereas short vowels incline to lower (Labov 1994: 116). Such patterns lead Labov to posit general principles of change, among which is the claim that vowel shifts are gradient and predictable in direction. It is also hypothesised that shifts are induced by the linguistic system itself, for example in response to the threat of a merger impairing communication (see Watt & Milroy this volume). Studies of vowel mergers are therefore often rightly claimed to be studies of change in progress, in that they show a phonological system in a state of flux. In a merger, a phonological contrast is in the process of being eradicated, with some members of the community more affected than others. Such a change can be situated near the top of the familiar S-curve of diffusion (see e.g. McMahon 1994: 52).

Our consonantal findings, however, do not appear straightforwardly amenable to a similar account. As such they also force into question the overall validity of Labov's principles, formulated as they are primarily on vowel data.

First, consonantal variables are not always easily placed in linear continua. Stops in particular are multiplex articulations, and the variation exemplified in our data involves complex manipulation of the temporal co-ordination and degree of stricture of several discrete articulatory gestures. Secondly, structured variation in our data occurs in a variety of directions, which makes it difficult to model in predictable linear terms. This is most striking in the case of canonical tokens of [t]: in both Derby and Newcastle these are mainly characteristic of female speech, but in Derby they are increasing whereas in Newcastle they are becoming less common.

Thirdly, it is difficult to link the variation apparent in our data to any pressure on the linguistic system. No phonemic contrast is threatened, and no radical redistribution of allophones is under way. All speakers are producing the same accent-appropriate allophones: Newcastle speakers continue to produce inter-sonorant /t/ as a glottalised form, while pre-pausal /t/ in both Derby and Newcastle continues (for most speakers) to be non-glottalised. The only difference is that subgroups within the accent community are realising these accent-specific allophones in slightly different ways. What we are seeing is subgroups within a community adopting what we may term different *phonetic realisation strategies* (PRSs). The net outcome of the variation is simply one of widening the range of possible allophonic realisation. It is not transparent how the linguistic system can be held responsible for inducing such variation.

A more appealing account of our data comes in terms of speaker-control rather than system-control. J. Milroy (1992) argues that linguistic change originates with *speakers*, and not with linguistic *systems*. Speakers constantly produce innovations, i.e. phonetic variations, which in the majority of cases are fleeting and random. Some innovations, though, may be adopted by the community at large. If this happens, the ultimate result may be that the system is affected and a linguistic change can be said to have taken place, e.g. through the loss of a phonemic contrast.[3] Thus what we usually observe in vowel studies is the stage of change at which an innovation has successfully penetrated a community, to the extent that the majority of the community is now operating with a different linguistic system from that which was operative before the innovation was adopted.

Such a stage has clearly not been reached by our consonantal variables. Instead, our variables appear to represent the stage in the development of a change which precedes the one just described, and which may be placed at the beginning of the S-curve. Here we see the stage in which innovations are no longer random but have begun to cluster, having been adopted by subgroups within the accent community. An order is beginning to emerge from the natural phonetic variation, guided perhaps by the 'invisible hand' (Keller 1994). In Labov's terms we may be seeing incipient changes on the verge of becoming indicators.

If we are right, our findings present a problem for phonological modelling. PRSs amount to a learned set of conventions which clearly play a significant part in identifying a speaker as a member of a particular speech (sub)community. But they are subsystemic, and thus presumably qualitatively different from the conventions which are learned in the mastering of a *language*-specific

phonological system. Variation in PRSs has no immediate effect on the phonological system itself, since the system of contrasts remains unchanged.

The general consensus amongst phonologists, however, is that 'there is no
well-defined allophonic level of representation . . . phonological representations should be mapped directly into speech output without passing through a
"buffer" level of allophonic representation' (Clements 1992: 183). Just how the
discrete phonological representation 'drives' the continuous speech output has
long been a central problem within phonology, of course. But structured variation of the subtlety we have seen takes the problem into another dimension.
The problem is particularly acute for any model which operates with phonemic
or segmental units, which are unlikely to be able to predict with sufficient resolution the degree of variation found in our data. Space prevents a detailed
critical discussion of the non-segmental alternatives available on the phonological market, although Articulatory Phonology appears as strong a candidate as any to cater for our data (Browman & Goldstein e.g. 1992a; for
an overview see McMahon, Foulkes & Tollfree 1994; see also Tollfree this
volume).

In variationist work the preferred form of phonological analysis largely
remains phonemic or segmental. However, one outcome from recent work on
the relationship between phonetics and phonology is that there has been a significant discrediting of segmental representation, because of the concern that
this may have more to do with the analytic categories of the investigator than
with the activities of the speaker-listener. This is not to say that it is necessarily
inappropriate to model vowel variables in segmental terms. Nonetheless, we feel
it imperative to raise this general issue in order to encourage variationists, phonologists and phoneticians to converge and communicate more than usually
occurs at present.

There is not only clear scope for variationists to avail themselves of insights
from phonetics and phonology: work within laboratory phonology, for example,
is overwhelmingly based on a much smaller amount of data from a much
smaller number of informants than is usual in sociolinguistics. Similarly it is
rare for phonologists to take an interest in variation (notable exceptions are
Harris 1985 and Kiparsky 1988), and we have argued previously that phonology
has much to gain from the fully accountable analysis characteristic of variationist work (Docherty *et al.* 1997).

We end with another comment on the methodology used in variationist sociolinguistics. Stages rooted at the foot of the S-curve have rarely been observed
before. Trudgill (1988) suggests that the reason for this lies in the methods usually employed within quantitative studies. To paraphrase Milroy (1992: 171), we
tend only to investigate variables characterised by variants which are different
enough to be easily noticed. This may mean, for example, that some speakers
have merged two vowels, or have adopted an allophone from a supra-local
source. But differences this obtrusive are usually symptomatic of the final stages
of a change: the patterns indicate that the system is already undergoing modification, and the differences can be interpreted as indicating different effects of

the linguistic system on the speakers (e.g. in terms of some speakers operating with more or fewer contrastive units).

In suggesting that our consonantal data illustrate the 'missing link' in the path from actuation to change, the contribution of instrumental phonetics is obvious. The structured differences which have been uncovered are very hard to identify auditorily, and the phonetic differences are so subtle as to be hardly noticeable, certainly insofar as they would not strike one's ears as obvious candidates for investigation as potential sociolinguistic variables. This is not a new position to take: Kerswill & Wright (1990) and Nolan (1992) pursue exactly this line. However, the lack of instrumental studies of consonants in the variationist literature is startling, and may well in part explain why these early stages have been so elusive. We may have found just the sort of methodology required to identify them.

Notes

1 Thanks to Paul Kerswill, Jane Stuart-Smith, Dominic Watt and Ann Williams for helpful suggestions on early drafts of this chapter. Thanks also to Suzanne Gaskell, who performed the full analysis of the GOAT vowel. We are grateful to the UK Economic and Social Research Council for financing the project Phonological Variation and Change in Contemporary Spoken British English (grant R000234892), and to the co-workers involved in that project: Jim Milroy, Lesley Milroy, Penny Oxley and David Walshaw. We must particularly thank David Walshaw for his expert advice on statistical matters. Where statistical values are given, ANOVA was used.
2 The data we concentrate on here display very clear effects, with some of the acoustic features correlating with non-linguistic speaker characteristics. We have not subjected the data to formal statistical analysis because of their exceedingly complex nature. The various acoustic features can occur in 29 logically possible combinations, of which 21 occur at least once in our data.
3 'Change', of course, is used with many definitions in (socio)linguistics. We consider change to equate with an effect on the linguistic system, and thus we restrict the term to what Milroy (1992) specifies as 'linguistic change'.

4

Sheffield dialect in the 1990s: revisiting the concept of NORMs

Jana Stoddart, Clive Upton and J. D. A Widdowson

4.1 *Introduction*

This chapter explores the concept of nonmobile older rural males (NORMs), often employed by sociolinguists (Chambers & Trudgill 1980: 33–5) to designate the sample of informants in the network of 313 localities in England and Wales investigated in the Survey of English Dialects (SED) between 1950 and 1961. Criteria for the selection of informants are spelled out in some detail in the Introduction to *The Linguistic Atlas of England*:

> The selection of the informants was made with especial care. The fieldworkers were instructed to seek out elderly men and women – more often men, since women seemed in general to encourage the social upgrading of the speech of their families – who were themselves natives of the place and both of whose parents were preferably natives also. They were to be over 60 years of age, with good mouths, teeth and hearing, and of the class of agricultural workers who would be familiar with the subject matter of the questionnaire and capable of responding perceptively and authoritatively. (Orton, Sanderson & Widdowson 1978: [3])

While at first sight the characterising of such speakers as NORMs seems entirely reasonable, closer examination of SED data reveals a rather different and certainly more complex picture. First, by no means all those interviewed fulfilled the nonmobile criterion, even discounting temporary absence during war service and the like, nor were they all agricultural workers (Kirk, Sanderson & Widdowson 1985: 45). Second, whereas the bulk of informants were indeed elderly, their ages varied considerably. Easson (Chambers, personal communication) recognises an age range of 50–90 in the SED speaker sample (Easson 1998: 5). Third, the SED included four urban localities in its network. Fourth, no fewer than 118 women were interviewed during the fieldwork, their occupations including domestic servant, factory worker, school cleaner, cook and singer (Kirk *et al.* 1985: 45).

The following discussion focuses primarily on data from an urban area to illustrate the dangers of over-generalisation and oversimplification inherent in the characterisation of SED data exclusively in terms of NORMs. Drawing on SED material from the Hillsborough area of Sheffield collected in 1952 and 1953, and on data recorded in various parts of the city in 1997, it allows the exploration of whether the rural/urban dichotomy is relevant to decisions on fieldwork sampling methods in regional dialect research and to the evaluation of the resulting data.

The SED data for Sheffield were contributed by a 64-year-old steelworker from Hillsborough, both of whose parents came from Sheffield, and whose wife was originally from Surrey. He is described as 'A good informant, fluent and broad in speech. A helper who realises [the] importance of [the] Survey and regards the duller parts of the Questionnaire as necessary to obtain all words' (Ellis 1952/53).

The more recent material on which the present study is primarily based comprises a ten-hour corpus tape-recorded by two fieldworkers, James Oldfield and Jana Stoddart, and deposited in the archives of the National Centre for English Cultural Tradition at the University of Sheffield. The fieldwork was carried out in various parts of the city, using two low-density social networks. The data were collected from a total of 24 speakers, the sample being divided into three age groups: 12–30, 31–55, 56 and over, four males and four females being recorded in each age group. Speakers were recorded responding to a questionnaire based on a selection from the SED questionnaire, reading a word-list, and in free conversation. In the conversational section of the interview, speakers were asked to talk about the city of Sheffield and to give their views on it as a place to live. The material was analysed to determine characteristic phonological features and to explore salient examples of phonological change by means of comparison with equivalent data in the SED Basic Material for Sheffield. The characteristic phonological features of the 1997 fieldwork data are detailed in section 4.2 below.

4.2 *Descriptive material*

4.2.1 Vowels

Table 4.1 Sheffield vowels – summary

KIT	ɪ	FLEECE	ɪiː > iː ~ ɪi(ː)	NEAR	iə
DRESS	ɛ > ë > ɪə	FACE	eː > eːˡ	SQUARE	ɛə
TRAP	a > ɒ	PALM	aː	START	aː ~ ɑː
LOT	ɒ	THOUGHT	ɔː > oʊ ~ ɔʊ	NORTH	ɔː > ɔə ~ ʊə
STRUT	ʊ > ɒ	GOAT	ɔː > oʊ > əʊ	FORCE	ɔː > ɔə > ʊə
FOOT	ʊ	GOAL	oʊ ~ ɔʊ > əʊ > ɔː	CURE	jʊəː
BATH	a > ɑː	GOOSE	uuː ~ ᵁuː > ʉu	happy	ɪ > e/ɛ
CLOTH	ɒ	PRICE	ɑɪ ~ ɑːˡ > aɪ	letter	ə
NURSE	əː	CHOICE	ɔɪ	horses	ə > ɪ ~ ï
		MOUTH	aː ~ aʊ ~ aᵁ	comma	ə

Comments

DRESS

[ɛ] is normal for all age groups, but is occasionally lowered and/or centralised, particularly before laterals, e.g.: [ɪmsɛ̈lf] *himself,* [spɛ̈ɫ] *spell* (= *splinter*), [wɛ̈l] *well.* [ɪə] is possible, especially with older speakers as in [ɪəd] *head.*

TRAP

[a] is the normal realisation; [ɒ] is used especially by females of all age groups in words such as *grandma.*

STRUT

[ʊ] is by far the most common variant, and is clearly the local norm; [ə] is found in weak position in rapid speech in all groups; [ɒ] occurs in words such as *one, none, once,* and can be heard occasionally in words such as *money, slush, other, mother,* particularly with females of middle age.

BATH

[a] for all groups, and particularly for older speakers; [ɑː], sometimes slightly centralised, for younger speakers.

FLEECE

[ɪiː] is common for all age groups; [iː] competes with [ɪiː]/[ɪi] especially among younger speakers; [ɪ̈] is heard mainly in the middle and younger age groups; [eɪ] or [ɪə] are possible with older speakers – [eɪ] in e.g. *key, speak, eat,* [ɪə] in e.g. *heat, sweet, leaves.*

FACE

[eː] for all groups, sometimes with a slight [ɪ]-glide [eːⁱ], and/or more open [ẹ]; half-open and shortened variant [ɛ] in words such as *make, take;* [ɛɪ] in words such as *eight, straight, weight* for all groups.

THOUGHT

[ɔː] for all age groups, rarely [oʊ]/[ɔʊ] for males in words which historically contained a velar fricative; [a ~ æ] in words such as *water.*

GOAT

[ɔː] for all age groups, particularly males; [oʊ] or with more open first element [ɔʊ]/[ɒʊ] for older males; [əʊ] is possible in all age groups, particularly for females; [ʊ] in words such as *go, goes, going, ago, over,* and a more traditional realisation [ʊə] in e.g. *don't* is possible, particularly with older speakers; words such as *windows, willow, pillow* have [ə] in the second syllable.

GOAL

[oʊ ~ ɔʊ] more typical for males; [əʊ] for females, especially in middle and younger age groups; [ɔː] is also possible for all age groups; [ɒː] or even [ɒʊ] is possible in the word *cold* with older male speakers as well as the traditional [ɔɪ] or [ɒɪ] in words such as *coal, hole*.

GOOSE
[ʊuː] or [ᵁuː] for all groups; [ʉu] mainly among older speakers.

PRICE
[ɑɪ] or [ɑːⁱ] for males; fronted starting point [aɪ] possible with females; [aⁱ], [aː] or sometimes [aːᵊ] is a typical realisation of the pronoun *I*, but the pronunciation is commonly reduced to [a] in weak position in all groups; [eɪ] in *right* and [iː] in words such as *night, right*, are typical for older speakers.

MOUTH
[aː] common for all age groups, but it faces strong competition from [aʊ] or [aᵁ]; [æʊ] in words such as *house, owl*, [əʊ] in e.g. *about, round, down*, especially among older speakers, where also centralised [äː] is possible.

SQUARE
[ɛə] for all groups; sometimes the first element can be half-long; [ɪə] in *where, there*, particularly with older males.

START
[aː ~ ɑː] for all groups: individuals vary between the two pronunciations.

FORCE
[ɔː] for all groups; [ɔə] for some middle-aged and younger speakers; [ʊə] in words such as *door, floor* or [ɔə] in words such as *four* for older speakers.

happY
Final [ɪ] is common for all groups, but [e]/[ɛ] are possible, more with speakers in the middle age group, rather less so with older speakers; more typical for females, e.g. [tʃɪmnɛ] *chimney*, [bɪzɛ] *busy*; younger speakers commonly have [ï]. The final vowel in words ending in *-day* is also frequently realised as [ɛ] and occasionally as [e]: [wɛnzdɛ] *Wednesday*, [jɛstədə] *yesterday*.

commA
Generally, strong vowels tend to be retained in the positions in which they are weakened in RP, e.g. [sʊpɔːzd] *supposed*.

4.2.2   Consonants

STOPS, FRICATIVES and AFFRICATES
[ʔ] is used for non-initial /t/ much more frequently by younger speakers (two to three times more than older speakers), particularly by males (among older speakers males used [ʔ] approximately four times more than females); /p, k, tʃ/

and especially /t/ are liable to glottal replacement or reinforcement mainly in final position (*shop, get, back* etc.) or at the boundary of two elements in a compound (*nightlife*); the definite article *the* is often glottalised or preglottalised, or, when followed by a dental, can be assimilated to [t] (*t'tram*).

Medial /t/ is often realised as [ɹ]: [gɛɹɪn] *getting*, [bʊɹ ɪf] *but if*. Initial /t/ is occasionally affricated by younger speakers.

Final /d/ has a tendency towards devoicing, especially among females in the middle age group: [ɹaɪtandɪd̪] *right-handed*; /d/ is occasionally assimilated either together with or following [n]: [fɹɛnz] *friends*, [gɹamɑː] *grandma*.

Omission of final stops /t, d/ and fricatives /f, θ, ð/, mainly in function words, is common for all groups; [dʒʊs] *just*; [an]/[ən] *and* – universal; [maˈsɛl] *myself*; [wɪ] *with*; [ɒ]/[ə] *of* – more common for males.

/k, g/ are often realised as [t, d] in initial position in words such as [tlʊmzɛ] *clumsy*, [dlʊvz] *gloves*; typical particularly for older females.

[f, v] are possible realisations of the dental fricatives /θ, ð/ for younger speakers, particularly males, in medial and final positions: *brother* [bɹɒvə], *mouth* [maːf]; [θ, ð] for older speakers. [d] can also be found in initial position, mainly in function words such as *then, than, there*, and the pronouns *they, those*; more typical for older males.

Final /z/ commonly tends to be devoiced or to be lengthened and devoiced: [z̥s], a feature especially obvious in the marking of plurality: [dʒɔːmz̥] *jambs*. It occurs mainly among speakers of the middle and older age groups, but also occasionally in the younger group.

NG
Final *-ing*: [ɪn] for all groups, [ɪŋ] possible, but not common, for younger speakers; [ɪŋg] is found occasionally, mainly in the middle and younger age groups, the [g] being sporadically devoiced or realised as [k].

H
H-dropping is fairly regular among older speakers and common among younger speakers as well; however, younger females normally use initial [h].

R
Approximant [ɹ] as in RP is common for all groups; a tapped [r] is occasionally pronounced by males; linking and intrusive R are common for all groups.

L
Laterals are normally clear, but dark [ɫ] is found occasionally in final position: [spɛ̈ɫ] *spell* (= *splinter*), [skʊˈəɫ] *school*, and before final [t]/[d]: [boʊɫt] *bolt*, [əʊɫd] *old*, [koʊɫd] *cold*, and in [apɫz̥] *apples*, among female speakers of the middle and older age groups.

4.2.3   Suprasegmentals

No significant intonational difference from RP; no evidence of rising or high level patterns at the end of declarative utterances.

4.2.4   Discussion

These characteristic features differ in a number of ways from those recorded for the SED. At that time the vowels in the TRAP, STRUT and BATH sets exhibited no variation from [a], [ʊ] and [a] respectively. The final vowel in the happy set was usually [ɪ], though there are a number of forms with a more open [ɪ] and with [e] – [slɪpe] *slippy* (= *slippery*), [jɛstəde] *yesterday* – indicating a potential trend towards the lowering which characterises pronunciation in the 1997 data. In the GOAT set [ʊə] was normal in such words as *both, coat, go, home*, and in the GOAL set we find [ɒʊ]: *cold, older*. The competition between [aː] and [aʊ] in the MOUTH set in the 1997 data was already in evidence in the early 1950s. The SED field-worker revealingly states that the [aʊ] form was used when words such as *round* were elicited as citation forms in response to the questionnaire, but the normal conversational form was [aː]. A transition is clearly taking place from earlier [a] to [ɑː] in the BATH set, and from [ʊə] and [ɒʊ] to [oʊ]/[əʊ] in the GOAT and GOAL sets, but in spite of this trend towards standard pronunciation the vowel sounds remain surprisingly conservative, especially of course among older speakers. A telling example of this is the SED fieldworker's comment on the [ᵘuː] vowel in such words as *school*: 'the second element of slightly diphthongised vowels is not so close as Cardinal 8 nor so close as vowel in RS [skuːl]' (Ellis 1952/53). This description is equally applicable to the vowel sounds in this set today. The SED fieldworker's transcription also frequently indicates nasalisation of [ɑˑɪ], but this is not in evidence in the 1997 data. The vowel in such SED forms as [fɹiːtn̩d] *frightened*, [nˡiːt] *night* has become [aɪ]/[ɑˑˡ]/[aɪ], and [bɹɒk] *broke* has become [oʊ]/[əʊ].

Rather more change is evident when the consonants are compared. Glottali-sation has increased dramatically, notably among younger speakers. While glot-tal stops appear only rarely in the SED data, the incipient later developments are foreshadowed by the fieldworker's incidental remarks on [klɪəɹɪnᵗ teːbl] *clear-ing the table*, when he comments that in the Hillsborough informant's speech the definite article 'is very often an unexploded t' (Ellis 1952/53). He also notes that unexploded glottal stops occur initially in such words as [ˀuðə] *other*. The initial aspirate is absent in the SED data, even in such forms as [ə ɒlɪdɪ] *a holiday*, while in the 1997 data there is a clear tendency for [h] to be pronounced in the middle and younger age groups, especially among female speakers; older male speakers occasionally substitute a linking [j] in such phrases as [miˑ jɛd] *my head*, or a linking [ɹ], e.g. [mɛdəɹɔːl] *Meadowhall*.

Final *-ing* was invariably realised as [ɪn] in the SED data, and is yielding only slowly to [ɪŋ], especially in the speech of younger females, but also to some degree among older females. The realisation of initial [ð] as [d] is in rapid decline and is now retained mainly by older males. By contrast, it is mainly older females who retain [t] and [d] for [k] and [g], especially initially and preceding [l] in such words as [tlʊmze] *clumsy* and [dlʊvz] *gloves*, though evidence from other recent surveys reveals that younger middle- and working-class speakers, both male and female, continue to substitute [t] for [k], for example in [maïtl] *Michael*, and [d] for [g] in [stɹʊdl̩] *struggle* (Survey of Language and Folklore; see also Docherty & Foulkes this volume). There are very occasional indications of the devoicing of final/penultimate [d] and [z] in the SED data, e.g. [bakəd̥z̥] *back-wards*, [fɔɹəd̥z̥] *forwards*, perhaps presaging the more recent developments. In sum, with the notable exceptions of greatly increased glottalisation throughout the sample, and clear tendencies towards more standard pronunciation in final [ŋ], initial [h] and initial [ð] for older [d] among younger speakers, consonantal usage remains fairly conservative.

4.3   *The concept of NORMs*

It is interesting to speculate why, in phonological terms, the dialect of the Sheffield area appears to have experienced comparatively limited change over the past half century. By contrast, the 1997 data reveal significant lexical erosion on a par with the degree of loss in other SED localities. Such loss is not confined, as might be expected, to the more specific or technical aspects of agriculture, but extends across the range of everyday usage. For example, the notion *left-handed* is represented in the SED data by [ˌdɒlɪ ˈpɔːd] *dolly pawed*. Data from the Survey of Language and Folklore (SLF), however, reveal that this form is typical of the north-west area of the city, of which Hillsborough forms a part. The SLF records that the normal variant in central Sheffield, where the informant was born, was [ˌdɒlɪ ˈpɒʃ] *dolly posh*, and that to the north of the city the variants were [dɒlɪ] *dolly* and [ˌdɒlɪ ˈandəd] *dolly handed*. The *dolly* group appears to be unique to the area, but the SED records only one variant which, as it happens, was not the dominant older local form. However, the 1997 data record only *left-handed* across the whole sample, showing that the *dolly* group is in terminal decline, though there is evidence from the SLF of the introduction of *cack-handed*, itself originally having a mainly south-eastern distribution in the SED. Its recent appearance locally serves to fill the gap following the erosion of the *dolly* group, though its meaning usually suggests physical awkwardness or ineptitude rather than applying literally to left-handedness. Other SED words not recorded in the 1997 sample include: [badlɛ] *badly* (= *ill*), [bandɪlɛgd] *bandy-legged* (= *bowlegged*), [baːmɛ] *barmy* (= *silly*), [tʃeːmə] *chamber* (= *bedroom*), [dʒeːlɛgd] *jay-legged* (= *knock-kneed*), [lɪgd daːn] *lay down* (past tense), [ɹamɪl] *rammel* (= *rubbish*), [sʊpɪn] *supping* (= *drinking*), [tabz] *tabs* (= *ears*), [klamd]/[tlamd] *clammed* (= *hungry*); [kɒkã·ɪd] *cock-eyed* (= *askew*), [gɔːpɪn] *gawping* (= *gaping*). The use of such words as [mʊkɪ] *mucky* (= *dirty*), [snɛk] *sneck* (= *lock, door-catch*), [spël] *spell* (= *splinter*), [staːvd] *starved* (= *cold*) appears to be very much in decline, along with the second person singular pronoun forms *thee* and *thou*, the latter's reduced forms [ða], [ta] and [tə], and such reflexives as [mɪ'sɛn] *myself* and [ɪz'sɛn] *himself*. *Thee, thou* and their accompanying verbal forms were in any case traditionally male preserves in the locality and largely eschewed by women. Indeed, as is well attested in the SLF data, women strongly objected to men using these pronouns to address them: [ðiː ða: ðɪsɛn ən si: ɒu ða laɪks ɪt] *thee 'thou' thyself and see how thou likes it*, in which incidentally the female speaker uses the *thee* form herself. The SLF also records that the older local traditional pronunciation of *thee* and *thou* with initial [d] lay behind the stereotypification of Sheffielders expressed in the soubriquet [diː daːz] *thee-thous*.

Characteristic features of the dialect grammar recorded in the SED have inevitably moved towards the standard, although the past tense of the verb *be* stubbornly maintains a paradigm diametrically opposed to that of standard English, the *were* forms being normal in the singular, and the *was* forms (though decreasingly) in the plural. Such syntactic features as the postpositioned adjective as in [taɪmz mɛnɪ av tould jə nɒtʔ tə duu ðat] *times many I've told you not to do that*, frequently recorded in the SLF in the 1960s and 1970s, have virtually disappeared. However, many older Sheffielders continue to *put the light on* rather than to *put on the light*, and prefer the *five-and-twenty* forms to the *twenty-five* forms when telling the time. A particularly interesting feature well attested in the SLF data for Sheffield is the addition of an emphatic objective personal pronoun at the end of an utterance, substituting for a standard reflexive: [am guin aːtʔ tənaɪʔ miɪ] *I'm going out tonight, me*, [ɪz ɒf uəm tədeɪ ɪm] *he's off home today, him*.

While there have clearly been changes in Sheffield speech at the lexical, grammatical and syntactic levels, the dialect retains most of the essential characteristics recorded almost half a century earlier. Leaving aside for the moment the oversimplification implicit in the designation of NORMs, it appears that the methodology of the SED was as appropriate for investigating this particular urban area as it was for the rural localities on which it was primarily focused. Given the criteria for the selection of informants, the choice of the Hillsborough speaker proved to be both judicious and revealing. Apart from a few minor highly localised variations such as the *dolly-pawed* response, his speech appears to be archetypal, and accurately representative of older working-class males in the area at that time. Subsequent research has shown that it was in many ways an inspired choice, providing a mid-century benchmark in the development of a dialect whose progress has been charted for more than two hundred years (Widdowson 1992/93). This unusually long history also offers further evidence of the surprisingly low rate of change. The SED speaker fulfils the criteria of nonmobility, age and gender, differing only by virtue of his urban rather than rural location. With this exception, for the purposes of the SED he is a characteristic informant, in this case a nonmobile older urban male, a NOUM. His responses to the questionnaire are as full, rich and varied as those of his rural counterparts, even when dealing with the detailed agricultural and specialised material in Books I to IV of the questionnaire. The fieldworker notes significantly that the speaker 'showed a certain restlessness' when answering this section of the questionnaire and 'admitted constantly that this was something he knew very little about' (Ellis 1952/53). This was not entirely true of all the agricultural sections, however, as he had an acquaintance who was a horse breeder, and he himself could handle a horse. The incidental material includes his comment [am nɒt ə gaːdnə] *I'm not a gardener* during the questions about plants (Ellis 1952/53), but in spite of such disclaimers he manages to answer fully and in detail. This is all the more remarkable in that he was a first hand melter in charge of a steel furnace – again an appropriate choice to represent the city, just as agricultural workers typified the rural occupations.

It should also be borne in mind that the expansion of Sheffield following industrialisation led to the incorporation of originally outlying villages, many of which retained a degree of individual identity until at least the 1950s. The influx of population came largely from the surrounding rural areas, bringing with it a knowledge of the countryside, later manifested in a proliferation of small farms and market gardens on the fringes of the city, and in allotments and domestic gardens, where animals and poultry were not uncommon. The rural/urban dichotomy implicit in the concept of NORMs may therefore be less absolute than might appear at first sight. Furthermore, recent research has shown that, notwithstanding the complexity and mobility of population which characterise any modern city, Sheffield retains a substantial core of longstanding family networks which exercise a stabilising influence on aspects of local identity (Hey 1993, 1997). It is reasonable to assume that this influence extends to the dialect, itself the key mode of expressing allegiance to place. In these respects the essential stability and continuity implicit in the SED's criterion of nonmobility are equally valid as in a rural community.

As far as age is concerned, the Sheffield informant is ideal for the purposes of the SED, both in theoretical and in practical terms. At 64 he is at the younger end of the age range, the majority of informants being a decade or so older, but old enough to remember the varied experiences of the first half of the century. The fieldworker describes him as 'A good informant, fluent and broad in speech. A helper who realises [the] importance of [the] Survey' and is 'a highly intelligent man' who was 'all the time co-operative' (Ellis 1952/53). These positive qualities also mark the informant out as bridging the gap between older traditional pre-war dialect and later usage influenced by developments in education and the advent of the mass media. It is also interesting to speculate what influence his wife's southern speech may have had on his own. By virtue of his age and his awareness of the SED's aims his evidence is crucial to the interpretation of more recent data in both the historical and the contemporary context.

As already noted, the informant copes well with what is essentially a rurally oriented questionnaire, raising the interesting possibility that the SED might well have been successfully extended to a representative network of urban localities in the 1950s. At that time many towns and even cities still preserved a certain homogeneity and an established sense of community which have since tended to fragment. In Sheffield, however, despite the many recent changes and developments, many older local people continue to identify strongly with the city, typically greeting friends, acquaintances and even strangers in the street with a friendly informality. It would be interesting to compare the Sheffield SED data with those of the other three urban localities included in the Survey – Leeds, York and the London borough of Hackney – not least to discover whether the questionnaire was equally successful in these places. Furthermore, most rural localities in the SED have also experienced major changes since the 1950s. Among many other developments the advances in agricultural technology have disrupted the comparative stability and continuity previously evident in the rural population. The resultant drift to urban centres has been counterbalanced by the movement of commuters into rural areas, with inevitable consequences such as the blurring of dialect boundaries and the contingent contribution which language makes to distinctive local identity.

In terms of gender, as would be expected, the Hillsborough informant conforms with the SED's emphasis on male speakers. This has the advantage of comparability with the predominantly male respondents from the other localities investigated, both rural and urban. Its obvious disadvantage, quite apart from the selection of a single individual to represent the characteristic regional speech of a whole city, is the lack of any counterbalancing of the data which might have been contributed by female respondents. As we shall see later, more recent research challenges the assumption that 'women's speech tends to be more self-conscious than men's' (Chambers & Trudgill 1980: 35) and that by implication they are less likely to speak the dialect than their male counterparts. While it may well be true that in England 'men speak vernacular more frequently, more consistently . . . than women' (Orton, quoted in Chambers & Trudgill 1980: 35), it is questionable whether they speak it 'more genuinely'. It would be difficult to deny, for example, that many working-class women, in both rural and urban areas, speak as broadly as the men. Although for various reasons, for example their responsibilities in teaching children appropriate language for use in more formal contexts, they may opt for more standard grammar and syntax, and certain more standard lexical choices, they often maintain most if not all of the phonological features of local dialect. As already noted, no fewer than 118 women contributed to the SED and several of them were also tape-recorded. In the Basic Material volumes (Orton & Halliday 1963; Orton & Wakelin 1967; Orton & Barry 1969; Orton & Tilling 1970) and other publications derived from the SED, their contributions have been treated in the same way as the material from male respondents. As yet there has been no separate analysis of the data contributed by these women and this would be a fruitful ground for further investigation, especially to discover whether there are any significant distinctions between the responses of males and females. It might well be expected, for example, that women would be more knowledgeable about the subject of Book V of the questionnaire, *The House and Housekeeping*, than would the men, and the same might also be true of the following three books on

The Human Body, Numbers, Time and Weather, and *Social Activities*. In rural areas women would of course be familiar with the daily activities on the farm and with the natural world of the countryside, together with the relevant local terminology. The inclusion of a substantial number of women as respondents indicates that the fieldworkers were fully aware that nonmobile older rural females, NORFs, possessed such knowledge and were able to express it in the vernacular in the same way as the male informants. In an urban locality where women even in the 1950s would have less familiarity with agricultural matters they would still be able to make a significant contribution in response to the SED questionnaire. There is also the open question of what influence, if any, wives may have on the speech of their husbands, especially if, as is the case with the Hillsborough informant, the wives come from another part of the country.

When considering the relevance and ramifications of the concept of NORMs for current and recent linguistic investigation, we of course take it as read that dialectology has outgrown the methodological approaches which characterised it at least until the planning of the SED. Stemming originally from a diachronic and philological base, it is hardly surprising that these approaches had been focused primarily on capturing the oldest and/or most conservative usage. They were often strongly motivated by a desire to rescue such information before it disappeared in the tide of progress. Fuelled by survivalist notions of dialect as a lively fossil that refuses to die, much of the early research aimed to reconnect the present with the past, using the evidence of living speech to establish patterns of historical development in the evolution of the language, in short 'to reflect the speech of a bygone era' (Chambers & Trudgill 1980: 35). This preoccupation with the past, as in other branches of language study, was swept away by the advent of the discipline of linguistics, with its emphasis on synchronic approaches to language in social context. Although some major surveys such as that of the *Atlas Linguarum Europae* maintained the older methodology into the 1970s, the powerful influence of sociolinguistics was instrumental in revealing the inadequacies of the earlier approach: 'However clear the motivation seems, it is nevertheless true that the narrow choice of informants in dialect geography is probably also the greatest single source of disaffection for it in recent times. Readers and researchers have questioned the relevance of what seems to be a kind of linguistic archaeology' (Chambers & Trudgill 1980: 35). Following the pioneering work of Houck in Leeds in the late 1960s (Houck 1966, 1967) – when incidentally the Basic Material of the SED was being edited for publication – and the groundbreaking work by Labov (1966) and Trudgill (1974), there was an inevitable sea change in approaches to the study of dialect, whether regional or social. Trudgill (1974: 4) succinctly articulates the reasons for such a shift as follows:

> Sociological urban dialectology can also have the function – particularly in Britain, where little attention has so far been paid to this kind of work – of providing a description of the linguistic characteristics of the vast majority of the country's population. It would seem that the considerable amount of rural dialectological work that has been

carried out in Britain has left the linguist singularly ignorant about the way in which most of the people in Britain speak. The aims of rural dialectology have, of course, been of a different nature. Many dialectologists have, legitimately, been concerned to record older dialect forms before they are lost for good. The result has been, however, a neglect of current speech forms which could have provided an excellent 'laboratory' for the testing of linguistic hypotheses. Rural dialectologists, too, can be accused of having neglected the heterogeneity that is present even in rural speech communities.

Dialectologists were initially wary of the new approach, just as devotees of traditional grammar resisted the onslaught of structural linguistics in the early 1960s. After an early standoff, occasioned in part by unwarranted attacks on 'traditional' dialectology, an uneasy truce eventually ensued. Once the two sides recognised that they had much to learn from each other, a rapprochement has been effected in recent years which in many respects has been mutually beneficial.

In view of these developments it is unlikely that dialect studies in the future, certainly in England, will focus exclusively on NORMs, except perhaps for purposes of comparison with analogous 'traditional' studies. In the future, dialectologists will draw increasingly on the various models put forward in sociolinguistic studies, especially with respect to sampling and modes of analysis, as will be the case in the Survey of Regional English (SuRE: Kerswill, Llamas & Upton forthcoming; Upton & Llamas forthcoming). The static model exemplified by concentration on NORMs has given way to dynamic models which investigate variation across the spectrum of age, gender and social class. The older approach not only played down the potential contribution of women to the study, but also completely ignored the younger generations. As Chambers & Trudgill (1980: 35) put it:

> Young people who have been natives of a particular region for their entire lives have often been disturbed to discover that the speech recorded in field studies of their regions is totally alien to anything that seems familiar to them. That discovery is not at all surprising when one considers that nowadays the greatest proportion of the population is mobile, younger, urban and female, in other words, the diametrical opposite of NORMs. The NORM population has been rapidly dwindling for several generations now. The important works of dialect geography recorded their speech faithfully and in a sense enshrined it, but it is likely that the future of dialect studies will have to be directed toward other, less rarefied populations.

In the light of these remarks it now remains to comment briefly on the 1997 data in terms of the four criteria characterising NORMs: mobility, age, domicile and gender. The three groups, each comprising four females and four males in the sample of respondents, are designated as older (O), middle (M), and younger (Y), females being represented as (F) and males as (M), plus an individual informant number, as in Table 4.2.

Table 4.2 Informant profiles: designation, age group, locality
and social class

Informant	Age	Locality	Social class
Older			
OF1	77	Netherthorpe	WC
OF2	78	Handsworth	WC
OF3	81	Netherthorpe	WC
OF4	60	Greystones	WC
OM1	83	Netherthorpe	WC
OM2	67	Stocksbridge	WC
OM3	82	Ecclesall	WC
OM4	78	Walkley	WC
Middle			
MF1	43	Hillsborough	WC
MF2	46	Wadsley	WC
MF3	47	Walkley	MC
MF4	45	Firth Park	MC
MM1	42	Wadsley	MC
MM2	32	Burncross	WC
MM3	47	Stannington	WC
MM4	31	Hunter's Bar	WC
Younger			
YF1	12	Beighton	WC
YF2	20	Ecclesall	MC
YF3	23	Mosborough	MC
YF4	25	Stocksbridge	MC
YM1	21	Nether Edge	WC
YM2	23	Broomhill	WC
YM3	22	Beighton	MC
YM4	21	Banner Cross	WC

The 12 females and 12 males are drawn from 17 localities across the city. Using occupational criteria and self-perception as a guide, seven of the females and ten of the males can be designated as working-class, while five of the females and two of the males can be described as middle-class. The typical characteristics of the phonology of the whole sample have been presented in summary form in the first section of this paper. Using the concept of NORMs as a starting point, some of the more salient features will now be discussed in greater detail.

4.3.1   Mobility

All 24 informants were born and bred in Sheffield, and most had lived all their lives in the part of the city where they were born. A few had moved to various places within the city boundaries. One of the males in the middle age group (MM3) had worked in London for seven years in the recent past, but this experience appears to have had no perceptible influence on his speech, which retains all the typical local features. Another (OM4) had spent time in the armed forces in the Second World War, again with no apparent effect on his speech in comparison with others in his age group. This raises the question of what effect, if any, military service had on the speech of SED informants, many of whom by virtue of their age may have served in two world wars. As with so many other aspects of the SED, this merits further investigation. Only one of the female speakers in the 1997 data, YF4, had spent any significant time away from the city, in this case living in Newcastle for two years while undertaking a higher education course. In the transition from a working-class background to a middle-class occupational and social status, her pronunciation has moved towards the standard, but only to a limited extent. There appears to be a strong tradition of retaining the main features of local phonology on the part of those living and working in the city, even among professionals in the middle classes. The 1997 interviews largely reaffirmed the evidence from the SLF that Sheffielders, especially those of the older generation, are reluctant to modify their accent if they move away from the city. This suggests a degree of local pride in identifying with the region through the shared connections of speech. On the other hand, several of those interviewed believed that local people lose their accent quickly when they move away. These conflicting views invite further study.

Other recent local surveys such as the Survey of Sheffield Usage (SSU) in the 1980s confirmed the underlying stability of the population, but point to an uneven distribution of native speakers from one part of the conurbation to another. In a sample of adult speakers across the south-western and north-western sectors of the city, from Sharrow, through Ecclesall, Crookes and Walkley to Hillsborough, for example, approximately 50% were native to Sheffield, 40% were originally from other localities in the United Kingdom, and 10% were from overseas. In a parallel sample from the geographically more tightly clustered Parson Cross area in the northern sector, on the other hand, more than 80% of interviewees were natives of Sheffield. As far as the two groups interviewed in 1997 are concerned, not only did the sample conform to the nonmobile criterion, but over 95% of the interviewees' parents were born and bred in Sheffield, an interesting exception being the father of YM3 who was born in Dublin. Nonmobility therefore seems to be a dominant factor in the comparative stability and conservatism in the speech of the locality.

4.3.2   Age

As regards age, the 1997 data present a wide spectrum, from 12 to 83. It so happens, however, that in the older group (56 →) the speakers cluster in the higher range 77–83, only two being in the sixties and below. The middle group (31–55) bunches in the 42–47 range, with only two speakers in their (early) thirties. In the younger group (12–30) all speakers apart from the 12-year-old are in their twenties. This unevenness in the sampling presents difficulties in making categorical statements about the relationship between phonology and age, except by reference to each of the three groups as a whole. Nevertheless, age difference seems to be the most important factor influencing phonological variation in vowels across the sample, as indicated in Table 4.3, in which the characteristic vowel sound(s) for each set are found at the head of the relevant column within each group, followed by a list of variants.

First, it is clear that the older group exhibits significantly more variation than is the case in the middle and younger groups. A number of conservative features noted in the SED data, including [ɛɪ] in such words as *key, eat, speak*, [ɪə] in *heat, sweet, leaves*, [ɔʊ ~ ɒʊ] in the THOUGHT set, [ɒʊ] in the GOAT and GOAL sets, [aː ~ aːᵊ ~ eɪ ~ iː] in the PRICE set, [ɪə] in the SQUARE set and [ʊə] in the FORCE set, are found only in the older age group. Significantly, several younger male speakers used [ɔʊ] in the GOAT and GOAL sets when reading the word-list, but [ɔː] in free conversation. Of particular interest is the loss of the [ɒː ~ ɒʊ ~ ɔɪ ~ ɒɪ] variants of the GOAL set in the middle and younger groups. The [ɔɪ ~ ɒɪ] pronunciations of such words as *coal, hole* have been emblematic of local speech, but are clearly yielding to northern standard [oʊ] and RP [əʊ], although an older [ɔː] is still tenacious across all groups. Northern [a] in the BATH set remains firmly entrenched but, as already noted, is beginning to face competition from [ɑː] among younger speakers. One surprising feature is that the final vowel in the happy set is typically realised as [ɪ] in the older group, but as [ɛ] in the middle and younger groups. For many speakers, especially females, final [ɪ] appears to be in free variation with [e]/[ɛ], especially in listing the days of the week: [mʊndɪ tiuːzdɪ wɛnzdɛ] *Monday, Tuesday, Wednesday* (MF2). Some younger speakers seem also to be adopting a further variant: [ɪ̈]. Overall, however, there is a clear drift towards more standard pronunciations, mirroring the gradual erosion of lexical variation.

4.3.3   Locality

The fact that the 1997 sample is drawn from widely scattered parts of the city might have been expected to reveal variation. Closer examination, however, shows that slightly over 50% of speakers are located in the south-west to north-west sectors. While central parts of the city are quite well represented, only four informants come from the eastern sector. This bias of course facilitates comparison with the SED data for Hillsborough in the north-west of the city, but precludes detailed analysis of the possible relevance of locality to phonological variation in the area as a whole. Such comparison as can be made, however, suggests that in this sample there is little if any significant difference in pronunciation from one part of the city to another. It is hoped that analysis of SSU data may in due course establish whether or not such variation exists.

Table 4.3. Vowel distribution according to age group

	DRESS	TRAP	STRUT	BATH	HAPPY	FLEECE	FACE	THOUGHT	GOAT	GOAL	GOOSE	PRICE	MOUTH	SQUARE	START	FORCE
Older	ɛ	a	ʊ	a	ɪ	iː	eː	ɔː	oʊ	oʊ	ʊu /uː	ɑɪ/ɑɪ	aː	ɛə/eə	aː	ɔː
Plus:	ε̈	ɑ	ɐ		e	iː	eˡ	ɔʊ	ɔʊ	ɔʊ	ʉu	aɪ	æːɪ	eɪ	ɒː	ɔʊ
	eɪ		e		ɛ	ïː	ɛɪ	ɒʊ	ɒʊ	ɒʊ		aː	aʊ			ɔə
						ɪə			ɔː	ɔː		eᵊ	aːᵊ			
						eə			ʊ (go)	ɒː		ɪə (right)	æʊ			
										ɔɪ		iː (night)	ʊə			
Middle	ɛ	a	ʊ	a	ɛ	iː	eː	ɔː	oʊ	oʊ	uːu	ɑɪ	aʊ	eə	aː/ɑː	ɔː
Plus:	ε̈	ɑ	ɐ		ɪ	iː	eˡ		ɔː	ɔː	ʉu	aɪ	ᵊʊ		ɒː	ɔə
			ɑ		e	ïː	ɛɪ		ɐʊ	ɐʊ	ʉᵿ		æː			
Younger	ɛ	a	ʊ	a	ɛ	iː	ɪə	ɔː	oʊ	oʊ	uːu	ɑɪ	aʊ	eə	ɑː	ɔː
Plus:		ɑ	e	ɑː	ɪ	ɪi	eˡ		ɐʊ	ɐʊ	ᵿuᵿ					
					ïɪ	ïː	eː		ɔː	ɔː						

4.3.4   Gender

In addition to the general points raised in the introductory summary of characteristic features, some interesting differences can be observed, notably in vowels. The most significant of these are presented in Table 4.4, which reveals gender-specific choices in the vowel sounds of eight of the sets under discussion.

Male speakers retain a larger number of conservative pronunciations in the THOUGHT, GOAT, GOAL, PRICE and SQUARE sets, giving the impression that female speakers employ less variation. Indeed, in purely numerical terms, this is the case overall, males using nine more pronunciation variants in these sets than females. On the other hand, females uniquely use the [ɒ] variant in the TRAP and STRUT sets, though only on an occasional basis. The [ɒ] variant in the STRUT set is of particular interest, as it is somewhat closer to standard [ʌ] and, given the existence of [ə] in weak position for this set, opens up the possibility of a move from [ʊ] towards [ʌ]. This is reinforced by evidence from the SLF which records fallback variants such as [ə] and even [əː] for strongly stressed words in this set, e.g. [bət ~ bəːt] *but*, in addition to the [ə] in weak position. Even so, the situation is complicated in the pronunciation [slɒʃ] as a variant of [sluʃ] *slush* by the fact that *slosh* was recorded as a lexical variant of *slush* in the SED fieldwork in various parts of the country, including Yorkshire, although the Hillsborough informant used [sluʃ] (Upton, Parry & Widdowson 1994: 373–4). The vowel realisations in the GOAT and GOAL sets are similar in profile to those in Table 4.3, demonstrating that women in the middle and younger age groups employ a much reduced range of pronunciation in which the characteristic [oʊ] is under increasing pressure from [əʊ].

Table 4.4 Vowel distribution according to gender

	TRAP	STRUT	HAPPY	THOUGHT	GOAT	GOAL	PRICE	SQUARE
Females	a	ʊ	ɛ	ɔː	oʊ	oʊ	ɑɪ	ɛə
Plus:								
	ɒ	ɒ	ɪ		ɔʊ	ɔʊ	aɪ	ɛˑə
		ə	e		əʊ	əʊ	aː	
			ï		ɔː	ɔː	aːə	
					ʊ (*go*)			
Males	a	ʊ	ɪ	ɔː	oʊ	oʊ	ɑɪ	ɛə
Plus:								
		ə	e	ɒʊ	ɔʊ	ɔʊ	ɑˑɪ	ɛˑə
			ɛ	ɔʊ	ɒʊ	ɒʊ	aː	ɪə
			ïɪ		əʊ	əʊ	aːə	
					ɔː	ɔː	eɪ	
					ʊ (*go*)	ɒː	iː (*night*)	
						ɔɪ		
						ɒɪ		

4.4 *Conclusion*

In conclusion, it is clear that, with the modification of 'rural' to 'urban', the concept of NORMs/NOUMs serves a useful purpose in characterising the ideal informant originally sought by the SED and similar surveys which focused primarily on the usage of older conservative speakers. Indeed, the Sheffield respondent not only fulfilled all but the 'rural' criterion, but also proved to be as knowledgeable and informative on all aspects of the SED as his counterparts in the countryside. Most of the speakers in the 1997 fieldwork in Sheffield were also nonmobile, and the older generation retained a significant number of the phonological features recorded in the early 1950s. Even so, however representative the Hillsborough SED respondent might have been, interviewing a single nonmobile older urban male to characterise the speech of a large conurbation inevitably gave a very limited picture of local speech as a whole. The present study has sought to demonstrate that there is much to be gained by comparing the language of older conservative speakers with that of other age groups, and by exploring variation not only over time but also taking account of such factors as locality, gender and social class.

A preliminary study such as this can do no more than open up possible avenues for exploration. Using only a small sample drawn from two social networks, the discussion has obvious limitations. Nevertheless, it is able to reveal continuity and change in local usage over the past few decades and to present a range of data on current speech in the city. Above all, it makes available for the first time a corpus of material from this urban area which extends and augments that recorded for the SED, and offers scope for more detailed study in the future. In raising more questions than can be immediately answered, it invites the re-examination of the concept of NORMs and a reappraisal of the past and present use and relevance of the term.

5

West Wirral: norms, self reports and usage

Mark Newbrook

5.1 *Introduction*

The data were collected in 1980 for the author's PhD thesis, in Heswall/Irby, Hoylake, West Kirby and Neston (see Newbrook 1982, 1986). 'Labovian' (one-to-one) interviews were carried out with 68 randomly selected informants (42 male, 26 female) aged 11–80. The sample covered the entire social class range in the area (which is considerable; see below). The interviews lasted 45–80 minutes in all, and included biographical questions, word-list and passage reading, (relatively) spontaneous speech and a minimal group exercise.

In addition, subjects were asked a series of questions aimed more directly at the informant's language attitudes. This section included a subjective evaluation/self-assessment exercise, in which informants were asked to identify, for each variable, one of a series of variants as the 'best' usage, and also to identify their own usual usage. The variants selected for the exercise covered the entire relevant dialectological range: RP, 'broad' and less 'broad' Liverpool usage, and 'broad' and less 'broad' Cheshire usage. The results were analysed auditorily, and the numerical data relating to usage (especially usage in conversation as opposed to exercises) were subjected to multiple regression analyses. Informants' usage and attitudes are discussed at length in sections 5.3 and 5.4 below.

5.1.1 West Wirral

West Wirral – regarded here as including most of Hoylake and the whole of West Kirby, Heswall (with Irby and other smaller surrounding settlements) and Neston (with hinterland) – extends along the south-west coast of the Wirral peninsula in Cheshire/Merseyside. It is a mixed rural/suburban area which was mainly rural, with mining in Neston, until the rise of commuter networks (from the early twentieth century for rail; from the 1940s onwards for better-surfaced roads and more frequent bus services). There is some light industry, mainly in Neston, and Hoylake and West Kirby function as minor seaside resorts and sailing and fishing centres. In 1974 most of the area (excepting Neston) was incorporated as the Borough of Wirral into the new urban county of Mersey-side; this reflected the increasingly central role of Liverpool.

During the last few decades such employment opportunities as have existed have been centred in inner Merseyside, as have major shopping and entertainment facilities. There has also been some migration into the area from inner Merseyside, including (a) upwardly mobile middle-class commuters (and retirees) seeking a more rural living environment and (b) (especially around 1945–1960) working-class overspill population relocated after the partial demolition of areas in inner Merseyside suffering from urban decay. This latter particularly affected the Pensby area of Heswall, where the population exploded in the immediate post-war years. Parts of central Heswall have also become more and more heavily built-up with middle-class housing. However, there has also been some out-migration, especially in more recent times, with younger people seeking employment of all kinds outside the region. In fact, the population of West Wirral has for several decades been stable at around 80,000; compare the 350,000 (also stable) in the entire Borough of Wirral including north-east Wirral (Birkenhead, Wallasey, Bebington etc.).

5.1.2 Dialectological background

The speech of West Wirral was originally largely similar to that of the rest of West Cheshire, but has increasingly fallen under the influence of Liverpool (as, at an earlier date, did that of north-east Wirral).[1] Liverpool usage was originally close to that of Lancashire (which forms a continuum with Cheshire usage), but was more cosmopolitan owing to the city's port role, and from the 1840s onwards was heavily influenced by Irish English, owing to massive migration to and through the city as a result of the Irish famine.[2] In consequence, major isogloss bundles have come to surround Liverpool and inner Merseyside.

5.1.3 Methodology

The study reported here was aimed at examining the current patterning of variation associated with some phonological isoglosses of this nature in the West Wirral area. The general direction of change is obviously towards Liverpool/Birkenhead usage. The area is distinctive in that it is particularly middle-class in character (it is part of Liverpool's 'stockbroker belt') and thus displays larger proportions of high-prestige usage (including RP-like phonology) than most areas in north-west England. On the other hand, there are also large numbers of working-class speakers with strong local accents of various kinds, including both overspill arrivals with their offspring and families resident in the area for longer periods.

The presence of RP, Cheshire and Liverpool/inner Merseyside (henceforth 'Liverpool') forms results in a system of three 'extreme' varieties, and hence – in the case of certain variables – of three 'extreme' variants (though this does not, of course, apply where two of the varieties share a feature, as quite frequently occurs). A two-dimensional scoring system was set up to accommodate this complexity: briefly, each relevant variable was scored on two scales, a 'horizontal' one reflecting the variation between Cheshire forms (scoring 0%) and Liverpool forms (scoring 100%) and a 'vertical' one reflecting the range from the broadest non-RP forms – either Cheshire or Liverpool – scoring 0% to the RP forms scoring 100%. For each variable in each style/informant combination, the two scores are, of course, partly independent of each other, and the sum of the two percentages may easily exceed 100 (see Figure 5.1).

A typical score for such a variable is shown in Figure 5.1. 40% on the horizontal dimension reflects usage which is rather more Cheshire than Liverpool; 67% on the vertical dimension is fairly high on the scale in respect of the typical degree of standardness or resemblance to RP of the relevant forms. Depending on the variable, both scores might represent summaries across a range of several variants, including some with intermediate scores (on either or both dimensions) as well as the three extreme variants. The precise breakdowns for the various variants are sometimes of great interest; the percentages themselves provide only a general impression of the nature of the usage of each informant (or, averaged, of each group of informants). In some cases (see below) there are rival forms even at the extremes. This is especially true for the Liverpool extreme, notably in the cases of some vocalic variables. Details for some of the individual variables are given below.[3]

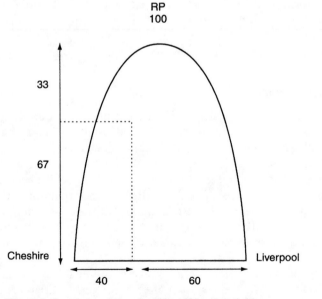

Fig. 5.1 Scoring system for West Wirral variables, showing a score of 40:67

5.2   *Descriptive material*

Twenty-one variables were analysed in detail in respect of stylistic variation. Of these, 17 were used in the subjective reaction/self-assessment exercise, and 14 were fully analysed in respect of the statistics of their correlation with non-linguistic factors. For seven of these last 14 variables, both horizontal and vertical dimensions were relevant, and for the other seven only vertical (no significant difference between Cheshire and Liverpool). The main statistical values cited below for these 14 variables are *t*-tests, in which scores of 1.0 or better may be taken as indicative of statistical significance, with scores of 2.0+, 3.0+ etc. indicating higher degrees of significance.

References below to 'the leading 21/17/14' variables relate to these various sets. However, the results for the individual variable features studied have been re-grouped for the purposes of the main discussion of specific phenomena so as to reflect (where appropriate) Wells' (1982) word sets.[4]

There was, overall, a considerable preponderance of indicator patterns showing little or no stylistic shifting (and thus, probably, limited social salience) over markers displaying appreciable stylistic shifting (and thus, probably, higher levels of social salience).[5] This was not entirely unexpected, given the middle-class nature of the area and the high scoring which was therefore typical on the vertical dimension; in the cases of many informant–variable combinations, the score was 80%+ in the least formal style and had little scope for rising further in more formal settings. However, in calculating variable-specific (and overall) breakdowns of indicators and markers, such cases have been excluded, since the classical marker patterning involving substantial increases in the score as formality increased would not have been possible. Across the leading 21 variables 258 of the relevant 1416 informant–variable combinations had to be excluded in this way (as 'high-scoring "indicators"'). Across the remaining cases there were 496 indicators, 455 markers and 207 anomalous stylistic patterns. 123 of these 207 were direct reversals (highest scoring in least formal style); many of these were concentrated on certain variables and apparently involved variations in attitudes as to norms (such as are discussed below).

There is thus still a (small) majority of indicators over markers even when the 258 high-scoring 'indicators' are excluded, suggesting that in many cases usage is not especially sensitive to style and remains quite markedly local in character even in rather formal settings. One of the most striking cases of this was – not surprisingly – the northern shibboleth variable BATH, where as many as 51 of the 68 informants produced genuine indicator patterns, with six high-scoring 'indicators' and only eight markers (see below on attitudinal factors which are highly relevant here). Even for STRUT (normally a marker in Northern England), the indicator–marker breakdown was 28 genuine indicators to 34 markers. One variable where markers did – not entirely expectedly – predominate was the variable THOUGHT, where the variation appears to involve only phonetic realisation, not phonological structure; there were 46 markers, with the vowel tending to be somewhat higher and considerably more rounded (as in RP) in more formal styles. In such cases the variable appears to be more socially salient than might have been anticipated, though where the issue is realisational it is rare for informants to comment explicitly, and indeed few did so here.

As noted, stylistic variation of these kinds relates closely to the relative and absolute salience of variables and also to attitudes to their key variants. The relevance of this will become apparent later in our discussion of informants' beliefs about and subjective attitudes to the variables and their variants, including self-reports.

In the variable-specific statements which follow, it should be assumed – except where otherwise noted – that variables patterned as mid- or high-scoring (relatively RP-like) indicators, and that there was general acceptance of the RP norm. Despite these facts, where there was evidence of change in progress this generally appeared to be change away from RP and, predictably, towards Liverpool; see below on the one clear exception (BOOK), and compare the findings of earlier scholars such as Heath (1980) and Trudgill (1974). In some cases a large minority of informants produced divergent patterning in some respect or other; for instance, variables which patterned mainly as indicators might still manifest marker patterning for some informants, who did display appreciable stylistic shifting. Numbers of marker patterns are noted below for the various variables. Totals of informants are usually out of 68 (but a few borderline cases have been omitted).

5.2.1   Vowels (usage)

Table 5.1 presents a summary of the typical realisations of keyword vowels produced by West Wirral speakers in everyday (vernacular) interaction. Stylistic and other variations and attitudinal responses are discussed in detail below.

Table 5.1 West Wirral vowels – summary

KIT	ɪ	FLEECE	iː	NEAR	ɪə
DRESS	ɛ	FACE	eɪ ~ ëɪ ~ ɛɪ	SQUARE	ëː ~ əː
TRAP	a	PALM	aː	START	aː
LOT	ɒ	THOUGHT	ɔː	NORTH	ɔː
STRUT	ʊ	GOAT	ɔʊ ~ ʌʊ ~ ɛʊ ~ oʊ	FORCE	ɔː
ONE	ɒ	GOOSE	ʉː	CURE	jɔː > jʉ(w)ə
FOOT	ʊ	BOOK	ʊ > ʉː	happy	i > ɪ
BATH	a ~ aː	PRICE	aɪ	letteʀ	ə
CLOTH	ɒ	CHOICE	ɒɪ	horses	ə > ɪ
NURSE	əː ~ ëː	MOUTH	aʊ	commA	ə

Comments

TRAP (and BATH where relevant) (realisation of /æ/; local form [a])
This vowel was generally realised around [a], differing from PALM/START (/ɑ:/)
mainly in length (as in Northern England generally). The mean score in the least
formal style was 39%. However, there were as many as 36 marker patterns, suggesting surprisingly high salience. There were a few cases of hyper-correct /ɑ:/ in
words such as *maths* (see under BATH).

STRUT (/ʌ/–/ʊ/; local form [ʊ] = /ʊ/)
The contrast with FOOT was maintained only at 27% in the least formal style.
This indicates quite 'broad' usage for this sample, but there was still a good deal
of marker patterning (34 informants), demonstrating a reasonably high level of
salience (if not as high as might have been expected).

ONE (with ONCE, NONE, -ONE) (/ɒ/–/ʌ/(–/ʊ/); local form [ɒ] = /ɒ/)
This variable obviously involves lexical incidence. All 68 informants mainly
showed north-western /ɒ/ in this set (and 11 had some traces of /ɒ/ in *nothing*);
25 had some /ʌ/–/ʊ/. The RP form with /ʌ/ is quite unfamiliar to many local
people, and the variant in /ɒ/ is very resistant to RP influence.

BATH (/ɑ:/–/æ/; local form [a] = /æ/)
This northern shibboleth variable (very resistant to RP influence) involves lexical incidence, but the degree of predictability on the basis of environment is
high, with the result that the patterning somewhat resembles that of a distributional variable (except that hyper-correct forms in /ɑ:/ for RP /æ/ in the TRAP set
– which are not dealt with here – are much more frequent than would be the case
with a genuine distributional variable). In the BATH set itself, RP /ɑ:/ was used
only at 13% in the least formal style (/æ/ at 87%). There were 51 genuine indicator patterns and only eight markers; the variable is not salient in the sense that
/ɑ:/ is much more heavily used in formal styles (it is not), and in fact there is a
major issue in respect of norms (see below).

NURSE (/ɔ:/ in RP; main local forms [ɔ:] or [ë:]) and SQUARE (/ɛə/ in RP; main local
    forms [ë:] or [ɔ:])
The contrast between SQUARE (usual realisation [ë:]) and NURSE (usual realisation [ɔ:]) was maintained by 40 informants. Eleven informants showed a merger
of these two classes (four around [ɔ:], the other seven around [ë:]). There was
one (dubious) case of (allegedly) Liverpool-style 'flip-flop', i.e. 'reversed'
phonemic incidence (/ɛə/ = [ɔ:], /ɔ:/ = [e:]). In respect of stylistic differentiation, there were only 16 marker patterns for SQUARE, 21 for NURSE. Both SQUARE
and NURSE manifested surprisingly low salience (little reference was made to
them in discussion), though perhaps the rather strong local middle-class tendency to preserve the RP contrast makes this issue less salient than elsewhere in
Merseyside.

GOAT (realisation of /əʊ/; main local forms [oʊ] or [ʌʊ]/[ɛʊ])
Forms approaching RP [əʊ] occurred at 52% in the least formal style; Liverpool forms of various kinds at 79%. Females (overwhelmingly; 25–0) and younger males preferred (originally) hyper-correct [ʌʊ]/[ɛʊ] to older Liverpool [oʊ]; all the males as a group narrowly preferred the latter, 22–20. This is as one might predict. There were only 15 marker patterns (salience was low, confirmed by a dearth of references to the variable in discussion).

FACE (realisation of /eɪ/; main local forms [ëɪ] or [ɛɪ])
Forms approaching RP [eɪ] occurred at 59% in least formal style, Liverpool forms of various kinds at 79%. Males preferred older Liverpool [ëɪ] to (originally) hyper-correct [ɛɪ] by a margin of 38–3, while females (perhaps predictably) preferred the latter, 16–6. There were only 17 marker patterns, indicating low salience.

PALM/START (and BATH where relevant) (realisation of /ɑː/; local form [aː])
This vowel was generally realised around [aː], differing from TRAP (/æ/) mainly in length, as in Northern England generally. However, there was typically a greater tendency towards RP-like realisations (here, retracted forms around [ɑː]) in this case; the mean score in the least formal style was higher, at 58%. There was virtually no non-prevocalic /r/ in START. Here only 24 informants produced marker patterns (perhaps in part because scoring was higher than for TRAP even in more informal styles).

THOUGHT/NORTH/FORCE (inventory/realisation; main local form [ɔː])
Here there is (a) an issue of inventory (whether all three or any two of these sets are in contrast or not; NORTH/FORCE appear as /ɔə/ and THOUGHT as /ɔː/ in some (more conservative) non-rhotic accents, but in many all three appear as /ɔː/); and (b) an issue of realisation (how the phoneme(s) is/are realised). The older contrast between /ɔː/ and /ɔə/ (as manifested in pairs such as *paw* and *pore/pour*) was maintained by 47 informants in one or more styles (nine produced anomalous/confused patterning, 12 had no contrast). However, only 10 of these 47 maintained the contrast in all styles, and 35 of the remaining 37 maintained it only in formal styles. RP-like phonetic realisations centring on [ɔː] occurred at only 28% in the THOUGHT set in the least formal style, with most realisations being somewhat more open and less rounded than this, as is usual on Merseyside (more centralised, characteristically Liverpool forms, specifically, occurred at 74%). This is very 'broad' usage for this sample, but there were surprisingly many marker patterns (46) given the apparently very low level of salience (there were no overt references at all in discussion, for example).

GOOSE (and BOOK where relevant) (realisation of /uː/; local form [ʉː])
RP-like forms occurred at 67% in the least formal style, fronted Liverpool forms such as [ʉː] at 80%. There were only 13 marker patterns (low salience).

BOOK, etc. (/ʊ/–/uː/; local form [ʉː] = /uː/)
This variable obviously involves lexical incidence. General English /ʊ/ occurred at 86% (traditional northern /uː/ at 14%) in the least formal style. There was only one marker pattern (45 high-scoring 'indicators') but there were as many as 18 anomalous stylistic patterns (17 reversals); see below on the issue of rival norms.

CURE (/ʊə/–/ɔː/; main local forms [ʉ(w)ə] or [ɔ̈ː])
As in Northern England generally, there was sporadic maintenance of contrast between /ʊə/ and /ɔː/, but most younger informants used /ɔː/ in most words in this set.

happY ([ɪ] = /ɪ/ – [i] = /iː/ (?); main local form [i])
Liverpool/general southern [i] occurred at 83% (older RP/rural northern [ɪ] at 17%) in the least formal style. Assuming a rather simplistic analysis taking the RP form to be [ɪ], there were 25 anomalous stylistic patterns (21 reversals) but only seven markers (see below on the effect of rival norms).

horsES (/ɪ/–/ə/; local form [ə] = /ə/)
Liverpool-like /ə/ occurred at 70% (older RP/general northern /ɪ/ at 30%) in the least formal style. There were 27 anomalous stylistic patterns (seven reversals; 20 more complex patterns) and as many as 28 markers (surprisingly high; see below on the issue of rival norms).

5.2.2 Consonants (usage)

T (local (Liverpool) form [ts])
Pre-consonantal/final /t/ was often glottal/glottalised as it is increasingly in many areas (quite unlike the traditional Liverpool pattern); intervocalically and initially there were some affricate/fricative/heavily aspirated Liverpool forms. Patterning in this second set of environments showed fairly strong correlation with the non-linguistic 'Merseysidisation' index; i.e., the Liverpool forms were used mainly by those with heavier contact with inner Merseyside (this was in fact the most striking case in this study of this last effect). There were also as many as 61 marker patterns for pre-consonantal and final /t/ but only 14 for /t/ in other positions (but the dialectology is more complex than this suggests and in the latter case most 'indicators' were in fact high-scoring).

K (local (Liverpool) form [x] or [kx])
Affricate/fricative/heavily aspirated Liverpool /k/ (most usually fricative [x]) occurred at 8% (92% stops with milder aspiration or none, depending on position) in the least formal style. Only four informants produced marker patterns (scoring was, of course, very high in all styles).

NG
-*ing* (local form [-ɪn] = /-ɪn/): /ŋ/ occurred at 60% in the least formal style (high

for such a style). 40 informants showed marker patterning across styles, not surprisingly given that the variable is obviously very salient. Most of the rest were high-scoring 'indicators'.

-thing (*something*, etc.; local forms [-θɪn] = /-θɪn/ or [-θɪŋk] = /-θɪŋk/): there was considerable use of /-θɪŋk/, especially among younger subjects, and 21 cases of marker patterning (this also involved /-θɪn/ in informal styles), as against 19 genuine indicators.

-ng (*king*, etc.; local form [-ŋg] = /-ŋg/): there was considerable use of /-ŋg/, with 32 genuine indicators and only 15 markers. This suggests limited salience; but see below on the effect of rival norms.

-ng- (*singer*, etc.; local form [-ŋg-] = /-ŋg-/): there was heavy use of /-ŋg-/, again with frequent indicator patterning (all 41 apparent cases were genuine) and only 17 markers. This again suggests limited salience; but see below on the effect of rival norms.

H (local form Ø)
77% of potential /h-/ was realised in the least formal style (very high for such a style); with the high-scoring 'indicator' patterns excluded, all remaining informants manifested marker patterning (except one who produced an anomalous stylistic pattern). The variable is very salient indeed.

R (local (Liverpool) form [ɾ])
There was almost no non-prevocalic /r/. In other positions, tapped Liverpool [ɾ] occurred at 12% (88% [ɹ]) in the least formal style. There was unusually strong correlation here between horizontal dimension scoring for this variable and the non-linguistic 'Merseysidisation' index. Surprisingly, there were few tokens of [ʋ], which is to all appearances a fairly common variant in and around Merseyside (though it is perceived locally as defective). Only five informants produced marker patterns (scoring was, of course, very high in all styles).

5.2.3   Other issues regarding usage

The scores for these variables generally correlated more significantly with the age of the informant in respect of the 'horizontal' Cheshire–Liverpool dimension than in respect of degree of standardness. This is not surprising; the former dimension is a much more obvious locus of linguistic change in the area, and correlation with age was most typically associated, as it seemed, with linguistic change (though see Newbrook 1987).

More specifically: all of the seven variables out of the leading 14 where the 'horizontal' dimension was relevant yielded *t*-scores of 1.0 or higher (four of them yielded 4.0 or higher), whereas only nine of the leading 14 variables (including these seven) yielded such *t*-scores on the 'vertical' dimension. None of these correlated at a *t*-score of 4.0 or higher, and the one variable which correlated at 3.0+ was the vowel of BOOK, where, uniquely for this study, the direction of change was apparently towards rather than away from RP. In the cases of a few variables (and some specific combinations of variables and particular groups of informants) it was not entirely clear whether stable age-grading or change in progress was at issue (again, see Newbrook 1987).

In the cases of a number of variables (notably FACE, GOAT and happY) the younger females appeared to be leading in the introduction of Liverpool features – in the former two cases, introducing very specific, originally hyper-correct variants (see above). On the other hand, the older women frequently produced much more RP-like usage than other groups – although the small sizes of the relevant groups do cast some doubt on any formulation of the precise degree to which this pattern might be confidently identified. This specific pattern has not been heavily instantiated in earlier surveys, and those factors which might be adduced to explain it in this case (such as the shrinking of social networks on widowhood) would also, it seems, have been just as valid (or invalid) in those earlier cases, thus calling any such explanation into question.

In cases where the RP and Liverpool forms are very similar and the Cheshire variant different, the latter was almost always moribund; an example is non-prevocalic /r/.

5.3   Variables: patterning of beliefs, subjective evaluations, self-reports; stylistic patterning

Informants generally categorised variants in very simple dialectological terms, using only one of the two main dimensions of variation. Perhaps surprisingly, this was usually the horizontal dimension distinguishing Liverpool from Cheshire usage – or, more usually in this context, other non-Liverpool usage. Non-RP forms were generally labelled Liverpool/Scouse, even where they are clearly shared with Cheshire and other northern usage. Some informants appeared to regard typical Cheshire usage in particular as closer to RP than it really is, perhaps basing this notion on the high average income typical of mid-Cheshire, the prestigious image that the county has acquired and the greater concentration of more RP-like accents that is typical (or regarded as typical) of parts of Cheshire, notably the city of Chester itself. This occurred, for instance, with STRUT, BATH, H and -*ing*, as well as with the interesting variable BOOK; in none of these cases is 'normal' Cheshire usage materially different from that of Liverpool (other than – perhaps – statistically). Even glottal variants of /t/ were identified as Scouse, which is possibly increasingly accurate but certainly does *not* reflect the traditional situation. Furthermore, RP forms were often identified geographically rather than socially, as 'southern', etc. – in some cases (as with BATH) accurately, in others (as with /h/) inaccurately as far as most non-RP southern English accents are concerned. This pattern of identification is familiar from anecdotal observation.

The main subjective reaction test in the study involved informants being presented orally with a short series of key variants (of all relevant dialectological types) for each of the principal variables investigated, and invited to identify (a) which of these variants (preferably one; more if necessary) was/were their own 'normal' usage, and (b) which (if any) they believed/felt to be the 'best'/'most correct' usage. The results of this test form the basis of the following sections.

5.3.1 Norms

The term *norm* refers here to those forms regarded as prestigious and/or as targets for emulation (in, for instance, formal settings).

Across all 17 variables studied in the main subjective reaction test, there were 941 statements (out of 1,156) endorsing RP forms as norms, 186 endorsing non-RP forms and 29 indicating inability to distinguish the forms as presented. See Table 5.2 for the detailed breakdown.

As is apparent from the table, the general pattern was for the RP norms to be accepted/endorsed. This applied even to cases such as STRUT where percentages of RP-like forms were low (especially in the more informal styles) and to those variables where indicator patterning was common. Acceptance of the RP norm was sometimes accompanied by heavy **over-reporting** (claims to use high-prestige forms – here, RP – which the informant apparently does not normally use): 41 instances for STRUT, even more for GOAT. Naturally there was typically far less **under-reporting** (claims to use low-prestige forms – here, non-RP – which the informant does not normally use).[6] This pattern of acceptance of RP usage is typical of data collected in Northern England. However, there were exceptions;

Table 5.2 Norms

Variable	Endorse RP	Endorse non-RP	Cannot distinguish
STRUT	65	3	0
BATH	21	47	0
NURSE	67	1	0
FACE	66	0	2
GOAT	67	1	0
GOOSE	67	1	0
BOOK	64	4	0
SQUARE	68	0	0
START	68	0	0
happY	13	51	4
horsEs	57	4	7
T (non-final/pre-C)	63	1	4
-ing	67	0	1
-ng	42	22	4
-ng-	13	50	5
H	67	0	1
R	66	1	1
Total	941	186	29

for instance, in the case of ONE there was little evidence in this study of awareness of a norm in /ʌ/, and in the case of BATH there was only limited support for RP /ɑː/. In this latter case, more use of and support for the RP form might have been expected in such a middle-class area.

It is, of course, possible (indeed likely) that the significance of RP *per se* in areas such as West Wirral may have declined in the period since 1980, and a new study conducted now might yield rather different patterns in this respect. Nevertheless, it is probably still the case that accents which are more similar to RP, at least up to a point, attract more overt prestige than those which differ sharply from it.

In some cases, however, the RP forms were apparently rejected as norms (by some) even in 1980; and we now turn to an examination of such patterns of reported attitudes.

In a number of instances, informants appeared to attach overt prestige to certain local variants (Liverpool, Cheshire or shared), to the point of identifying them as 'correct' or 'good' usage in preference to the RP equivalents. On some occasions, this was done, as it seemed, in full knowledge of which forms are found in RP, rather than out of any ignorance or confusion about the dialectological facts. Such cases are labelled here as **conscious rejection**. More typically, however, the main factor appeared to be sheer ignorance or confusion as to what the RP form might actually be; RP itself was accepted as the source of norms, but there was uncertainty or error as to the appropriate forms. Indeed, this latter phenomenon apparently accounts for most such responses in the cases of most such variables. The overall breakdown in this respect favoured ignorance over conscious rejection, 134–52 (total = 186 as in Table 5.2).

Overwhelmingly the main instance of conscious rejection of RP as a source of norms was BATH, where the local [a] = /æ/ form was preferred to the RP form by 47 out of the 68 informants; only 21 clearly endorsed the RP form. Across all the remaining 16 variables there were only five clear cases of the conscious rejection of an RP norm.

The heaviest clustering of cases of ignorance/confusion involved:

-ng-   endorsement of the cluster with /-g-/ by around 50 informants; some responses unclear

happY   endorsement of /-iː/ by 51 informants; but the dialectological facts are complex and the interpretation of responses is often debatable

-ng   endorsement of the cluster with /-g/ by 22 informants

These three variables are among those for which heavy endorsement of non-RP forms would not be unexpected, given anecdotal evidence. However, some other variables, in particular BOOK, might also have been expected to manifest similar patterns, but did not. There were in fact only about 10 clear cases of this kind across all the remaining 13 variables (including BOOK). Indeed, no more than four informants, in the case of any one of these variables, overtly endorsed a non-RP form. This figure includes both ignorance/confusion and conscious rejection. In these cases, local variants had only covert prestige, if indeed that.

As will be clear from the foregoing, there was a fairly marked tendency for anomalous stylistic patterning to cluster on some of the variables just listed, for each of which there was a major issue in respect of norms. This applies in particular to happy. The other main locus of anomalous patterning was horses, where this may be the only strong indication of a local norm which is not otherwise made very overt (compare the case of book).

5.3.2   Self-reporting (claims)

In terms of self-reporting, 729 claims out of 1,127 (the 1,156 just identified minus the 29 where the distinction between the variants was not perceived) were claims to use an RP form, 395 were claims to use a non-RP form, and three were equivocal. See Table 5.3 for the detailed breakdowns.

The largest majority claiming an RP form was 61 (for nurse). In the cases of two of the three variables where there was a clear overt local norm (bath, -ng-), and also for the more complex case of happy, 50 or more informants claimed to use the non-RP form identified as the norm. For -ng, the breakdown in favour of the local form was 36–28 (surprisingly close given the pattern reported above for subjective evaluation). In the case of horses, only 25 claimed to use RP [ɪ]. In some dialectological respects horses resembles happy but the two variables are related in a complex way. The variable horses is one of the best candidates

Table 5.3 Self-reporting (claims) A

Variable	Claim RP	Claim non-RP	Equivocal claim
STRUT	53	15	0
BATH	10	58	0
NURSE	61	7	0
FACE	38	28	0
GOAT	52	16	0
GOOSE	58	9	1
BOOK	50	18	0
SQUARE	56	12	0
START	58	10	0
happy	7	56	1
horses	25	35	1
T (non-final/pre-C)	51	13	0
-ing	51	16	0
-ng	28	36	0
-ng-	12	51	0
H	59	8	0
R	60	7	0
Total	729	395	3

for a local norm involving covert rather than overt prestige; there was no tendency to endorse the non-RP form overtly. These last two variables (-*ng* and horsEs) warrant further study (as does happY, and also BOOK – which was, however, quite orthodox in *this* respect).

5.3.3 Norms and accuracy in self-reporting

Of the 1,127 claims just discussed, 660 appeared substantially accurate (basing this judgement on the scoring in the least formal style) and 467 inaccurate. See Table 5.4 for the detailed breakdown across all 1,127 cases.

Of the 467 inaccurate claims, 32 also involved non-standard reactions with respect to norms (they were among the 186 responses of this latter type referred to above). They are thus awkward to classify in terms of the usual schema involving over- and under-reports, which implies that informants tend to work with the prestige standard variety as a source of norms. However, only six of these 32 cases involved an inaccurate claim to use an RP form not recognised as the norm (labelled a **pseudo-over-report**). That is, in 26 of the 32 cases a non-standard form, not an RP form, was inaccurately claimed: 25 cases labelled **pseudo-under-reports** where a non-standard form was claimed and an RP form not recognised as the norm was generally used, and one **dialect error** (see below on the latter). These 32 cases were concentrated on the interesting variable horsEs (see above) and on three of the variables where non-standard reactions in respect of norms were clustered (happY, -*ng* and -*ng*-). Such cases were

Table 5.4 Self-reporting (claims) B

Variable	Accurate claim	Over-report	Under-report	Dialect error
STRUT	26	41	1	–
BATH	59	4	4	1
NURSE	29	36	2	1
FACE	30	10	7	19
GOAT	8	46	3	11
GOOSE	32	31	3	2
BOOK	47	11	10	–
SQUARE	47	12	8	1
START	41	25	2	–
happY	52	4	5	3
horsEs	26	23	11	1
T (non-final/pre-C)	40	15	9	–
-*ing*	45	17	5	–
-*ng*	23	18	22	1
-*ng*-	49	10	4	–
H	54	10	3	–
R	52	11	4	–
Total	660	324	103	40

particularly numerous in the case of *-ng*. In fact, across only 22 cases of non-standard reactions in respect of norms involving this variable (compared to 50+ for each of the other three such variables), a total of 13 such inaccurate self-reports (out of the 32 found across all these variables) occurred – including 12 of the 25 'pseudo-under-reports'.

The 'over-report' column in Table 5.4 includes 318 orthodox over-reports and the six inaccurate claims to use RP forms not recognised as the norm which have just been discussed; the 'under-report' column likewise includes 78 orthodox under-reports and the 25 inaccurate claims to use non-RP forms recognised as the norm which have just been discussed (the 6 + the 25 make up 31 of the 32 cases where an inaccurate claim as to an informant's own usage was combined with a non-standard reaction with respect to a norm). The 'dialect error' total of 40 includes 39 of the 435 (467 minus 32) and the one (the remaining member of the 32).

Not very surprisingly, BATH was not represented in the 32, apparently because endorsements of non-RP forms in respect of this particular variable involve conscious rejection of the RP form rather than sheer error and are thus much less likely to involve confusion. All nine inaccurate self-reports for BATH were among the 21 cases where informants (apparently or definitely) accepted the RP norm; all 47 who endorsed the local form self-reported correctly.

The breakdown across these 32 cases (six pseudo-over-reports, 25 pseudo-under-reports, dialect error) makes a marked contrast with the patterning of the much larger group of cases of inaccurate reports (435) where the RP norm was endorsed (out of the total of 941 such cases). The direction of this difference is not unexpected but its degree is perhaps worthy of note. Across those 435 more straightforward cases, a predictably large majority of 318 were over-reports (inaccurate claims to use RP forms), 78 were under-reports (inaccurate claims to use lower-prestige forms) and (as noted) 39 were dialect errors (claims to use one non-standard local form while generally using another – here, by claiming either to use forms characteristic either of Cheshire or of Liverpool while generally using forms of the other type, or – for FACE or GOAT – to use one Liverpool form while generally using the other).

Thirty of the 40 dialect errors (made up of 39 of the 435 inaccurate claims paired with endorsement of the relevant RP form + 1 of the 32 inaccurate claims paired with endorsement of a non-RP form) were clustered on the complex realisational variables FACE and GOAT. However, the under-reports were spread rather evenly across the relevant variables (the striking total of 22 cases for *-ng* includes 12 of the 25 pseudo-under-reports, as noted). The especially difficult realisational variable GOAT, as well as producing the only dialect error among the 32, generated an especially large total number of inaccurate self-reports: 60 in all, including 46 over-reports. The other very high total of over-reports was (perhaps predictably) the 41 recorded for the very salient variable STRUT (though see above on the level of salience actually found here). The next highest total was 36 (NURSE) and the mean was around 27 (including means of 19 over-reports and six under-reports).

Dialect error is obviously possible only where the two local varieties differ (or, for FACE and GOAT, where there are two 'Liverpool' variants); hence the blanks in some of the rows under this column.

5.4 *Conclusion*

Despite the 'dirtiness' of the data, a considerable number of patterns did emerge from the 1980 material – some more predictable than others. The situation in 1980 was, however, clearly a very complex one, and generalisations across the variables often proved difficult. Many of the points to emerge from the study related to specific variables/variants, involving both usage *per se* and – often more strikingly – patterns of attitudes and beliefs.

More generally, however, it may be said that the process of linguistic assimilation into Merseyside was already well advanced in West Wirral in 1980. Future developments are likely to involve the continuation of this process, perhaps to the point where almost all traces of traditional Cheshire usage disappear and the speech of West Wirral becomes virtually indistinguishable from that of other parts of Merseyside. There will, presumably, continue to be a higher than average proportion of RP-like or other higher-prestige usage, because of the socio-economic character of the area. However, recent changes in the national status of RP may mean that RP 'paralects' or other less regional non-RP accents occupy some of this ground. There is also evidence in the data that even in 1980 non-RP forms (some general northern but others more narrowly local) had considerable measures of covert prestige and at times overt prestige.

On the other hand, various scenarios are in fact possible; a follow-up study conducted in the next few years, some twenty years after the collection of the data analysed here, would be of great interest. Interesting comparisons might also be made with areas in West Cheshire more remote from Liverpool (such as the city of Chester or the neighbouring villages), or with areas at a similar distance from Liverpool itself but on the Liverpool side of the Mersey, where there appears to be a higher degree of isogloss-bundling, notably in the area north and east of Huyton. Further work on all these fronts – including work on attitudes and beliefs with respect to the relevant variants and the identification of norms – is to be eagerly anticipated.

Notes

1 On Cheshire usage, for the nineteenth century, see Darlington (1887), Ellis (1889), Wright (1905), and for the earlier twentieth century, see Orton & Barry (1969), Anderson (1975), Walters (1955) on Hoylake, Barry (1958) on Neston. For Liverpool usage ('Scouse'), see Knowles (1974, 1978), De Lyon (1981).
2 In addition, there was a considerable amount of in-migration from North Wales, and

in consequence Liverpool English appears to have undergone some influence from Welsh and/or Welsh English. However, most of the relevant features are either much less salient (even in West Wirral, adjacent to Wales) or only putatively of Welsh origin.

3 The process of accommodation towards Liverpool usage was being observed, as it emerged, at a rather late stage, and many of the older Cheshire forms had already been lost. For instance, the interesting phonological patterning involving /eɪ/ and /iː/ (as manifested in 'reversed' phonemic incidence, for instance in /greɪn griːn/ = *green grain*) had disappeared without a trace, and non-prevocalic /r/, traditionally reported for Cheshire, survived only vestigially. The details given below thus relate mainly to the precise extent to which usage, where not RP-like, approached the Liverpool pattern; and, of course, to the relative prominence of RP-like forms (as opposed to local forms of either kind) in the data.

4 One widespread feature of the patterning of variants (which may perhaps relate to the fact that the process was captured near its end-point) involves the relative 'dirtiness' of the data, which manifested degrees of quasi-haphazard variability and rather low levels of correlation between dependent and independent variables. However, this factor did not altogether prevent the drawing of well-founded conclusions, and many patterns of considerable interest did emerge in the analysis of the usage – although there was seldom any clear correlation between the degree to which Liverpool usage predominated and the non-linguistic 'Merseysidisation' index derived from informants' scores on a range of dimensions of social variation involving degree of contact and identification with Liverpool/Merseyside (see below for the two main exceptions).

5 Indicators are variables which correlate with social class and the like but display little or no stylistic variation; as opposed to markers, which also display stylistic variation.

6 See section 5.3.3 below on both types of inaccurate self-reporting.

6

Sandwell, West Midlands: ambiguous perspectives on gender patterns and models of change

Anne Grethe Mathisen

6.1 *Introduction*

Of all the West Midland boroughs, Sandwell has the greatest variety of Black Country accents, including the Birmingham-types from Great Barr, Smethwick and Soho/Victoria. The complete corpus on which this chapter is based includes speakers from all 24 electoral wards. However, limits were imposed on the diversity of accents by choosing a fairly small number of adjacent wards the greatest distance from Birmingham because the intention in the present investigation was to study social rather than geographical variation.

The present description is based on a 30-hour corpus collected in 1984 by the late Michael Walton (University of Oslo), a native of Dudley Port and long-time citizen of Oldbury (Sandwell). Fieldwork was carried out in Wednesbury, Tipton and Rowley Regis. The 57 informants included in this survey represent male and female speakers, two social classes (MC, WC), and four age groups (teenagers = 16 yrs, young = 30 yrs, middle-aged = 50 yrs, and elderly = 70 yrs; all adult ages are centre points). The recordings comprise conversational speech (CS), a reading passage (RPS), a word-list (WLS) and a list of word-pairs (WPS).

6.2 *Descriptive material*

6.2.1 Vowels

Comments

TRAP
More front than the [a] generally heard in Northern varieties. It is usually very short, as in *glass*. The old and very long form [æːː], as in [tʃæːːmpiən] *champion*, is heard occasionally, even among teenagers.

Table 6.1 Sandwell vowels – summary

KIT	i	FLEECE	iː > ɪi > əi	NEAR	iə
DRESS	ɛ	FACE	æi > ɛi	SQUARE	ɛː
TRAP	æ > æː	PALM	ɑː	START	ɑː
LOT	ɒ > ɔ	THOUGHT	ɔː	NORTH	ɔː
STRUT	ɒ > ʊ > ə	GOAT	aʊ ~ ɔʊ	FORCE	ɔː
FOOT	ʊ	GOOSE	uː	CURE	juːə > jɔː
BATH	æ > a	PRICE	ai ~ ɑi > ɔi	happy	i
CLOTH	ɒ > ɔ	CHOICE	ɔi	letter	ɛ > ə
NURSE	ə̝ ~ ə̝ː	MOUTH	æu ~ ɛu	horses	i
				comma	ə

STRUT

The most common variant for all generations is [ɒ], especially in monosyllabic words where most Northern varieties have [ʊ]. It occurs very frequently with the elderly, in all phonetic contexts. *Long/lung* and *doll/dull* are frequently homophones in word-pairs lists. For younger speakers, it is more frequent before /l/ and /ŋ/. But it also appears as more close, in the area of [ʊ], especially when used in disyllabic words (*lucky*, *brother*), and quite frequently by teenagers in more conscious speech styles. Very occasionally it can be more centralised and perceived in the area of [ə], especially in *but*.

BATH

The predominant variant is a short, front and very open [æ], as in *laugh, chance, master*, in all social groups and ages, though it may vary in length. The Northern form [a] is less common, but present in older male speech. [ɑː] is infrequently used by some speakers in the middle class, mostly by females in conscious speech styles. In certain items, such as *France*, the vowel is occasionally long [fɹæːns]. *Can't* is often [kɔː], as in *can't have it* [kɔːɹ ævit] in the speech of elderly WC speakers, usually men.

CLOTH

Little variation in this vowel, but *soft* is pronounced [saft] by many WC adults. The typical old pronunciation in Sandwell was [æ] (or [ɛ] in some communities), as in *it's your turn to wash the fode (fold)* [its jaʊ tɛːn tə wæʃ ðə faʊd]. But this is not heard in the speech of the elderly in this group of informants.

NURSE

A close but fairly central variant [ə̝ː] is typical for teenage and elderly speakers, though the variation in teenage speech signals a marked preference for the RP-type realisation [ɜː] in this age group, especially by the girls. This variant is also preferred by MC speakers in general. For some speakers, especially elderly and WC, also a less close but quite front and [e]-like variant [ə̞ː]. The stylistic differentiation for this vowel is very clear. Whilst the RP-like variant [ɜː] has a strong position in CS, the closer variant [əː] has equal or higher scores in all reading styles indicating that the local variant may carry more significance as a local prestige/standard form than the RP-standard.

FLEECE
The diphthongal variants are often heard, especially with WC speakers and elderly.

FACE
A wide diphthong with a very open and front starting point, *day* [dæi], *cake* [kæik] versus [kʌik] in Birmingham. For elderly speakers also [ɛi], or [ɛ] as in *taking* [tɛkɪn]. Some realisations may be classed as triphthongs, as in *age* [æiədʒ], *sale* [sæiəɫ], or *days* [dæiəz], where [ə] or [ə̯] is more noticeable than as a mere glide-off. [æiə] may even be disyllabic in [dæi $ əz]. In *sale* it may be perceived as a vocalisation of /l/, but the articulation of the /l/ is usually present following the schwa. This particular phonetic detail occurs in the speech of male and female speakers, all age groups and both social classes, but is slightly more frequent in more conscious speech. In fact, [ə] also occurs with more diphthongs (see PRICE, CHOICE, MOUTH, GOOSE). It has a certain characteristic 'drawl' to it, although the speech is not necessarily very slow.

GOAT
A wide diphthong, mostly with a central rather than back starting point, *go* [gau], *road* [ɹaud], *coal* [kauɫ]. Also [ɔu], as in *broke* [bɹɔuk], increasing in frequency with age for this variant, and mostly used by men, who also add a schwa in a few items such as *road* [ɹɔuəd]. [əu] for some MC speakers, especially in more conscious speech. There is no systematic record of vocalic split in L-final items.

GOOSE
Diphthongised variants mainly for older speakers. Some items may have an additional schwa as in *shoes* [ʃuːəz] (see FACE).

PRICE
Occasionally [ɔi]. The additional schwa is found in more items with this diphthong than with any of the other vowels mentioned above. Typical items are *night* [naiət], *side* [saiəd], time [taiəm] (see FACE).

CHOICE
May have an additional schwa: *boys* [bɔiəz], *coins* [kɔiənz] (see FACE).

MOUTH
A very wide diphthong with a front and open or half open starting point and a very close ending point, as in *out* [æut] and *about* [əbæut]. Occasionally an even closer starting point [eu], *house* [heus], *down* [deun], particularly with WC males.

Occasionally, the diphthongised GOOSE vowel [ə̞u] in *shooting* may become homophonic with [ɛu ~ eu] in *shouting*. Example with schwa: *town* [tɛuən] (see FACE).

NEAR
[iə] for all speakers; also [iː] with linking R, *near him* [niːɹ ɪm].

SQUARE
Monophthong for most speakers. [ɛə] occasionally for elderly speakers.

CURE
Has a very close, back and rounded starting point; sometimes a close central starting point, [pə̞uːə], *poor*. Also [pʊə] and [pɔː].

lettEr
The unstressed vowel is frequently less central than schwa and has the front quality of [ɛ].

6.2.2   Consonants

T
The standard realisation is a fully released aspirated/non-aspirated alveolar stop [t]. The glottal stop is very frequent in teenage speech and also variably in young adult (30 yrs) speech, especially in MC, but very infrequent in the speech of the elderly. Age is the main social factor, but female and MC speakers, in that order, are at the front of this ongoing change. The score for [ʔ] in word-final and word-medial position (all phonetic contexts included) is 23% for female speakers and 18% for males. The equivalent scores for [ʔ] before approximants only, however, are 53% and 44% respectively. In word-final position only, the scores rise to 58% and 50%, in pre-approximant positions (see further below).

The glottalised variant, [ʔt], plays a more modest role within all social groups, with the MC teenagers and the young adult (30 yrs) female MC speakers displaying the highest frequencies. Glottalisation in general, as a boundary marker or in emphatic speech, is more common for teenage and young adult groups than the elderly.

The tap [ɾ] is a male variant with higher frequencies increasing with age (20% for the 70 yrs old). Within the female groups, this realisation is WC, and not age-sensitive.

K, P
Glottalisation of /k/, [ʔk], is quite frequent (also in RPS), but less so for /p/.

NG
[ŋg, ŋ] word-finally as in *sing*; before a vowel-initial suffix in *singer* [sɪŋgə], and

singing [siŋgiŋ]. NG is subject to a great deal of regular stylistic variation (see further below). In teenage speech [ŋg] occurs on average in 50% of tokens in CS, and particularly with women it seems to be a local prestige form. It is clearly preferred in more conscious speech by both males and females.

In verbal endings, e.g. sing*ing*: [n, ŋ, ŋg]. [n] is used on average in 80% of the tokens by teenage and elderly speakers, but only 60% by the middle-aged. In fact, the highest frequencies are provided by the teenage females and the elderly males. But [n] is hardly present in more conscious speech. [ŋ] shows clear social differentiation with an occurrence of 55% for MC and 10% for WC. [ŋg] is virtually absent in CS speech but marked in both WC and MC reading style speech. The presence of this variant is substantial in the reading style speech of the MC, comparable to variant [ŋ], and it obviously has local prestige.

TH

[θ, ð] for adult speakers; [f, v] for an increasing number of teenagers and nearly categorical with some boys. [f, v] are mainly found in initial and medial position: *three* [fɹiː], *brother* [bɹʊvə], but are not heard in function words.

H

H-dropping is typical for teenage and WC speech (all ages): *house* [aʊs], *hundred* [ʊndɹəd], and also occurs in reading style speech.

J

J-dropping does appear (especially with *new* [nuː]). It is more frequent in teenage speech but also present in the speech of the elderly, and when reading.

R

Sandwell has a non-rhotic accent. Mainly post-alveolar [ɹ], but occasionally a tap [ɾ] before vowels. The alveolar tap [ɾ] occurs mainly as a prevocalic variant for /t/; it is quite frequent for males and more so for the younger speakers. Linking R is categorical and intrusive R is very frequent in all groups. Few examples of labiodentals, [ʋ].

L

L is frequently dark in all positions in male speech, although clear varieties occur. L is usually clear in female speech in pre-vowel position. Dark L is also present in monitored speech. Most examples are found before front vowels and closing diphthongs, *lean* [ɫiːn], *lace* [ɫɛis], also following /p/, *place* [pɫæis], but this distribution is still under-investigated. L-vocalisation is very frequent for young speakers, but common in most groups. Also in highly conscious speech (WLS). Occurs in word-final position, *mile* [maɪʊ]; before consonants, *hills* [iʊz]; word-medial, *children* [tʃiʊdɹən]; as syllabic consonant, *cycle-cross* [sæikʊ kɹɪɒs].

6.3   *Sandwell speech and the role of gender in change*

Most quantitative studies working in the sociolinguistic tradition of Labov have included gender as one of several social categories, thus including both female and male speakers of accents that display differential use of both standard and non-standard linguistic forms. Awareness of and documentation on gender differences go back a long way. Fischer's (1958) analysis of (NG) in participles (*walking*) in New England schoolchildren's speech, one of the earliest sociolinguistic studies, suggested that the standard form [ŋ] was predominantly characteristic of females, whilst males tended to use the non-standard [-ɪn]. This gender correlation has been supported in numerous studies of (NG) throughout English-speaking communities. Glottal replacement of /t/, although mostly interpreted in relation to social class and style, is another sound change strongly associated with male speakers (e.g. Macaulay 1977; Lodge 1984: 22).

Hudson (1996: 195) declares that the findings in sociolinguistic research on gender and variation are so robust and clear that we can call them facts. They support the generalisation that 'females use standard variants of any stable variable which is socially stratified for both sexes more often than males do', even to the extent that we can call this 'Sex/Prestige Pattern' universal (Hudson 1996: 202). This basic finding is expressed by Labov as 'Principle I: For stable sociolinguistic variables, men use a higher frequency of nonstandard forms than women' (Labov 1990: 210).

6.3.1   Assumptions on gender in innovation and change

Although changes may be introduced at any social level they are likely to spread from:

(i) lower to upper social classes
(ii) less formal to more formal styles of speech
(iii) less salient phonetic environments to more salient environments.

The process of change relating to glottal realisations of (T) is a good example of the direction of change listed above, a direction of change towards a vernacular, non-standard norm. As such, glottal replacement of (T) has been regarded as both stigmatised and predominantly a feature of male speech. And as a vernacular sound change it is only reasonable to expect the men to head the hunt for more glottal arenas. However, when a new vernacular form, either a regional or a class variety, has been adopted by an attractive social group in the community, it may come to lose its traditional features and become reinterpreted.

It is an established sociolinguistic fact that women are likely to be leading the changes that are standardising. And according to Labov (1990: 213), these changes take place at a high level of social consciousness and share many of the properties of stable variables, expressed in his 'Principle Ia: In change from above, women favor the incoming prestige form more than men'.

While women are often found to be early adopters (Milroy & Milroy 1985b), and leading linguistic changes where they introduce prestige forms, men are typically leading changes that introduce or revitalise vernacular forms (see also Watt & Milroy this volume). According to Chambers & Trudgill (1980: 97–8), 'changes away from the prestige norm . . . will have working class (. . .) men in the vanguard'. In Martha's Vineyard (Labov 1972: 36–7), the fishermen lead the change to a more conservative pronunciation using centralised vowels (in *light* [ləit] and *house* [həus]). In Norwich, the men are leading a similar sound change away from the RP vowel [ɛ] to the more local [təːl] or [tʌl] in *tell* (Trudgill 1974, this volume). Milroy & Milroy (1985b: 356) also report on the domination of men in the backing and rounding of /a/ in Belfast.

In raising changes in Toronto, Vancouver and Victoria, age-grading is also gender-graded so that the females lead the males in all age groups (Chambers 1989: 80–3). Although it is basically a change away from the Canadian standard, more broadly, it can be viewed as a change towards the American standard and thus the role of females leading a change that is standardising is supported also in this case. The same linguistic change in progress is reported in MC Canadian English in Vancouver (Chambers 1993: 148). Mechanisms of change are not clear and simple. But according to Labov, another principle of change, based on clear and consistent results in sociolinguistic research, states that women are generally instrumental in linguistic change: 'Principle II: In the majority of linguistic changes, women use a higher frequency of the incoming forms than men' (1990: 206). His conclusion seems to be that women are the chief agents of differentiation, both adopting new prestige features more rapidly than men, and also reacting more sharply against the use of stigmatised forms (Labov 1990: 240). 'The number of cases where men are in the lead is relatively small' (Labov 1990: 219). Various vernacular speech forms have often been regarded as markers of solidarity linked to working-class speech. But since men are known to use more vernacular forms than women in every social class, gender may be the primary marker.

6.3.2 New accounts of gender and prestige

Whilst the findings of several studies from many British locations, over a period of approximately 20 years, in general support the characteristics of glottalisation as a male, lower-class and stigmatised norm (e.g. Trudgill 1974; Macaulay 1977; Reid 1978; Lodge 1984), more recent studies in British English, however, provide information contrary to the traditional gender pattern of linguistic change. It appears that glottalisation, frequently reported as the ultra-stigmatised speech form, is now being adopted by female speakers. They have taken on the role of innovators in various speech communities in Britain and elsewhere (e.g. New Zealand, Holmes 1995: 446–7), and this time they are in the forefront of a vernacular change.

In Cardiff English, Mees (1983; see also Mees & Collins this volume) found that glottalisation of (T), which is a relatively new feature in Wales, is a high prestige feature with increasing scores from low to high social status groups in adolescent speech. The scores for glottalisation are more or less equal between boys and girls in the interview style with the girls showing a slightly higher frequency for glottal replacement in all three phonetic environments, pre-C, P and V (Mees 1987: 30–5). The combination of gender/stylistic patterns indicates 'a degree of uncertainty about the prestige associated with the use of glottalisation'.

In Tyneside English, however, sociolinguistic analyses reveal a disjunction between glottaling (replacement) and glottalisation (reinforcement) (Milroy, Milroy, Hartley & Walshaw 1994; see also Watt & Milroy, and Docherty & Foulkes this volume). Whilst glottalisation is well established in the local dialect, its presence having been observed in several generations (Milroy, Milroy, Hartley & Walshaw 1994: 350), and it is a preference for local male speakers, the glottal replacement of (T) is an innovation led by middle-class and female speakers. The authors argue that the males are associated with the diffusion of more localised changes (i.e. maintenance) in Tyneside, e.g. glottalised variants of (P), (T) and (K). The females, by contrast, are instrumental in the diffusion of supra-local changes exemplified by the glottal stop. The status of the glottal stop has changed from a local vernacular form to a general non-localised innovation in British English speech. In keeping with Labov, i.e. interpreting in prestige terms, the glottal replacement of (T) becomes a **change from above**. Thus the female preference for glottal replacement of (T) is an adjustment to what has become a prestige/standard form. In this respect, the explanation of female linguistic speech patterns is kept well within the frame of gender-based differentiation documented in the literature and reported above. In contrast to the general model of prestige/stigma associated with social class and change, Milroy, Milroy & Hartley (1994) suggest a model where gender is prior to class in linguistic change. The diffusion of a variant favoured by female speakers brings about a reversed evaluation of that variant. In this respect the women *create* the prestige and the variants favoured by women become the prestige forms through this process (Milroy, Milroy & Hartley 1994: 26). So, through its diffusion the glottal stop can then be characterised as a change from above. Female speakers are also reported to prefer glottal replacement in Coleraine, Northern Ireland (Kingsmore 1995: 171; 184), although the glottal stop is here strongly associated with rural speech.

The question of what process makes a sound change move from vernacular to prestige standard, in this case the glottaling of (T) in New Zealand English, and the particular role of women in the process of change, is discussed by Holmes (1995). In the data on glottal replacement, the stylistic and social class differentiation demonstrate that the status of the glottal variant of (T) is changing from vernacular to standard, that the leading edge of change is the conversational speech of young women and that it is being introduced into standard New Zealand English through the speech of young middle-class women. Although glottal stops were more frequent in WC speech than in MC speech, the young women produced higher scores than the young men in both social classes, whilst the middle-aged women produced fewer than the men in the same age group (Holmes 1995: 446–7). It is concluded that women play an important part in the de-stigmatisation process and the change of the sociolinguistic status of the glottal stop in New Zealand.

6.3.3 Variable (T) – a sound change from outside

6.3.3.1 Linguistic context

The results of the analysis of (T) are based on 3817 tokens in CS speech. Glottalisation of (T) followed by homorganic /tʃ/, /dʒ/, /d/ or other stops was not included. Although there is a lot of glottal activity going on in these environments, it is very difficult to distinguish auditorily whether the glottal stop is actually followed by an oral closure, a geminated homorganic stop articulation, an assimilated stop (very often), or simply by one or perhaps two deleted stops. It was decided that the patterns of distribution could be kept under control by only including cases where the following segments could be checked and correctly identified. The most important variants of (T) are:

   (i)   [t]   – fully released aspirated/non-aspirated stop
  (ii) [ʔt] – glottalised variant
 (iii) [ʔ]   – glottal stop variant
 (iv) [ɾ]   – tapped realisation, or variants which sound like [d]
  (v) [ɹ]   – realisation of the T-to-R rule type

According to Table 6.2, the amount of glottaling in the data depends to a large extent on the position of (T) in the word, as well as the phonetic context. In most reports on glottaling, glottal replacement is more common in pre-consonantal position. This study, however, reveals considerable phonetic variation even within this phonetic context. The pre-approximant position score for word-final [ʔ] is 54%; i.e. 20% (or more) higher than in other pre-consonantal positions. Pre-approximant position includes word-final (T) before word-initial /j/

Table 6.2 Percentage of [ʔ] by following phonetic segment, all informants (N = 3,817 tokens; VLong = long vowel; VDiph = diphthong; VShort = short vowel)

Word position	Phonetic context (%)						
	Approx	**Nasal**	**Fricative**	**VLong**	**Pause**	**VDiph**	**VShort**
Word-Final	54	33	26	19	16	16	13
Word-Medial	33	18	–	–	–	–	5

(*let you*), /w/ (*it will*), /l/ (*cut loose*) and /r/ (*put right*); and word-medial (τ) before /l/ (*battle*). Glottaling before pause or vowel is usually considered non-standard and the results in this study also show less frequent use of [ʔ] in these contexts, with the lowest score of 13% in word-final position before short vowels. In word-medial position, the use of [ʔ] is more frequent before syllabic consonants (*battle* 33%, *button* 18%) than before vowels (*butter*, *getting* 5%). In word-medial pre-approximant position, the 33% score indicates that τ-glottaling before syllabic lateral consonant (*battle*) is less stigmatised than expected, especially compared to pre-vocalic and (word-final) pre-pausal positions.

It is evident from the data that the glottal replacement of (τ) is being diffused in Sandwell speech through a pattern which is comparable to its use by RP/near-RP-speakers (Wells 1982). Thus, the higher frequencies of [ʔ] are in pre-consonantal positions, and the lower frequencies in pre-pausal and pre-vocalic positions. This applies to glottaling of (τ) in word-final positions. The more extensive use of glottal articulations in a phonetic context which must be considered to fall within the pattern of current mainstream RP, may support the view that it is modelled on a non-local standard which is appreciated as a prestige versus a vernacular or stigmatised form of speech. The extended use of τ-glottaling, to pre-vocalic, pre-pausal and pre-syllabic consonant positions, indicates a more complex situation, however, but the interpretation of the actual prestige of this current sound change will become clearer through information on its social differentiation.[1]

6.3.3.2   Sociolinguistic patterns

(i) Age
Sociolinguistically, two of the variants (ii and iii) revealed interesting patterns. The sociolinguistic distribution of the glottal stop variant raises a couple of questions relating to the type of prestige and/or status generally associated with this feature. As a change from outside, the higher scores for [ʔ] in the teenage group are expected.

The scores in Table 6.3 show that the glottal stop is more frequent in CS

Table 6.3   Percentage of [ʔ] by age, phonetic context and gender

Age	Word-medial	Word-final (all phon. contexts)	Word-final (pre-approx. only)	Word-final (pre-approx. only)	
				Female	Male
16	21	30	69	73	65
30	5	17	48	53	44
70	0	4	13	18	8
All	12	24	54	58	50
N	*839*	*2,978*	*553*		

speech for the teenage group than for both the adult groups. Depending on the phonetic embedding, the young adult group scores are also worth looking into. The elderly speakers, however, show very little interest in this feature, and only in the phonetically high-frequency contexts. The difference between age groups is systematic, highly significant ($p < 0.001$)[2] and also confirming that glottal replacement is an innovation in Sandwell speech.

Glottalisation of word-final /t/, variant (ii) [ʔt], seems to be part of a general process of *lenition*. In Table 6.4, the glottalised /t/, [ʔt], is more frequent for working-class speakers than middle-class speakers in the elderly group. For the young adults, the male working-class speakers also have higher scores (35%) than the male middle-class speakers (21%), whilst the scores for the female speakers are level (24–25%) in both social classes, and much higher than for the elderly women. In teenage speech, the highest scores for this variant are in the middle-class groups of both girls and boys, with 23% and 26% respectively, twice as high as in the working-class groups of the same age. The speech of young female adult speakers seems to be a transition zone and glottalisation of /t/ in teenage speech is now associated with middle-class rather than the more conservative working-class speech.

(ii) Gender
The distribution of glottal stop by gender suggests that it is more frequent in female than male speech. Table 6.5 makes it clear that men and women differ within both age groups but in varying degrees. The score of 37% for [ʔ] in teenage female speech is quite high compared to 25% for male speakers in the same age group. The young adult groups, however, are more equal in their use of the glottal stop in word-final position: i.e. a score of 17/18%. The use of glottalised [ʔt] seems to follow the same gender pattern with more frequent use of [ʔt] in female groups than in male groups, but the generational difference is reversed in the use of glottal stop as the young adults use more of glottalised [ʔt] than the teenage speakers. Interestingly, for both [ʔ] and [ʔt], the interaction between gender and age shows that the female speakers have higher scores than the male speakers in both age groups. Also in pre-approximant position, as reported in Table 6.3, the female speakers have higher frequencies for the glottal

Table 6.4 Percentage of glottalisation [ʔt] by age, gender and class in word-final, pre-approximant position (N = 553)

| | Age | 70 | | 30 | | 16 | | 16–70 |
	Gender	M	F	M	F	M	F	M & F
Class	MC	4	5	21	24	26	23	18
	WC	8	14	35	25	13	10	14

Table 6.5 Percentage of glottalisation by age and
gender in word-final contexts (N = 2,978)

Age	Phon. variant	Male		Female
16	[ʔ]	25	<	37
	[ʔt]	8	<	12
	[ʔ] + [ʔt]	33	<	**49**
30	[ʔ]	17	~	18
	[ʔt]	12	<	19
	[ʔ] + [ʔt]	29	<	**37**
16 + 30	[ʔ] + [ʔt]	31	<	**43**

stop variant than the male speakers in all age groups, the highest score being 73%, for 16-year-old female speakers.

Treating [ʔt] and [ʔ] as different degrees of the same process, and thus combining the scores, the total scores for glottalisation of word-final /t/ are higher for women than for men in both age groups, a difference of 8% and 16% for young adults and teenagers respectively. The relationship between age and gender again shows that whilst the increase in the use of glottalisation in male speech between the two generations is very small (4%), the scores for the female speakers show a marked increase (12%) for the teenage girls, who have reached 49%. It is interesting to note that the female speakers are in the lead of this innovative change, with the male speakers being more conservative. Whether this gender pattern, across age groups, indicates that glottal articulation for word-final /t/ is carrying, or gaining, prestige, i.e. being chosen by women for its prestige, or being given prestige in being chosen by the women, is not really obvious from the analysis. To explore this question further it is useful to examine the interaction between gender and social class.

(iii) Social class
For all informants, the use of glottal stop or [ʔt] in word-final position is higher for female than for male speakers in both social classes, but more so in the groups of middle-class speakers. Figure 6.1 illustrates scores of frequency for the glottalisation of word-final /t/.

The very high score of 59% for teenage middle-class girls is a clear marking of the linguistic choice of variant for word-final /t/. It is twice as high as for the middle-class boys. The pattern of higher scores for the female speakers is repeated in young adult group as well, and in both age groups in the working class. Although the differences are smaller in the other groups, the pattern is consistent. And although the considerably lower score of 46% in the young adult group of female speakers suggests the age-graded use of glottalisation in Sandwell speech, the scores in both middle-class female groups are well above those of their counterparts in the working class; i.e. 40% for the 16-year-olds and 27% for the 30-year-olds, a difference of 19% in each case ($p < 0.001$). That the middle-class females use significantly more glottal articulations for /t/ than

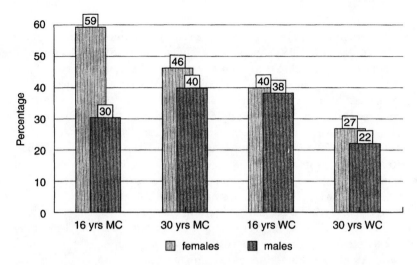

Fig. 6.1 Glottalisation of /t/ by age, gender and class in word-final context

the working-class females may be interpreted as class-marking, certainly within the female group.

In comparison, the class differentiation in the male groups is somewhat blurred. For the young adult males, the score of 40% for the middle-class speakers is 18% higher than for male working-class speakers ($p < 0.001$). In the teenage group, however, the male working-class speakers have a slightly higher score (of 38%) than the male middle-class speakers ($p < 0.04$). The class-marking is thus minimal and in an opposite direction in the teenage group, but quite considerable for the young adult males.

The standard interpretation would no doubt evaluate glottalisation of word-final /t/ as a middle-class feature of speech on the basis of the pattern in which it is diffused in the young adult groups of speakers in Sandwell. What is even more consistent, however, is the dominance of female speakers at the forefront of this sound change. The female scores are higher than the male scores in both social classes within each age group, with the teenage middle-class girls having a considerable lead of 29% over their male counterparts. The glottalisation of /t/ in word-final position is thus well established in female speech. Whilst there is only moderate class variation in male speech patterns of this feature, class is, however, a marked feature in female speech, suggesting that the middle-class female speakers lead the change.

6.3.4 Variable (NG) – a sound change from within

Not all linguistic changes involve adopting new forms from outside the speech community. The word-final non-NG-coalescing (NG) variant [ŋg] is a well-established and traditional feature of Black Country accents (including Sandwell English) as well as in western parts of the midlands and the middle-north of

England (Wells 1982). Conservative local pronunciations associated with the past tend to linger in the most casual types of speech and within the older age groups. Macaulay (1985: 184) characterises East Central Staffordshire as a 'relic area' where the voiced velar stop occurs regularly after a velar nasal.

For non-NG-coalescing accents, the voiced velar stop /g/ following the velar nasal /ŋ/ is used by speakers of all social classes, except 'the very small layer of RP speakers at the top' (Wells 1982: 365–6). Knowles (1978: 86) reports from Liverpool that the velar stop 'is even used by middle-class women', and both he and Heath (1980) found that [ŋg] was used almost throughout the social scale (see also Newbrook this volume).

In Sandwell, [ŋg] occurs word-finally (*among, during, moving*), and word-medially before vowels (*Birmingham, singing*), but not before word-internal consonants. Evidence from this location shows that, based on its sociolinguistic distribution, this variant is far from being a relic or in recession. Table 6.6 illustrates the dynamic pattern of a linguistic change in progress, identifies its innovators, and confirms the stability and significance of this variant, in this region.

Table 6.6 shows that the velar stop pronunciation is more favoured by women than men, particularly with teenage speakers (64% versus 37%). In fact, whatever age group, and whatever social class, the female speakers quite clearly display a significantly higher proportion of [ŋg] than their male counterparts. The difference in scores between all adult female and male speakers in CS is 11%, and 27% in the teenage group. The interaction between gender and social class, however, complicates the pattern. It is evident that the difference in the use of [ŋg] is smaller between gender groups in the middle class than within the working class. Whilst the difference in adult male and female group scores hovers around 7% in the middle class, it is approximately 14% in the working class. Thus the middle-class speakers seem to form a more homogeneous group across both gender and age divisions.

Although the effect of class is present, it is not primary in all generational groups. The scores in the group of elderly speakers show an average of 44% for [ŋg], with only minor class and gender differentiation. At the age of 50, the male speakers are lagging behind, especially in the working class with only 17%. The

Table 6.6 Percentage use of [ŋg] in *-ng* in CS by age, gender and class (N = 381)[3]

Class	Gender	Age				All adults
		16	30	50	70	
WC	Female	–	57	45	46	50
	Male	–	45	17	45	36
MC	Female	–	36	35	46	39
	Male	–	30	27	38	32
WC + MC	Female	64	46	4C	46	45
	Male	37	38	22	42	34

younger adults of 30, however, show a more stratified use of [ŋg] and social class is more marked than gender. Even so, the role of the female speakers is again quite clear in both classes, especially the preference of 57% for [ŋg] in the female working-class group. The gender pattern observed in the adult groups is repeated in the teenage group where the female score for [ŋg] has increased by 18% compared to the 30-year-old women. This difference, however, is modest beside that of gender in this particular age group, i.e. 27%. The use of this local pronunciation seems to be the more advanced choice in conversational speech styles for young girls. With the consistent pattern of gender differentiation across social class and generations, it is clear that [ŋg] must be characterised as a female form rather than a working-class form.

Table 6.7 Percentage use of [ŋg] in
-ng by gender and style

	CS	RPS	WLS	WPS
Female	51	58	86	95
Male	35	50	60	88
N	381	98	162	134

The analysis of the use of [ŋg] in different speech styles confirms that this variant is the primary choice for both men and women in monitored speech.[4] The stylistic distinctions are clear and quite consistently rising from conversational speech to the style of the word-lists. The rise in scores for the male speakers is in fact 10% larger than for female speakers, but on every level the female score is higher than the male score. The preference for the regional variant in the more conscious speech styles, and the particular female lead, is an interesting marking of a form that represents a direction towards (or maintenance of) a local standard rather than towards the southern British standard, or RP. This suggests that it is the women who are the more active part in the revitalisation of this particular regional form of pronunciation, and that the teenage girls are edging this process. The data cast doubt on the general notion that the females universally favour the less localised forms. Even the club of elderly middle-class women, eagerly practising their RP in the presence of the interviewer, cannot resist letting the velar stop filter through to a percentage score of 46 (Table 6.6). One is reminded of the Martha's Vineyard effect, the local male inhabitants leading the other inhabitants in the process of regaining local dialectal superiority in the land. Although both men and women are locally oriented here, the men are less so, especially in conversational speech.

6.4 Conclusion

As in many urban accents in Britain, the complex interaction of social and linguistic factors in Sandwell speech is both interesting and challenging in view of earlier and current research and interpretation of phonological variation and change. On the basis of the data presented here, the social class model related to prestige and stigma does not satisfactorily account for the patterns of variation illustrated in the analyses of (T) and (NG) in this community.

It appears that glottalisation of /t/ is an innovation in Sandwell English and currently involved in linguistic change in this location. There are no indications in the data that glottal reinforcement and glottal replacement are best viewed as discrete categories rather than as points on a single continuum, as discussed with reference to Newcastle variants by Docherty, Foulkes, Milroy, Milroy & Walshaw (1997). Both glottalisation and glottal replacement of /t/ are favoured more by female than by male speakers. Glottalisation, traditionally associated with stigmatised, vernacular speech and in Labovian terms characterised as a change from below, is thus implemented and diffused via female speakers of both social classes rather than by working-class males. It can hardly be characterised as prestigious in social terms and is not a change towards the RP standard. Gender-marking, however, seems to be overriding class-marking in a sound change which is introducing a non-local form and is being led by young women, especially women in the middle class. The social influence of female speech in general may be causing a change in the evaluation of this feature, turning the process into a change from above, or, as suggested by Milroy, Milroy & Hartley (1994: 27), *creating* rather than favouring prestige forms. Clearly, it is a change which is bringing Sandwell speech closer to a national urban British pronunciation.

The pattern of distribution for (NG), however, suggests that the female speakers are the active part also in a change away from both RP as well as from any other non-local urban standard, with the teenage girls in the lead. The variant [ŋg] is not an innovatory form; it represents a change from within, and there is no sharp differentiation across the groups of elderly speakers. Although both gender and class are implicated in the change, it is the female speakers who favour the localised variant in both social classes in the younger age groups, and especially in the teenage group. The highest frequencies in adult speech occur in the female working-class groups which is to be expected in a localised change. Interpreted in prestige terms, this variant represents a direction away from the 'standard' norm associated with prestige and the role of women in linguistic change, and towards a localised form, a direction traditionally associated with male speakers. Variable (NG) is stratified for both men and women, so that the standard form [ŋ] is used more in MC than WC of the same gender. In terms of Labov's Principle I, (NG) can be considered as a stable variable. But it is, all the same, the women who use a higher frequency of the non-standard form [ŋg], in both social classes. However, the contextual diffusion of this variant, with higher scores in more conscious speech in both male and female groups, illustrates the prestige-related use of a localised variant. With even higher scores for female speakers, also in this context, it is relevant to suggest that the female speakers are approximating to a local norm of prestige, which is an orientation away from the national standard, and from RP.

Neither of these changes are in the direction of standard English. Whilst glottalisation of /t/ is established as a middle-class norm in Sandwell English (in fact it is an integrated feature in the speech of younger teachers in the schools of the area), the velar stop, although highly frequent in female teenage speech, is still more characteristic of working-class speech among adult speakers. As illustrated by the data in the present study, these changes are largely brought about by the females. The speech patterns of these variables for male speakers are relatively conservative. But it is clear that age is the most important social factor in the data, and the teenagers are by far the most heavy users of features that are spreading in Sandwell speech, from without and within their own urban accent.

Notes

1 The analysis of the variable (T) includes data from 44 informants, 28 in the 16-year-old group, and eight in each of the other age groups. The full analysis, including stylistic analysis, will be presented in Mathisen (forthcoming).
2 Significance levels have been evaluated by ANOVA for (T) and chi-square for (NG).
3 The analysis of (NG) is based on 36 informants, 12 in the 16-year-old group, and eight in each of the other age groups. The 12- to 16-year-olds are not assigned social class but are treated as one group (Mathisen 1992).
4 It might be argued that the use of [ŋg] is influenced by the effect of spelling. However, this would not explain why the WC speakers are more prone to it than their MC counterparts, nor why younger speakers use more [ŋg] than the older speakers, nor why the same pattern is not found more commonly in other varieties.

7

Norwich: endogenous and exogenous linguistic change

Peter Trudgill

7.1 *Introduction*

Research on which this chapter is based consists of fieldwork carried out in 1968, as reported in Trudgill (1974), with a random sample of 60 informants born and brought up in or around Norwich; and a follow-up study carried out in 1983, as reported in Trudgill (1988), with a quota sample of 17 informants. It is also based on 54 years of residence in the city as an observer and as a native speaker of one form of Norwich English.

7.2 *Descriptive material: Norwich phonology*

Rhythm is a somewhat elusive concept in phonology, but there is no doubt that one of the most distinctive characteristics of Norwich English, and indeed of East Anglian English as a whole, is precisely its rhythm. This in turn would appear to be due, at least in the main, to the lengthening – in comparison with other varieties of English – of stressed syllables and the consequent shortening, reduction to schwa, and even loss of unstressed syllables, e.g. *forty four* [fɔ::ʔ:fɔ:], *half past eight* [ha::pəs æiʔ], *have you got any coats?* [hæ:jə gɑʔnə kʰuʔs], *shall I?* [ʃælə], *walking* [wɔ:kn].

7.2.1 Vowels

The segmental phonology of Norwich is clearly that of a south of England variety: the vowels of STRUT and FOOT are distinct, and the lexical sets of BATH and START have the same vowel. It is also clearly that of a south-eastern rather than south-western variety in that the accent is non-rhotic.

Comments

Checked vowels: KIT, DRESS, TRAP, LOT, STRUT, FOOT
For most speakers, the system of checked vowels is thus the normal south of

Table 7.1 Norwich vowels – summary

KIT	ɪ	FLEECE	ii	NEAR	ɛː		
DRESS	ɛ > e	FACE	æi > ẹ	SQUARE	ɛː		
TRAP	æ ~ æɛ	PALM	aː	START	aː		
LOT	ɑ > ɒ	THOUGHT	ɔː	NORTH	ɔː		
STRUT	ɐ	GOAT	ʊu > ʊ	FORCE	ɔː		
FOOT	ʊ	GOOSE	ʉu > ʊu	CURE	ɜː		
BATH	aː	PRICE	ɑɪ	happy	ii > ɪ > ə		
CLOTH	ɔː	CHOICE	ɔɪ	letter	ə		
NURSE	ɜː	MOUTH	æʉ	horses	ə		
				comma	ə		

England six-vowel system involving the lexical sets of: KIT, DRESS, TRAP, LOT, STRUT, FOOT. Older forms of the dialect, however, have an additional vowel in this sub-system. If we examine representations of words from the NURSE set in twentieth-century Norfolk dialect literature, we find the following (for details of the dialect literature involved, see Trudgill 1996a):

Item	Dialect spelling
her	*har*
heard	*hard*
nerves	*narves*
herself	*harself*
service	*sarvice*
earn	*arn*
early	*arly*
concern	*consarn*
sir	*sar*
fur	*far*
daren't	*dussent*
first	*fust, fasst*
worse	*wuss*
church	*chuch, chatch*
purpose	*pappus*
turnip	*tannip*
further	*futher*
hurl	*hull*
turkey	*takkey*
turn	*tann*
hurting	*hatten*
nightshirt	*niteshat*
shirts	*shats*
girl	*gal*

On the subject of words such as this in East Anglian dialects, Forby (1830: 92) wrote:

> To the syllable *ur* (and consequently to *ir* and *or*, which have often the same sound) we give a pronunciation certainly our own.

> Ex.   *Third word burn curse*
>   *Bird curd dirt worse*

> It is one which can be neither intelligibly described, nor represented by other letters. It must be heard. Of all legitimate English sounds, it seems to come nearest to *open a* [the vowel of *balm*], or rather to the rapid utterance of the *a* in the word *arrow*, supposing it to be caught before it light on the *r* . . . *Bahd* has been used to convey our sound of *bird*. Certainly this gets rid of the danger of *r*; but the *h* must as certainly be understood to lengthen the sound of *a*; which is quite inconsistent with our snap-short utterance of the syllable. In short it must be heard.

My own observations of speakers this century suggest that Forby was quite right, although he had no access to phonetic terminology, and that the facts are as follows. Earlier forms of East Anglian English, including the dialect of Norwich, actually had a checked vowel system consisting of seven vowels. The additional vocalic item, which I represent as /ɐ/, was a vowel somewhat more open than half-open, and slightly front of central, which occurred in the lexical set of *church, first*. Dialect literature, as we have seen, generally spells words from the lexical set of *first, church* as either <fust> etc. or <chatch> etc. The reason for this vacillation between <u> and <a> was that the vowel was in fact phonetically intermediate between /ʌ/ and /æ/. This additional vowel occurred in items descended from Middle English *ur, or* and *ir* in closed syllables. Words ending in open syllables, such as *sir, fur*, had /aː/, as did items descended from ME *er*, such as *earth, her* (as well as items descended from *ar* such as *part, cart*, of course). The vowel /əː/ did not exist in the dialect until relatively recently.

Since the mid-twentieth century, the /ɐ/ vowel has more or less disappeared from the Norwich phonological inventory. In my 1968 study, /ɐ/ was recorded a number of times, but the overwhelming majority of words from the relevant lexical set had the originally alien vowel /əː/. Only in lower working-class speech was /ɐ/ at all common in 1968, and then only 25 per cent of potential occurrences had the short vowel even in informal speech. The vowel did not occur at all in the 1983 corpus.

As far as the other checked vowels are concerned, we can note the following.

KIT

One of the most interesting features of the older Norwich dialect checked vowel system was that, unlike most other varieties, /ɪ/ did not occur at all in unstressed syllables. Unstressed /ə/ continues to be the norm to this day in words such as *wanted, horses, David, naked, hundred*. I have hypothesised (Trudgill 1986) that this feature of East Anglian English may have had some input into the formation of southern hemisphere Englishes such as Australian English, where schwa also occurs in such words.

More striking, however, is the fact that /ə/ was the only vowel which could occur in any unstressed syllable in the earlier dialect. This was true not only in the case of word-final syllables in words such as *water, butter*, which of course also have /ə/ in RP, and in words such as *window, barrow*, which are pronounced [wɪndə, bæɹə] in very many other forms of English, but also in items such as *very, money, city* which were /veɹə, mʌnə, sɪtə/. In the modern dialect, dedialectalisation has taken place in that words from the *very* set are now pronounced with final /ɪ/ by older speakers and /iː/ by younger speakers (see below), as is now usual throughout southern England.

It is also noteworthy that the KIT vowel occurred not only in items such as *pit, bid* in the older dialect but also in a number of other words such as *get, yet, head*. There is little predictability as to which items have or had the raised vowel, but in all the words concerned the vowel was followed by /t/ or /d/. The modern dialect has seen increasing dedialectalisation through a process of transfer of these words from KIT to DRESS (see further below).

DRESS

The vowel /ɛ/ in the older dialect was a rather close vowel approaching [e]. During the course of the twentieth century, it has gradually opened until it is now much closer to [ɛ]. I have hypothesised that this close realisation may also have had some role to play in the development of the short vowel systems of the southern hemisphere (Trudgill 1986), where all three front checked vowels have closer realisations than in England.

In older forms of the dialect, /ɛ/ occurred not only in the expected *bet, help, bed* etc. but also in a number of items which elsewhere have /æ/, such as *catch, have/has/had*.

TRAP

The vowel /æ/ appears to have undergone a certain amount of phonetic change. For older speakers for whom /ɛ/ was [e], it is probable that /æ/ was closer to [ɛ], as in Australian English, while in the modern dialect it is a good deal more open. In Norwich it has now also undergone a further change involving diphthongisation in some phonological environments: *back* [bæɛk] (see further Trudgill 1974).

LOT

The low back vowel /ɑ/ of *pot* is unrounded [ɑ] rather than rounded [ɒ] in the older Norwich accent. This unrounded realisation is gradually disappearing from Norwich apparently under the influence of both RP and the rounded vowel found in dialects further south (see Trudgill 1972).

The lexical set associated with this vowel was formerly rather smaller in that, as in most of southern England, the lengthened vowel /ɔː/ was found before the front voiceless fricatives, as in *off, cloth, lost*. This feature survives to a certain extent, but mostly in working-class speech, and particularly in the word *off*.

STRUT

As far as the vowel /ʌ/ is concerned, there have been clear phonetic developments, with the vowel moving forward from an earlier fully back [ʌ] to a more recent low-central [ɐ], as in much of the south of England, though the movement has not been nearly so extensive as the actual fronting which has taken place in London (see Wells 1982: 305).

FOOT

The FOOT vowel /ʊ/ was much more frequent in the older East Anglian dialect than in General English (in the sense of Wells 1982). Middle English **ou** and **ō** remained, and indeed still remain (see below), distinct in the dialects of Norfolk, e.g. *road* /ɹuːd/, *rowed* /ɹʌud/. However, there has been a strong tendency in East Anglia for the /uː/ descended from Middle English ō to be shortened to /ʊ/ in closed syllables. Thus *road* can rhyme with *good*, and we find pronunciations such as in *toad, home, stone, coat* /tʊd, hʊm, stʊn, kʊt/. This shortening does not normally occur before /l/, so *coal* is /kuːl/, but otherwise distribution is unpredictable: /ʊ/ does not occur in *foam, load, moan, vote*, for example. On the other hand, the shortening process has clearly been a productive one, suggesting that knowledge of the stylistic relationship between the two vowels has continued to be part of the competence of local speakers: Norwich, for example, until the 1960s had a theatre known as *The Hippodrome* /hɪpədɹʊm/, and trade names such as *Kodachrome* can be heard with pronunciations such as /kʊdəkɹʊm/. The feature thus survives quite well in modern speech, but a number of words appear to have been changed permanently to the /uː/ set as a result of lexical transfer (see below). Trudgill (1974) showed that 29 different lexemes from this set occurred with /ʊ/.

The vowel /ʊ/ also occurs in *roof, proof, hoof* and their plurals, e.g. /ɹʊfs/. It also occurs in middle-class Norwich sociolects in *room, broom*; working-class sociolects tend to have the GOOSE vowel in these items.

The checked stressed vowel system
The older checked stressed vowel system of Norwich English was thus:

/ɪ/ *kit, get*	/ʊ/ *foot, home, roof*
/e/ *dress, catch*	/ʌ/ *strut*
/ɛ/ *trap*	/ɑ/ *top*

/ɐ/ *church*

The newer system is:

/ɪ/ *kit*	/ʊ/ *foot, home, roof*
/ɛ/ *dress*	/ʌ/ *strut*
/æ/ *trap, catch*	/ɑ/ *top*

Upgliding diphthongs: FLEECE, FACE, GOAT, GOOSE, PRICE, CHOICE, MOUTH
Characteristic of all of the upgliding diphthongs, of which there is one more
than in most accents of English (see below), is the phonetic characteristic that,
unlike in other south of England varieties, the second element is most usually a
fully close vowel, e.g. the FACE vowel is typically [æi] rather than [æɪ].

FLEECE

The /iː/ vowel is an upgliding diphthong of the type [ɪi], noticeably different from
London [əɪ]. The modern Norwich accent demonstrates happY-tensing, and, as
we saw above, this vowel therefore also occurs in the lexical set of *money, city*
etc. Unstressed *they* also has /iː/: *are they coming?* /aːðiːkʌmən/.

FACE

The most local pronunciation of this vowel is [æi], but qualities intermediate
between this and RP [eɪ] occur (see Trudgill 1974). Older forms of Norwich
English, although this is now vestigial and is heard mainly from older speakers,
have an additional vowel at this point in the system: /æi/ in these lects originally
occurred only in items descended from ME **ai**, while items descended from ME
ā had /eː/ = [eː ~ ɛː]. Thus pairs such as *days–daze, maid–made* were not
homophonous. The /eː/ vowel is currently being lost through a process of transfer of lexical items from the one vowel to the other (see below, and Trudgill &
Foxcroft 1978).

GOAT

There are in fact two vowels at this point in the Norwich vowel system. Paral-
leling the vestigial distinction in the front vowel system between the sets of *made*
and *maid*, corresponding to the distinction between the ME monophthong and
diphthong, so there is a similar distinction in the back vowel system which, however, is by no means vestigial (see Trudgill forthcoming, on why the one distinction has survived longer than the other). The distinction is between /uː/ = [ʊu],
descended from ME **ọ̄**, and /ou/ = [ɐu], descended from ME **ou**. Thus pairs such
as *moan: mown, road: rowed, nose: knows, sole: soul* are not homophonous. One
small complication is that adverbial *no* has /uː/ while the negative particle *no* has
/ou/: *no, that's no good* /nou ðæs nuː gʊd/. (Note that there is no vocalic split in
Norwich between the sets of GOAT and GOAL.)

There are two additional complications. One is that, as we have already seen,
words descended from the ME monophthong may also have /ʊ/, i.e. *road* can be
either /ɹʊd/ or /ɹuːd/.

Secondly, as was mentioned briefly above, many words from the set of GOOSE
which are descended from ME **ọ̄** may have /uː/ rather than /ʉː/. That is, words
such as *boot* may be pronounced either [bʉːt] or [buːt]. In the latter case, they are
of course then homophonous with words such as *boat*. Therefore *rood* may be
homophonous either with *rude* or with *road* which, however, will not be
homophonous with *rowed*. It is probable but not certain that this alternation in
the GOOSE set is the result of lexical transfer (see below), perhaps under the

influence of earlier forms of RP, from /ʉː/ to /uː/. (I say earlier forms of RP because more recent pronunciations of the GOOSE vowel in RP involve much more fronted vowels than was formerly the case.)

Forms in /uː/ are more typical of middle-class than of working-class speech, and phonological environment can also have some effect: /ʉː/ before /l/, as in *school*, has much lower social status than it does before other consonants. There is almost no stylistic variation, however: speakers do not generally alternate between one vowel and another from social context to social context. Words which in my own lower-middle-class speech have /ʉː/ rather than /uː/ include: *who, whose, do, soon, to, too, two, hoot, loot, root, toot, soup, choose, lose, loose, through, shoe.* I have no explanation at all for why, for example, *soon* and *moon* do not rhyme in my speech. There is also considerable individual variation: my mother has /uː/ in *choose*, for instance, and my late father had /uː/ in *who.*

Note that this alternation never occurs in the case of those items such as *rule, tune, new* etc. which have historical sources other than ME ǭ – for very many speakers, then, *rule* and *school* do not rhyme.

Two modern developments should also be noted. First, the phonetic realisation of /uː/ is currently undergoing a rather noticeable change (see below), with younger speakers favouring a fronter first element [ɵu] (see Trudgill 1988). Secondly, there are some signs that the *moan: mown* distinction is now finally beginning to break down, though this awaits further research.

GOOSE

The vowel /ʉː/ is a central diphthong [ʉʉ] with more lip-rounding on the second element than on the first. Since Norwich English demonstrates total ȷ-dropping (see below), there is complete homophony between pairs of words which have this vowel such as *dew: do, Hugh: who, cute: coot.* Many words in this set may also occur with the vowel /uː/ (see above).

PRICE

There is considerable variation in the articulation of the /ai/ vowel, as described in detail in Trudgill (1974, 1988). The most typical realisation is [ɐi], but younger speakers are increasingly favouring a variant approaching [ɑi] (see further below).

CHOICE

It is still possible to hear from older speakers in Norwich certain words from this set, notably *boil,* with the PRICE vowel, although this is now very recessive. The vowel /oi/ itself ranges from the most local variant [ʊi] to a less local variant [ɔi], with a whole range of phonetically intermediate variants.

MOUTH

The most typical realisation of the /æu/ vowel is [æ̈ʉ], although there is some variation in the quality of the first element.

Long monophthongs: BATH, NURSE, PALM, THOUGHT, NEAR, SQUARE, START, NORTH, FORCE, CURE

There are no ingliding diphthongs in modern Norwich English, monophthongisation having converted them all into monophthongs (see also below on smoothing).

BATH/PALM/START

The vowel /aː/ is in its most local realisation a very front vowel approaching [aː] but in more middle-class speech more central variants occur. Typical London and RP back variants around [ɑː] are not found.

NURSE/CURE

As we saw above, the vowel /əː/ is a relative newcomer into Norwich English. Its phonetic realisation is perhaps a little closer than in RP. It occurs in all items from the set of NURSE, but it also occurs in words from the CURE set that are descended from ME **iu** or **eu** before **r**, so that *sure* rhymes with *her* (see also below on smoothing). Note also that, because of J-dropping (see below), the following are homophones: *pure: purr, cure: cur, fury: furry*.

THOUGHT/NORTH/FORCE

The /ɔː/ vowel has a realisation which is approximately [ɔ:] without, however, very much lip-rounding. It occurs in items such as *poor, pore, paw*. As we saw above, as is typical of more conservative south-of-England varieties, it also occurs frequently in the lexical set of CLOTH.

NEAR/SQUARE

These two lexical sets are not distinct in Norwich English, although there is some evidence that this is the result of a merger that is quite recent (see Trudgill 1974). The most usual realisation of this single vowel, which I symbolise as /ɛː/, is [e̞ː ~ ɛ̞ː]. It is possible that some speakers thus pronounce items such as *fierce* and *face* identically.

Smoothing

We have already noted that earlier ingliding diphthongs have become monophthongs: /ɪə/ > /ɛː/ in *near*, /ɛə/ > /ɛː/ in *square*. This is also true of /ʊə/ > /ɔː/ in *poor*, /ɔə/ > /ɔː/ in *pore*, and (presumably) /ʉə/ > /əː/ in *pure*. This development also occurred in original triphthongs, giving *tower* /taː/, and, in middle-class speech, *fire* /faː/. (In working-class speech, *fire* has a different vowel /ɑː/ which occurs only as a result of smoothing.)

This historical process involving lowering before /ə/ and then loss of /ə/ is paralleled by a synchronic phonological process which carries across morpheme and word boundaries, and extends to additional vowels. (In examining the following examples, recall that Norwich has /ə/ in most unstressed syllables where most other accents have /ɪ/.) The full facts can be summarised as follows:

Vowel + /ə/	Example	Output
/iː/	*seeing*	/sɛːn/
/æi/	*playing*	/plæːn/
/ai/	*trying*	/tɹaːn ~ tɹɑːn/
/oi/	*annoying*	/ənɔːn/
/uː/	*do it*	/dəːt/
/uː/	*going*	/gɔːn/
/ou/	*know it*	/nɒːt/
/æu/	*allow it*	/əlaːt/

Thus, *do it* is homophonous with *dirt* and *going* rhymes with *lawn*. The vowels /æː/, /ɑː/, /ɒː/ occur only as a result of smoothing. Interestingly, some speakers pronounce *towel* as [təːl].

7.2.2 Consonants

P, T, K
Intervocalic and word-final /p, k/ are most usually glottalised. This is most audible in intervocalic position where there is simultaneous oral and glottal closure, with the oral closure then being released inaudibly prior to the audible release of the glottal closure, thus *paper* [pæip͡ʔə], *baker* [bæik͡ʔə].

This also occurs in the case of /t/, as in *later* [læit͡ʔə], but more frequently, especially in the speech of younger people, glottaling occurs: [læiʔə]. East Anglia (see Trudgill 1974) appears to have been one of the centres (see below) from which glottaling has diffused geographically in modern English English. Trudgill (1988) showed that [ʔ] is the usual realisation of intervocalic and word-final /t/ in casual speech, and that it is now also increasingly diffusing into more formal styles. There is an interesting constraint on the use of [ʔ] and [t͡ʔ] in Norwich English in that these allophones cannot occur before [ə] if another instance follows, i.e. *lit it* has to be [lɪtʰəʔ] rather than *[lɪʔəʔ].

In /nt/ clusters, the /n/ is frequently deleted if (and only if) the /t/ is realised as a glottal stop: *twenty* [twɛʔɪi], *plenty* [plɛʔɪi], *going to* [gɔːʔə].

TH
TH-fronting was completely absent from Norwich English in 1968. By 1983, however, it had become very common indeed (see below and Trudgill 1988).

V
The present-tense verb-form *have* is normally pronounced /hæ ~ hə ~ ə/, i.e. without a final /v/, unless the next word begins with a vowel: *have you done it?* /hæ jə dʌn ət/. This has the consequence that, because of smoothing (see above), some forms involving *to have* and *to be* are homophonous: *we're coming* /wɛː kʌmən/, *we've done it* /wɛː dʌn ət/. There is no trace at all in the city of the older rural East Anglian merger of /v/ with /w/, as in *very* [wɛɹə].

H

As I have pointed out before (see Trudgill 1974), traditional dialects in East Anglia did not have H-dropping. Norwich, however, has had H-dropping for many generations. The 1968 survey showed that levels of H-dropping correlate with social class and style, ranging from 0 per cent for MMC in formal speech to 61 per cent for LWC informants in casual speech. It is interesting that these levels are much lower than in other parts of the country, and that hypercorrect forms do not occur.

J

Norwich, like all of Norfolk and adjacent areas of Suffolk, Cambridgeshire, Lincolnshire and even parts of Leicestershire and Bedfordshire (see Trudgill 1990), demonstrates total J-dropping (Wells 1982). That is, a probable earlier /j/ has gone missing before /ʉː/ not only after /r/, as in *rule*, as in all accents of English; and not only after /l, s, n, t, d, θ/, as in *lute, sue, news, tune, duke, enthuse*, as in many accents of English; but after all consonants. Pronunciations without /j/ are therefore also typical in items such as: *music, pew, beauty, few, view, cue, hew*. The word *ewe* now begins with /j/, although this was formerly not the case, and *education* is now /ɛdʒəkæiʃn/ although it was formerly /ɛdəkeːʃn/.

R

There has been a remarkable change, as elsewhere in England, in the pronunciation of /r/ in recent years: as many as one third of informants born between 1959 and 1973 (see Trudgill 1988) used a labiodental approximant realisation [ʋ] of /r/, which before 1959 was used by only a handful of idiosyncratic speakers, rather than the more usual alveolar approximant [ɹ]. The latter is still the most common variant in the community as a whole, but the prevalence of the former amongst younger speakers suggests that this picture is likely to change soon.

Intrusive /r/ is the norm in Norwich English. It occurs invariably where the vowels /ɛː, aː, ɔː, ə/ occur before another vowel across both word and morpheme boundaries: *drawing* /dɹɔːɹən/, *draw it* /dɹɔːɹət/. (Its occurrence is utterly automatic. In my 1968 study, I initially set up intrusive /r/ as a phonological variable but had to abandon it because there was no variability!) Because of the high level of reduction of unstressed vowels to /ə/ (see above), intrusive /r/ occurs in positions where it would be unusual in other accents: e.g. *give it to Anne* /ɡɪv ət təɹ æn/. Linking /r/ is essentially the same phenomenon and occurs additionally after /əː/.

L

/l/ was traditionally clear in all positions in rural East Anglian dialects, but Norwich has the same distribution of 'clear' and 'dark' allophones as RP. Vocalisation of /l/ does not occur.

7.3   *Endogenous and exogenous change*

Clearly, Norwich English, like any other variety, during the course of the twentieth century has undergone, and is undergoing, a number of linguistic changes. We have mentioned the major phonetic and phonological changes in our survey above. An interesting problem for historical linguistics and sociolinguistics that a relatively detailed survey of this type in a relatively well-defined geographical area can help throw some light on is whether it is possible to distinguish between changes which appear to be internal to the system itself and changes which are in some way the result of influence from other external varieties. We can refer to these changes as respectively **endogenous** and **exogenous** phonological changes. (If some changes can be shown to be truly endogenous, this will shed some doubt on the argument (see J. Milroy 1992) that all change is the result of contact.) Exogenous changes, moreover, will be further subdividable according to the source and the nature of the external influence.

7.3.1   Endogenous changes

Among changes which appear to be good candidates for the description of endogenous phonetic and/or phonological changes are the following.

TRAP
The 1968 survey revealed a strong trend on the part of middle-aged and younger working-class speakers for this vowel to be diphthongised, particularly before velar consonants. Its absence from the speech of older informants, together with the fact that the older dialect in any case (see above) had a vowel closer than [æ], suggests a relatively recent innovation. Its absence from RP and from neighbouring dialects – as far as is known – suggests that this is a spontaneous, internally produced change. The innovative forms typical of Norwich English are, for example, *back* [bæɛk], *bag* [bæɛg], *bang* [bæɛŋ].

GOAT
One of the most interesting changes in Norwich English in recent times can be dated, in a rather remarkable way, quite precisely. This change involves the vowel /uː/ of *goat, home, moan* (but not *know, old, mown* – see above), and consists of the fronting of the first element [ʊu] > [ʉu]. This first came to my attention as the result of some work by William Labov. My 1968 fieldwork resulted in my 1971 Edinburgh University PhD thesis, which formed the basis of Trudgill (1974). The first publication to emerge from this research was Trudgill (1972), which was submitted to the journal *Language in Society* in the spring of 1971. This article aroused the interest of Labov, who was one of the editors, and who was planning a field trip to Britain that summer. During August 1971 he paid a surprise visit to my parents in Norwich, and, in my absence, asked to see a copy of my thesis. He also, during the course of his visit to Norwich, made a number

of field recordings of speakers of the local dialect. He was intrigued by the realisation of the vowel of *road* etc., which he could not at first – a common problem for non-natives of the area who have only one vowel themselves in this phonological area – distinguish from the vowel of *rude* etc. To my surprise, however, he discovered in commutation tests that at least two natives of Norwich also had this problem. He carried out this work less than a mile from my own home with two boys, friends aged 11, who were thus born in 1960/61. One of them was unable consistently to distinguish between the vowels of *toe* and *two* in the speech of the other. I personally found this hard to believe, but when I heard the recordings, I understood why: the /uː/ vowel the second boy was using in *toe, road* had a pronunciation which was new to me and which had a fronted first element which brought it noticeably closer to the pronunciation of the vowel /uː/ of *two, rude*. The distinction was no longer between [ʊu] and [ʉʉ] as in my own speech but between [ʉu] and [ʉʉ]. This pronunciation, which has now become the norm amongst younger Norwich speakers, did not occur at all in my 1968 sample, in which the youngest speakers were born in 1958. We are therefore able to say with an unusual degree of accuracy that it first occurred in Norwich English in the speech of those born around 1960.

NEAR and SQUARE
Speakers with typical local phonology in Norwich do not distinguish between these two lexical sets. Words such as *here* and *hair* are total homophones. (On leaving Norwich and going to university at the age of nineteen, I attempted to introduce this distinction into my own accent, but had considerable difficulty since spelling is no help with, for example, pairs such as *near* and *pear*. Indeed, I am still not always sure what the General English pronunciation of words such as *tear* is, and have to ask others for confirmation.) By the time of my 1968 survey, the normal pronunciation of the single vowel which applies to both these lexical sets was typically [ɛ̝ː ~ e̞ː] (see above). However, the very oldest informant in the sample, a lady in her nineties, used a diphthongal pronunciation [e̞ə]. This monophthongisation should perhaps be seen as related to the widespread south of England and RP trend involving the SQUARE vowel [ɛə] > [ɛː], the CURE vowel [ʊə] > [ɔː], and the FORCE vowel [ɔə] > [ɔː]. This merger appears to be a Norwich innovation – it is not found in any other accents in southern England – and indeed does not actually cover even all of East Anglia. It is clearly therefore an endogenous change. It is a change which is not surprising in view of the low functional load of the two vowels (see Trudgill 1974), and similar changes elsewhere in the English-speaking world, such as the merger of the same two vowels in New Zealand English (see Wells 1982: 608), are likely to be spontaneous and historically unrelated.

7.3.2 Problematic cases

PRICE
As described above, the older pronunciation of this vowel, [ɐi], typical also of rural Norfolk dialects, appeared in the 1968 study to be in competition with a

newer and audibly different pronunciation, [ɑi], as illustrated in the speech of a relatively small number of teenage informants. The 1983 study confirmed this and showed that it was becoming the norm for younger speakers. It is not entirely clear whether this is an internally generated change or if it reflects the influence of the speech of the Home Counties, where back first elements are rather common in this diphthong.

Smoothing

The process of smoothing – the monophthongisation of triphthongs – has been well described by Wells (1982) for the accents of English English. It is certainly found in a wide range of English English accents, especially in the south of England, and including in RP. There is good reason to suppose, however, that this phenomenon represents an endogenous change in Norwich English. The fact that it is found in areas of England beyond Norwich or East Anglia does not necessarily mean that it has spread to Norwich from elsewhere. In fact, the reverse seems likely to have been the case. That is, smoothing probably spread from the Norwich area outwards. One reason for arguing this is that smoothing is much more extensive in the Norwich region than anywhere else. As described by Wells for other accents, it typically affects only /aiə/ and /auə/. In Norwich, on the other hand, as we have seen, it affects a much wider range of triphthongs than this. Trudgill (1986) also shows that in East Anglia itself, smoothing is more prevalent the nearer one comes geographically to Norwich.

Glottaling and glottalisation

The glottaling of intervocalic and word-final /t/ is one of the most dramatic, widespread and rapid changes to have occurred in British English in recent times. It is still spreading geographically into areas such as South Wales (see Mees 1990; Mees & Collins this volume) from which it was formerly absent. It is spreading socially from lower-class to higher-class accents. It is spreading stylistically from informal into formal speech. (Trudgill (1988) showed that Norwich is no exception to this particular trend.) And it is spreading phonologically from more favoured to less favoured environments. London is sometimes cited as the geographical source of this innovation, which would make it an exogenous change from the point of view of Norwich English. There is some reason to suppose, however, that this may not necessarily be the case. The records of the Survey of English Dialects (see Trudgill 1974) show that northern East Anglia was in the 1950s the only rural area in southern England in which glottaling and glottalisation of intervocalic /t/ were at all prevalent. It is therefore possible that this is a feature which has spread from – and not to – the area of Norwich in the last century or so.

7.3.3   Exogenous changes: dedialectalisation and lexical redistribution

It is a widespread occurrence in dedialectalisation that influence from standard, prestigious or metropolitan varieties does not immediately affect the phonological systems as such of lower-status or more peripheral areas. Rather, the phonological system remains intact, at least initially, while lexical items are transferred from one set to another in order to more closely match the distribution of lexical items in the external variety. There is much evidence in Norwich English that the influence of London and RP has taken this form. Examples mentioned above include *get* /ɪ/ > /ɛ/; *catch* /ɛ/ > /æ/; *off* /ɔː/ > /ɒ/.

Notice, however, that unsystematic transfer as a result of external influences can eventually have systematic consequences. In Trudgill & Foxcroft (1978) it was argued that this was happening in East Anglia in the case of the vowel /eː/ of FACE. Lexical items such as *face, gate, name* were gradually and somewhat spasmodically being transferred from the set of /eː/ to the set of the already existing vowel /æi/, which in the original dialect was confined to items such as *play, main, day*. The reason for this transfer was clear: the English of London had a vowel which phonetically closely resembled East Anglian /æi/ in words from the *gate* set as well as words from the *day* set. The motivation of individual speakers was to make their pronunciations of individual words more closely resemble those of speakers of the influential external variety. In our 1978 paper, however, we predicted that the end result of this process historically would eventually be the total loss from the phonological system of the vowel /eː/. Twenty years later, this has now happened in Norwich. The two vowels have merged as /æi/, and the merger, which was effected by means of the process of lexical transfer, has gone to completion.

7.3.4 Other exogenous changes

H-*dropping*
East Anglia is well known to be one of the very few dialect areas in England to have resisted the innovation of H-dropping. The records of the Survey of English Dialects show very clearly that this is the case. On the other hand, it is clearly also the case that for quite some time this has been true only of rural dialects. The 1968 Norwich survey showed that H-dropping was normal in Norwich, and Trudgill (1973) demonstrated that this was true also of other urban areas of East Anglia such as Ipswich, Yarmouth and King's Lynn. As recently as the 1970s it was still a matter of common knowledge in the Norwich area that 'City people drop their h's, country people don't', though, with the more recent spread of H-dropping also to rural areas, this awareness no longer survives so strongly. This suggests, then, that H-dropping arrived in East Anglia from outside quite recently and, according to the normal pattern of the geographical diffusion of linguistic innovations, spread first to the major urban areas and only subsequently to rural areas dominated by the particular towns and cities. This view is strengthened by the fact that, at least in 1968, H-dropping in Norwich was quantitatively at a much lower level than in other areas of England investigated by sociolinguists.

TH-*fronting*
TH-fronting in modern England is a remarkable phenomenon. Formerly confined to the London area and to Bristol, it has in the 1980s and 1990s begun to

spread enormously rapidly across England. It was totally absent from the 1968 Norwich corpus, but by the time of the 1983 survey it had made amazing inroads into the local dialect. None of the Norwich informants born before 1958 had this feature. Of informants born between 1959 and 1973, 70 per cent had some degree of loss of /θ/ and /ð/ through merger with /f/ and /v/, and 29 per cent had no instances of /θ/ at all. The mechanisms by which this change from outside has occurred remain mysterious – see the discussion in Trudgill (1986) – but it is clear that this is a change which has spread into Norwich from elsewhere.

Labiodental R

A similar phenomenon is provided by the case of labiodental /r/. This is also becoming very common in many parts of England. In the 1968 survey, 7 per cent of the informants had this feature, while in 1983 it had risen to 31 per cent.

7.3.5   Problematic cases

LOT

As we saw above, the original unrounded [ɑ] realisation of this vowel in Norwich is gradually giving way to the more usual – in English English – rounded vowel [ɒ]. There seems no doubt that this is an exogenous change. The only problem would seem to be its source. In Trudgill (1972) I argued that the source was *both* RP *and* the neighbouring local dialects. The justification for this was that the newer rounded variant had, surprisingly, been shown in the 1968 survey to be most prominent in two different social groups in the community: middle-class women, and working-class men. This unusual pattern of class and sex differentiation could be explained in the following way. The new vowel was being introduced into Norwich English simultaneously from two different sources: RP, which was most influential in the case of the middle-class female speakers; and the dialects of neighbouring Suffolk, which were most influential in the case of the working-class male speakers.

STRUT

This was not a variable dealt with in the 1968 survey, and it is not a feature which the Survey of English Dialects records are sufficiently phonetically detailed to help us with. Nevertheless, as we noted above, my own observations make it clear that the quality of this vowel has changed in Norwich English over the past hundred years. Older speakers have a vowel which is fully back and close to the true cardinal value of [ʌ], i.e. [ɔ] without lip-rounding. The most usual pronunciation from younger speakers, however, is close to that of RP which, in spite of the fact that it is still usually symbolised as /ʌ/, is actually phonetically a central vowel around [ɐ]. This change is problematic to categorise since it probably represents an example of Norwich English simply following a wider trend. RP, too, together with certain other south of England varieties, has clearly undergone a similar lowering and fronting in the same period. In any case, there is no sign as yet in Norwich English of the more fronted variants of /ʌ/ typical of London English.

happy-*tensing*

Similar comments can be made about happy-tensing in Norwich. Two successive changes have occurred in Norwich in recent times in the lexical set of *happy, city, money*. First, final /ə/ gave way to /ɪ/: /hæpə/ > /hæpɪ/. This is clearly to be interpreted as Norwich English being influenced from outside by the national mainstream. Secondly, however, in the speech of people born after around 1930, /hæpɪ/ has been replaced by the more recent /hæpiː/. This latter is part of a much wider south of England-based change (see Wells 1982) which is, perhaps, now beginning to find its way into RP. It seems rather pointless to argue whether this change happened first in, say, London, and then spread to Norwich, or whether it is something which happened all over southern England more or less simultaneously.

7.4 *Conclusion*

Some of the phonetic and phonological changes we have observed in Norwich English appear to be truly endogenous. The diphthongisation of the TRAP vowel, the fronting of the GOAT vowel, and the merger of the vowels of NEAR and SQUARE are without parallel anywhere in neighbouring or metropolitan or national prestige varieties. The only possible way to argue that they are nevertheless the result of contact would be to show that they are hyperadaptations – possibly hyperdialectisms accentuating already existing differences with neighbouring dialects – of some kind. This does not appear to be possible. We seem forced to accept the possibility that change can be truly system-internal.

Moreover, at least NEAR/SQUARE can be regarded as, as it were, a blow for heterogeneity in that it is a change which is taking Norwich English away from the national mainstream. Also, in a few other cases, we have argued that Norwich (which until the nineteenth century was one of the four largest cities in England and is still the largest city within a radius of 120 miles) may have been the source, or at least *a* source, for the innovations of glottaling and smoothing.

Exogenous changes, although they are obviously important, are always somewhat harder to argue for in particular cases, as we saw with the STRUT vowel, because there is always the possibility that they would, as it were, have 'happened anyway'. Many of the exogenous changes we have described above seem to be the result of Norwich English falling into line with the national mainstream – part of a widespread homogenisation process. Thus the examples of lexical transfer we described can be seen as a result of the influence of RP and of other varieties of English English generally, as can the rounding of the LOT vowel.

Other exogenous changes, on the other hand, involve the diffusion of clearly non-RP features into the area: H-dropping, TH-fronting and labiodental R come into this category. These three features, however, also seem to be part of a general process of homogenisation in that they are bringing Norwich English into line with other regional accents and, as other papers in this book also make clear, the latter two features are currently spreading very rapidly into many or most parts of England.

One change, however, which has not (yet) taken place in Norwich is the vocalisation of [ɬ]. This is a feature which has already spread into southern East Anglia, so this may just be a matter of time. During the course of the twentieth century, the dialects of Norfolk have abandoned their original clear [l] in syllable-final position, as revealed by the Survey of English Dialects, and replaced it with [ɬ], so we can perhaps expect this phonetic trend to continue, thus gradually leading to at least a partial loss of distinctiveness for this currently very distinctive East Anglian urban variety of English.

8

Dialect levelling: change and continuity in Milton Keynes, Reading and Hull

Ann Williams and Paul Kerswill

8.1 *Introduction*

This chapter deals with the accents of three towns, Milton Keynes, Reading and Hull, chosen in order to illustrate and attempt to explain the phenomenon of dialect levelling in England. Data for the chapter were recorded as part of two ESRC-funded projects conducted at the University of Reading: *A new dialect in a new city: children's and adults' speech in Milton Keynes* (henceforth referred to as the MK project; 1990–94, ESRC ref. R000232376) and *The role of adolescents in dialect levelling* (the DL project; 1995–98, ESRC ref. R000236180). Details of each corpus are given below.

The Milton Keynes project

Approximately 100-hour corpus; 48 working-class children were recorded (age groups of 4, 8 and 12 years by two sexes, giving eight speakers per cell). All the children were native-born or had arrived within the first two years of life. Additionally, one caregiver was recorded for each child (all except one were female; of the 47 females, 46 were the child's mother; five caregivers were born in the Milton Keynes area). Recordings of the children were made in structured sessions in pairs with the fieldworker, consisting of a semi-structured interview, a word-list reading, and a range of tasks tailored to the age group and designed to elicit specific words, including a quiz, a map task, a picture story retelling, a 'spot the difference' game, and the identification of objects in a bag. Recordings of adults were conducted as informal interviews, mainly in their homes.

The Dialect Levelling project

Approximately 90-hour corpus; 96 adolescents aged 14–15 in three towns, Hull, Reading and Milton Keynes (one age group, three towns, two sexes, two classes ('working class' and 'middle class'), giving eight speakers per cell). Recordings of the adolescents consisted of (1) individual interviews with the fieldworker, including a word-list reading, (2) a discussion in pairs with the fieldworker, and

(3) a group discussion with four to six adolescents in a single-sex group, guided by the fieldworker. Additionally, four elderly working-class persons aged 70 or over (two male, two female) were recorded in each town. All subjects were native-born or had arrived within the first four years of life. Survey of English Dialects (SED) materials (Orton & Halliday 1963; Orton & Wakelin 1967; Orton & Tilling 1970) were used for comparison (for Reading: Berkshire site 5, Swallowfield; for Milton Keynes: Buckinghamshire site 2, Stewkley; for Hull: Yorkshire sites 25 and 28, Newbald and Welwick).

8.2   Descriptive material

8.2.1   Vowels

A study of the vowels of the three accents reveals the similarities between the accents of the southern towns of Milton Keynes and Reading, as well as the converging direction of change. These similarities will be discussed in the main part of this chapter. The account of Hull reveals that it has in most respects a typical northern accent, with, for example, no contrast between STRUT and FOOT and the vowel of TRAP in BATH. On the other hand, it has two very distinct variants of the PRICE vowel, a monophthong before voiced consonants and a diphthong elsewhere; this pattern is restricted in England to Humberside and parts of East Yorkshire as well as an area in the Fens (Britain 1997b). Yet Hull shares with the southern towns changes in a number of consonants, involving the spread of the glottal stop between vowels, the use of [f] for [θ] in words such as *thing*, and the use of [v] for [ð] as in *brother*.

Note: The main variants listed in Table 8.1 are those of young, working-class people, especially adolescents. Where there is significant age, gender or class variation, this is pointed out in the following text.

8.2.1.1   Milton Keynes

KIT
While [ɪ] is the most commonly heard variant, a lowered variant [ɪ] is also frequent, particularly among females. Older speakers may have a raised variant [i].

DRESS
Raised variants, e.g. [ẹ], may be heard before velars.

TRAP
A raised variant [a̦] may be heard. Noticeably lengthened variants are heard before some voiced consonants.

STRUT
More central variants [ʌ]and [ɐ] may be heard. Some elderly speakers use [ə].

Table **8.1** The vowels of Milton Keynes, Reading and Hull – summary

	Milton Keynes	Reading	Hull
KIT	ɪ > ɪ̞ ~ i̠	ɪ > ɪ̞ ~ e̝	ɪ
DRESS	ɛ̝ > e̝	ɛ̝ > e̝	ɛ
TRAP	a ~ a̠	a ~ a̠	a̠ > a
LOT	ɒ̝	ɒ̝ ~ ɑ	ɒ̝ ~ ɑ
STRUT	ʌ > ʌ̟ ~ ɐ	ʌ > ʌ̟ ~ ɐ ~ ɔ̞ː	ʊ̞
FOOT	θ > ʊ̞ ~ ø ~ ʏ	θ > ʊ̞ ~ ø ~ ʏ	ʊ̞
BATH	ɑː > ɑ̟ː ~ a̠ː	ɑ̟ː > a̠ː	a̠ > a
CLOTH	ɒ̞	ɒ̞ ~ ɑ	ɒ̞ ~ ɑ
NURSE	ə̝ː	ə̝ː	ɛ̝ː
FLEECE	ˡi > ᵊi	iː ~ ˡi > ᵊi	ˡi ~ e̝i
FACE	ɛi ~ æi ~ ɐi ~ e̝i	ɛi > æi ~ e̝i	ɛ̝ː
PALM	ɑː > ɑ̟ː ~ a̠ː	ɑ̟ː > a̠ː	aː > ɑ̟ː
THOUGHT	ɔ̝ː > oʊ̞	ɔ̝ː > oʊ̞	ɔ̝ː ~ ɔ̞ː
GOAT	əʏ ~ ɐʏ ~ əɪ ~ ɐɪ	əʏ ~ əɪ ~ ə̝ʏ ~ əʊ	ɔ̈ː ~ əː > əʊ ~ əʊ
GOAL	ʌʊ > ɔ̝ʊ	ʌʊ > ɔ̝ʊ	ɔ̈ː ~ əː > əʊ ~ əʊ
GOOSE	ʉː ~ ʉ̈ː ~ ʏː ~ yː > ᵊʉ̈ː	ʉː ~ ʉ̈ː ~ ʏː ~ yː > ᵊʉ̈ː	ʊu ~ əʉ
PRICE	ɑɪ > ɑ̟ɪ ~ ɑː ~ ɔɪ ~ ʌ̟ɪ	ɑɪ ~ ɔɪ ~ ʌ̟ɪ > ɑː	a̠i̠ ~ a̠ː
CHOICE	ɔɪ ~ oɪ	ɔɪ ~ oɪ	ɔɪ
MOUTH	aʊ > aː ~ ɛː ~ æʊ	aʊ > aː ~ ɛɪ ~ ɛ̝ʊ	aʊ ~ ɐʊ
NEAR	e̝ː ~ eə	e̝ː ~ eə	e·ɛ
SQUARE	ɛː ~ ɛ̝ə	ɛː ~ ɛ̝ə	ɛ̝ː
START	ɑː > ɑ̟ː ~ a̠ː	ɑ̟ː > a̠ː	aː > ɑ̟ː
NORTH	ɔ̝ː > oʊ̞	ɔ̝ː > oʊ̞	ɔ̝ː ~ ɔ̞ː
FORCE	ɔ̝ː > oʊ̞	ɔ̝ː > oʊ̞	ɔ̝ː ~ ɔ̞ː
CURE	jɔ̝ː	jɔ̝ː	jʊɛ
happY	i̠	i̠	ˡi
lettER	ɒ̝ ~ ə̝	ɐ ~ ə̝	ɛ
commA	ɒ̝ ~ ə̝	ɐ ~ ə̝	ɛ
horsES	ɪ	ɪ	ɪ

FOOT
More conservative, less centralised variants such as [ʊ̞] may be heard, as can fronted [ø] and [ʏ].

BATH, PALM, START
A fronted variant [ɑ̟ː] is frequent, particularly among MC young people. Elderly WC people tend to use [a̠ː] in BATH and PALM.

FACE
A more open variant [æi] or [ɐɪ] is also found. MC people are likely to use [e̝ɪ].

GOAT
Older speakers have a more raised onset and a less fronted offset, e.g. [ə̝ʊ̞]. Girls and young women tend to have greater fronting and/or unrounding of the

offset, giving [ɐɪ]. MC speakers participate in the same fronting process, but their vowel onset remains higher, e.g. [əʏ].

GOAL
The onset may be higher and/or rounded, giving e.g. [ɔ̞ʊ], especially among MC speakers.

GOOSE
More fronted variants, such as [ʏː] or even (in palatal environments such as in *huge*) [yː], may be heard, particularly in young female speech. Elderly speakers use [ʉː]. For some speakers, a slight central on-glide can also be heard, e.g. [ᵊʉː].

PRICE
Many speakers (particularly MC) use a fronted [ɑ̟ɪ]. The rising/fronting offset may be very slight in fast speech, giving rise to a near-monophthong [ɑ]. Elderly speakers tend to have a raised-centralised onset, giving [ʌɪ].

CHOICE
MC variant is [ɔɪ].

MOUTH
A fast speech variant [a] is commonly used. A few younger speakers (particularly those with London origins) use a monophthong [ɛː]. Speakers aged 30–50 may use [æʊ]; elderly speakers [ɛɪ]; SED records [ɛʊ̈].

NEAR
Older speakers have [eə].

SQUARE
Older speakers have [ɛ̝ə].

commA
MC and older speakers use [ə̝].

8.2.1.2 *Reading*

KIT
While [ɪ] is the most commonly heard variant, lowered or centralised variants [ɪ̞] or [ï] are also frequent, particularly among females. Elderly speakers have a lowered or centralised variant [ɪ̞] or [ë].

DRESS
Raised variants, e.g. [e̞], may be heard before velars.

Table **8.1** The vowels of Milton Keynes, Reading and Hull – summary

	Milton Keynes	Reading	Hull
KIT	ɪ > ɪ̞ ~ i̞	ɪ > ɪ̞ ~ e̞	ɪ
DRESS	ɛ > e̞	ɛ > e̞	ɛ
TRAP	a ~ a̠	a ~ a̠	a̠ > a
LOT	ɒ̞	ɒ̞ ~ ɑ	ɒ̞ ~ ɑ
STRUT	ʌ > ʌ̞ ~ ɐ	ʌ > ʌ̞ ~ ɐ ~ ə:	ʊ̞
FOOT	ɵ > ʊ̞ ~ ø ~ ʏ	ɵ > ʊ̞ ~ ø ~ ʏ	ʊ̞
BATH	ɑ: > ɑ̟: ~ a̠:	ɑ̟: > a̠:	a̠ > a
CLOTH	ɒ̞	ɒ̞ ~ ɑ	ɒ̞ ~ ɑ
NURSE	ə̞:	ə̞:	ɛ:
FLEECE	ˡi > ᵊi	i: ~ ˡi > ᵊi	ˡi ~ e̞i
FACE	ɛi ~ æi ~ ɐi ~ e̞i	ɛi > æi ~ e̞i	ɛ:
PALM	ɑ: > ɑ̟: ~ a̠:	ɑ̟: > a̠:	a: > ɑ̟:
THOUGHT	ɔ̞: > oʊ̞	ɔ̞: > oʊ̞	ɔ̞: ~ ɔ̞:
GOAT	əʏ ~ ɐʏ ~ əɪ ~ ɐɪ	əʏ ~ əɪ ~ əʏ ~ əʊ̞	ɔ̈: ~ ə: > ɵʊ ~ əʊ
GOAL	ʌʊ > ɔ̞ʊ	ʌʊ > ɔ̞ʊ	ɔ̈: ~ ə: > ɵʊ ~ əʊ
GOOSE	ʉ: ~ ʉ̞: ~ ʏ: ~ y: > ᵊʉ̞:	ʉ: ~ ʉ̞: ~ ʏ: ~ y: > ᵊʉ̞:	ʊu ~ ɵʉ
PRICE	ɑɪ > ɑ̟ɪ ~ ɑ: ~ ɔɪ ~ ʌɪ	ɑɪ ~ ɔɪ ~ ʌɪ > ɑ:	a̞i ~ a̠:
CHOICE	ɔ̞ɪ ~ ɔɪ	ɔ̞ɪ ~ ɔɪ	ɔɪ
MOUTH	aʊ > a: ~ ɛ: ~ æʊ	aʊ > a: ~ ɛɪ ~ ɛʊ̞	aʊ ~ ɐʊ
NEAR	e̞: ~ eə	e̞: ~ eə	eˑɛ
SQUARE	ɛ: ~ ɛ̞ə	ɛ: ~ ɛ̞ə	ɛ:
START	ɑ: > ɑ̟: ~ a̠:	ɑ̟: > a̠:	a: > ɑ̟:
NORTH	ɔ̞: > oʊ̞	ɔ̞: > oʊ̞	ɔ̞: ~ ɔ̞:
FORCE	ɔ̞: > oʊ̞	ɔ̞: > oʊ̞	ɔ̞: ~ ɔ̞:
CURE	jɔ̞:	jɔ̞:	jʊɛ
happ**Y**	i̞	i̞	ˡi
lett**ER**	ɒ̞ ~ ə̞	ɐ ~ ə̞	ɛ
comm**A**	ɒ̞ ~ ə̞	ɐ ~ ə̞	ɛ
hors**ES**	ɪ	ɪ	ɪ

FOOT
More conservative, less centralised variants such as [ʊ̞] may be heard, as can fronted [ø] and [ʏ].

BATH, PALM, START
A fronted variant [ɑ̟:] is frequent, particularly among MC young people. Elderly WC people tend to use [a̠:] in BATH and PALM.

FACE
A more open variant [æi] or [ɐi] is also found. MC people are likely to use [e̞ɪ].

GOAT
Older speakers have a more raised onset and a less fronted offset, e.g. [ə̞ʊ̞]. Girls and young women tend to have greater fronting and/or unrounding of the

offset, giving [ɐɪ]. MC speakers participate in the same fronting process, but their vowel onset remains higher, e.g. [əʏ].

GOAL
The onset may be higher and/or rounded, giving e.g. [ɔ̝ʊ], especially among MC speakers.

GOOSE
More fronted variants, such as [ʏː] or even (in palatal environments such as in *huge*) [yː], may be heard, particularly in young female speech. Elderly speakers use [ʉː]. For some speakers, a slight central on-glide can also be heard, e.g. [ᵊʉː].

PRICE
Many speakers (particularly MC) use a fronted [ɑ̟ɪ]. The rising/fronting offset may be very slight in fast speech, giving rise to a near-monophthong [ɑ]. Elderly speakers tend to have a raised-centralised onset, giving [ʌɪ].

CHOICE
MC variant is [ɔɪ].

MOUTH
A fast speech variant [a] is commonly used. A few younger speakers (particularly those with London origins) use a monophthong [ɛː]. Speakers aged 30–50 may use [æʊ]; elderly speakers [ɛɪ]; SED records [ɛʊ̈].

NEAR
Older speakers have [eə].

SQUARE
Older speakers have [ɛ̝ə].

commA
MC and older speakers use [ə̞].

8.2.1.2   *Reading*

KIT
While [ɪ] is the most commonly heard variant, lowered or centralised variants [ɪ̞] or [ï] are also frequent, particularly among females. Elderly speakers have a lowered or centralised variant [ɪ̞] or [ë].

DRESS
Raised variants, e.g. [ẹ], may be heard before velars.

TRAP
Retracted variants, e.g. [a̠], are common. Noticeably lengthened variants are heard before some voiced consonants.

LOT, CLOTH
Elderly people may use [ɑ].

STRUT
Some young WC people use a central [ə], as do many elderly speakers. Otherwise [ɐ] or [ʌ] are common.

FOOT
More conservative, less centralised variants such as [ʊ] may be heard, as can fronted [ø] and [ʏ].

BATH, PALM, START
Some WC adolescents use [a̠ː]; this fronting is less marked among the elderly, who use [ɑ̟ː].

FACE
A more open variant [æɪ] is also found. MC people are likely to use [e̞ɪ].

GOAT
The onset may be raised or fronted, giving e.g. [əʏ]. Elderly speakers have less fronted offsets, giving e.g. [əʊ]. MC speakers have similar variants, and participate in the same fronting process.

GOAL
The onset may be higher and/or rounded, giving e.g. [ɔ̝ʊ], especially among MC speakers.

GOOSE
More fronted variants, such as [ʏː] or even (in palatal environments such as in *huge*) [yː], may be heard, particularly in young female speech. Elderly speakers use [ʉː]. For some speakers, a slight central on-glide can also be heard, e.g. [ʉ̈ː].

PRICE
The onset is variably rounded. The rising/fronting offset may be very slight in fast speech, giving rise to a near-monophthong [ɑ]. Elderly speakers favour [ʌ̟ɪ].

CHOICE
MC variant is [ɔɪ].

MOUTH
A fast speech variant [aː] is commonly used. Older WC speakers use [ɛʏ] and [ɛɪ]

which are still used by a minority of WC children. Speakers may switch between [ɛɪ] (or [ɛʊ̞]) and [aʊ] according to context, with no intermediate variant.

NEAR
Older speakers have [eə].

SQUARE
Older speakers have [ɛ̞ə].

commA
MC and older speakers use [ə].

8.2.1.3 *Hull*

STRUT
More central variants, e.g. [ə], are found among MC speakers.

NURSE
Merger with SQUARE is common.

FLEECE
Elderly speakers may have [e̞i].

FACE
In the words *eight* and *eighty,* [ɛɪ] is used. Older speakers also use this vowel in *weight*; thus, *wait* and *weight* form a minimal pair.

PALM, START
MC speakers may use [ɑ̟ː].

THOUGHT, NORTH, FORCE
MC speakers use [ɔ̞ː]

GOAT, GOAL
The central variant is associated with female, particularly MC, speech, though other females use it, too. A diphthong [ɵʊ] or [əʊ] may be used by many MC speakers. There is usually no distinct allophone for this vowel before /l/.

GOOSE
MC speakers may use [ɵʉ].

PRICE
In WC speech, [ai̞] is used before voiceless consonants, [a̠ː] elsewhere. This distinction is not found in MC speech, which uses the diphthong throughout. The monophthong has the potential for merger with the PALM/START vowel.

MOUTH
The offset is strongly labialised.

8.2.2 Consonants

There is considerable evidence of convergence in the consonant systems of British accents. Studies such as the *Phonological Variation and Change* project (see Docherty & Foulkes, and Watt & Milroy this volume), as well as our own, show that т-glottalling and the fronting of /θ/ and /ð/ to [f] and [v] are widespread and show increasingly similar phonological and sociolinguistic patterning throughout the country. Here, we will underline this convergence by discussing all three towns together.

T, P
Glottal replacement of non-initial /t/ is the norm among young working-class people in all three towns, with males using the feature a little more (see Table 8.8, below). Among middle-class young people, girls use the feature more in Reading and Hull, while in Milton Keynes it is the boys who have the higher frequency. Pre-consonantal environments, as in *let me*, favour the process the most. Older speakers in Hull use less glottal replacement of /t/ than younger people, suggesting a recent introduction of the feature. In Reading and Milton Keynes, the glottal stop may replace medial /p/ in some items, such as *stupid* and *paper*.

K
Final /k/ in Hull may be pre-aspirated, giving [klɒhkʰ] for *clock*.

TH
/θ, ð/ are realised as [θ, ð] by older speakers; [f, v] are increasingly used by younger speakers ([v] is not used initially in function words, such as *that*). See discussion below, Table 8.8.

H
In all three towns н-dropping is the norm for older speakers, though it is less common among young speakers in Reading and Milton Keynes than in Hull (see Figure 8.1).

R
The main variant in all three towns is [ɹ]. Labiodental [ʋ] is common among children and young adults. Linking and intrusive r are the norm, but are rare in Hull after [ɔː] as in *law and order*. In Reading and Milton Keynes, older speakers are variably rhotic. Thus the vowels in NURSE, NORTH, FORCE, NEAR, SQUARE, letER and START may be followed by a weakly articulated [ɹ]. In Reading, rhotic pronunciations are the norm among working-class speakers over the age of 50, and among younger speakers in the case of the NURSE vowel only. In Milton Keynes, rhoticity is restricted to much older speakers.

L

In Reading and Milton Keynes, syllable-final /l/ is strongly labiovelarised and variably vocalised; in Hull, /l/ is lightly velarised in both syllable-initial and syllable-final positions.

8.2.3   Suprasegmentals

It is beyond the scope of this chapter to give an exhaustive description of intonation in the three accents. Instead, we give an example of the characteristic intonation of declarative sentences in a narrative style.

Both Reading and Milton Keynes have patterns that are close to what is described for RP (e.g. O'Connor & Arnold 1973; Cruttenden 1997), and appear very similar to each other. The basic pattern is for a mid or rising head followed by high falling nuclear tone.

Example 1: Reading

I sees them on a Tuesday and a Thursday night and most of the time

I'm with my boyfriend

Example 2: Milton Keynes

Their mum goes with like their uncle or something and then

everyone ends up dead in the end

For Hull, the basic pattern involves a low head followed by a low-to-mid or low-to-high rise starting on the nuclear syllable. If the nuclear syllable is utterance-final, the rise takes place on that syllable. If there are unstressed syllables following the nucleus, the nucleus is low and the first unstressed syllable is mid or high, any subsequent syllables remaining high.

Example 3: Hull

There's a little park over there and they leave broken bottles in the

park where little kids go.

8.3 *Levelling: change and continuity in three urban English accents*

The above descriptions strongly suggest that the accents of Milton Keynes, Reading and Hull are converging in both inventory and realisations. Yet, there are still marked differences between them, especially, of course, when we compare Hull with the southern towns. What we are witnessing is the phenomenon of **dialect levelling** and by extension **accent levelling**, a process whereby differences between regional varieties are reduced, features which make varieties distinctive disappear, and new features emerge and are adopted by speakers over a wide geographical area (see also Cheshire, Edwards & Whittle 1993).

Explanations for levelling have been sought in the changing demographic patterns of the last 40 years, which have seen an increase in geographical mobility: the populations of inner cities have declined as inhabitants move out to the suburbs and dormitory towns, while the populations of smaller towns and cities, such as Cambridge, Norwich, Ipswich, Reading and Oxford, have increased (Dorling & Atkins 1995; Giddens 1997). In addition, post-Second World War efforts to rehouse those displaced by the war or living in sub-standard accommodation in inner cities led to the creation of 35 'new towns' across the country (Schaffer 1972). Evidence of an increase in social mobility is less clearly quantifiable but individual studies have shown a recent decrease in downward mobility, accompanied by an increase in the number of young men from blue-collar backgrounds taking up white-collar work (Marshall, Newby, Rose & Vogler 1988). Both vertical social mobility and lateral (geographical) mobility are likely to lead to the breakdown of the close-knit social networks associated with traditional working-class communities and thought to be influential in maintaining local linguistic norms (Milroy & Milroy 1992).

The projects discussed here were designed to explore the links between such geographical and social factors and dialect levelling. The MK project was a study of the emergence of a new dialect in the new town of Milton Keynes (Kerswill 1994a, b, 1996a; Kerswill & Williams 2000). In the second (the DL project), three towns were chosen as research sites, similar in size but differing in their geographical location, demographic characteristics and social composition. The choice of town was informed by the claim that highly mobile populations give rise to diffuse social network structures which in turn promote rapid dialect change (Trudgill 1986, 1992, 1996b) and that the kind of stable communities we find in old-established urban populations promote the enforcement of local conventions and norms, including linguistic norms (L. Milroy 1987b). Milton Keynes, designated in 1967 and built on a green-field site adjacent to the M1 motorway, lies within an 80-kilometre radius of several important urban centres, including London, Oxford, Coventry, Leicester and Cambridge. It is Britain's latest and fastest growing new town with a population that has increased from 40,000 in 1967 (MKDC 1990) to 176,000 by the time of the 1991 Census. Some 75% of the in-migrants to the town moved from other areas in the south-east, including London. In Milton Keynes, then, we have a socially fluid population made up of newcomers with aspirations to improve both their housing conditions and their employment prospects. Moreover, having arrived in the town, many residents continue to move within Milton Keynes itself (Williams & Kerswill 1997). Such instability hinders the formation of strong local ties and the kind of close-knit, stable social networks which reinforce linguistic norms and inhibit language change.

In complete contrast, Hull is a city of limited social and geographical mobility. Out-migration exceeds in-migration and a combination of related factors including high unemployment, poverty and poor educational achievement in the local schools means that both geographical and social mobility are severely curtailed. In addition, its geographical position 400 kilometres north of London on the extreme eastern seaboard, cut off from the south by the River Humber and remote from other large conurbations, means that, unlike for example Norwich, York or Reading, it has few commuters. In Hull, then, we expected to find speakers with strong local ties and the kind of networks that reinforce local norms.

Reading shares characteristics with both Hull and Milton Keynes. It is an old established town with a stable, local population, but its location in the prosperous M4 corridor, 60 kilometres west of London, has attracted international companies and new industries and, as a consequence, considerable numbers of in-migrants from a wide range of socio-economic groups.

Levelling has been shown to occur in mobile populations where there is a high level of dialect contact. In such areas individuals regularly find themselves in face-to-face interaction with speakers of other varieties, and in their efforts to accommodate to their interlocutors, tend to avoid features that are unusual or markedly regional, or which might lead to comprehension difficulties (Trudgill 1986: 25). Such individual acts of accommodation replicated throughout a population can lead to permanent language change as marked variants gradually disappear while the forms with the 'widest geographical (and social) usage' are retained (Trudgill 1986: 98). However, while first-generation migrants will adapt in minor ways to their new linguistic environment, they are nevertheless already adults who have passed the 'critical stage' of language acquisition (Lenneberg 1967; Kerswill 1996b) and are not likely to make major grammatical and phonological changes to their speech. Studies have reported the acquisition of 'easy features' and small changes in vowel quality as well as lexical and morpholexical borrowing in adult migrants (Yaeger-Dror 1994; Kerswill 1994a), but it is their children, the second-generation migrants, who are central to the linguistic focusing (i.e. a reduction in the amount of linguistic variability in a speech community; see Le Page 1980) that precedes the formation of a homogeneous variety.

In a new town such as Milton Keynes, children, who at the pre-school stage acquire their parents' accent, will encounter a range of accents as they start school and begin to expand their social contacts. By adolescence, a period when the need for autonomy from parents is accompanied by increasing loyalty to the peer group and strong pressure is exerted to conform to peer group norms, focusing can be expected to occur and features of the new levelled variety begin to emerge (Kerswill & Williams 2000). While levelling in a new town context can be explained in terms of second-generation speakers settling on forms already present in first-generation speakers, the spread of certain southern features to areas remote from London (e.g. Stuart-Smith this volume) is less easily accounted for. Moreover, if we accept that levelling results from accommodation between speakers in face-to-face interactions (Trudgill 1986: 54), it becomes difficult to account for the presence of southern features in the speech of, for example, northern teenagers who have little contact with southerners. Tourists, in-migrants and football supporters, considered to be instrumental in the diffusion of new features, can be discounted in the case of Hull. A more acceptable explanation may lie in the presence of 'language missionaries' (Trudgill 1986: 57) combined with attitudinal factors (see below for discussion). Thus, although levelling has been identified as a widespread phenomenon, the form it takes and the mechanisms by which it operates will differ according to local demographic and social factors, and it is to these that we turn our attention.

8.3.1 Milton Keynes: discontinuity and rapid change

The processes of focusing and levelling in areas of high social and geographical mobility can be illustrated with data from the MK project. While the data collection employed a cross-sectional or apparent time model, it was nevertheless possible to construct a chronological record of ongoing phonological change in an area that has seen massive demographic upheaval. The main body of data comprised recordings of two generations: children who had been born in Milton Keynes and their caregivers who had come to the town as migrants. They formed a socially homogeneous working-class sample, living on adjacent housing estates and attending three neighbouring schools. Samples of the pre-new town dialects of the small towns now incorporated into the new conurbation were collected in interviews with elderly men and women born in the early years of the century and resident in the area ever since. In addition, transcriptions of speakers born in the 1870s and 1880s were available in the form of SED data collected in the 1950s in the village of Stewkley, now on the outskirts of Milton Keynes (Orton & Tilling 1970). Thus, we have evidence from speakers whose birth dates span 100 years.

Changes in one vowel sound, in particular, illustrate the transition from distinct regional feature to levelled form. This is /aʊ/, the vowel in MOUTH (Table 8.2). Taking the elderly speakers' realisations as representative of an earlier stage (corroborated by the SED symbol used in words containing /aʊ/, as shown), we can see that the accent has changed radically with respect to this vowel: there is almost no overlap between the caregivers and children on the one hand and the elderly speakers on the other. But, in Milton Keynes, we cannot assume that this is a 'normal' community-based change, in which younger people either adopt forms from other varieties or produce innovations of their own. The rapid

Table 8.2 Percentage use of variants of MOUTH in Milton Keynes: interview data

	[ɛʊ̞]	[ɛɪ]	[ɛː]	[aː]	[æʊ]	[aʊ]
SED informants	✓					
Elderly						
(N = 4)	63.2	25.6	9.8		1.2	
Caregivers						
(N = 48)			11.7	17.2	38.6	31.5
Children						
(N = 48)			10.5	8.7	13.9	65.9

Note: The scores given for interview data are obtained by finding a mean score for each subject based on approximately 20 tokens per speaker, and calculating the group mean.

change that has taken place in Milton Keynes is due to the lack of social continuity between the young speakers and the old: most of our child subjects had grandparents living elsewhere, a discontinuity that we believe is reflected in the distribution of variants for this vowel. In place of continuity, we have an incoming group of adult first-generation migrants bringing with them a spectrum of variants, ranging from the London monophthong [ɛː] to the Scots [ʉ], with [æʊ], the variant used by many south-eastern speakers, being the most common. While all the parental variants occurred in the children's data, especially in that of the 4-year-olds, it was clear that the older children were rejecting the more marked variants of their parents' accents, including [æʊ], which presumably spread from London, and were settling on the RP-like, non-regional variant [aʊ]. In sum, the establishment of the new town has led to a rapid shift consisting of three distinct stages: first, before the advent of the new town there was a period of stability during which [ɛʊ̞] predominated; second, we find a shorter period during which [æʊ], the form used by the migrants of the 1970s, was favoured; finally, this variant gave way to the non-regionally marked [aʊ] of the new generation of native-born young people – a form which, as our research in Reading shows, is increasingly characteristic of a wide area in the south-east. Later in the chapter we return to the issue of geographical dialect levelling in this region.

Changes in the GOAT diphthong, however, present a somewhat different picture. While there is a similar break between the pre- and post-new town forms, we find that the discontinuity is overlaid by the spread of an innovation at the expense of older variants. At the time of the SED research, GOAT was represented by two phonemes given phonetically as [ʌʊ] and [ʊə], the former used in words such as *throat* and *dough* and the latter in a lexical set including *road* and *coat*. In the audio recordings of the elderly Milton Keynes residents, the former has replaced the latter, and the result is centralised to [əʊ] or [əʊ̞]. None of these older variants was at all common in the recordings of our parent cohort, however, the majority of whom, being from London and the south-east, favoured [ʌʊ] (Table 8.3) which Wells (1982: 308) cites as the main Cockney variant. As might be expected, [ɐʊ] was also the most common variant in the recordings of the 4-year-olds, who were clearly modelling their speech on that of their caregivers. However, as Table 8.3 demonstrates, the older children appeared to be moving away from the central-to-back diphthong favoured by their parents and to be settling on a new variant with a central onset but a high front offset, typically [əʏ] or [ɐʏ] and sometimes unrounded to [əɪ] or [ɐɪ]. These fronted variants are new, since they are not part of the older rural dialects of the region, nor are they characteristic of traditional RP or older London speech. The children along with some of the younger caregivers are introducing these new variants to Milton Keynes. As with MOUTH, this vowel is in fact participating in a change affecting the whole south-east region (Torgersen 1997), a point we return to below.

8.3.2 Demography, network type and change in three towns

The results described above illustrate a number of principles that might be derived from studies of areas of intensive dialect contact (see also Chambers 1992): there is normally no historical continuity with the locality; marked regional forms are disfavoured; majority rather than minority forms win out; and, from initial diffusion, focusing takes place over one or two generations. The Milton Keynes data, however, could only partially illustrate two further principles (Kerswill & Williams 2000). The first is that the structure of the new speech community is seen in adolescents, not in pre-adolescent children. As the oldest children in the Milton Keynes project were just 12, it was not possible to make strong predictions about adolescent behaviour. We could only assume that the tendencies they exhibited as young teenagers would be confirmed in later adolescence. The follow-up Dialect Levelling project focused on adolescents, an age group who are approaching maturity in their *knowledge* of adult linguistic norms, including style shifting, and yet who experience strong peer group

Table 8.3 Percentage use of variants of GOAT in Milton Keynes

	[əɪ]~[ɐɪ]	[əʏ]~[ɐʏ]	[ɐʊ]~[ɐʊ] also [oː]
Caregivers (N = 48)	3.5	37.3	60.0
4-year-olds (N = 16)	13.5	30.2	55.7
8-year-olds (N = 16)	12.9	53.6	33.3
12-year-olds (N = 16)	3.0	68.6	28.2

Note: The children's data are taken from the elicitation tasks; those of the caregivers are taken from the interviews. The caregivers' scores include the [oː] used by five mothers from outside the south-east of England.

pressure to differentiate themselves from the older generation and to adhere to the norms of their own age group. It was assumed, then, that evidence of linguistic innovation, including levelling tendencies, would be apparent among the subjects recorded for this study.

The second principle that could not be fully explored in the Milton Keynes project concerns the relationship between network characteristics and language change. Milton Keynes offered limited scope for the study of *differences* between social network types. By its very nature, a new town population is composed of mobile individuals who, in adapting to life in a new environment, contract numerous weak and uniplex ties. Elements that are necessary for the formation of strong local networks, such as links with close kin living in the neighbourhood, a common work-place with friends and neighbours, and shared out-of-work activities with workmates (Milroy 1987b), are rare. Thus, while the Milton Keynes data enabled us to demonstrate that loose and diffuse network structures promote rapid language change (see Milroy & Milroy 1992; Kerswill & Williams 2000), there was no opportunity to explore the opposite claim that close-knit networks inhibit language change. By extending the project to include Hull and Reading it was possible to compare towns whose contrasting demographic characteristics give rise to a range of network types.

The city of Hull provides a complete contrast with Milton Keynes. Its remote location on the east coast limits geographical mobility, and upward social mobility is restricted by one of the highest unemployment rates in the country. In the district where the research was conducted, 44% of the heads of household were 'not in the labour market' compared with a national average of 16% (OFSTED 1993). The teenagers who took part in the project had all grown up in close proximity to each other on the extensive council estate situated on the periphery of the city. In many cases, as Table 8.4 indicates, parents and even grandparents had spent most of their lives on the same estate. Thus, the teenagers' and their parents' networks were dense and multiplex and anchored very firmly in North Hull. The Milton Keynes families, in contrast, had migrated from many parts of the country and a number of the children had been born elsewhere, moving to the new town in the first few years of their lives. Reading shares characteristics with both towns. It has stable, long-established local communities as well as a mobile population of commuters and workers in the new high technology industries. Unlike Hull, however, it has near full employment and the potential, at least, for social mobility.

In the DL project, we have supplemented the ethnographic information obtained in the interviews by using subjects' birthplaces together with the birthplaces of their parents as a simple analogue of social network density. This gives us a measure of the *localness* of the network, which can be expected to correlate with density. Furthermore, instead of looking at individual speakers, we obtain a picture of the localness of the networks in each sampling district as a whole. Table 8.4 shows this information for the working-class subjects in each town. As can readily be seen, Milton Keynes is clearly differentiated from Hull and Reading, both of which have a large majority of families with strong local ties.

Table 8.4 Birthplace of working-class adolescents and their parents in Hull, Milton Keynes and Reading (DL project)

	HULL			MILTON KEYNES			READING		
	BORN	Mother's b'place	Father's b'place	BORN	Mother's b'place	Father's b'place	BORN	Mother's b'place	Father's b'place
Girls									
1	Hull*	Withernsea		Scotland	Scotland	Scotland	Reading	Reading	Reading
2	Hull*	Hull*	Hull*	Milton K	Halifax	London	Reading	Reading	Reading
3	Hull*	Hull	Hull	Luton	Hampshire	Watford	Reading	Guyana	Guyana
4	Hull*	Hull*	Hull*	London	London	London	Germany	Reading	Reading
5	Hull*	Hull*	Hull*	Milton K	Bletchley	Bletchley	Reading	India	Reading
6	Hull*	Hull*	Hull*	Lancashire	Lancashire	Liverpool	Reading	Cambridge	Reading
7	Hull*	Hull	Hull	Blackpool	London		Reading	Reading	Reading
8	Hull	Hull	Spain	Bletchley	Stevenage	Ireland	Reading	Reading	Reading
Boys									
1	Hull*	Hull*	Hull*	Milton K	Bletchley	Bletchley	Reading	Reading	Reading
2	Hull	Hull	Hull	London	Essex	London	Reading	Reading	Reading
3	Hull*	Hull*	Hull*	Milton K	London	London	Reading	Reading	Reading
4	Hull	Hull	Hull	Milton K	Suffolk	Ireland	Reading	Reading	Reading
5	Chester	Hull*	Lincs	Newbury	Berkshire	Tadley	Reading	Reading	Reading
6	Hull*	Hull*	Hull*	Ireland	Halifax	Ireland	Reading	Reading	Reading
7	Hull*	Hull*	Hull	Milton K	London	London	Reading	Reading	London
8	Hull*	Hull*	Hull	Milton K	London	Jamaica	Reading	Reading	Ireland

* born and still resident on the estate

Table 8.5 Percentage use of variants of PRICE in Reading: interview data

	[a̠ɪ]	[ɒ̣ɪ]	[ɑɪ]	[ɔɪ]	[ʌ̣ɪ]	[ʌɪ]
Elderly (N = 4)		12.4	47.8	21.8	1.7	15.7
Girls (N = 8)	2.8	21.2	45.1	21.1	4.3	5.1
Boys (N = 8)	0.6	19.1	63.7	13.7	2.7	

Table 8.6 Percentage use of variants of PRICE in Milton Keynes: interview data

	[a̠ɪ]	[ɒ̣ɪ]	[ɑɪ]	[ɔɪ]	[ʌ̣ɪ]	[ʌɪ]
Elderly (N = 4)			24.4	56.6	15.3	3.4
Girls (N = 8)	25.4	44.6	29.2	0.5		
Boys (N = 8)	1.0	38.0	60.0			

As might be expected, the linguistic results reflect the demographic patterning found in the three towns. Tables 8.5 and 8.6 show the results for the PRICE vowel for Reading and Milton Keynes. Table 8.5 suggests that there has been little change in the pronunciation of this vowel in traditional Reading English over three generations. The predominant variant is a back, diphthongal [ɑɪ]: however, there are also raised back/centralised variants which, though occurring less in teenage speech than in the speech of the elderly, nevertheless reflect the continuity that is present in the community and the close contact many of our teenage informants had with the older generation. This continuity is not present in Milton Keynes, where the migrant families have little connection with the old people of the area. The results shown in Table 8.6 chime with our findings for MOUTH and GOAT: the old dialect forms have all but disappeared, with the raised back/centralised variants preferred by the elderly speakers almost completely absent from the speech of the young people.

8.3.3   Hull: continuity and resistance to change

It is in Hull, however, that the strongest evidence of close-knit networks acting as a conservative force and resisting change can be seen. The realisation of the PRICE vowel in Hull is quite distinctive. Characteristic of the old dialect of Hull and the surrounding area of Holderness is an allophonic distinction between a diphthong [aɪ̞] and a monophthong [aː] in this vowel (Trudgill 1990: 69). The former precedes voiceless consonants in words such as *bright, like, pipe*, and the latter, voiced consonants as in *bride, five, mind*. The following description was published by the English Dialect Society in 1877:

> *Long i* as in night, tribe, &c. This has two distinct powers [aa...y] or [aa...] and [ey]. To a stranger it seems as if these were used indiscriminately, but such is far from being the case. Each follows certain well defined and fixed rules.
>
> (1) When this long *i* is followed (*a*) by a flat consonant, *i.e.* by the letters *b, d, g* hard, *j*, (or *g* soft) *v, z* (or *s* with *z* sound); (*β*) the liquids *l, m* and *n* ; (*γ*) another vowel; it has the sound of [aa...y], which in N. and W. has a great tendency to become [aa...].

tribe	[thraa...yb] or [thraa...b]
rive	[raa...yv]
...	

> (2) When, on the other hand, long *i* is followed by a sharp consonant, *i.e.* by one of the letters *c* (or *s* with sharp sound) *f, k, p, t*, or the remaining liquid, *r*, it is pronounced [ey], *e.g.*: –

rice	[reys]
tight	[teyt]

(Ross, Stead & Holderness 1877: 9)

Today, the distinction between two distinct allophones in these environments is maintained, although the quality seems to have changed in that the monophthong is near-categorical before voiced consonants, while the diphthong preceding voiceless consonants has been lowered – if we can accept Ross *et al.*'s transcription [ey] as representing IPA [eɪ]. Thus, in the Hull teenagers' speech, the two vowels are typically pronounced [aː] and [aɪ̯]. Table 8.7 shows their distribution in both middle-class and working-class groups. Of the 16 middle-class teenagers in the sample, only one observed the distinction between voiceless and voiced contexts. The older working-class speakers on the other hand observed the rule categorically, as did all the young working-class students with the exception of one boy. Thus, while the two allophones are merged in middle-class Hull speech, working-class children appear to be preserving some of the more complex patterning of the older local variety.

Further evidence of the strength of local linguistic norms in Hull can be seen in the distribution of H in lexical words, as in *house, home, hand*. Milton Keynes, Reading and Hull are all located in the extensive area covering most of central England where H-dropping is a feature of the traditional dialects (Upton & Widdowson 1996). As might be expected, the elderly speakers in all three towns had few instances of initial [h]. In contrast, the working-class adolescents in both Reading and Milton Keynes showed a surprisingly high use of the standard form. It might be suggested that since H is a very salient feature, the young people were style shifting and accommodating to the fieldworker. This

Table 8.7 The PRICE vowel with following voiceless and voiced consonants: middle-class and working-class speakers in Hull (%)

(a) With following voiceless consonant, e.g. *bright*

	[aḭ]	[aˑɪ]	[aː]
MC boys	100	0	0
MC girls	100	0	0
WC boys	100	0	0
WC girls	100	0	0
WC elderly	100	0	0

(b) With following voiced consonant, e.g. *bride*

	[aḭ]	[aˑɪ]	[aː]
MC boys	75.0	20.0	5.0
MC girls	92.5	7.5	0.0
WC boys	7.5	10.0	82.5
WC girls	0.0	25.7	74.2
WC elderly	0.0	0.0	100.0

Note: Each adolescent subject read the following words: *bright, knife, lighter, bike, whiter; bride, five, pint, smile, wider.* Scores for the elderly are derived from the interview data: 20 tokens per speaker were transcribed.

was clearly not the case in Hull, however, where the adolescents matched the older speakers in their use of the non-standard variant, as shown in Figure 8.1. An explanation for the differences, however, might lie in the very salience of this feature. In such a close-knit, territorially bounded community as the Hull estate, use of the standard form is perceived as 'posh' (see Kerswill & Williams 1997)

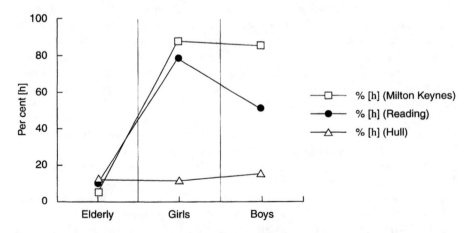

Fig. 8.1 Percentage use of [h], working-class speakers: interview data

and there is strong pressure to avoid it. We discuss further explanations for the contrasting patterns of Hull and the two southern towns in the next section.

To judge from the data so far presented, working-class teenagers in Hull appear to be resisting any movement towards standardisation of accent features; the close-knit and territorially defined nature of their community appears to inhibit language change. However, one of the motivations for studying adolescent speech was that it was in this age group that we expected to find evidence of linguistic innovation along with levelling tendencies. Data on a group of consonantal variables indicated that the Hull teenagers can be as ready to adopt innovations as their southern counterparts.

For some years now, researchers have been documenting the progress of a series of consonantal features which originated in London, and are rapidly being adopted by young speakers across Britain. The replacement of /t/ by a glottal stop [ʔ] in word-medial, intervocalic position (as in *letter*) and in word-final position (as in *cut it out*) is a feature of London or Cockney English which has spread so widely across both geographical and social space that it has come to be 'perceived as a stereotype of urban British speech' (Milroy, Milroy & Hartley 1994: 3), present not only in the working-class varieties but also making inroads into RP (Wells 1994). The extent of glottalisation in the interview data of the Milton Keynes and Reading adolescents described here was not surprising, given (a) that these two towns are close to London and (b) that T-glottalling is a common feature in southern English English, present both in older Reading speech and in the speech of the majority of new migrants to Milton Keynes, who originate from London or the south-east of England. More surprising were the results for Hull, where T-glottalling does not form part of the original dialect nor of the dialect of the surrounding East Riding, according to the SED (Orton & Halliday 1963), though it is now used to some extent by middle-aged and elderly speakers. Young people in Hull appear to be using glottals as frequently as their southern counterparts, as shown in Table 8.8.

Similar patterns can be seen in the analysis of two further London features, the merger of /θ/ with /f/ (as in *thin*) and of /ð/ with /v/ in word-medial and word-final positions (as in *brother*; see Table 8.8). Like T-glottalling, these features appear to be spreading rapidly out of London. In Norwich, the mergers were totally absent from the speech of 11-year-olds in 1968, whereas they were 'very common indeed in the speech of working-class 16 year olds in 1983' (Trudgill 1986: 54). It was expected that the mergers would be present in the adolescents in Milton Keynes, given that Londoners account for 35% of in-migrants to the town, and the proximity of Reading to London would account for their adoption there, although they are absent from the speech of older residents. However, the data given in Table 8.8 demonstrate quite clearly that the mergers are now also found in working-class adolescent speech in Hull. The mergers form part of a group of features which also includes T-glottalling and the use of labiodental [ʋ] which seem to constitute a set of 'youth norms', adopted by young people in many areas of Great Britain (see Docherty & Foulkes, and Stuart-Smith this volume). Like their peers

Table 8.8 Three consonantal variables currently spreading in British English: interview data

		Middle Class		Working Class	
		Girls	Boys	Girls	Boys
Milton Keynes	% [ʔ] for intervocalic /t/	25.4	48.6	75.2	83.0
	% [f] for /θ/	7.1	36.1	55.8	87.8
	% [v] for non-initial /ð/	14.3	46.9	70.8	89.5
Reading	% [ʔ] for intervocalic /t/	29.5	14.1	92.2	100.0
	% [f] for /θ/	0.0	11.4	76.4	83.7
	% [v] for non-initial /ð/	0.0	6.4	87.4	93.7
Hull	% [ʔ] for intervocalic /t/	30.9	20.0	71.8	82.7
	% [f] for /θ/	9.6	16.5	63.2	90.7
	% [v] for non-initial /ð/	27.1	23.7	77.7	95.5

in other parts of Britain, young Hull speakers are adopting these innovative features in full measure.

8.3.4 Regionalism, mobility and youth norms

The patterns emerging from the data appear to point to a north–south divide, with young people in the southern towns rejecting older, regionally marked forms in favour of non-regional variants used over a wide area, while the working-class northern teenagers continue to adhere strongly to certain conservative local forms. The linguistic differences possibly reflect more general north–south divisions that have been widening since the late 1970s (Smith 1994), with the south of Britain, especially the south-east, experiencing increased economic activity and wealth while the north has undergone a corresponding decline in its prosperity. In a survey which ranked 280 British towns according to their prosperity (Champion & Green 1990), Milton Keynes and Reading are in third and ninth places respectively. Although Hull, as a city, is not listed, Smith (1994: 133) points out that 'even the worst performing towns in the south east scored higher than a substantial proportion of those in, say, Yorkshire and Humberside'. The relative prosperity of the southern towns makes social mobility an achievable goal. In Hull, however, where school leavers face one of the highest unemployment rates in the country, the 'intense pressure to reject non-standard dialects through routes such as the educational system' (Milroy & Milroy 1993: 60) has little impact on children who remain unconvinced of the value of education as a passport to social mobility and have little incentive to modify their accents.

Closely linked to increased economic prosperity are the population movements that have taken place in Britain since the 1970s. The main trends show an
overall movement from north to south, with the result that at present 58% of the
population live in the south, in an area which occupies only 40% of the land area
of the United Kingdom (Smith 1994). Important for a study of the spread of
accent features are the socio-economic characteristics of the migrants. According to Smith (1994: 232), 'migrants tend to be young, and the most mobile
among the population are those in their 20s. They are generally well educated
and are predominantly in professional and other non-manual jobs.' Thus, while
Milton Keynes and Reading have seen in-migration of all social classes including professional cadres, there has been little migration of any kind into Hull.
These factors are reflected in the school populations. In Milton Keynes, there
are two extensive secondary school campuses attended by most of the children
living in the town, an arrangement which results in a good deal of mixing at educational and social levels. A very different situation is found in Hull, where the
middle classes tend to live outside the city in the surrounding villages. 'Working-
class Hull is crammed within tight local authority boundaries with almost no
middle class hinterland – those families school their children in the East Riding'
(*The Observer*, 3 May 1998). Thus, there is little or no social mix in many of the
schools within the city and consequently little opportunity for the children to
interact regularly with a range of social groups. In addition, the remote location
of the housing estates, built on the very outskirts of the city, combined with the
strong tendency for families to remain on the estate for several generations,
means that in their early years children have little experience of coming into
contact with speakers of different varieties.

While structural factors can be advanced to account for some of the rapid
dialect changes in Milton Keynes and Reading, as well as for the more conservative speech patterns of the Hull youngsters, it is difficult to see how such factors might explain the enthusiastic adoption of the non-standard southern
consonantal variants [ʔ], [f] and [v] by working-class young people in northern
areas, as demonstrated in Table 8.8. It has been suggested that new variants can
be introduced by 'language missionaries' (Steinsholt, cited in Trudgill 1986), i.e.
individuals who move away from their native area for a period and then return,
having acquired new dialect features. As these individuals are still considered to
be 'insiders', their language is not rejected as that of outsiders might be (Trudgill
1986: 56). Although initially it appeared that the working-class Hull adolescents
had little or no contact with outsiders (Table 8.4), the ethnographic analysis
revealed that this was not uniformly the case. Two of the teenagers had spent
several months living in Lowestoft and Somerset respectively, and still visited
friends in these areas. While we have no evidence to suggest that these two particular adolescents were responsible for introducing new variants to Hull, they
permit us to demonstrate that even in areas of low population movement,
mobile individuals do exist. Other 'language missionaries' in the Hull context
might be older siblings serving in the armed forces or working outside the area.

It is also likely that affective factors play a part in the rapid spread of the southern features. Firstly, it has been suggested that this set of consonantal variables can be identified as 'youth norms' (Foulkes & Docherty in press). The tremendous increase in radio and TV stations and programmes directed at young people has led to the widespread use of informal and non-standard registers in the broadcast media, many of which emanate from London and the south. Adolescents throughout Britain are regularly exposed to southern accents, which in turn are associated with young people and youth culture. Second, the changes observed in the pronunciation of this group of consonants are from standard to non-standard, and are thus likely to be more acceptable to working-class speakers. Finally, variation in the consonants T and TH is possibly less salient for Hull speakers than, for example, variation in the realisation of H and of the vowels in STRUT or BATH. The adoption of southern, non-standard variants of T and TH does not affect a northerner's sense of regional identity. As for H-dropping, its continued use by the Hull adolescents is, we have argued, due to the strongly local nature of the networks of this group. Thus, by adopting non-standard southern features, the young Hull speakers are able to signal their identification with the peer group and youth culture, while at the same time retaining their strong links with both their social class and their region of origin. Cohen (1972: 26), in his work on subcultures, identifies the motivation that may lie behind the Hull adolescents' choice of linguistic forms when he suggests that young people 'negotiate a space for their own culture within the parent class culture. In this way they both create and express autonomy and difference from parents and maintain ... the parental identifications which support them.'

8.4   *Conclusion*

The data presented here for Reading and Milton Keynes show similarities between the varieties used by the current generation of adolescents in the two towns, although the mechanisms by which changes take place are quite different. In Milton Keynes, massive demographic change has resulted in discontinuity of dialect transmission followed by focusing in the first native-born generation, while in Reading linguistic changes are more gradual. The resulting forms are quite similar, however, and strongly suggest a gradual move in the southern counties to adopt more standard-like or at least less localised variants. Hull, with its greater geographical isolation and relative lack of opportunities for young people, is linguistically more conservative. Yet its adolescents remain open to non-standard linguistic innovations coming from outside. A comparison of language variation in the three towns shows that levelling is present in each, but that the underlying processes differ. Structural factors, such as migration patterns, economic prosperity, geographical distance, social class and social network type, clearly play important roles, but these can be mediated by affective factors, such as, for teenagers, identification with the peer group and the locality on the one hand, and with a wider youth culture on the other.

9

South East London English: discrete *versus* continuous modelling of consonantal reduction

Laura Tollfree

9.1 *South East London English: introduction*

London covers a vast area and it is impossible to include a comprehensive study of its linguistic features here.[1] The data referred to derive from a survey carried out for Tollfree (1996). Labovian interviews were recorded during 1990–4 with 90 informants from the South East London region encompassing Peckham, Sydenham and Penge (representing largely working-class communities), and Dulwich, Beckenham and Bromley (middle-class communities). The remarks made in this chapter pertain only to these suburbs, although I draw comparison throughout to Wells (1982), bearing in mind his claim that the working-class accent of London is 'the most influential source of phonological innovation in England and perhaps in the whole English-speaking world' (1982: 301).

The suburbs studied radiate out progressively on a south-eastern axis, falling short of the green belt area in Kent. There is much internal differentiation in the general South Eastern urban/suburban region, in terms of a strong inner versus outer London contrast. Peckham, Dulwich, Sydenham and Penge have a truly London identity, while Beckenham and Bromley show more diversity. Some Beckenham and Bromley residents rarely visit the city centre, preferring Bromley and environs for recreation and shopping. Others commute daily to central London for work, and/or spend leisure time in the city, and identify more as Londoners than as suburban South Easterners.

Inner-city Peckham has long been a working-class area. Its progressive decline as a strategic centre for shopping and commerce has been apparent since the 1960s, but there is still a busy High Street. Peckham is served by major railway and bus routes to central London, which contributes to its 'inner-city' ambience. Sydenham and Penge were popular residential districts in the first half of the twentieth century, with a mixed upper-middle-, middle- and working-class population. Today, they have a marked working-class population and, like Peckham, a somewhat 'inner-city' character. Dulwich divides into the middle- and upper-middle-class residential areas of West Dulwich and Dulwich Village, and working-class East Dulwich. Dulwich, Sydenham and Penge are all served by frequent rail and bus links to central London, and are popular commuter areas.

Beckenham and Bromley are important commuter residential zones, which until recently were almost exclusively middle-class. Bromley in particular has a higher working-class population than in the late 1970s. Thirteen miles from London city centre, Bromley forms one of a number of important foci for commerce and retail in the southern metropolitan zone. This may have contributed to its present-day social diversity. There was considerable migration to the Bromley area in the inter-war period, notably from London and urban Essex. Bromley has flourished at the expense of neighbouring centres, succeeding in attracting more high-threshold outlets, and has undergone a large-scale centre improvement in the 1990s. Its future development is almost guaranteed with the opening of the Channel Tunnel and the new rail link from central London throughout the south-east (Hamilton 1991).

9.1.1   Methodology

Informants were randomly selected and grouped according to suburb, accent group, and age. Across the suburbs, informants' speech fell along an accent continuum ranging from maximally to minimally broad regionalised varieties. In order to embody a useful data set for theoretical investigation (rather than to constitute a typologically balanced study), two general accent groups were distinguished. One group encompasses medially to maximally broad varieties (South East London English, or SELE). The other covers regionalised forms of RP which fall towards the minimally broad end of the continuum (South East London Regional Standard, or SELRS, the local form of near-RP).[2] Accents falling part-way between the two groups were assigned to an accent group on the basis of conversational material. There was some overlap, but no direct correlation, between accent group and socio-economic group (i.e. SELE and working class, SELRS and middle class). 25 SELE informants and 37 SELRS informants aged 15–30, and 7 SELE informants and 21 SELRS informants aged 54–89 were interviewed. Interviews were conducted over two meetings of approximately 45 minutes each, and were carried out under different speech situations ranging from formal to informal. Finally, the interviewer discussed the informant's perception of his/her system, to explore how this compared with attested results from earlier recordings, and to identify attitudinal factors. The recordings were transcribed auditorily using a standard IPA system. A subpart of the recordings was re-analysed after an interval to provide a measure of consistency.

9.2 *Descriptive material*

9.2.1 Vowels

Comments

KIT
Older speakers have [ɪ]; the younger group have [ɪ] or a slightly centralised [ï].

DRESS
Older speakers have [ɛ], and some variants with schwa-type offglide [ɛᵊ].
Younger speakers have [ɛ] or a more open form [ɛ̞].

Table 9.1 South East London vowels – summary

	SELRS	SELE
KIT	ɪ ~ ï	ɪ ~ ï
DRESS	ɛ ~ ɛ̞	ɛ ~ ɛ̞
TRAP	æ	æ
LOT	ɒ ~ ö	ɒ ~ ö
STRUT	ɐ ~ ʌ	ɐ ~ a
FOOT	ʊ ~ ü̞	ʊ
BATH	ɑː ~ ɑ̈ː ~ ɒ̈ː	ɑː ~ ɑ̈ː ~ ɒ̈ː
CLOTH	ɒ ~ ö	ɒ ~ ö
NURSE	ɜː ~ əː	ɜː ~ əː
FLEECE	iː ~ ï(ː)	iː ~ ï(ː) ~ ᵊiː ~ iːᵊ
FACE	eɪ ~ ɛ̞ɪ ~ ë̞ɪ	aɪ ~ aɪ ~ aɪ
PALM	ɑː ~ ɑ̈ ~ ɒ̈ː	ɑː ~ ɑ̈ ~ ɒ̈ː
THOUGHT	ɔː ~ o̞ː	ɔː ~ o̞ː ~ ɒʊ ~ o̞ː
GOAT	ʌʊ⁽ʷ⁾ ~ ɤʊ ~ ɤə ~ ə̞ʊ	ʌʊ ~ ʌɤ ~ ɐɤ ~ aː
GOAL	ɒʊ⁽ʷ⁾ ~ ɒɤ ~ a̱ʊ	ɒʊ⁽ʷ⁾ ~ ɒɤ ~ a̱ʊ
GOOSE	ʉ⁽ʷ⁾ː ~ ʉ̈ː ~ ʉ̱ː	ʉ⁽ʷ⁾ː ~ ʉ̈ː ~ ʉ̱ː
GHOUL	ʊː	ʊː
PRICE	aɪ ~ a̱ɪ ~ äɪ	ɑ̞ɪ ~ ɑː ~ ɑ̈ː
FIRE	aɪ(j)ə	ɑɪ(j)ə ~ a̱ɪ(j)ə ~ a̱ː ~ ɑ̈ː
CHOICE	ɔɪ ~ oɪ	ɔɪ ~ oɪ
MOUTH	aʊ ~ aɤ	æː⁽ʊ⁾ ~ ɛː
POWER	aʊə ~ aɤə	æʊwə ~ æː ~ æ̞ː
NEAR	ɪː ~ ɪᵊ	ɪː ~ ɪᵊ ~ iːa
SQUARE	ɛ̞ː⁽ᵊ⁾ ~ e̞ː⁽ᵊ⁾	eː ~ eː⁽ᵊ⁾
START	ɑː ~ ɑ̈ː ~ ɒ̈ː	ɑː ~ ɑ̈ː ~ ɒ̈ː
NORTH	ɔː ~ o̞ː	ɔː ~ o̞ː ~ ɒʊ ~ o̞ː
FORCE	ɔː ~ o̞ː	ɔː ~ o̞ː ~ ɒʊ ~ o̞ː
CURE	jʉə ~ jʊ̞ə ~ jɔː	jʉə ~ jʊ̞ə ~ jʉː ~ jʊ̞ː ~ jɔː
happy	i(ː)	i(ː)
letter	ə ~ ə̞	ə ~ ə̞ ~ ɐ
comma	ə ~ ə̞	ə ~ ə̞ ~ ɐ
horses	ɪ ~ ï	ɪ ~ ï

TRAP

TRAP has [æ] or [æ:] for all speakers. This is slightly lower than the variant found by Hughes & Trudgill (1996) for Cockney: [ɛ]. They also identify a diphthong [ɛi].

LOT/CLOTH

For all speakers a fully back, rounded [ɒ] or, especially in less formal styles, a slightly centralised variant [ö].

STRUT

For SELRS speakers [ɐ] or [ʌ] (cf. the fully back [ʌ] standardly given for RP or near-RP, e.g. Wells 1982: 305). SELE has [ɐ] or [a], similar to East End Cockney [ɐ̞]/[a] (Wells 1982: 305) or [æ] (Hughes & Trudgill 1996).

FOOT

Older speakers use [ʊ], as standardly given for the London region and RP. Younger speakers of SELE maintain the use of [ʊ], but SELRS speakers under *c.* 30 typically have unrounded, centralised variants, e.g. [ÿ]. The contrast between the two age groups of SELRS is very marked, and all local (and many non-local) speakers are highly sensitive to it.

BATH/PALM/START

All speakers demonstrate variation within a range of fully low variants: fully back [ɑ:], slightly advanced [ɑ̟:], and for the broader speakers back/slightly fronted variants with light rounding, such as [ɒ̈:]. (Fully back, unrounded realisations have been given for the London region generally, e.g. Wells 1982: 305.)

NURSE

[ɜ:] for older speakers, and [ɜ:] or a centralised [ə:] for the younger group. There is no rounding for the NURSE set. (Wells (1982: 305) finds lightly rounded variants for Cockney.)

FLEECE

Typically [i:] for both age groups. In older speech, a laxed, centralised vowel [ï] or [ï:] may also occur, especially in casual styles. Broader varieties also have [ᵊi:] or [i:ᵊ] with schwa-like on- or off-glides for all age groups.

FACE

Older SELRS speakers use either [eɪ]/[e¹], or [ɛɪ]. The first element of these variants may be slightly centralised. There is invariably a more open, and also sometimes a centralised, start to the diphthong in younger speech: [ë̞ɪ]. For SELE speakers, the first element of the diphthong is usually further lowered to [ɐɪ] or [aɪ], and may be slightly rounded: e.g. [ɒ̈ɪ]. Wells (1982: 307) reports similar rounded variants ([ɛ̈ɪ]), as well as unrounded forms ([ɐɪ]), for 'Popular London' speech. He supplies [æɪ] and [aɪ] for broader (Cockney) speech, for which Hughes & Trudgill (1996) give [æɪ].

THOUGHT/NORTH/FORCE

The findings support Wells (1982: 310) and Hughes & Trudgill (1996) regarding a distinction present in London, but absent in RP, between pairs such as *pause* and *paws*, *board* and *bored*. Specifically, across the social continuum, there is a small phonetic distinction for both age groups between items with a closed syllable, such as *lord* (in the region of [oː]), and those with an open syllable, such as *law* (in the region of [ɔː]). Inflected items retain the nucleus of the underived form, hence *paws* and *bored* have the [ɔː] of *paw* and *bore*. Variants are typically slightly advanced for younger speakers: [o̞ː]/[ɔ̞ː]. Realisations are monophthongal in SELRS, but may be slightly diphthongal in SELE, e.g. [ɔ̞ᵘ]. (Hughes & Trudgill (1996) also report a diphthongal realisation for this set in Cockney.) Broader speakers also use unrounded variants: [ʌ̞ː]/[ɔ̞ː].

GOAT

For older SELRS speakers, the typical realisation in GOAT is [ʌʊ], with a fully back first element (compare the RP variants [ɜʊ] or [əʊ]; Wells 1982). Sometimes the diphthong is accompanied by strong labialisation, [ʌʊʷ]; or has a raised start, [ɤʊ]; or has a centred second element, e.g. [ɤə]. For younger speakers, the start is typically advanced and closer, e.g. [əʊ] (but for none of these speakers are there variants with starting points as advanced as those reported by Hughes & Trudgill (1996) for Cockney, [æʉ]). The difference between the age groups indicates a centring change for the first element (in the direction of RP [əʊ]). For all SELE speakers there are variants in the region of [ʌʊ], [ʌɤ] and [ɐɤ], and long monophthongal realisations [aː], especially in frequently used items such as *no*. Wells (1982: 309) also reports monophthongs for Cockney, but these are more in the region of 'a frontish [ʌː]'. The diphthongal realisations are similar to those given by Wells (1982: 308) for Cockney, which start in the region of [æ] or [ɐ], and move towards [ɤ̈].

Where the GOAT vowel is found in word-final position, as in e.g. *barrow*, it may be reduced to schwa or open [ɐ].

The split between GOAT and GOAL appears to be categorical in South East London for all speakers (including near-RP speakers). This phenomenon is also known as the *Roland-roller* rule (Wells 1982), and is characteristic of the London vernacular. Whilst the variation between the variants is discrete, continuous variation is demonstrated within each of the categories.

GOAL

GOAL items are realised with [ɒʊ], [ɒʊʷ], [ɒɤ] or [aʊ]. Even in local RP, this alternation appears to be categorical. The *Roland-roller* rule involves the realisation of /l/ in syllable rhymes as either a velarised consonantal reflex, or a vocoid in the region of [ɤ] or [ʊ]. The realisation of underlying /l/ triggers the shift of the nucleus of the GOAT class of words in a specific way: in morphologically underived forms the nucleus is realised as [ɒʊ] before tautosyllabic underlying /l/, whilst surfacing as [ʌʊ] elsewhere. Taking morpheme boundaries into consideration, [ʌʊ] and [ɒʊ] are in complementary distribution. *Roland* therefore has [ʌʊ] rather than [ɒʊ] because the vowel + /l/ sequence is not tautosyllabic. This pattern breaks down in morphologically complex (derived) forms, e.g. *roller*, in which the [ɒʊ] of the underived stem *roll* is retained despite the fact that /l/ is no longer tautosyllabic on the surface.

GOOSE

Older speakers of both SELRS and SELE have in GOOSE a high vowel which is back, but not fully so: [ʉ:], [ʉ̈:] or [ʉ̈:]. In open syllables it may be accompanied by strong labialisation: [ʉ:ʷ]. Younger speakers typically have more open variants, in the region of [ʉ̈:]. The vocalic split between GOOSE and GHOUL is apparently complete in this region (including near-RP speech). Presumably this distinctiveness is a development of the allophonic variation between *two* and *tool* noted by Wells (1982: 303) for London and the South East generally (but not for RP).

GHOUL

This item is included to investigate the extent of vocalic split in /l/-final items of the GOOSE set. For older and younger speakers, GHOUL items typically have vowels in the region of [ʊ:] for both accent groups. Note that whilst the variation between the variants is discrete, variation within the categories is continuous (as with the GOAT-GOAL split above).

PRICE

For older and younger SELRS speakers, PRICE has [aɪ] or [a̱ɪ], with a slightly retracted start, or [äɪ] with a somewhat centralised start. The first element often has rounding, which is more marked in broader speech: [ɒ̞ɪ]. Across the age range in SELE, PRICE typically has a retracted, somewhat rounded starting element, which can be fully back: [ɑɪ]. The second element can also be centralised, and is often very brief or wholly lacking. This renders PRICE monophthongal: [ɑ̞] or [ɑ̞:]. Hughes & Trudgill (1996) give [ɑɪ] for Cockney PRICE, with an unrounded starting point. Wells reports [ɑ] or, 'in more vigorous, "dialectal" Cockney', a rounded [ɒ] as starting points. He also finds that the second element can be absent, and in compensation the first element may be lengthened (1982: 308).

FIRE

FIRE has [aɪə] or [aɪjə] for older and younger SELRS speakers. This is consistent with Wells' (1982: 303) observation of less smoothing in FIRE in London Regional Standard than in RP. In SELE the first element may be retracted as far back as [a̱] or even [ɑ], or may be centralised, [ä]. The first element may also be lightly rounded in broader speech. Particularly in broader speech there may be smoothing, e.g. to [a̱:] or [ɑ̞:].

CHOICE

Typically, the nucleus ranges between [oɪ] and [ɔɪ]. Younger speakers, especially in less broad varieties, also use variants with an advanced or centralised first element: [öɪ].

MOUTH

For the older SELRS group the diphthong for the MOUTH set is [aʊ] or [aɤ]. SELE speakers tend to use variants with a closer start and a second element of very short duration, [æːᵁ], or a long monophthong, [æː] (as is reported for Cockney by Wells 1982: 309). The younger speakers also have [aʊ] or [aɤ] at the less broad end of the continuum. At the broader end, however, there is [æʊ], a variant with a very close start, sometimes even as high as [ɛ]. It is also sometimes retracted, e.g. [ɜʊ].

POWER

For the SELRS speakers, POWER has a triphthong, [aʊə] or [aɤə]. This includes regionalised near-RP speech. This is in accord with the corresponding observation by Wells for POWER in London Regional Standard speech, and can be contrasted with RP where there is more smoothing (1982: 303). For SELE speakers, there are variants with a closer start, often with glide insertion: [æʊwə], or a long monophthong [æː]. Broader speakers, however, have [æʊwə], a variant with a very close first element, and again the long monophthong [æː], or a raised version, [æː].

NEAR

There is much variation in the nucleus used for NEAR, from [ɪː] to [ɪːᵊ]. The monophthong can be quite open: [ɪː]; a small number of tokens were also found of a more open variant, [eː]. In young SELE speech there is also a diphthong with a very open second element, [iːa] (similar to the 'almost [iə]' realisations reported for Cockney by Wells 1982: 305).

SQUARE

Older SELRS speakers have a long monophthong [ẹː] or [ɛ̣ː], perhaps with a schwa-type off-glide, e.g. [ɛ̣ːᵊ], [ɛ̣ᵊ]. Younger speakers have either [ɛᵊ] or a slightly more open version, [ɛᵊ]. SELE speakers tend to have closer variants, [eː], [eᵊ] or [eːᵊ].

CURE

In terms of lexical incidence, CURE items divide into two categories (a dichotomy is also noted for RP by Wells 1982: 287). Items in which the nucleus is preceded by [j] typically have [ʉə]/[ʊ̈ə], e.g. *pure*. There may be smoothing to [ʉː] or [ʊ̈ː], especially in broader speech. Other items typically have [ɔ] or [ɔː] (thereby merging with THOUGHT/NORTH as realised in open syllables). Whilst there is inter- and intra-speaker variation in lexical incidence, it is more predictable (although not categorical) for younger speakers. This is in accord with Wells' (1982: 287) remarks for RP that 'speakers who pronounce some or all of *poor, more, your* and *sure* with /ɔː/ . . . are on the increase'. Social class is apparently not an influencing factor in the patterning of lexical incidence.

happY

[i] and [iː] are the preferred realisations in happY for older and younger speakers across the accent continuum (RP has [ɪ]: Wells 1982: 319; Hughes & Trudgill

1996 give /i/ for Cockney). Wells (1982: 319) finds a range of diphthongal realisations from [əi] to [ɪi] (less broad) in the London speech he examined, but no diphthongs were found in the South East London survey.

lettER/commA
The vowel in commA and lettER ranges between [ə] and [ə̝] for all speakers. Broader SELE speakers also have a rather open variant [ɐ], which is particularly noticeable utterance-finally.

9.2.2   Consonants

P, T, K
Speakers in both age groups demonstrate variable glottal reinforcement/ replacement of /p/ and /k/. This occurs pre-consonantally and pre-pausally, e.g. *stopcock* [stɒˀpkɒˀk], *keep* [kʰiːˀpʰ]; intervocalically, e.g. *hacker* [hæˀkɐ]; and before a nasal, e.g. *thanks* [hæŋˀks], *happen* [hæʔn̩]. The association of [ʔ] with [p] in intervocalic contexts (e.g. in *paper*) is reported for Cockney by Hughes & Trudgill (1996). Aspiration and affrication may co-occur with glottalisation. However, by far the most widespread glottal reinforcement/replacement (henceforth T-glottalisation) is to be found in the representation of /t/.[3] This is a characteristic feature of London English. Wells (1982: 303) notes that one of the primary differences between RP and London dialects is that London-influenced forms have a degree of '/t/-glottalling' in pre-vocalic contexts. Hughes & Trudgill (1996) report that [ʔ] is extremely common in Cockney for /t/ between vowels and before a pause.

The results of the South East London survey indicate that the distribution patterns of T-glottalisation are very complex. In particular, T-glottalisation is highly sensitive to prominence patterns, and these restrictions cut across the patterns of behaviour in segmental context. These patterns are discussed in detail below. First, two other common phonetic variants will be discussed: affricated/fricated, and voiced tap variants.

In SELRS, a fricated [tˢ] occasionally arises pre-vocalically, and in word-final position (particularly utterance-finally, where it may also be glottalised).[4]

The plosive [t] is the prestige form, but according to informants fricated variants have a similar high status. In fact they are not distinguished from plosive variants by most speaker-hearers. Fricated forms are used mainly by older speakers, and are particularly associated with a confident, or affected, speech style. The fricated variant is occasionally found in broader varieties, where it is generally associated with an emphatic production, most frequently in pre-pausal or word-internal intervocalic environments.[5]

In SELRS, tapped variants [ɾ] may also occur in intervocalic position, either across a word boundary (particularly in phrases involving commonly used lexical items, e.g. *but I, lot of, get a, quite a, what is, that is*) and word-internally in certain items (e.g. *getting, better*). In SELE, taps are found intervocalically, particularly in cross-word boundary cases, but also word-internally. Sivertsen (1960: 119) also reports a flap in accelerated speaking styles in a small-scale study of Bethnal Green London speech. T-tapping has the same distribution pattern as T-glottalisation with regard to prominence relations (see below). However, in segmental contexts where both T-tapping and T-glottalisation occur (i.e. intervocalic contexts), glottalisation is favoured over tapping.

Glottalised variants are used frequently by both SELRS age groups in pre-consonantal position (where they are minimally perceptible by speaker-hearers). This is the case both in word-internal contexts (e.g. *nightmare*) and cross-word boundary contexts (e.g. *trinket box*). There is frequent use, particularly by older SELRS speakers, of glottalised variants preceding syllabic /n̩/ (e.g. *button*), but not preceding syllabic /m̩/ (e.g. *bottom*), or before a syllabic lateral (e.g. *bottle*), where T-glottalisation is stigmatised. Individuals vary in their preference for a syllabic /n̩/ over a vowel plus non-syllabic /n/ sequence. Younger SELRS speakers tend to prefer the vowel plus non-syllabic /n/ sequence. Since this renders /t/ intervocalic, T-glottalisation is blocked (as in other word-internal intervocalic contexts in this accent). T-glottalisation may be heard, but only sporadically, in pre-vocalic cross-word boundary and pre-pausal position in older SELRS speech. This represents the greatest disparity between the two age groups, and suggests a change in progress: the phonologisation of T-glottalisation in SELRS. The results for older speakers of SELRS seem to reflect the traditional stigma of T-glottalisation, particularly in intervocalic contexts; children are still corrected by carers.

In SELE, the distribution of glottalised variants is more widespread. T-glottalisation is near-categorical in pre-consonantal and pre-pausal positions. By contrast with (especially older) SELRS speakers, there is also a high incidence of T-glottalisation in word-final pre-vocalic position, and in word-internal intervocalic position where the prominence of the preceding syllable is greater than that of the subsequent syllable (see below). There is no particular evidence that T-glottalisation is on the increase in this last context, suggesting that the progression of a T-glottalisation sound change may either be very slow, or else has stabilised, at least for the present.[6] In morphological terms, T-glottalisation is attested before a range of (Lexical Phonology Level II) suffixes (e.g. *debtor, squatter*), and in verbs with the regular *-ing* suffix (e.g. *heating, sorting*). It is more restricted before other (Lexical Phonology Level I) suffixes (e.g. *theoretic, automatic*). T-glottalisation also operates freely between the stems of compound items (e.g. *butthead, a put-on, a get-up*), as well as in phrasal verbs (e.g. *get away*). For many speakers, it arises consistently in specific lexical items (e.g. *better, getting, letter, sitting*).

T-glottalisation is blocked when /t/ is preceded by a non-resonant consonant in coda position (e.g. *project, sister, chapter*), but frequently arises following resonants (e.g. *violent, moult, present, knelt, pentax, printer, guilty, magenta*). An explanation based on phonetic conditioning is likely.

The effect of prominence has a strong influence on T-glottalisation, cutting across both the intervocalic and post-resonant environments. T-glottalisation is blocked in foot-initial onset position generally, both word-initially (e.g. *tiny*) and word-internally (e.g. *attend*).[7]

т-glottalisation is generally blocked in word-internal foot-initial onset position (i.e. where the following nucleus bears greater prominence than the first, e.g. *particular, botanical*).[8] However, it is widely attested in word-internal non-foot-initial onset position (i.e. where the preceding syllable is the more prominent, e.g. *magenta, printer, guilty, natter, Betty, botany, Saturday*). This suggests that /t/ is properly syllabified as part of the preceding stressed syllable by means of a strategy which attracts to the stressed syllable as many consonantal entities as possible.

It is evident that т-glottalisation is highly sensitive to prominence patterns, and that these restrictions cut across the patterns of behaviour in segmental context. Where the segmental conditions are right, т-glottalisation may operate in an item with prominence relations of, for example, [1 2] (*litter, butler*), [1 3 2] (*senator, habitat*), or [3 1 2] (*magenta*) etc. By contrast, in cases with a prominence relation of [2 1] (*pretend*) or [2 1 3 4] (*contemptible*), for example, the process is blocked. The generalisation can then be made that т-glottalisation is optional where the stress on the syllable following /t/ is less than that borne by the preceding syllable, i.e. in non-foot-initial onset position.

т-glottalisation seems not to be affected by whether the following vowel is weak or full. In other words, other things being equal, т-glottalisation is equally likely before schwa (e.g. in *senator,* which has a prominence relation [1 3 2]) as it is before a full vowel such as [iː] (e.g. in *obscenity* [2 1 3 4]).

NG

In broader varieties there is frequent realisation of /-ɪŋ/ as [ɪn] (e.g. *swimming*). There are occasional instances in accelerated-style minimally broad speech.

TH

In the broader speech of both age groups, there is variable use of [f] and [v] for /θ/ and /ð/. This is stigmatised in the region: children are 'corrected' by carers. There is, however, no significant difference between the two age groups with regard to these features, and it seems there has been no recent change. The use of [f] for /θ/ and [v] for /ð/ was not found to be as widespread as was reported for Cockney by Hughes & Trudgill (1996). They find that the contrast between /θ/ and /f/ is 'invariably lost', and that the contrast between /ð/ and /v/ is 'often lost', medially and finally. In initial position, [d] or zero are more likely realisations of /ð/, although contrary to Wells' (1982: 328) findings, [v] *can* appear for initial /ð/ (for example, there were several instances of [vɪs] for *this*).

In broader speech, [h] is also a variant of /θ/ (e.g. *thanks* [hæŋˀks]), and a frequent realisation of initial /ð/ is zero (e.g. *all that stuff, older than*). Word-internal /θ/ was also found to be replaced by [ʔ] in a number of instances of the item *something* [sɐmʔɪŋ].

H

In older SELRS speech, like RP, there is variable н-loss, largely restricted to closed-set items, specifically unstressed auxiliaries (e.g. *have, has, had*) and unstressed pronouns (e.g. *him, her, his, he*).[9] Unlike RP, there is also occasional H-loss in unstressed items which are not members of the closed sets, producing homophonous sets (e.g. *hat – at, hone – own* etc.).

Younger SELRS systems appear to have progressed further. There is variable H-loss in the pronoun and auxiliary sets, occasional H-loss in metrically unstressed position in non-closed set items, and occasional H-loss in metrically stressed position in non-closed set items. It seems that H-loss is most inhibited in, though not excluded from, foot-initial onset position (e.g. *behind, happy*). The incidence rises in a position of reduced sentence stress.

The greatest difference between young and old SELRS speech is between intervocalic cross-boundary and post-consonantal word-internal contexts, although older speakers are found to exhibit occasional H-loss in post-consonantal cross-word boundary contexts (in metrically unstressed positions). There is some evidence, from the young especially, that H-loss proceeds most freely in post-consonantal contexts. Utterance-initial H-loss is only very rarely attested (and is then frequently self-corrected, demonstrating the traditional social stigma attached to 'H-dropping'). The environments most resistant to H-loss for all speakers are utterance-initial and word-internal intervocalic, corresponding to foot-initial onset position.

Loss of H is markedly more widespread in SELE. In particular, it is less restricted in the word-internal categories than it is in nearer-RP forms. Importantly, the incidence of H-loss is not inhibited in metrically stressed positions, and for many individuals is frequent in foot-initial onset position (as in *hospital*). It is possible that, by contrast with SELRS, there has been a generalisation across prosodic environments, such that the differentiation between differing metrical strengths is not so sharp. When [h] deletes, vowel lengthening may be promoted in compensation, and <h>-initial items behave as though they were vowel-initial. For H-loss in <h>-initial nouns, a preceding indefinite article most commonly becomes *an*, but may be *a* followed by [ʔ], or more rarely weak *a* followed by intrusive [ɹ] (e.g. *a* [ɹ](*h*)*orse*).

Loss of H is higher in younger SELE, although not profoundly so. This suggests that any change in progress is a slowly developing one, or that it is stabilising, or has stabilised, without affecting the entirety of the possible contexts. The category exhibiting the highest rate of H-loss in each age group is the class comprising auxiliaries and pronouns; this incidence is closely followed by the post-consonantal application across word boundaries. It is not banned from personal pronouns; speakers variably pronounce [h] in their own names (e.g. *Harry, Helen*). There is some indication of lexical selectivity (e.g. *here, help, head, horrible, house* and *behind*). There is at least one lexical exception: *ahead*.[10] In other items the process is variable. There are no pre-vocalic environments in which H-loss is blocked. Some hypercorrection in pre-vocalic contexts is attested, although this is usually restricted to the older speakers, e.g. *dozen* [h]*eggs;* [h]*old Bill.*

The data distinguishing young and old speakers may indicate either a slowly progressing or stabilising sound change which has not gone to completion, and/or the consequences of stylistic factors.

GLIDES

In minimally broad forms no /-j/-cluster reduction was attested. In broad forms, for all speakers, there is variable ȷ-dropping after /h, n, m, s, d, t, l, b/, but no reduction was attested after /p, f, v, k, g/. Another option for items such as *huge* is the loss of /h/ from the cluster to leave /j/ (Sivertsen (1960: 142) finds only [j] for /hj/). Wells (1982: 330) reports that in London English, /b/ is one of the small number of segments which is freely followed by /j/ (the others are /p, v, g/). Wells also lists reduction in London /fj, kj/ but this was not attested in the South East London survey.

The glides /r, w, j/ may be formed in the appropriate vocalic environment, to avoid vowel hiatuses created by syntactic concatenation, or by processes such as ʜ-loss or ʟ-vocalisation. Vowel hiatuses are disfavoured in this accent, and are typically avoided, either by means of glide formation (e.g. [w]: *legal earnings* [ligɣwəːnɪŋz]; [ɹ]: *a house* [ɐɹæːs]; [j]: *he is* [hᵊiːjɪz]) or by inserting [ʔ] (across word boundaries, e.g. *Michael ate it* [mɑːkʰöʔɛʔɪʔt]). Utterance-final items such as *do they* [dʉ ðaɪj] also often end with a [j] glide, especially in broader speech.

R

ʀ is typically realised as [ɹ]. Linking and intrusive ʀ are almost categorical following /ɔː/, /aː/, /ə/ and /ɜː/. According to informants, suppression of ʀ-insertion phenomena sounds affected. When the product of other processes forms the correct vocalic environment, this often promotes ʀ-insertion phenomena. Examples are ʟ-vocalisation (e.g. with ʀ-intrusion in *I'll*[ɹ] *eat it*), ʜ-loss (e.g. *the idea*[ɹ] *(h)e's got*), and monophthongisation of MOUTH and GOAT (e.g. *now*[ɹ] *I will*) and deletion of /ð/ (e.g. *older*[ɹ] *(th)an Dad*).

Some individuals demonstrate variable use of a labiodental approximant [ʋ] for ʀ. Four informants in the younger age group demonstrate a consistent use of [ʋ].

L

SELRS and SELE exhibit a continuum of clear [l]–dark [ɫ] alternation, with clear, slightly palatalised variants tending to arise in syllable onsets (e.g. *listen, yellow*) and darker variants in syllable rhymes (e.g. *held, pool*). Dark [ɫ] is velarised and involves back vowel resonance.[11]

In addition, all speakers demonstrate variable, context-dependent ʟ-vocalisation. The product of vocalisation is a back vocoid, articulated in the velar or pharyngeal region.[12] It is not associated with specific lip positioning: the lips may be rounded, neutral, or weakly spread. The incidence of vocalisation is higher in the younger group, which may be indicative of change. The environments in which vocalisation has been attested are: word-final pre-consonantal (e.g. *all right* [o̞ːɹɒɪʔ]), word-internal pre-consonantal (e.g. *filthy* [fɪɣfiː]), word-final pre-pausal (e.g. *will* [wɪɣ]), syllabic /l/ (e.g. *people* [pʰiːpɣ]), and word-final intervocalic (e.g. *legal info* [ligɣwʷɪnfɐɣ]). Vocalisation in this last context was found only in the speech of the younger group. By contrast, Wells (1982: 321) suggests this is not a possible environment for vocalisation in London English.

In all systems, vocalisation is blocked in word-initial contexts, and word-internal intervocalic contexts regardless of morphology (e.g. *pullover, shallow, Eleanor*).

The disparity between the age groups in SELE is small, except in one noticeable context. As mentioned, in addition to the contexts standardly observed for vocalisation, vocalised forms were observed in the younger speech in word-final pre-vocalic position (e.g. *Muswell Hill* [mazweɤʷɪɤ]), although the incidence of vocalisation here is less than in other contexts. This suggests a recent extension.

SELRS and SELE informants were not normally sensitive to the vocoid–consonant alternation, and perhaps as a consequence, vocalised forms are not particularly stigmatised in these varieties. This said, vocalisation can be unconsciously suppressed when accommodation towards the regional standard occurs.

9.3 *Discrete versus continuous modelling of consonantal reduction*

The remainder of this chapter focuses on the reducing behaviour of /l/. The implications of the data for current phonological theory are outlined, in particular regarding the provision of a unified, principled account of the full range of surface variation attested, the identification of the motivation behind this variation, and the distinction of phonetic processes from those which are phonologically productive (see further Tollfree 1996).

Sociolinguistics is *a priori* concerned with variable patterns of behaviour. By contrast it is fair to say that variation has not been the central concern of most work in phonology. Indeed, as will become apparent during the discussion, the very tools of phonology (e.g. the nature of phonological primitives, and of procedures) can preclude close analysis of variable material. The discussion considers analyses in two diverse models, with the aim of highlighting the disparity in aims and methods between sociolinguistics and phonology.

The survey demonstrates that there is a clear subset of distinguishable surface variants of /l/ (clear, dark, vocoid), but within each category there is substantial variation (in backing of /l/, and in the precise realisation of the vocoid). Whilst the alternation between consonantal and vocoid forms is phonological, variation both within a category, and between the clear and dark variants, seems to operate at a more superficial, i.e. phonetic, level. The phonological alternation would at first glance seem to lend itself to analysis within a categorical (discrete) model, but the gradation between clear and dark forms, and the range of variability in the vocoid, might be better explained in a continuous model. The discussion which follows addresses this apparent intractability.

Two diverse analyses of the data are presented, based on quite different sets of criteria. The first discussed is based on Government Phonology, essentially a licensing framework in which phonology is cognitive, and discrete in procedural terms. Analysis in this model is centred on deducing what speakers know about their global system. Consonantal reduction patterns are explained in minimally distinct terms as a single phonological operation arising in a unified segmental/prosodic environment.

The second analysis is based on Articulatory Phonology, a continuous model in which the focus is on what speakers do, and synchronic consonantal reduction is explained in terms of relative (re)arrangement of articulatory gestures (alterations in gestural magnitude, duration and overlap).

A full description of these two models cannot be provided here for reasons of space (references for further reading are supplied). It will be necessary, however, to introduce a considerable bulk of technical material for the purpose of outlining the main points of this paper.

9.3.1   Government Phonology

Government Phonology (GP) (Kaye, Lowenstamm & Vergnaud, e.g. 1985, 1990; Kaye 1990) is effectively a segmental derivative of phoneme theory. It embodies a universal approach to phonological organisation, in which syntagmatic constituent structure is bound by the phonological property of **government** in a monostratal plane (following Government and Binding Theory, e.g. Chomsky 1981, 1982). Government is a binary, asymmetric relationship in most cases holding between two skeletal positions. Locality and directionality are criteria for assessing the well-formedness of structures. Some segments are awarded governing skeletal positions, and this is in turn what determines syllable position.

Three basic ground rules govern the way in which structures are organised:

- **universality**
- **privativeness** (which permits only univalent spreading processes)
- **non-arbitrariness** (an operation must be motivated in the context in which it applies).

These are accompanied by a range of universal principles, and, where necessary, language-specific parameters (for an overview see e.g. Carr 1993).

One of the central assumptions of GP is that a theory cannot be developed by means of direct reference to phonetic material. Phonological representation, however, is in terms of discrete acoustic **elements**. Invoking a chemical metaphor, GP conceives of segments as being composed of lone elements or combinations of elements. Each element consists of a number of properties, one being **marked** (its determining attribute), the remainder being unmarked. Elements are **autonomous** in that they have a unique stand-alone phonetic interpretation. For example, the Coronal element R is said to be independently realised as a coronal tap. Elements combine in a specified manner (by **fusion operations**), with the consequence that a purely categorical output is predicted. A fusion involves two elements. One element is defined as the **head**, and the other as the

operator. In fusion, the operator contributes only its salient property; the remaining properties are contributed by the head element.

A configuration for consonantal /l/ includes the elements R **(Coronal)**, ʔ **(Stop)** and U **(Labial)**. Their phonetic correlates are:

- R: tongue tip/blade gesture or front-bunching of dorsum
- ʔ: abrupt decrease in overall amplitude; occlusion along the mid-sagittal line of the oral tract
- U: maximal expansion of oral and pharyngeal cavities.

ʔ as head position indicates occlusion. R in operator position contributes its salient property of alveolarity, thereby defining the place of articulation. A third fusion connects U and gives sonorancy. (1) below shows the internal segmental structure of /l/:

(1) Unified lexical representation of /l/

$$
\begin{array}{ll}
O & \text{(Onset skeletal position)} \\
| & \\
x & \text{(timing unit)} \\
| & \\
R^{\circ} & \\
| & \\
\underline{ʔ}^{\circ} & \\
| & \\
U^{\circ} &
\end{array}
$$

Explanation in GP is most valued if it accounts for a number of like phenomena (following the principle of universality). A range of consonantal reduction (lenition) patterns are economically explained in terms of a single operation, **element loss** (internal segmental depletion), in a unified segmental and prosodic environment (e.g. Harris & Kaye 1990). Element loss relates up to three surface-distinct variants of /l/. Elements cannot be inserted (following the principle of privativeness). Accordingly, the base form of /l/ is the most complex structure (the clear variant), and less complex segments (the back variant and the vocoid) are formed via element loss.

In order for non-arbitrariness to be satisfied, there must be rationale for element loss in the context in which it is observed, and elemental configurations must be related to each other in a direct way, at the level of both base forms and surface-distinct configurations. These issues are now examined.

'Coda' licensing (Kaye 1990) ensures that word-final consonants occur in an onset position followed by an empty nucleus. Syllabic structures are maximally binary (i.e. lack a coda: Kaye, Lowenstamm & Vergnaud 1990: 203); thus /l/ in *bill* is internuclear in position, as shown in (2). Interconstituent government (indicated by the dashed arrow) operates from left to right, following proper government and constituent and nuclear government (Kaye, Lowenstamm & Vergnaud 1990: 210):[13]

(2)   *Syllabic structure of* bill

O   N   O   N
| | | |
x   x   x   x
| | | |
[b   ɪ   l   v°]

According to Harris (1990a), lenition is favoured in internuclear contexts (**prime lenition sites**). For example, /t/ lenites when it is internuclear in position, due to its weak licensing status: in other words it has a diminished ability for holding internal complexity. A parallel prime lenition site for /l/ is given in (3):

(3)   *Prime lenition site for* /l/

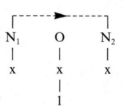

The governing relationship in (3) is licit as it is local, but not strictly so (according to projection government: Charette 1990). The direction of government is subject to parametric variation: in this case left-headed government operates at the level of nuclear projection.

   Given this, /l/ may lenite (velarise/vocalise) whenever it is in an internuclear site, and the following nucleus is empty. This development is internally driven by a requirement for internal structural stability (the maintenance of governing relations, determined at the lexical level). ʔ ceases to function as the head of the configuration, and is replaced by the vocalic element, U° (head alignment). This derives the back variant, [ɫ]. Element loss is then sanctioned: ʔ and R are forfeited, constituting true lenition (Harris 1990a), as shown in (4). This move is in line with the **complexity condition** (Kaye, Lowenstamm & Vergnaud 1990).

(4) L-*vocalisation*

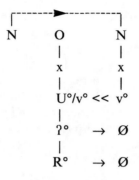

Thus, in the sequence *bill in* given in (5), /l/ is clear or vocalised:

(5)   bill + in

```
r---►---1
O   N   O   N   O   N   O   N
|   |   |   |       |   |   |
x   x   x   x       x   x   x
|   |   |   |       |   |   |
[b  ɪ   l   v°]     [ɪ  n]  v°
```

(5) allows for the attested vocalisation in items such as *built, bill,* and *bill in,* and correctly excludes it in the case of *lit*. Due to universality, however, (5) falsely predicts vocalisation in word-internal intervocalic instances (e.g. *fellow*).

Segmental depletion is a binary process, and GP therefore predicts a purely categorical phonetic output. This falls short of explaining the observed phonetic gradation of clear–dark /l/ (and incomplete vocalisation forms: Wright 1986, 1989). Further, the implication that the relationship between clear, velarised and vocalised /l/ is strictly phonological, and that velarised and vocalised /l/ are phonologically reduced forms of the clear variant, is inappropriate for South East London English (and any other accents) where clear–dark /l/ alternation is phonetic.

9.3.2 Articulatory Phonology

Articulatory Phonology (AP) (Browman & Goldstein e.g. 1986, 1989, 1990a, b, 1991, 1992a, b) is a non-segmental approach in which contrast among lexical units is described in terms of **gestures** and their continuous interrelations. Gestures are abstract, and in theory cognitive, units of contrast among lexical items, and parallel the continuous movements of a small set of quasi-independent articulators (for an overview see e.g. McMahon, Foulkes & Tollfree 1994).

Gestural manoeuvres (sliding and acoustic hiding) are invoked in this analysis of the surface variation in /l/, which also incorporates claims by Sproat & Fujimura (1993) regarding the bi-gestural nature of English /l/.

Sproat & Fujimura (1993) present acoustic and X-ray microbeam data for English /l/ in initial position and preceding various phonological boundaries, in the context /i_ɪ/. They propose that English /l/ is bi-gestural, consisting of a vocalic dorsal gesture corresponding to dorsal retraction and lowering, and a consonantal tongue tip gesture corresponding to tongue tip extension. According to Sproat & Fujimura, vocalic gestures show a strong affinity for syllabic nucleii, whilst consonantal gestures are attracted to the margin. This renders the two articulatory gestures making up /l/ inherently asynchronous. For syllable-final /l/s, the vocalic gesture precedes the consonantal gesture; in other words the vocalic gesture is nearer to the nucleus. The situation is reversed for syllable-initial /l/s.

Sproat & Fujimura's results suggest that certain distributions are favoured by universal tendency. Their work supports claims that backing of /l/ is a matter of degree (e.g. Lehiste 1964; Bladon & Al-Bamerni 1976), and they explicitly reject the notion that dark [ɫ] and clear [l] should be treated as distinct entities. For example, in the context of high front vowels, /i_ɪ/, they found that darker /l/s may involve a greater retraction and lowering of the tongue dorsum (as opposed to *raising*, as might be expected from the traditional term velarisation). This occurs along with an earlier occurrence of the dorsal retraction extremum relative to the tongue tip advancement extremum. In contrast, lighter variants show a dorsal extremum which is later in relation to the tongue tip extremum. Sproat & Fujimura suggest that this is a duration effect because a sequence such as /il/ will generally have a longer duration in pre-pausal position than it will in phrase-medial position, which might in turn be due to a failure of tongue retraction to attain its full target (Crystal & House 1988).

If Sproat & Fujimura are correct, a prediction is made that the degree of backness in South East London English /l/ depends on the degree of retraction and lowering of the vocalic dorsal gesture, and its timing relative to the tongue tip gesture. In syllable-initial /l/ the consonantal (tongue tip) gesture precedes the vocalic (tongue body) gesture. This is shown in (6), where the gestures and their temporal relationships are represented by overlapping boxes.

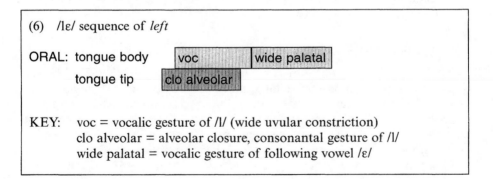

(6)   /lɛ/ sequence of *left*

ORAL: tongue body

tongue tip

KEY: voc = vocalic gesture of /l/ (wide uvular constriction)
      clo alveolar = alveolar closure, consonantal gesture of /l/
      wide palatal = vocalic gesture of following vowel /ɛ/

For syllable-final /l/s, however, the vocalic gesture precedes the consonantal gesture, and is nearer to the nucleus. For a consistently dark syllable-final /l/, the consonantal gesture co-occurs with the vocalic gesture for /l/ for the entire duration of the consonantal gesture.

---

(7) /il/ sequence of *heel*

ORAL: tongue body | narrow palatal | voc |

      tongue tip | clo alveolar |

KEY: narrow palatal = vocalic gesture of preceding vowel /i/

Thus, in terms of gestural composition, /l/ can be seen as a single phonological entity, constituted by two gestures, which will be phonetically implemented as a clearer or darker variant, depending on such factors as the position of /l/ in the syllable and the duration of the prosodic context containing the /l/. The surface alternation is then the consequence of a purely low-level gestural manoeuvre.

---

(8) *Gesturing sliding and hiding of* clo alveolar

ORAL: tongue body | voc |

      tongue tip | clo alveolar |
                          | cons |

↓

(9) *Deletion of* clo alveolar

ORAL: tongue body | voc |
                          | cons |

KEY: cons = any following consonantal gesture

A straightforward proposal for vocalisation follows. For /l/ in the syllable-final context illustrated in (7), the early vocalic (voc) darkness, originally heard as a cue for /l/, becomes reinterpreted as having an independent status in the sequence. For instance, the preceding vowel might be heard as a diphthong, or as having an off-glide, thereby promoting the perception of /l/ as vocalic.[14] The consonantal (tongue tip) gesture of /l/ is shielded by following consonantal gestures, by a process of relative gestural sliding and subsequent hiding (Browman & Goldstein 1990b, 1992a), as shown in (8). Hidden gestures are inaudible, and a phonological vocalisation development involves cross-generational non-specification (loss/deletion) of the consonantal tongue tip gesture, illustrated in (9).

There are a number of drawbacks to this approach to surface variation in /l/. In general terms, there is no rationale for gestural sliding and loss of the tongue tip gesture. More specifically, in order for gestural sliding and acoustic hiding to be principled, there has to be evidence that vocalisation originates in pre-consonantal positions. This is not unequivocally supported by the South East London data. In SELE (broader) speech, with predominantly vocoid realisations in syllable-final position, an initiation site can no longer be readily identified. Vocalisation has progressed too far: it is equally likely in all appropriate contexts except word-final pre-vocalic contexts, where it is disfavoured, and which thus can be excluded as an initiation site. In SELRS (minimally broad) speech, the process occurs freely in pre-consonantal position, yet there is no conclusive evidence to suggest that vocalisation is more likely pre-consonantally than in word-final pre-pausal position (in which case there would be no following consonantal gesture to shield the tongue tip gesture of /l/).[15]

Despite these limitations, the AP explanation of surface variation in /l/ is *a priori* more constrained than the modelling via element loss in GP and other non-continuous models, to the extent that gestural sliding involves maintaining consistent numbers and ordering of gestures, and synchronic modification only of the relative arrangement of the gestures. Within AP the full range of variants and variation can be demonstrated. Surface variation between clearer and darker /l/ depends on syllabic position and phonetic duration of the prosodic context. The vocoid variant is phonologically distinct from the consonant, and is explained as a consequence of low-level gestural rearrangement (sliding) and subsequent acoustic hiding.

9.4   *Concluding remarks*

The theoretical discursive has raised a number of questions pertinent to current phonological thought, centred on the apparent incompatibility of categorical (discrete) and continuous approaches. It has also served to highlight the disparity in focus between sociolinguistics and phonology.

Traditional analyses characterise the overall shapes of the vocal tract, or acoustic products ('outputs' in the terms of Browman & Goldstein 1992a). GP provides an output, but no explanation of the relationship between abstract phonological representations and phonetic behaviour. On this view, phonology is purely cognitive (categorical), all 'changes' are by definition phonological and internally motivated, and surface variation is an epiphenomenon.

By contrast, AP provides 'a description of the (local) articulatory gestural organisation' (Browman & Goldstein 1992a: 163). Phonetic motivation for surface variation in /l/ is identifiable. There is provision for gradation of description in backing of the consonantal form, and synchronic vocalisation is explained in terms of the relative (re)arrangement of articulatory gestures (alterations in gestural overlap). Gestural sliding and acoustic hiding account for transition to the phonological domain, thereby enabling assessment of the material in terms of sound change progression.

Neither the tools of GP nor those of AP enable the full modelling of variation patterns, and whilst this is not a task that either model was strictly designed to satisfy, it is evident that an interest in variation, such as exists in sociolinguistics, forces many basic assumptions in phonology into question.

Notes

1 This chapter was largely written during the course of a Study Abroad Studentship awarded by the Leverhulme Trust, to which I am greatly indebted.

2 SELRS serves as a more appropriate reference standard than the minority RP form in this region where even middle-class speakers have some regional characteristics (see below on the *Roland-roller* rule). The viability of RP (e.g. as characterised in Wells 1982) as a living language system is in doubt, and it may be better viewed as an ideal form which has become somewhat fossilised. See e.g. Milroy & Milroy (1985a), Leith (1983) and Crowley (1991) on the development and status of 'standard' forms.

3 The auditory analysis carried out on this data set does not discriminate between glottal stop and glottalised variants, thereby obscuring any variation patterns which might exist between them (see Docherty & Foulkes this volume).

4 Wells (1982: 323–6) also reports affrication of /d/ and use of [ʔ] for /d/ in London English.

5 Beaken (1971) finds affrication accompanying word-final glottalisation of /p/, /k/ and in particular /t/ in Bromley English.

6 Bowyer (1973) finds for Bromley that only five out of 34 informants showed glottalling. т-glottalisation now appears more widespread in the area. This may reflect accommodation in the direction of London English, and/or the migration of (central) Londoners to the suburbs.

7 A few exceptions were found in phrases containing unstressed word-initial /tə-/ items: *tomorrow, today, to,* e.g. *by tomorrow, swear to go.* т-glottalisation was also attested in *sometimes.* In these examples, /t/ is preceded by a more prominent syllable, with which the first syllable of the /t/-initial item may be said to form a foot, thus maintaining a unified prosodic environment for т-glottalisation.

8 A number of exceptions to this generalisation were identified, e.g. *seventeen.* This can be explained in terms of a restricted lexical set (of numerical *-teen* items), the other members of which conform to the prosodic (and segmental) structural description for т-glottalisation described above (i.e. *thirteen, fourteen, eighteen*). A generalisation may have been formed, entailing that *seventeen* has come to fit this pattern of behaviour and is subjected to т-glottalisation. In isolation items such as *thirteen* have the prominence relation [2 1], but they show stress shift behaviour to [1 2] in e.g. the phrase *thirteen girls.* In such cases, т-glottalisation was blocked, with three exceptions: two instances of *fourteen* and one of *thirteen.* The item *seventeen* also undergoes stress shift from

[2 3 1] in isolation to [1 3 2] in *seventeen men*, where two instances of ᴛ-glottalisation were attested.

9 Instrumental research by Pierrehumbert & Talkin (1992) shows that ʜ-loss is a scalar, rather than binary, process.

10 Forms such as [əɛd] or [ə?ɛd] are not attested. ʀ-intrusion is blocked word-internally in this accent, hence forms such as [əɹɛd] are not found. Speakers with a largely ʜ-less inventory prefer to use [əhɛd].

11 'Velarised /l/' may not, as the term suggests, involve raising of the back of the tongue towards the velum (Sproat & Fujimura 1993). See later discussion.

12 It is unlikely that ʟ-vocalisation is strictly binary. For example, Wright (1986, 1989) reports incomplete vocalisation in Cambridge English.

13 The notation v° indicates the 'cold vowel', effectively an underspecified syllable nucleus (Kaye, Lowenstamm & Vergnaud 1990).

14 In Old English, breaking is thought to have initiated a similar vocalisation process in [lC] environments (Jones 1989).

15 As it stands, AP is organisationally inadequate to model phonologisation of low-level manoeuvres. See McMahon, Foulkes & Tollfree (1994) and Tollfree (1996) which consider the integration of AP with Lexical Phonology for the purpose of modelling phonological variation and change.

10

Cardiff: a real-time study
of glottalisation

Inger M. Mees and Beverley Collins

10.1 Introduction

10.1.1 Background

The information in this description is derived from a longitudinal project on the sociophonetic variation of a group of Cardiff informants whose linguistic development is being traced over a period beginning in 1976.[1] So far four corpora of material have been assembled of which three have been utilised for this survey. Recordings were made of 80 primary schoolchildren (aged 9–11) in 1976. In 1981 it was possible to trace 75 of these. In 1990, 54 of the informants were tracked down and recorded together with a new sample of approximately 70 Cardiff children of primary school age (not used for this study). It is hoped to obtain a further set of data in 2001. Where language change is noted, this refers not only to a comparison of the first and subsequent recording sessions but also to observations made of a small group of Cardiff speakers of the older generation (65 plus).[2]

The latter portion of this chapter (sections 10.3 and 10.4) deals with a study of glottalisation in the speech of a micro-group of working-class female informants, concentrating on social ambition as a likely factor in promoting linguistic change.

10.1.2 Types of Welsh English

Historically, one can distinguish between three types of linguistic area in Wales (Collins & Mees 1991: 75–6; see Williams 1990 for a history of anglicisation in Wales, and Coupland & Thomas 1990: 8–9 for a slightly different typology of Welsh English):

Type 1. The present-day Welsh heartlands where Welsh was overwhelmingly the majority language until 1900 (e.g. most of Gwynedd and Dyfed, together with parts of Clwyd and fragments of West Glamorgan and Powys).[3] In these regions, this is either still the case or otherwise a large percentage of the population remains bilingual.

Type 2. Areas which were largely Welsh-speaking until about 1850 but rapidly passed through stages of bilingualism towards English monolingualism in the early twentieth century, e.g. the industrialised former coal-mining valleys of south-east Glamorgan and south-west Gwent and border areas of Clwyd.

Type 3. Border or coastal areas where English has been spoken by the vast majority of the population since well before 1800, in some cases possibly from the time of the Norman Conquest. This category includes not only marginal regions such as southern Pembrokeshire, south Gower, Powys and eastern Gwent, but also crucially the densely populated low-lying parts of southern Glamorgan and Gwent.

This chapter will deal with the core area of the last-named region, i.e. the city of Cardiff. But note that the speech of much of South Glamorgan and southern Gwent (well beyond Barry to the west and at least as far as Newport and its surroundings to the east) are very similar in most respects. In fact, the Barry-Cardiff-Newport area should be regarded as constituting a single accent continuum (Coupland 1988: 4–5) speaking what we shall henceforth refer to as 'Cardiff English' (CE), taking in at least half a million speakers. CE is sharply demarcated from the (mainly Type 2, peripherally Type 1) speech of the rest of industrial South Wales, which we shall term General South Wales English (henceforth GSWE).

10.1.3 South Wales characteristics

A pioneering survey of what he termed 'Glamorgan English' is to be found in Windsor Lewis (1964), who provided the first linguistic description to distin-

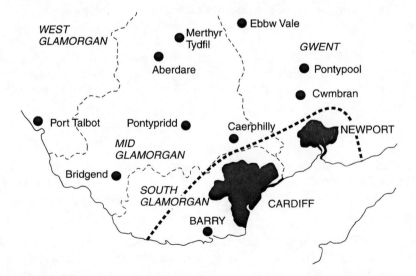

Fig. 10.1 Map of the approximate extent of the Cardiff English accent continuum

guish clearly between the Type 2 and Type 3 varieties of South Wales English mentioned in section 10.1.2 above ('Cymric' and 'Cardiff' respectively, in his terms). Later descriptions of individual varieties of GSWE have been provided by Tench (1990) for Abercrave; Connolly (1981, 1990) for Port Talbot; while Mees (1977, 1983), Coupland (1988), and Collins & Mees (1988, 1990) have produced descriptions of CE. Wells (1982) also includes a description of Welsh English with much useful detail on the speech of South Wales. But perhaps the most accessible source of information for the general reader is Hughes & Trudgill's (1996) basic but influential textbook on British English accents where South Wales English is exemplified by the speech of Pontypridd (Type 2).

However, as we have pointed out (Collins & Mees 1988: 17–18), much of what Hughes & Trudgill mention does not apply to CE, as this variety does not fit the general stereotype of South Wales English. Although there are certainly connections between CE and GSWE, the former also has much in common with the accents of the English Severnside area of Gloucestershire and Somerset (notwithstanding the difference in the matter of rhoticism). This can be seen in, for example, the presence in CE of a clear/dark /l/ allophonic patterning; the general absence of the so-called 'lilting' intonation tunes typical of GSWE (see 10.2.4 below); the lack of extra vowel contrasts, particularly the absence of the GOOSE–JUICE split (see 10.2.1 below); and the extensive use of assimilation and elision. In an accent typology of the British Isles, CE can logically be regarded as forming a linguistically distinct and numerically significant *subcategory* of Welsh English (Coupland 1988: 46–51, 98; Collins & Mees 1988: 18). The speech of the Barry-Cardiff-Newport area ought not to be lumped in with the rest of South Wales any more than, say, Merseyside should be left undistinguished from the speech of the remainder of Lancashire.

10.2 *Descriptive material*

10.2.1 Vowels

Table 10.1 Cardiff English vowels – summary

KIT	ɪ	FLEECE	iː	NEAR	jøː > iːə		
DRESS	ɛ	FACE	ei	BEER	iːə		
TRAP	a	PALM	æː	SQUARE	ɛː		
LOT	ɑ	THOUGHT	ʌː	START	aː		
STRUT	ə	GOAT	ɤu	NORTH	ʌː		
FOOT	ɤ	GOOSE	uː	FORCE	ʌː		
BATH	a ~ æː	PRICE	əi	CURE	juːə ~ jʌː		
CLOTH	ɑ	CHOICE	ʌi	happy	i		
NURSE	øː	MOUTH	ʌu	letteʀ	ə		
				horsɛs	ɪ		
				commʌ	ə		

Comments

Systemic variation: STRUT, GOOSE, NEAR, BEER, SQUARE, NORTH, FORCE, CURE, commA

In CE, the NEAR and CURE vowels can be regarded as sequences /iːə/ and /uːə/ whilst SQUARE is typically realised as a steady-state vowel – which implies that the accent has no centring diphthongs. Note that Table 10.1 contains two keywords which in RP and similar varieties have /ɪə/. NEAR represents a small set of words: *near, mere, year, ear, here* and *hear* (and their derivatives). Although these words may have /iːə/ they are (more commonly) pronounced with a rising diphthong [jøː], e.g. *near* [njøː]. It is not unusual for *year, ear, here* and *hear* all to be pronounced in the same way, [jøː]. BEER represents all other words with /ɪə/. These, unlike the NEAR words, are heard only with vowel sequences [iːə], e.g. *Ian, idea, real* [ˈiːən əiˈdiːə ˈɹiːəl]. Before intervocalic /r, l/ followed by a vowel, they are monophthongised to [iː], e.g. *cereals, really* [ˈsiːɹiːəlz ˈɹiːli].

Though Windsor Lewis (1964: 23) took CE to have an independent STRUT vowel, we regard STRUT and commA as being in allophonic relationship, i.e. /ə/ is employed here to cover both the commA vowel and also, when stressed, the STRUT vowel. It is problematical, even in RP and similar varieties, whether the stressed variant should be considered as a separate phoneme, because of the absence of minimal pairs. See the discussion in, for example, D. Jones (1967a: 58–62) and Wells (1970: 233–5; 1982: 385–6).

CE lacks many of the GSWE vowel features described by other investigators. There are no *toe–tow* or *mail–male* contrasts (Connolly 1981: 52–3). Nor does the accent possess what we have previously termed the GOOSE–JUICE split (Collins & Mees 1991: 84), i.e. an additional phoneme /ɪu/ (see also Wells 1982: 385–6). As is the case in English outside Wales, CE *brewed* is identical with *brood, blew* with *blue,* and *goose/juice* is a good rhyme.[4]

In GSWE, the NORTH–FORCE contrast (as described by Wells 1982: 159–62) appears overwhelmingly to be maintained; see, for example, Connolly (1990: 123), Tench (1990: 137–8). Notwithstanding Windsor Lewis (1964: 19), we have not ourselves been able to find any consistent evidence for the NORTH–FORCE distinction from any of our Cardiff informants. We conclude that if it formerly existed, it is now virtually extinct.

Thus, overall, the CE vowel system – even in its broadest forms – is much closer to that of southern English varieties than is GSWE.

Lexical-incidental variation: TRAP, BATH, PALM, THOUGHT, CURE, happY

The final vowel of happY patterns with FLEECE rather than KIT. As with speakers of other English varieties who use FLEECE in this context (Cruttenden & Gimson 1994: 98–9), the CE happY realisation is generally shorter and somewhat more open. The internal unstressed vowel in examples such as *anniversary, universe* also has FLEECE in the speech of broad CE individuals. Mainstream CE usually chooses /ə/ in these cases.

CE exhibits a complex alternation between the TRAP vowel /a/ and the PALM vowel /æː/ in BATH words such as *class, pass, grass, bath, laugh, answer, chance, dance.* TRAP appears to be favoured before nasal + consonant, whilst PALM is the preference before fricatives (as appears to be the case in most Australian English; Wells 1982: 599). Certain words, e.g. *bath, laugh, rather, father, master* and the suffix *-graph* in *photograph,* etc., appear almost always to have PALM. Other items, e.g. pre-nasal *answer, chance, dance* (and also pre-fricative *castle, nasty)* are overwhelmingly said with the TRAP vowel.

Apart from any social pressure to produce PALM in these words in the speech of the middle class (presumably under the influence of other southern varieties of 'England English'), broad and mainstream Cardiff speakers still show confusing idiolectal variation. In fact, the same speaker may even produce TRAP and PALM vowels for the same word in succeeding sentences (to give an example from our corpus, *France* as [fɹans] and [fɹæːns]). CE distribution is very different from that of northern English accents (Wells 1982: 353–6, 387); on the other hand, there does appear to be some similarity to the patterning in south-western varieties of England English, and also to that of much Australian English (Wells 1982: 599).

In CE, unlike most other Welsh varieties (Wells 1982: 164), the THOUGHT vowel is frequently used in preference to the CURE vowel in words such as *sure, cure, tour.* The patterning is complex but it would appear that what may be termed 'THOUGHT replacement' is the norm for certain common items, e.g. *tour, sure, insure* (Mees 1983: 78–9). Other words, e.g. *pure, cure* (i.e. words containing a consonant + /j/), are also regularly found with the THOUGHT vowel in the speech of mainstream Cardiffians.

Realisational differences
Checked vowels: DRESS, TRAP, LOT, STRUT, FOOT
DRESS is around open-mid and somewhat centralised. TRAP is variable, but is typically almost open, and often a little retracted (though never as obviously as its counterpart in GSWE). Like many other southern varieties of British English (D. Jones 1956: 235–6; Fudge 1977), CE has a longer type of TRAP vowel in a small number of lexical items (e.g. *man, mad, bad, bag*). Nevertheless, this prolonged [aː] is distinct from the PALM vowel. LOT [ɑ] is unrounded in much basilectal CE (but see 10.2.3.1 for Social variation), while FOOT tends to be unrounded and centralised [ɤ̈] (a vowel of similar type – noticed first perhaps by Daniel Jones (1950: 42) – is also to be heard in present-day RP; Cruttenden & Gimson 1994: 112).

CE stressed /ə/ (equivalent to STRUT) covers a wide area of the vowel diagram and shows considerable idiolectal variation. It is, however, always relatively close, regularly reaching close-mid; it is on average closer than its counterpart in most GSWE accents.

Free steady-state vowels: NURSE, FLEECE, PALM, THOUGHT, GOOSE, SQUARE
FLEECE /iː/ is noticeably close and generally lacks any glide. SQUARE /ɛː/ is always a

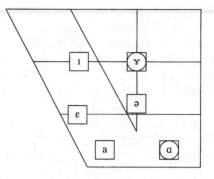

Fig. 10.2 CE checked vowels[5]

steady-state vowel and is raised, being well above open-mid. NURSE /ø:/ is typically front/central, regularly above open-mid tongue height, and potentially rounded. Surprisingly, the lip-rounding (deviant from most other English varieties) is more striking in middle-class speech (see 10.2.3.1 for sociolinguistic variation of lip-rounding resulting from setting characteristics). THOUGHT /ʌ:/ is unrounded, open-mid and centralised in the broadest forms of CE (though more sophisticated forms of the accent have a closer vowel with strong rounding; see 10.2.3.1).

PALM /æ:/ is the most characteristic vowel of the accent. In broad CE, it is generally a front open vowel, slightly closer than CV4. It is not true, however, for CE, to say that TRAP /a/ and PALM /æ:/ are typically distinguished by length, as claimed by Hughes & Trudgill (1996: 81) for South Wales English. There would appear always to be some difference of quality. CE /æ:/ is a salient accent feature, which, along with H-loss, suffers the greatest social stigmatisation (see Coupland 1988: 26–7, 141). We have chosen to symbolise PALM with /æ:/ (rather than /a:/) to call attention to the extent of this potential raising in broad varieties.

GOOSE is close and somewhat advanced from back, and typically lacking the glide variants found in most southern British varieties, except in one context. Following /j/, e.g. *few, music,* the vowel has an extended glide realisation (perhaps this is a lingering echo of a former JUICE vowel).

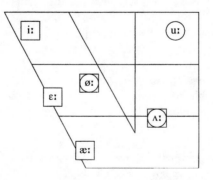

Fig. 10.3 CE free steady-state vowels

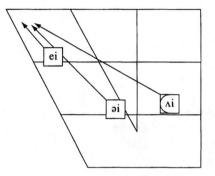

Fig. 10.4 CE fronting diphthongs

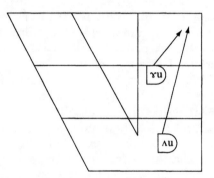

Fig. 10.5 CE backing diphthongs

Diphthongs: FACE, GOAT, PRICE, CHOICE, MOUTH

The final elements of all the glides are remarkably close. FACE /ei/ has a relatively close starting point, and reaches a very raised end tongue position. The corresponding back vowel GOAT has two realisations. Formerly, it was a potential diphthong of an [oᵁ] type (Mees 1983: 72); it is now much more frequently realised as a back/central glide [ɤu] – overwhelmingly so in the speech of younger Cardiffians (see Coupland 1980: 6). Consequently, unlike for most other Welsh English varieties, CE FACE and GOAT are nowadays full diphthongs.

All the remaining diphthongs (PRICE /əi/, MOUTH /ʌu/ and CHOICE /ʌi/), have noticeably centralised starting points. PRICE in addition seems to be acquiring some rounding (see Coupland 1988: 28). The starting point of MOUTH is low back rather than truly central, so we have chosen to represent it as /ʌu/ rather than /əu/ (cf. Wells 1982: 380). CHOICE tends to have an unrounded first element.

Like other Welsh accents, CE is resistant to 'smoothing' (Wells 1982: 238–42), and thus *buying* and *tower* will be pronounced as [ˈbəiɪn ˈtʌuə] rather than the [ˈbaːɪŋ ˈtɑːə] of traditional RP. Often a brief [j] or [w] glide is inserted [ˈbəːiʲɪŋ ˈtʌuʷə] even though these are neither as obvious nor as consistent as those to be heard in other South Wales accents. Exceptionally, the word *our* regularly has an alternative smoothed form [aː], not heard in GSWE.

10.2.2 Consonants

The CE consonant system is similar to most other types of native-speaker English. Unlike the rest of South Wales, it seems to be little affected by Welsh. (It is notable that some Cardiffians have difficulty with [x] in local Welsh place-names, replacing it with [k]; virtually all find a convincing Welsh voiceless [ɬ] an insurmountable problem.)

P, T, K
Initial fortis stops /p t k/ are strongly aspirated, but less so than in most Welsh varieties; similarly, final devoicing is not as obvious as in other Welsh accents, but appears more consistent than in most southern British varieties. In basilectal CE, /p t k/ normally lack glottalisation in final position, although more sophisticated speakers tend to adopt glottalisation along the lines of mainstream RP (Mees 1983: 84; 1987). CE stands out among British accents in having glottalisation as a prestigious rather than a stigmatised feature (Mees 1987). See 10.2.3.2 and 10.3 for elision of final alveolar stop consonants in a small set of high-frequency words. In medial position, T-voicing is common. Between a vowel and syllabic /l̩/, [ʔ] occurs regularly only in the word *little*. As in many other varieties, the sequence /tn̩/ is frequently [ʔn̩], e.g. *kitten* [kɪʔn̩]; glottalisation is auditorily weaker in the broader forms of the accent.

NASALS
As in most basilectal types of English, the ending *-ing* is generally pronounced as /ɪn/, e.g. *singing, ceiling* [ˈsɪŋɪn ˈsiːlɪn].

Words like *Canton* (local place-name), *lantern* are realised as [ˈkanʔn̩ ˈlanʔn̩] with glottal stop followed by syllabic nasal (cf. RP [ˈkantən ˈlantən]); in addition, syllabic [n̩] is found in the sequence /ndn/ as in *London* [ˈləndn̩] (cf. RP [ˈlʌndən]).

H
In CE, as in most English and Welsh basilectal accents, H-loss is a common phenomenon and suffers the usual social stigmatisation. The cluster /hj/ is /j/ in the broadest forms of the accent, e.g. *human* [ˈjuːmən], *huge* [ˈjuːdʒ]. Note also *here, hear* as [jøː]. More sophisticated speakers use [ç] instead, e.g. [çuːmən], a realisation of /hj/ also commonly found in standard varieties. The CE [ç] appears, however, to have a rather more front articulation, and closer narrowing resulting in stronger friction, making it sound rather conspicuous to non-Cardiffian ears.

J
As in many Welsh varieties, /j/ does not occur before /iː/, e.g. *yeast, yield* [iːst iːld]. See above for /jøː/ as an alternative to /iːə/ in words of the NEAR type.

R

CE is totally non-rhotic, with regular occurrence of R-liaison forms. In the broadest varieties, /r/ may be realised as a weak alveolar tap [ɾ], rather than as an approximant [ɹ], especially in intervocalic position.

L

Unlike other GSWE, CE /l/ exhibits the normal English allophonic patterning of clear [l] before vowels and [j], and dark [ɫ] before other consonants and pause. CE has obvious 'breaking' before dark [ɫ] (Wells 1982: 298), e.g. *meal* [miːəɫ], *school* [skuːəɫ], *old* [ɤuəɫd]. There is full central alveolar contact and little of the L-vocalisation characteristic of much modern English.

10.2.3 Features of connected speech

10.2.3.1 Articulatory setting

By 'articulatory setting' we mean the general posture of the vocal organs as they are held throughout the speech process (Honikman 1964; Laver 1980).

Impressionistically, the CE tongue shape seems characteristically 'alveo-larised', with general tongue advancement and the front/blade of the tongue held tense and close to the alveolar ridge with the sides somewhat raised. The posterior of the tongue is lax, giving a large pharynx cavity. The velum appears to be partly lowered throughout running speech, giving rise to semi-continuous nasality.

Basilectal speakers have a general lack of lip-rounding often with the corners of the mouth permanently slightly retracted. As a result, vowels that are rounded in most English varieties, e.g. THOUGHT and LOT, are unrounded or spread in CE. Mainstream and middle-class CE do not share this feature; not only is THOUGHT rounded but so is NURSE, as is typical of Welsh English generally (Wells 1982: 381). (Broader CE speakers appear usually to realise NURSE with little lip-rounding or none at all.)

The vocal folds appear to be tense, with a tendency to harsh anterior voice (as described by Catford 1977: 102–3). Creak is largely absent. The tenseness of the vocal folds is often combined with a breathy quality giving greater resonance and tension combined with an impression of hoarseness. The Cardiff accent is sometimes pejoratively labelled 'harsh' or 'rasping' (cf. Coupland 1988: 98).

10.2.3.2 Connected speech processes

CE is characterised by remarkably pervasive assimilation and elision. Not only is Cardiff assimilation typically English in form – unlike the more limited Welsh-influenced assimilation found in GSWE accents such as Abercrave (Tench 1990: 132) – but it appears to be even more extensive than in the majority of English accents, including RP (Brown 1977: 53–83). Although CE patterning is on similar lines, it is the extent and consistency that is striking – even at a slow speaking rate. CE place and lenis/fortis assimilation corresponds closely to that found in RP (see Cruttenden & Gimson 1994: 257–60); manner assimilation most frequently affects /ð/ in contexts following alveolars other than /t, d/, e.g. *all that* [ˈʌːl lat], *in the* [ɪn nə], etc. Although similar manner patterns are not unusual in RP (Ortiz Lira 1976), CE extends such usage regularly to strongly stressed contexts, e.g. *in these cases* [ɪn ˈniːz keisɪz], *although* [ʌːl ˈlɤu].

In utterances such as *wasn't, doesn't, isn't,* /z/ often emerges as [d] under the influence of the following nasal: [ˈwɑdn̩, ˈdədn̩, ˈɪdn̩]. This may be further reduced to [wɑn:, dən:, ɪn:].

Elision features are also similar to colloquial RP (e.g. Brown 1977: 60–72; Cruttenden & Gimson 1994: 261–2), though on a much more regular basis, even in slower speech modes. In addition, CE is notable for elision in a set of high-frequency words (for a list, see section 10.3 below), where alveolar stops may also be elided pre-pausally (e.g. *that's right* [ˈas ˈɹəɪ]) and intervocalically (e.g. *but I* [bə əi]). In addition, /t/ may be deleted in final /-nt/ clusters, not only before consonants, e.g. *don't drive* [dɤun ˈdɹəiv], but also before vowels, e.g. *can't handle* [kæːn ˈandl̩], *went up* [wɛn ˈəp]. Note that the vowel normally retains full length, but occasionally there may be potential confusion (e.g. between *can* and *can't*), at least for non-Cardiffians. /t/ in a final /-ts/ cluster is frequently elided with no compensatory glottalisation, e.g. *it's dead* [ɪs ˈdɛd], *gets some chips* [ˈgɛs səm ˈtʃɪps].

/r/ is occasionally elided in intervocalic position, e.g. *very* [ˈvɛːi], *America* [əˈmɛːɪkə]. A 'remnant' of the /r/ is seen in the lengthening of the preceding vowel.

10.2.4   Intonation and rhythmic features

On the whole, CE has vowel length patterns that are closer to southern English varieties than they are to the rather more syllable-timed effect of much GSWE. A feature of the accent which is reminiscent of some south-western varieties of English is the extended length of certain free vowels, especially /ɑː/, /ʌː/ and /øː/. On the other hand, the close vowels /iː, uː/ seem noticeably short.

Although CE does not regularly exhibit Welsh-type consonant lengthening (Connolly 1981: 59), there is frequently noticeable extra weight and pitch movement giving undue prominence to final unstressed syllables, e.g. *he's landed* [iːz ˈlandɛd]. It is perhaps in certain of these rhythmic features that CE can be shown to have most in common with GSWE accents.

CE intonation is recognisably Welsh, even though in some ways it shows more resemblance to the accents of England than it does to those of Wales. CE certainly lacks the close correlation with the pitch patterns of Welsh which is such a striking feature of the neighbouring GSWE varieties of Glamorgan and Gwent (Wells 1982: 392; Tench 1990: 138). The pitch range is considerably more compact than in GSWE and the characteristic nuclear tones of CE have counterparts in southern British varieties rather than in Welsh. The accent is notable for considerable use of rise–fall and fall–rise patterns, both of these being somewhat more extended than their counterparts in most other English accents.

A salient feature of CE intonation – particularly associated with narrative mode – is a rising or mid-level contour with a high-rise termination. A similar intonation tune, with comparable implications, is very common in Australian English (see, for example, Horvath 1985: 126–32), and has been noted of late to be spreading to British English varieties. But at least as far as Cardiff is concerned, such terminal rising patterns are certainly of greater time-depth. Not only are they consistently to be heard on our recordings as far back as 1976, but informal observations indicate that the phenomenon dates back much further. The Cardiff-born co-author of this chapter (BC) remembers from as early as the late 1950s that English visitors to the town regularly commented on the lines of 'Why do Cardiff people always seem to be asking questions when they're actually trying to tell you something?' See Coupland (1988: 32–3) for a more detailed discussion of this characteristically Cardiffian intonation feature.

10.3   *Glottalisation*

As noted above, CE, unlike most British urban varieties, has comparatively little glottalisation. Furthermore, glottalisation decreases as one moves down the socio-economic scale, so that the broadest accents are notable for the paucity of this feature (even though CE is still at variance with most other Welsh accents, especially those of Type 1, where glottalisation is hardly known; see Wells 1982: 388; Tench 1990: 131). Work carried out on Cardiff speech back in 1976 and 1981, based on a real-time study of the speech of schoolchildren, and reported in Mees (1983, 1987, 1990), showed that glottalisation following a pattern of distribution found in RP (Wells 1982: 260–1) appeared to be on the increase in Cardiff. An analysis of the class, style, gender and time variation revealed glottalisation of word-final /t/ to be a spreading prestigious feature, with the process of change being led by young middle-class females (see Docherty, Foulkes, Milroy, Milroy & Walshaw (1997: 303–4) for comparable findings in respect of Tyneside). However, there was little evidence of the change having passed into the speech of the working classes, where glottalisation remained sporadic.

The Cardiff research may be considered as a 'panel study'. This has been defined by Labov (1994: 76) as a type of project that 'attempts to locate the same individuals that were the subjects of the first study, and monitors any changes in their behaviour by submitting them to the same questionnaire, interview or experiment'. Labov continues:

This is an expensive and time-consuming procedure, if it is planned as a panel study from the beginning, for the initial sample must be large enough to take the inevitable losses into account. An unplanned panel study will be left with a reduced sample, perhaps too small for statistical significance, but nonetheless extremely valuable for the interpretation of the original observations.

Several linguists have returned to the community they originally studied and have replicated their work, but the pursuit of the same individuals was usually not a part of the basic design.

Fortunately, although the Cardiff project was indeed not originally envisaged as a panel study, it has nevertheless proved possible to track down an unusually high percentage of the original informants. Labov (1994: 97) regards 50% as 'a remarkably high proportion'; in Cardiff we managed to locate 67%. Work on the larger project is still in progress (see 10.1.1), but here we intend to concentrate on an in-depth scrutiny of a micro-group in order to investigate one aspect of the spread of glottalised variants.

Mees (1983) reports the results of a comparison of data collected in the 1976 and 1981 fieldwork. The analysis dealt with the speech of 36 informants, who had been selected from the original sample and assigned to three social classes (Middle Middle Class, Lower Middle Class and Working Class, henceforth MMC, LMC, and WC) on the basis of father's occupation – each class sample consisting of six boys and six girls. Two speech styles (interview style and reading passage style) were considered. An investigation was undertaken of co-variation of six variables with social class, gender, style and time. The present discussion is concerned more particularly with the speech of WC female subjects and it is on this that we shall primarily focus – specifically on their realisations of word-final pre-consonantal and pre-pausal /t/ in a small set of seventeen (mostly monosyllabic) high-frequency words, i.e. *it, bit, get, let, at, that, got, lot, not, what, put, but, might, right, quite, out, about*. Unlike other words ending in /t/, these items appear to behave differently in CE with respect to realisational possibilities; cf. the discussion in Docherty *et al.* (1997: 297), and Milroy, Milroy & Hartley (1994: 24), for whether words of this kind should also be conjectured as forming a subset in Tyneside. In CE, most word-final /t/s can be produced as [t] or [ʔ, ʔt], but for this set of common words there is a third possible variant, namely elision (∅), whereby /t/ is either completely elided or else realised as a very weakly articulated stop with inaudible release.

Tables 10.2 and 10.3 present the distribution of [t], [ʔ, ʔt] and ∅ as realisations of pre-consonantal and pre-pausal /t/ for the females in three social classes at two points in time. From Table 10.2 it is clear that glottalised variants are favoured by the girls in the higher social classes at both points in time, whereas elided forms are characteristic of the working class. Pre-pausally, the picture is much the same, as illustrated by Table 10.3. Again, the high percentage of glottalised forms in the middle classes is striking. Conversely, the working-class girls clearly have a preference for the elided variant.

Results from the fieldwork undertaken in 1990 allowed us to investigate the extent to which CE middle-class glottalisation has infiltrated into working-class speech. We selected from the original (1976) sample a micro-group of four working-class females for more intensive study, noting the occurrence of glottalisation in approximately 20 minutes of informal speech of each individual spread over the fifteen-year time span of the survey.[6] We observed the pronunciation of word-final /t/ in three potential glottalisation sites: pre-consonantal,

Table 10.2 Percentage of [t], [ʔ, ʔt] and
ø for pre-consonantal /t/ (in interview style) for all
females by social class at two points in time

	1976	1981
[t]		
MMC	14.3	7.5
LMC	34.5	25.5
WC	37.4	35.1
[ʔ, ʔt]		
MMC	79.2	84.6
LMC	30.8	47.6
WC	22.4	9.3
ø		
MMC	6.6	7.9
LMC	34.7	26.9
WC	40.2	55.7
N tokens analysed		
MMC	96	443
LMC	153	227
WC	198	281

Table 10.3 Percentage of [t], [ʔ, ʔt] and
ø for pre-pausal /t/ (in interview style) for all
females by social class at two points in time

	1976	1981
[t]		
MMC	33.9	8.5
LMC	46.4	20.6
WC	9.4	16.7
[ʔ, ʔt]		
MMC	51.4	83.2
LMC	25.8	62.4
WC	21.2	15.7
ø		
MMC	14.7	8.3
LMC	27.8	17.1
WC	69.4	67.6
N tokens analysed		
MMC	49	264
LMC	76	157
WC	127	208

pre-pausal and pre-vocalic. Table 10.4 shows the percentage of glottalised as opposed to other variants of word-final /t/ in the interview style of the subjects concerned.[7]

At first sight, it would appear that glottalisation is indeed beginning to invade the speech of Cardiff working-class females; the average scores for the group as a whole are considerably higher in 1990 than in the two earlier recordings. But there is actually more involved. Tables 10.5 and 10.6 present the percentage of glottalised and other variants of word-final /t/ in the interview style of each of the four working-class girls.

There is an apparently inconsistent pattern inasmuch as two informants (Carol and Judy) show a considerable glottalisation increase, whereas the others (Julie and Marilyn) do not.[8] However, social mobility and personal ambition (cf. Douglas-Cowie 1978) must be taken into account if the developing pattern is to prove liable to explanation. To do so involves abandoning for the moment quantitative research techniques and going beyond the statistical data to consider the personalities and backgrounds of the individuals concerned.

All four subjects spent their childhood and teenage years in Ely (a sprawling council house estate on the west side of Cardiff notorious for its image of criminality, high unemployment and social deprivation) and all were classified as working class on the basis of their father's occupation. All four informants had low glottalisation scores both in their first interviews as children (aged approximately 10) and in their teens (aged about 14). From then on, however, a dichotomy emerges, coinciding with widening differences in lifestyles and career prospects. In their interviews, two of the subjects gave considerable evidence of ambitious career plans and determination to improve their living circumstances. Both had indeed, in terms of their own or their husband's occupations, already

Table 10.4 Percentage of [t], [ʔ, ʔt], [t̴] and Ø for word-final /t/ (interview style) for three contexts at three points in time: four subjects

Word-final /t/	% [t]	% [ʔ, ʔt]	% Ø	% [t̴]	*N tokens*
Pre-consonantal					
1976	39.3	**13.9**	46.8		93
1981	31.7	**7.4**	61.0		165
1990	28.2	**31.7**	40.2		184
Pre-pausal					
1976	27.4	**23.8**	48.8		53
1981	16.9	**22.3**	60.7		73
1990	26.7	**44.7**	28.6		72
Pre-vocalic					
1976	21.9	**2.3**	10.3	65.5	60
1981	16.7	**2.3**	6.5	74.5	81
1990	30.0	**11.7**	8.3	50.0	131

Table 10.5 Percentage of [t], [ʔ, ʔt] and ø for pre-consonantal word-final /t/ (interview style) at three points in time: four subjects individually scored

Word-final /t/	% [t]	% [ʔ, ʔt]	% ø	N tokens
Carol				
1976	55.2	**20.7**	24.1	29
1981	47.2	**7.6**	45.3	53
1990	27.8	**37.5**	34.7	72
Judy				
1976	40.0	**20.0**	40.0	10
1981	31.8	**0.0**	68.2	22
1990	14.3	**74.3**	11.4	35
Julie				
1976	24.0	**8.0**	68.0	25
1981	13.5	**11.5**	75.0	52
1990	47.6	**11.9**	40.5	42
Marilyn				
1976	37.9	**6.9**	55.2	29
1981	34.2	**10.5**	55.3	38
1990	22.9	**2.9**	74.3	35

Table 10.6 Percentage of [t], [ʔ, ʔt] and ø for pre-pausal word-final /t/ (interview style) at three points in time: four subjects individually scored

Word-final /t/	% [t]	% [ʔ, ʔt]	% ø	N tokens
Carol				
1976	53.3	**26.7**	20.0	15
1981	38.1	**19.0**	42.3	21
1990	15.0	**60.0**	25.0	20
Judy				
1976	14.3	**14.3**	71.4	7
1981	0.0	**50.0**	50.0	20
1990	10.0	**85.0**	5.0	20
Julie				
1976	30.8	**15.4**	53.8	13
1981	0.0	**20.0**	80.0	15
1990	31.8	**13.6**	54.5	22
Marilyn				
1976	11.1	**38.9**	50.0	18
1981	29.4	**0.0**	70.5	17
1990	50.0	**20.0**	30.0	10

transferred to a higher socio-economic class. A quote from Judy's interview will serve as an example:

> It was a very good job – and if I'd been the type of person – who was prepared to just have a nice cushy little number and just stay there – I could have stayed there for the rest of my life – but er – I – I found that it wasn't fulfilling enough – that – you know – I – I felt I could do something more.

Judy is referring to the fact that she already had one successful career behind her as a dental technician and at the time of the interview was almost within sight of achieving her ambition of becoming a fully qualified chiropodist. The other young woman, Carol, had established herself in a career in office accounting while her husband was a qualified chartered accountant; the couple had moved into a new house in a leafy suburb to the north of Cardiff.

The remaining two subjects had experienced less in the way of good fortune. Marilyn, who was not in paid employment, was living in temporary rented accommodation in an inner-city area with her young daughter and her lorry driver partner. Julie was a lone parent bringing up her young son. She had remained in Ely, managing to find work as a part-time waitress/barmaid. The tone and content of both of their interviews contrast sharply with those of the two ambitious subjects. There is little evidence of long-term plans to change lifestyle or improve their socio-economic circumstances; Julie's references to her restaurant duties are indicative of the attitudes of both women:

> I'm just glad I got this now – you know – I'm on my feet again now – I'm working or whatever – a bit of pocket money I call it . . . you haven't got to bother with the till – they write it down on – what's on the menu – you know – what they're having with their meals – so you just pour the drinks – so you haven't got to work out anything – which is good.

This difference in general attitude is reflected in the distribution of the scores for the word-final /t/ variants so that by the time of the 1990 round of interviews (all by now were in their early twenties) the young women also show great divergence in their glottalisation scores: Carol and Judy exhibit a striking increase in glottalisation while the scores of Julie and Marilyn remain consistently low. The changes made by Carol and Judy to their pronunciation reflect a desire to gain higher socio-economic status – a desire that has led them to differentiate their speech from that of their peers.

10.4   *Conclusion – glottalisation and Cardiff accent group identity*

We are left with two questions to consider. Why is Cardiff peculiarly socially sensitive to glottalisation features as compared with the rest of South Wales?

And why should what appears at first sight to be simply a spread of such features to working-class speech need more analysis?

The significance of glottalisation in our study appears to be related to the wider question of the status of varieties of English in the Cardiff region. Here, as Coupland (1988: 40, 46–51, *et passim*) has pointed out, a perception of accent types exists which is quite different from that found elsewhere in South Wales. Cardiff does not have any prestigious form of Welsh English as an icon. Despite living in the capital city, Cardiffians in general, and working-class Cardiffians in particular, do not enthusiastically participate in the general revival of Welsh loyalty, nor do they consider themselves part of the new Welsh ethnicity which has been noted by some observers. The 1997 Referendum underlined the relationship between accent divisions and group identity, when districts included in the CE dialect area, i.e. Cardiff, Newport and the Vale of Glamorgan, voted in large numbers against the Welsh Assembly (ironically, it was nevertheless eventually decided to locate the Assembly in Cardiff itself).

Most speakers of Welsh English (Types 1 and 2, including GSWE, in our classification above) would appear to regard Welsh accented speech with approval. But, in Cardiff, broad GSWE varieties are regarded with opprobrium. Welsh speech features such as clear /l/, steady-state vowels in GOAT and FACE, and 'lilting' intonation are (in exaggerated form) frequently the butt of ridicule. In working-class Cardiff communities this negativism is likely to be far greater than that reserved for broad Cardiff accents. On the other hand, RP, near-RP and accents of similar type are regarded in Cardiff in much the same way as in England, and do not suffer the extreme negative reactions which have been reported for Type 1 and 2 areas of Wales (Coupland 1988: 51). The attitude of the media is suggestive here: on Cardiff local radio, the presenters overwhelmingly have RP (natural or acquired) accents or mild British regional accents without any Welsh associations.

Glottalisation may be attractive to ambitious CE speakers because it represents, at subconscious level, a move away from local Welsh accent characteristics towards more sophisticated and fashionable speech. While we have ourselves shown that glottalisation actually has considerable time-depth in RP (Collins & Mees 1996), there is no denying the extent of its recent expansion, perhaps under the influence of what has been dubbed 'Estuary English' (Rosewarne 1984). Nowadays, glottalisation is associated with London life, metropolitan fashions and trend-setting attitudes; it is to be heard from royalty as well as rock stars. It is not difficult therefore to account for the fact that in Cardiff and the adjacent area, where many inhabitants appear to look away from Wales towards England, glottal stop is a prestige feature. Apart from glottalisation, it is perhaps not mere chance that there are other recent linguistic changes in CE, e.g. the change of FACE and GOAT to obvious diphthongal glides and the rounding of PRICE, that can be associated with movement away from Welsh-accented speech and towards south-eastern English varieties.

Since Labov (1966: 495–6) it has frequently been confirmed that solidly working-class speakers are relatively secure in their speech norms, and make the least effort to change. So it is not surprising that our two non-ambitious subjects have not altered their speech habits. The ambitious working-class women, on the other hand, are eager to strive towards a new class status and to acquire the trappings that go with it. The upwardly mobile Cardiff females can be seen to acquire RP-style glottalisations together with a professional career, a suburban house and a well-qualified partner. Those who lack such aims are also likely to lack glottalised forms.

What superficially appears to be a straightforward linguistic change in our real-time study – the spread of a new feature to a South Wales working-class community – turns out to be rather more complex in at least two ways. Firstly, account must be taken of local linguistic attitudes and group identities. Secondly, the working class must not be considered as one amorphous whole, but it must be recognised that persons may shift social class or have ambition to do so. Their linguistic behaviour needs to be analysed accordingly.

Notes

1 We wish to thank Wim van der Wurff for reading and commenting on portions of this chapter, and Jack Windsor Lewis for help with an earlier version of the accent description.
2 We are grateful to Nikolas Coupland for providing us with this material.
3 We refer here to the names of the former regional divisions which are still in common use in Wales.
4 The GOOSE–JUICE split is reported to occur in the speech of Newport (Windsor Lewis, personal communication).
5 Note that in the vowel diagrams we employ the following conventions (Windsor Lewis 1969: 16): squares and circles indicate spread/neutral and rounded lips respectively. A D-shape is employed for diphthongs involving a change from spread to rounded lips; its reverse (ᗡ) indicates a change from rounded to spread.
6 Since we wanted to compare female speakers reared in a specific locality of the city (Ely), these are not a subset of the WC females in Tables 10.2 and 10.3, even though they are in other significant respects (i.e. age and social class) congruent. We are very grateful to Tina Pinnerup and Mette Rasmussen (formerly students at the Copenhagen Business School) for producing the orthographic transcripts of the four informants.
7 For the purposes of this article, it was decided not to utilise the individual results for pre-vocalic glottalisation since so little was found; as stated in 10.2.2, Cardiff speakers are much more likely to have ᴛ-voicing in this context (cf. Holmes's 1994 study of New Zealand).
8 The informants' names have been changed.

11

Glasgow: accent and voice quality

Jane Stuart-Smith

11.1 *Introduction*

Glasgow is Scotland's largest, and once most industrial, city. It has a strong sense of Scottish and specifically Glaswegian identity, which is expressed through its language, characteristic accent, and culture. This chapter offers first a brief description of the Glasgow accent, and then turns to an important aspect of accent which is rarely discussed by either phoneticians or sociolinguists – voice quality.

11.1.1 Glasgow: linguistic context

Glasgow, like much of lowland Scotland, is generally regarded linguistically as a 'traditional dialect' area (Wells 1982), where an alternative variety of English exists alongside a standard variety. In the Scottish context, the 'standard' spoken variety of English of many educated, middle-class (MC) speakers is Scottish Standard English (SSE). SSE is a variety of English whose grammar is very similar to that of standard English English, but which is spoken with a Scottish accent to a greater or lesser degree (Abercrombie 1979). The alternative variety is historically derived from Scots, and is more often spoken by working-class (WC) speakers (for a recent history of Scots see Jones 1997; see also Chirrey this volume). Aitken (e.g. 1979) provides a useful model of the relationship of Scots and SSE in terms of a linguistic continuum, with Scots at one end and SSE at the other. Scottish speakers can either move discretely to different points on the continuum (style-switchers), or show tendencies to move up and down the continuum (style-drifters). Style-drifting is very common in speakers in the central belt of Scotland, and in Glasgow in particular.

For descriptive purposes we acknowledge in Glasgow two varieties, each with a characteristic accent:

- Glasgow Standard English (GSE), the Glaswegian form of SSE, spoken by most MC speakers;
- Glasgow vernacular (GV), the dialect of many WC speakers, which is

historically based on West-Central Scots, but which shows strong influences from Irish English, its own distinctive slang, and increasing levelling towards GSE (Macafee 1983; 1994: 26f.).

The relationship between the two varieties – if these can indeed be defined in this way – must be seen as fuzzy and overlapping, particularly given the tendency for style-drifting according to social context. Glasgow also has the 'Kelvinside' accent (cf. the 'Morningside' accent in Edinburgh), which is spoken largely by older female MC speakers, and which is generally thought to be highly affected by other Glaswegians (Johnston 1985). RP has little status in Glasgow, and is regarded with hostility in some quarters. The position of other accents of English is less clear. Certain specifically English English features in the speech of some younger Glaswegians, such as TH-fronting, suggest that a non-standard English English model may be becoming more relevant.

11.1.2   Data for this study

This description of Glaswegian accent and voice quality is mainly based on a preliminary analysis of data collected in 1997.[1] The methodology for the data collection was adapted from that of the Newcastle/Derby study (see Docherty, Foulkes, Milroy, Milroy & Walshaw 1997; also the chapters in this volume by Watt & Milroy; Docherty & Foulkes). It resulted in good examples of casual, relaxed conversations from most speakers. Thirty-two speakers were recorded, with equal numbers of males and females, adults (40–60 years) and children (13–14 years), from two broadly different social and regional backgrounds of the Glaswegian conurbation: Maryhill, a working-class inner-city area stretching from the north-west of the city centre, and Bearsden, a leafy suburb further out to the north-west, inhabited mainly by the middle classes. The children for the study were approached through two schools, each markedly different in terms of three criteria: percentage of exam passes; percentage of school leavers going on to higher education; and percentage of children receiving clothing grants. The selection criterion for the children (and WC adults) was that they had been born and raised in the area. This was extended for the MC children, in that children born in the west end of Glasgow were also included. This same criterion was applied for the MC adults, the high proportion of university employees and white-collar workers reflecting Bearsden's status as an area of upward social mobility. The data comprise high-quality digital recordings of read word-lists and spontaneous conversations from same-sex pairs of up to 45 minutes. The word-lists were digitized into a Pentium PC running *Xwaves/ESPS* speech-processing software. The data are extensive; it is stressed that all comments made here are preliminary, and in many cases more auditory and acoustic investigation is required.

11.2   *Descriptive material*

While most comments here are based on the 1997 data, and especially the word-list data, the following description also draws on observations by Macaulay & Trevelyan (1973); Macaulay (1977); Abercrombie (1979); Wells (1982); Macafee (1983), who acknowledges the help of Paul Johnston for phonetic observations; Macafee (1994); and Johnston (1985, 1997b). An invaluable discussion of SSE is that of Abercrombie (1979).

Trudgill (1974: 185f.) argues that describing the voice quality of an accent can help account more generally for segmental variation. In this chapter the discussion of voice quality follows the segmental description. However, it will become clear that reference to some features of voice quality at this stage do enable certain aspects of segmental sociophonetic variation to be expressed more satisfactorily.

11.2.1   Vowels

Differences between the vowel systems of GSE and GV are now largely reflected in lexical incidence (for detailed discussion see especially Macafee 1994: 224f.). In the 1997 data, the MC speakers showed the SSE vowel system as described by Abercrombie (1979), with occasional instances of GV vowels in younger speakers, most often [ʉ] in a restricted set of words in the MOUTH set. When reading the word-lists, most WC speakers also showed the SSE vowel system, although with different qualities from the MC speakers. The retraction (and lowering) of vowels can be explained as the result of a backed tongue body setting, perhaps with pharyngealization, in WC speakers. In casual speech, WC speakers use GV vowels occasionally, though with clearly restricted lexical incidence, particularly in the younger speakers. The broadest speech in terms of Scots vowel incidence was found in the older WC female speakers (possibly because the fieldworker was female).

The sociophonetic realization of the stressed monophthongs is exemplified in the two formant plots shown in Figure 11.1.

Comments

RHOTICITY
The retention of underlying post-vocalic /r/ means that in comparison with many other accents of English, there are no centring diphthongs phonemically in words such as *near, hair*. The selection of vowels before /r/ varies considerably. In words such as *fir, fern, fur*, some speakers show one vowel /ɪ/ (or /ʌ/), others two /ɛ ʌ/ (*fern, fir, fur*), and still others three. There are also differences in the back vowel used before /r/ in START (for more discussion see Wells 1982: 407).

Table 11.1 Glasgow vowels – summary.

	Glasgow Standard	Glasgow Vernacular
KIT	ɪ	ï ~ i̵
DRESS	ɛ	ɛ
HEAD	ɛ	i
NEVER	ɛ ~ ë	ï
TRAP	a̠	a̠
STAND	a̠	ɔ
LOT	ɔ	o
STRUT	Ä	Ä
FOOT	ʉ	ï ~ i̵
BATH	a̠	a̠
AFTER	a̠	ɛ
CLOTH	ɔ	o
OFF	ɔ	a̠
NURSE	Ä	Ä ~ ɪ
FLEECE	i ~ i̞	i ~ i̞
FACE	e	e
STAY	e	e ~ ʌi
PALM	a̠	a̠
THOUGHT	ɔ	o
GOAT	o	o
MORE	o	e
GOOSE	ʉ	ʉ
DO	ʉ	e
PRICE	ʌi	ʌi
PRIZE	ae	ae
CHOICE	ɔe	ɔe
MOUTH	ʌʉ	ʉ
NEAR	i	i
SQUARE	e	ɛ ~ e
START	a̠	e
BIRTH	ɪ	ï ~ Ä
BERTH	ɛ	ɛ ~ ɪ
NORTH	ɔ	o
FORCE	o	o
CURE	jʉ	jʉ
happY	e	e ~ ï
lettER	ï ~ Ä	Ä
horsES	ɪ	ï ~ Ä
commA	Ä	Ä

VOWEL LENGTH

Scottish vowels can vary in phonetic length according to phonetic and morpho-
logical conditioning; this is described by the 'Scottish Vowel Length Rule', or
'Aitken's Law' (e.g. Wells 1982: 400f.; Scobbie, Hewlett & Turk this volume).
Vowels are short, unless preceding /r/, a voiced fricative, or a boundary, includ-

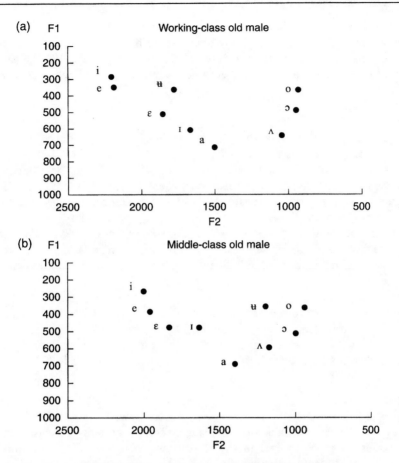

Fig. 11.1 Sociophonetic realization of stressed monophthongs illustrated by vowel formant plots of (a) a typical working-class man; (b) a typical middle-class man

ing a morpheme boundary. Thus [i] in *bead, beak* is short, but long in *beer, breathe, bee*; similarly [ʉ] in *brood* is short, but can be long in *brew* and *brewed* (*brew+ed*). This rule also accounts for the incidence of the diphthongs [ʌi] (in short environments, e.g. *side*) and [ae] (in long environments, e.g. *sighed*), though genuine minimal pairs occur in Scots, e.g. *aye* [ae], *ay* [ʌi]. In the 'Kelvinside' accent both diphthongs can be merged as [ae].

KIT
Sociolinguistic variation in the realization of the monophthongs /ɪ a ʉ/ was investigated by Macaulay & Trevelyan (1973), and Macaulay (1977). They identified a number of variants for the KIT vowel – [ɪ ɛ̣ ë̞ ə̣ ʌ] – but the main

class differences correlated with front–backness, with (lowered and) backed variants in WC speech. This correlates well with the analysis of voice quality which identifies a main setting difference between MC and WC speakers in degree of tongue backing (see comments by Scobbie, Hewlett & Turk this volume).

TRAP, BATH

Previous studies also show the pronunciation of /a/ to be backer in quality in lower-class speakers than higher-class speakers (e.g. Macaulay's Class I used the very front [æ], as in the 'Kelvinside' accent). In the 1997 data some backing was found in WC speech. A potential development noticed in the 1997 data is the alignment of allophonic variation of front and backer allophones with the lexical sets of southern English English, e.g. *cap* [kap] but *car* [kaɾ] in WC speakers. This is not necessarily to be expected, since as Abercrombie (1979: 61) has pointed out, the few SSE speakers who show a distinction between /a/ and /ɑ/ show a different lexical incidence from RP. They often have /ɑ/ in *salmon*, for example.

FACE, GOAT

The FACE and GOAT vowels tend to be monophthongs in GSE, and especially in GV. Apart from regular breaking especially before /r n l/, the 1997 data show very little evidence for the diphthongal realization of these vowels found in English English (or BBC Scotland newscasters; see also Macafee 1983: 35).

GOOSE

In previous studies the realization of the GOOSE vowel carried reverse connotation to that of TRAP: a backer quality was associated with higher class. This finding seems to be continued in the 1997 data, with the WC realization more fronted than the MC (see Figure 11.1).

SQUARE

In Glasgow there are signs of a merger of /er/ and /ɛr/. /ɛr/ is sometimes said to be a feature of Catholic rather than Protestant speakers, but Macafee (1994: 225f.) contends that the evidence for this is weak and that the merger is better regarded as a feature of GV in general at this time.

11.2.2   Consonants

STOPS

Stops are generally reported to be less aspirated in Scottish English (e.g. Wells 1982: 409) and this appears to be the case, at least auditorily for MC and WC speakers. Glottalling of non-initial /t/ is a strongly stigmatized yet extremely common feature of Glaswegian. Macaulay & Trevelyan's (1973) study (see also Macaulay 1977) revealed clear social stratification, with WC speakers producing more glottal stops than MC speakers. An initial investigation of the 1997 data reveals a significant increase in glottalling, and continued social differences in patterning according to phonetic environment (Stuart-Smith forthcoming). If /t/ is not replaced with a glottal stop, it can be realized as a tap, particularly when /t/ is final in a short-vowelled syllable, as in e.g. *get it, let it* (cf. Macafee 1983: 34). Glottalling of /p/ and /k/ is also reported, as are ejective realizations of emphatic utterance-final stops (Macafee 1983: 33).

The place of articulation of /t d/ can be dental (or pre-alveolar) in GSE (Wells 1982: 409); the predominant tongue tip/blade setting identified in the voice quality analysis was advanced, indicating a fronted articulation for /t d l n/ (though not always for /s/). Macafee (1983: 38; 1994) also notes specifically Scots features of GV which affect /d/ in certain words: the possible devoicing of /d/, and the loss of /d/ after /l/ and /n/, e.g. *aul* 'old', *staun* 'stand'.

TH

The analysis of voice quality identified lax supralaryngeal tension for WC speakers, and especially children. This is reflected in the very open approximation of most fricatives and approximants, and especially /θ ð/. A possible variant for /θ/ in GV is [h], in e.g. *think, something*, with a retroflex or alveolo-palatal fricative or [ɹ̩] in the initial cluster /θr/, in e.g. *three* (Wells 1982: 410; Macafee 1983: 33; Chirrey this volume).

Macafee (1983: 34, n. 26) notes sporadic instances of 'Cockney' /f/ for /θ/; this is found variably but frequently in the speech of WC children, in both word-list and conversational speech in the 1997 data. Similarly, /v/ is also found for /ð/ in e.g. *smooth*. More common local variants of /ð/ in GV are [r], particularly intervocalically, in e.g. *brother*, or complete elision word-initially (Wells 1982: 410; Macafee 1983: 33). Scots lexical incidence results in instances of the loss of /v/ intervocalically, in e.g. *de'il* 'devil', and of /θ/ word-finally, in e.g. *wi'* 'with' (Macafee 1983: 38).

S, Z

Macafee (1983: 34) notes a 'cacuminal' (apico-alveolar) realization of /s z/ in GV and links this to the articulatory setting of protruded jaw. In the 1997 data a distinctive realization of /s/ is particularly apparent, although usually in male speakers, especially boys (both WC and MC). The precise articulation is uncertain, but it seems to be produced with a retracted (and possibly lowered) tongue tip. Interestingly, speakers who show this form of retracted /s/ do not necessarily show protruded jaw.

WH, X

The consonantal phonemic systems of GSE and GV are essentially the same, but potentially differ from those of standard and other varieties of English English, primarily by having two additional phonemes /x/ and /ʍ/, as in *loch* /lɔx/ versus *lock* /lɔk/, and *whine* /ʍʌin/ versus *wine* /wʌin/ respectively (Wells 1982: 408; Chirrey this volume). The lexical frequency of /x/ is low, and it is often replaced by /k/ (Macafee 1983: 32), especially by young WC speakers. If /x/ was pronounced in the 1997 data, it was often realized as a strongly backed, almost uvular fricative, particularly by MC adults. A merger of /ʍ/ and /w/ is reported in younger speakers by Macafee (1983: 32), and this occurs in the WC children in the 1997 data (see further Lawson 1998; Chirrey this volume).

H, J

H-dropping is not generally reported for Scottish English (Wells 1982: 412), and is rarely apparent in these data (except in e.g. enclitic *him*, *her*). Similarly, J-dropping appears to function much as Wells states, i.e. after /l/ and commonly after /s/, with only sporadic instances elsewhere. Clusters with /j/, such as [tj] in *nature*, which have undergone coalescence to [tʃ] in English English and GV, are still retained by some GSE speakers (Wells 1982: 412; Macafee 1983: 32–3).

R

Scottish English remains rhotic (see above), although loss of post-vocalic R is reported in the speech of WC Edinburgh children by Romaine (1978) and in Glaswegian by Macafee (1983: 32). R-loss is also found in the 1997 data, mainly in the speech of WC children. Post-vocalically before a pause, in e.g. *car*, there is virtually no articulation beyond the open approximation of tongue backing in secondary articulation. Before a consonant, in e.g. *card*, a back approximant (velar/uvular/pharyngeal) is replacing the apical articulation. The loss of R is phonetically complex and deserves further investigation.

There is a range of realizations of R, commonly post-alveolar [ɹ], retroflex [ɻ] and a tap [ɾ], but rarely a trill. These variants are partly conditioned by place in the word and phonetic environment, but also by social factors (cf. Romaine 1978): in the 1997 data MC speakers show more instances of retroflex articulation, while WC speakers show more apical taps.

L

The secondary articulation of /l/ tends to be dark in all positions in the word, although some MC speakers use clear /l/ where this is expected in English English (Wells 1982: 411; Macafee 1983: 33). In the 1997 data velarized, and velarized and pharyngealized (see n.3), were the most usual secondary articulations for /l/ and also /r/. There is a clear link between the speakers (especially WC children) showing strongly retracted tongue body settings, and darker segmental secondary articulation.

L-deletion was a historical process in Scots, yielding common forms such as *hauf* 'half' (Macafee 1983: 38). More recently L-vocalization of the kind usually found in southern English, to a high back rounded vowel [ɤ] or [o] (Wells 1982: 258f.), has been reported in Glaswegian (Macafee 1983: 34, n. 26). This is clearly evidenced in the speech of WC children in the 1997 data.

11.2.3 Prosodic features

There is little published work on Glaswegian intonation, although this situation is likely to change once the results of the analysis of the Glasgow-based Map Task Corpus are published (for preliminary discussion see e.g. Mayo 1996). Nevertheless, we may note a common (and perhaps increasingly common) feature of Glasgow intonation which is shared by speakers of GSE and GV. This is in the use of a final rising intonation pattern (the 'high rise') (see Macafee 1983: 36; Cruttenden 1995). The 'high rise' is a long-standing feature of Glaswegian, as in e.g. Liverpool and Belfast, and is not necessarily related to the apparently rapid spread of high-rising terminal intonation in southern accents of English English.

Virtually nothing has been said about rhythm in Scottish English, bar Abercrombie's (1979: 67f.) comments that disyllabic words such as *table* are often pronounced with a short first syllable and long second syllable. (This is particularly likely for the FLEECE, GOOSE and PRICE vowels when in 'short' environments.) He also makes the observation that syllabification in SSE utterances tends to favour open syllables, so that e.g. [sṇt $ andrʉz] *St Andrews* is syllabified as [sṇ $ tandrʉz]. Little has been said either about Glaswegian voice quality, which is the subject of the rest of this chapter.

11.3 *Voice quality in Glaswegian*

Glasgow vernacular is well known for its distinctive voice quality. This 'Glasgow voice' is stereotypically exaggerated by television characters such as Rab C. Nesbitt, with phonetically slack articulation, jaw protrusion and harsh phonation. Glasgow vernacular in general is often impressionistically described with labels such as 'rough', 'ugly', 'harsh' and 'aggressive', and has been infamously associated 'with the unwashed and the violent' (Macaulay & Trevelyan 1973: 137). Apart from obvious links of a dialect with a large industrial city and its attendant social problems (Macafee 1983: 27), such opinions probably also reflect subjective impressions of stereotypical 'Glasgow voice', particularly given the paralinguistic association of both jaw protrusion and harsh voice with aggression and anger in many cultures (Laver 1994: 409, 420), and the tendency to judge individuals linguistically on the basis of stereotypical associations (Laver 1976; Brown, Strong & Rencher 1975). The extent to which such features of voice quality actually occur in Glaswegian speech has not been documented.

11.3.1 The phonetic analysis of voice quality

The term 'voice quality' refers here to the overall auditory quality which characterizes an individual's speech, including supralaryngeal and phonatory features. The most important contribution to the systematic phonetic analysis of voice quality has been made by Laver (see e.g. 1968, 1980, 1994). What follows is a brief outline of his approach; in all cases the reader is referred to Laver's more recent work (e.g. 1994: 391f.). Laver's work extends the thoughts of Abercrombie, who described voice quality as 'those characteristics which are present more or less all the time a person is talking: it is a quasi-permanent quality running through all the sound that issues from his mouth' (Abercrombie 1967: 91). Voice quality is taken to result from two main factors: the anatomy and physiology of the speaker (see Mackenzie Beck 1988),[2] and the 'long-term muscular adjustments, or articulatory settings (Honikman 1964), once acquired idiosyncratically, or by social imitation, and now unconscious, of the speaker's larynx and supralaryngeal vocal tract' (Laver 1968). Linguistic identification and membership of particular regional and social groups involves *acquired* speech traits, and thus sociophonetic voice quality is concerned with describing the habitual muscular settings over which speakers have a degree of voluntary control.

Much like the auditory description of vowel quality, a speaker's voice quality is described in terms of the interaction of a set of variable articulatory settings, facilitated by reference to a defined 'neutral' setting. Articulatory settings are characterized by their effects on particular phonetic segments, which are determined largely by shared physiology. For example, advanced tongue tip/blade setting will cause alveolar consonants to be fronted, making these 'key' segments for the identification of this setting. For descriptive purposes a relatively simple relationship between auditory impression and articulatory setting(s) is usually assumed. The acoustic correlates of the proposed settings have also been investigated (see e.g. Laver 1980; Nolan 1983; Esling & Dickson 1985; Pittam 1987).

11.3.2   Previous sociophonetic work on voice quality

Despite the recognized association of voice quality with particular regional and social accents (e.g. Wells 1982: 91), few descriptions of British urban accents have included more than informal remarks on voice quality. This is perhaps surprising, given that voice quality is often a clear social marker, particularly for class (Laver & Trudgill 1979), and that incorporating features of overall voice quality in a phonetic and phonological description can explain trends in segmental variation across social groups (Trudgill 1974: 190–1).

Three sociolinguistic studies have considered voice quality. Trudgill (1974) on Norwich English and Knowles (1974, 1978) on Scouse include discussion of voice quality in the vernacular. The typical settings of Norwich voice are: raised larynx, nasalization, high supralaryngeal tension, creaky phonation, loud with high pitch range. Scouse also shows raised larynx, but with velarization, faucalization, pharyngeal constriction, and close jaw; this combination of settings accounts for the characteristic auditory 'adenoidal' quality (Knowles 1978: 89). Esling's (1978a, b) examination of male speech in Edinburgh is the most detailed study. He found clear differences in voice quality correlating with social class. In particular, working-class speakers showed tongue blade articulation, protruded jaw, pharyngealization and raised larynx, with predominantly whispery and harsh voice. More recently, the sociophonetic nature of phonatory settings, specifically breathiness (Henton & Bladon 1985) and creak (Henton & Bladon 1988), has received attention. Both studies raise the important issue of what constitutes 'normal' (and hence 'abnormal') for a particular setting in a particular accent.

Apart from Esling on Edinburgh, there are only informal comments on Scottish English and/or Glaswegian voice quality. Abercrombie (1979: 68) refers to Sweet's claim of the 'pig's whistle' (possibly describing a type of harshness), though admits that he has never heard it. Knowles (1974: 100) mentions that velarization is found in some Scottish varieties, while Laver (1980: 131) comments on the frequent occurrence of harshness in some urban Scots accents and later (1994: 416) on a wider range of lingual articulation in 'many Scots accents'. If 'central' = 'lowland', apparently contradictory claims about laryngeal tension appear. Catford (1977: 103) refers to 'very lax, full-glottal, voice heard in Central Scotland', which contrasts with Wells' (1982: 92) comment that: 'the accent of lowland Scottish speakers typically involves tense voice'. Specific comments on aspects of Glaswegian voice quality refer to pharyngealization (Macafee 1983: 32), and in localized speech, to a protruded lower jaw setting (Macafee 1983: 35).

11.3.3 A perceptual analysis of Glaswegian voice quality

11.3.3.1 Methodology

Alongside the theoretical identification and classification of articulatory settings, a clinical tool was devised for the systematic perceptual analysis and transcription of voice quality, based on the Vocal Profile Analysis (VPA) protocol (see Laver, Wirz, Mackenzie & Hiller 1981; Mackenzie Beck 1988; Laver 1991: 268). The VPA protocol is particularly suitable for the transcription of voice quality, and so section 1 was used here (see Figure 11.2) with minor modifications.[3]

I established a VPA profile for each of the 32 speakers, for their conversational and read speech separately. It is important to note that the speakers were transcribed in random numerical order, which did not reflect their social grouping. This order was different for the two genres. While it would certainly have been desirable to have more judges to transcribe the data, the overall validity of the transcription would seem to be confirmed by a relatively high degree of consistency in setting, and setting values, in speakers across the two speech types.

Once the transcription was complete, I analysed the VPA profiles qualitatively and quantitatively. The qualitative analysis consisted of drawing up a verbal

Vocal Profile Analysis Protocol

Judge: . . . . **Tape:** . . . . **Sex:** . . . .

Date of Analysis: . . . . **Speaker:** . . . . **Age:** . . . .

I. VOCAL QUALITY FEATURES

CATEGORY	FIRST PASS			SECOND PASS						
	Neutral	Non-neutral		SETTING	Scalar Degrees					
		Normal	Abnormal		Normal			Abnormal		
					1	2	3	4	5	6
A. Supralaryngeal Features										
1. Labial				Lip Rounding/Protrusion						
				Lip Spreading						
				Labiodentalisation						
				Extensive Range						
				Minimised Range						
2. Mandibular				Close Jaw						
				Open Jaw						
				Protruded Jaw						
				Extensive Range						
				Minimised Range						
3. Lingual Tip/Blade				Advanced						
				Retracted						
4. Lingual Body				Fronted Body						
				Backed Body						
				Raised Body						
				Lowered Body						
				Extensive Range						
				Minimised Range						
5. Velopharyngeal				Nasal						
				Audible Nasal Escape						
				Denasal						
6. Pharyngeal				Pharyngeal Constriction						
7. Supralaryngeal Tension				Tense						
				Lax						
B. Laryngeal Features										
8. Laryngeal Tension				Tense						
				Law						
9. Larynx Position				Raised						
				Lowered						
10. Phonation Type				Harshness						
				Whisper(y)						
				Breathiness						
				Creak(y)						
				Falsetto						
				Modal Voice						

Fig. 11.2 Vocal Profile Analysis Protocol (reproduced from Laver (1991: 268) with permission of the author and the Edinburgh University Press)

description summarizing the VPA profile. Eight sociolinguistic groups of four speakers were assumed according to class (MC/WC), age (young/old) and gender (male/female). The verbal descriptions for each group were pooled, and settings observed in three or more speakers were noted. This produced an initial qualitative profile of shared features of voice quality for each group. These group profiles were then conflated in a similar way to give overall group characteristics, such as 'all MC speakers', or 'all WC female speakers' and so on. In this way shared and distinctive settings of voice quality could be identified for groups of speakers according to social factors of class, age and gender.

Observed degrees of settings were then quantified, giving simple descriptive statistics (e.g. mean, standard deviation) for each articulatory setting for groups of speakers (cf. Mackenzie Beck 1988: 188). Once the qualitative analysis had identified particular articulatory settings (or degrees of settings) as characteristic of social groups, these were then tested for statistical significance, using the non-parametric Mann–Whitney U Test. Thus in the following discussion, a setting is considered distinctive if (a) it was identified from the qualitative analysis (and was thus apparent in the majority of speakers in a group), and (b) if the difference in the group means was subsequently found to be statistically significant at $p < 0.05$.

11.3.4   Results

11.3.4.1   General points

The analysis of the VPA profiles of speakers confirmed characteristic constellations of articulatory settings for each group for both speech styles (see Tables 11.2 and 11.3). Even with such small numbers, speakers seem to conform broadly both to their assumed 'category' (e.g. WC men, MC girls, etc.), and to wider social groupings observed anecdotally in Glasgow.

The key findings can be summarized as follows:

- voice quality in Glaswegian differs with age, gender and class
- children showed laxer supralaryngeal articulation than adults
- overall, male speakers showed greater nasalization than female speakers; gender differences were also apparent in phonation: males showed more creaky voice; females more whispery voice
- a specifically WC Glaswegian voice quality can be identified (with more open jaw, raised and backed tongue body with possible retracted tongue root, whispery voice); MC voice quality is best described in terms of the *absence* of WC traits
- there is little evidence for the stereotypical 'Glasgow voice'
- all speakers shared a particular constellation of settings, which probably contributes to the overall impression of their speaking with a Glaswegian accent.

Table 11.2 Group characteristics of voice quality of speakers in conversational speech. (These are taken from the VPA protocols; characteristic is only mentioned when present in at least three speakers. Each group consists of four speakers.)

Gender	Age	Middle class	Working class
Male	*Old*	– mod. advanced tongue tip/blade – backed, sl. raised tongue body; sl. ATR; mod. nasal – mod. tense; whispery; mod. creaky voice	– lip rounding/protrusion; open jaw; advanced tongue tip/blade – mod. backed, raised tongue body; sl. RTR; mod. nasal; lax – tense; mod. whispery; sl. creaky voice
	Young	– advanced tongue tip/blade – raised tongue body; mod. nasal; tense – tense; whispery; mod. creaky voice	– lip rounding/protrusion; mod. open jaw; advanced tongue tip/blade – mod. backed, raised tongue body; sl. RTR; mod. nasal; v. lax – tense; whispery; creaky voice
Female	*Old*	– advanced tongue tip – sl. raised tongue body; nasal; tense – tense; whispery voice	– open jaw; advanced tongue tip/blade – backed, raised tongue body; nasal – mod. tense; mod. whispery; sl. creaky voice
	Young	– advanced tongue tip/blade – fronted, raised tongue body; nasal; lax – tense; mod. whispery; int. creaky voice	– open jaw; sl. advanced tongue tip/blade – v. backed, raised tongue body; RTR; nasal; v. lax – tense; v. whispery voice

Key: sl. = slightly; mod. = moderate; v. = very; int. = intermittent

Two settings were completely absent from both speech styles: labiodentalization and minimized jaw movement. The lack of labiodentalized setting correlates with the observed lack of a 'labial' pronunciation for /r/ in Glaswegian, which is becoming more widespread in urban accents in England (see e.g. Docherty & Foulkes this volume; Foulkes & Docherty in press).

Across both conversational and read speech a cluster of settings was shared by all speakers in the Glaswegian data: advanced tongue tip/blade, raised tongue body, nasalization, and tense, whispery voice. The advanced tongue tip/blade setting accounts for the observation that alveolar consonants may be realized as dental in Scottish English (Wells 1982: 409). The observation of nasalization and whispery voice, if to differing degrees, across all speakers is similar to the

Table 11.3 Group characteristics of voice quality of speakers in read word-lists. (These are taken from the VPA protocols; characteristic is only mentioned when present in at least three speakers. Each group consists of four speakers.)

Gender	Age	Middle class	Working class
Male	Old	– advanced tongue tip/blade – fronted, sl. raised tongue body; nasal; tense – tense; whispery; creaky voice	– sl. lip rounding/protrusion; open jaw; advanced tongue tip/blade – sl. backed, sl. raised tongue body; sl. RTR; nasal; tense – tense; whispery; creaky voice
	Young	– lipx; advanced tongue blade – fronted, raised, tongue body; mod. nasal – tense; whispery; sl.creaky voice	– lip rounding/protrusion; open and sl. protruded jaw; advanced tongue tip/blade – backed, sl. raised tongue body; int. RTR; nasal – tense; whispery; creaky voice
Female	Old	– advanced tongue tip/blade – sl. nasal; mod. tense – tense; mod. whispery voice	– lip rounding/protrusion; advanced tongue tip/blade – backed, raised, tongue body; nasal; tense – v. tense; whispery; voice
	Young	– lipx spreading; advanced tongue blade – mod. fronted, mod. raised, tongue body; nasal; tense – tense; sl. raised larynx; whispery; creaky voice	– open jaw; advanced tongue tip/blade – sl. backed, sl. raised tongue body; sl. RTR; nasal and denasal; lax – tense; mod. whispery; int. creaky voice

Key: sl. = slightly; mod. = moderate; v. = very; int. = intermittent; lipx = more extreme movement of lips

findings reported for 50 adult speakers by Mackenzie Beck (1988: 196f.). She also reports over half of the speakers as showing higher than neutral laryngeal tension. She offers a potential explanation for this in the unnaturalness of the recording situation, but given that 'tense voice' was found in relaxed conversational Glaswegian, it may also be a genuine feature of the (south-eastern) Scottish accents spoken by most of her informants.

11.3.4.2   Age and voice quality

The main aspect of Glaswegian voice quality which correlates with age is what is called here 'supralaryngeal tension'. In the VPA protocol it is possible to identify degrees of both 'tension' (SLtense) and 'laxness' (SLlax), although some caution must be exercised with these settings (for 'overall muscular tension' see e.g. Laver 1994: 416f.). In both conversations and word-lists children seemed to showed more laxness. WC young speakers in particular showed a high degree of laxness in conversational speech, and in read speech WC girls as a group showed laxness. This laxness is directly linked to the slacker articulation of obstruents, especially fricatives, observed in young WC speakers. All adults showed greater tenseness while reading the word-lists, perhaps due to the unfamiliar activity of reading aloud.

Young MC speakers showed two other characteristics – extensive lip movements and specifically tongue blade, as opposed to tongue tip, articulation. In general, little extensive (or minimized) movement was observed for the data as a whole, but this finding is not contrary to expectations for Scottish English (Laver 1994: 416). The use of blade articulation is reminiscent of Esling's Edinburgh results, since he also observed blade articulation in boys, as opposed to men, though this was restricted to the WC speakers. He ascribes this and the few other supralaryngeal age-related differences (palatalization, velarization, and advanced tongue root) largely to intrinsic differences resulting from boys' smaller vocal tracts (Esling 1978a: 184), and those of phonation to possible artefacts arising from his method of analysis (Esling 1978b: 20).

11.3.4.3   Gender and voice quality

Overall, gender differences in Glaswegian voice quality are mainly reflected in degrees of nasalization, creak and whisper. In both speech styles, greater nasalization was found in male than female speakers. This gender difference persists for WC speakers, and qualitatively but not quantitatively for MC speakers. The auditory quality of nasalization does not necessarily require velic lowering, and can be invoked by different interacting articulatory strategies (see Laver 1980: 68f.). This makes the finding of both nasalized and (auditorily) denasalized settings in the WC girls' word-list speech less contradictory than it might appear. The transcription reflects the observation that these girls' oral segments sound nasalized, but that their nasal segments are not fully nasal. Exactly this is reported for Scouse by Knowles (1974: 111f.), who reports both a 'nasal twang' and an 'adenoidal' quality occurring simultaneously. Nasalization is often used by male WC speakers to imitate a particular type of MC speech, associated with upward social mobility (also characterized by high pitch); a couple of such imitations occur in the recorded conversations.

The overall finding of more creaky voice in male than female speakers in both speech styles is similar to the reports for RP and 'Modified Northern'

English by Henton & Bladon (1988; see also Mackenzie Beck 1988: 199). The gender difference is increased in the word-lists, where all female speakers use more whispery voice. If 'whispery voice' is to be equated with Henton & Bladon's 'breathiness' (1985), this again would seem to agree with their observations for speakers from the same corpus. We note too that although more whispery voice is an indicator of WC in the conversational speech overall, WC women and girls still show substantially more whispery voice than their male counterparts.

A further gender difference in WC speakers is apparent qualitatively in the conversational data: more men and boys show lip-rounding or protrusion. In MC speakers greater supralaryngeal tension is found in women and girls than in men and boys in the word-list data. We also note that MC girls are identified as having slightly raised larynx and lip spreading when reading the word-lists. These settings with tongue blade articulation and tongue body fronting and raising together conspire to raise their auditory pitch. Interestingly, their conversational speech does not share this constellation of settings, suggesting that reading aloud is a separate linguistic activity for these speakers (cf. Esling 1978a: 188). We can only speculate as to whether the effect is intended to sound 'feminine'.

11.3.4.4   Social class and voice quality

The most complex and extensive differences in Glaswegian voice quality correlate with social class. As in Trudgill's description of Norwich English, differences in voice quality are very important for signalling existing and original social background in Glaswegian, although the relationship between class and language is somewhat different. The difference between e.g. WC and MC speech entails a potentially significant phonetic and phonological shift from a form of SSE to a form of Scots, which will include differences of lexical incidence and possibly of system. The different forms of speech also show substantially different voice qualities. Describing differences in articulatory settings will therefore allow a number of generalizations about segmental differences between WC Scots and MC SSE to be captured, but voice quality alone cannot complete the account (Abercrombie 1967: 89f.).

In conversational speech, WC speakers are distinguished from MC speakers by showing predominant degrees of open jaw, raised and backed tongue body, possible retracted tongue root, supralaryngeal laxness, and whispery voice. In adult speakers differences of open jaw and whispery voice are most apparent, while in children open jaw, backed tongue body with retracted tongue root and supralaryngeal laxness are typical of WC, as opposed to MC, speakers. Interestingly, MC voice quality can be defined almost entirely in terms of the absence of these settings, which recalls Johnston's (1983: 11) discussion of Scottish and Northern social accent climbing in terms of deletion of vernacular features (as opposed to the adoption of 'prestigious' ones). The only MC features are the possible presence of advanced tongue root in MC men, describing an impressionistically 'hollow' quality, and tongue body fronting in MC girls.

The results for the read word-lists are rather similar: overall, WC speakers show open jaw, backed tongue body, retracted tongue root, and lesser supralaryngeal tension. In adults only tongue backing is distinctive, but WC children show open jaw, tongue body raising and backing, and retracted tongue root. In read speech all MC speakers share one additional setting, fronted tongue body, potentially enhancing the difference between their speech and localized 'backed' speech (cf. Esling 1978a for social differences in read and 'narrative' speech in Edinburgh).

WC voice quality shows advanced tongue tip/blade setting combined with a backed tongue body setting. Such contradictory tongue settings are attested (Laver 1994: 411). They account for the impression of 'frontness' and 'backness' which is often apparent in broad WC speech. Since both MC and WC speech shares tongue body raising, the main difference in tongue body setting is along the horizontal axis, with WC speech showing backing (velarization), and MC occasional fronting (palatalization).

WC speech is also characterized by an auditory quality of pharyngealization, as also found by Esling (1978b) in Edinburgh WC speech, expressed here cautiously in terms of tongue root retraction. Only slight degrees of retracted tongue root are transcribed, partly reflecting the fact that the auditory quality of pharyngealization is most clearly noticeable during liquids and semi-vowels. This highlights the grey area between 'long-term' and 'short-term' settings (traditionally secondary segmental articulation). Secondary articulations must play some part in our overall impression of voice quality, particularly in Scottish English which is rhotic, and hence which contains far more opportunities for secondary articulation than a non-rhotic variety of English (cf. Honikman 1964).

There are few indications in these data of the stereotypical male 'Glasgow voice'. One similarity is in lax supralaryngeal tension combined with a higher degree of laryngeal tension, which would facilitate harsh voice, although this is rarely found (unlike Esling 1978a: 146; 1978b). The two speakers concerned are two WC men in their late fifties; they also show slight pharyngeal constriction. Impressionistically their voice quality is closest to the stereotype, although they do not seem to show jaw protrusion, but only open jaw. Open jaw is shared by all groups of WC speakers except WC women, for whom lip rounding/protrusion is noted instead. Jaw protrusion is only characteristic of WC boys (word-lists). There seems to be an anomaly here in terms of segmental pronunciation: jaw protrusion is often noticed through a distinctive articulation of /s/. In these data WC men, and WC and MC boys share a 'retracted' /s/. This may indicate jaw protrusion (Macafee 1983: 34), although this is only found in WC boys here.

Interestingly, MC boys are adopting a variant of /s/ which may help contribute to an impression of WC voice quality.

Apart from the isolated instances of harsh voice, the main phonatory difference between WC and MC voice quality is increased whisperiness in WC conversational speech (cf Esling 1978a: 146). Creak does not appear to correlate with class, as in Edinburgh, where higher-class speakers showed much creakier voices (Esling 1978b). In fact, if the settings characterizing Glaswegian WC voice quality are compared with those of Edinburgh there are few similarities, namely in pharyngealization, protruded jaw, and more whispery phonation.

Not surprisingly, not all speakers conformed to each of the eight social groups in all respects. Clearly idiosyncratic, organic factors of voice quality were involved, but there were also some anomalous cases. For example, the voice quality of one WC woman was unusual: she sounded in some respects rather MC, but her segmental pronunciation was closer to that of WC speakers, particularly in T-glottalling. Her similarity to MC voice quality is accounted for by her fronted and raised tongue body setting, typical of the voice quality of (read) MC speech. She is a good example of Abercrombie's (1967) claim that all three strands of indexical information are needed to signal social membership.

11.4   *Conclusions*

The investigation of Glaswegian voice quality presented here seems to be the first comprehensive sociophonetic examination of voice quality in a British urban accent since the mid-1980s. There is more work to be done in acoustically analysing these data (Stuart-Smith & Früh in progress), but what is given here is already sufficient to identify the existence of clear differences in voice quality according to age, gender, and above all social background. This analysis demonstrates clearly that understanding features of voice quality enables a more integrated description of an accent.

Notes

1 Thanks are due to Claire Timmins, who acted as the fieldworker, and to Grace Arthur, Joanne Cork, Eleanor Lawson and Barbara McGinley, who helped transcribe the word-list data. I am very grateful to John Esling, John Laver, Paul Johnston, Caroline Macafee, Ronald Macaulay, Janet Mackenzie Beck, Mike MacMahon, and Jim Scobbie, together with the editors, for constructive criticism on an earlier draft of this chapter. All subsequent errors and views remain my own.
2 This includes the effects of illness and habits such as smoking.

3 Additional settings of 'advanced' and 'retracted' tongue root (ATR/RTR) were used
   to describe auditory pharyngealization potentially arising from retracted tongue root
   (e.g. Laver 1994: 412) or pharyngeal sphinctering (J. Esling, personal communication),
   although identifying fine degrees of RTR is difficult (J. Laver, personal communication). I also used a more extended set of subdivisions to represent 'degree' of any particular articulatory setting.

12

Edinburgh: descriptive material

Deborah Chirrey

12.1 Introduction

This chapter aims to identify the characteristic features of the accent of the city of Edinburgh and its surrounding areas.[1] The data informing this study were gathered both by formal interview and by informal observation. The formal interviews produced six hours of recorded speech, gathered from fourteen speakers, women and men who ranged in age from 17 to 73. There were seven speakers in the younger age bracket (17–30), and seven in the older age group (40–73). The speakers were from a range of localities within the Edinburgh area, including the centre of Edinburgh and also Leith, Corstorphine and Currie. Based on factors such as education and employment, the speakers were judged as being lower- to upper-middle class.

12.1.1 The English language in Scotland

The history of English in Scotland is significantly different from its history in England.[2] As a result of this, we are confronted with a number of marked linguistic differences between the English of the two countries. To take the phonological system as an example, one can cite the survival of a number of archaic features in Scottish accents, such as the /x/ and /ʍ/ phonemes, which have mostly disappeared from other accents of English. Alternatively, one might draw attention to the smaller number of vowels that characterise Scottish accents.

Moreover, Scottish accents themselves display a complex interplay between two language varieties, usually referred to as Scots and Scottish English. In an attempt to represent this situation, Aitken (1981a: 74) has talked of a 'bi-polar continuum' along which most Scottish speakers operate, in which, theoretically at least, each speaker has access to features of both linguistic systems and possesses the ability to range from one to the other as occasion demands. It would appear that speakers make judgements about the appropriateness of a particular variety based on stylistic and contextual factors. In addition, certain sociolinguistic factors would seem to correlate with the use of Scots or Scottish

English (henceforth ScE) by a particular speaker: features of Scots are far more likely to be found in the linguistic systems of working-class speakers, as well as in the accents of older, rural speakers, especially those who have not been exposed to the normalising tendencies of the education system for longer than necessary (Aitken 1984b: 519–23).

Furthermore, Edinburgh can be described in general as more middle-class than Glasgow, and thus Edinburgh speakers are on the whole more oriented towards standard varieties than their Glasgow counterparts (see further Johnston 1983, 1984, 1985).

12.2   *Descriptive material*

12.2.1   Vowels

The system of vowels varies depending upon whether we are dealing with a Scots or ScE speaker. Most speakers will operate with the following system: /i, e, ɛ, ë, a, ɔ, o, ʉ, ɪ, ʌ, ae, ʌi, ɔe, ʌʉ/. Not every speaker has all of these phonemes, however. For example, not all speakers will have /ë/ (Aitken's vowel).

It is immediately obvious that Scottish accents possess a smaller inventory of vowel phonemes than English English (henceforth EngE) accents. One reason for this is the maintenance of full rhoticity, the loss of which caused many EngE accents to form new diphthongs. One result of this smaller set of vowel phonemes is that Scottish speakers do not make some vowel contrasts that English speakers do, thus e.g. *fool* and *full* are both [fʉl]. It should be noted that Scottish accents do not display phonemic vowel length distinctions in the same fashion as EngE accents (e.g. *heat* [hiːt] versus *hit* [hɪt]). However, most vowels (except /ɪ/ and /ʌ/) have long or short allophones which are conditioned by their environment and are entirely predictable. This is referred to as Aitken's Law, or the Scottish Vowel Length Rule (see, for example, Aitken 1981b; and the detailed discussion of Edinburgh vowel length by Scobbie, Hewlett & Turk this volume, which offers contradictory evidence). Essentially all vowels are short unless they are followed by /r/, a voiced fricative, a morpheme boundary, or are final in an open syllable. Thus there is a phonetic distinction between the vowels in pairs such as *mate* and *mare* [met, meːɹ] and *cute* and *queued* [kjʉt, kjʉːd]. Note that durational differences triggered by the SVLR are not indicated in Table 12.1 below.

The interplay between Scots and ScE results in a range of options for Edinburgh speakers, which Table 12.1 illustrates. Most Edinburgh English (henceforth EdinE) speakers will select from the first column, but may choose to use a Scots phone for stylistic purposes. Scots speakers may select from the second column for spontaneous informal speech, but choose the EdinE options in formal situations. Thus the same speaker may refer to a *house* as a [hʉs] or a [hʌʉs] depending upon the context of the situation. It can be seen that a number of the word classes are actually split between two or more phonemes, e.g. HEAD and PRICE.

Table 12.1 Vowels in Edinburgh – summary

	EdinE	Scots
KIT	ɪ	ï ~ ɨ
DRESS	ɛ	ɛ
HEAD	ɛ	i
NEVER	ɛ ~ ë	ï ~ ɨ
TRAP	a̠	a̠
LOT	ɔ	o
STRUT	Ä	Ä
FOOT	ʉ̠	ï ~ ɨ
BATH	a̠	a̠
AFTER	a̠	ɛ ~ e
CLOTH	ɔ	o
NURSE	Ä	Ä
FLEECE	i	i
FACE	e	e
STAY	e	e ~ ʌi
PALM	a̠	a̠
THOUGHT	ɔ	o
GOAT	o	o
MORE	o	e
GOOSE	ʉ̠	ʉ̠
PRICE	ae ~ ʌi	ʌi
PRIZE	ae	ae
CHOICE	ɔe	ɔe
MOUTH	ʌʉ̠	ʉ̠
NEAR	i	i
SQUARE	e	ɛ
START	a̠	e
BIRTH	ï	ï ~ ɨ
BERTH	ɛ	ɛ
NORTH	ɔ	o
FORCE	o	o
CURE	jʉ̠	jʉ̠
happʏ	e	e ~ ï ~ ɨ
lettɛʀ	ï ~ Ä	Ä
horsɛs	ï ~ Ä	ï ~ Ä
commᴀ	Ä	Ä

The phenomenon of 'breaking' is very common among Edinburgh speakers. This typically involves the vowel in a syllable being followed by a brief transitional vowel glide of an [ï] quality, e.g. [tɹeⁱl] *trail*. Vowels exhibit this process only before /r, l/ and /n/. (This seems to mark a difference from Glasgow varieties where breaking also occurs before /d/ and /t/, although this has not been formally tested.) The syllabicity of the word is not usually affected unless the original vowel is a diphthong. Then there is a strong possibility that the syllable will become disyllabic. Thus *sour* may be pronounced as a monosyllabic [sʌʉ̠ⁱɹ], but is more likely to be pronounced as a disyllabic word: [sʌʉ̠\$ ɹɪ] (where \$ indicates the syllable boundary).

Comments

NEVER
[ë] may be used in stressed position in a small class of words, including *seven, eleven, devil, next, heaven, bury, shepherd* and *earth* (Abercrombie 1954; McClure 1970).

TRAP, AFTER, BATH, PALM, START
In EdinE, but not Scots, this vowel tends to be realised as [ɔ̈] or [ɑ] before /r/.

FOOT, GOOSE, CURE
In general [ʉ], but for some EdinE speakers this vowel is fronted even further to something approaching [ø].

MORE
This set also includes *no, go, so, low, snow, stone.*

NURSE, BIRTH, BERTH
The distribution of variants before /r/ shows much variation. For some speakers [ï] is used in BIRTH, BERTH and NURSE. For others, by contrast, BIRTH and NURSE have [ʌ̈], while BERTH has [ɛ]. Variants around [ə] may also be found.

PRICE, PRIZE
Some upper MC EdinE speakers do not have a distinction between PRICE and PRIZE, using solely [ae].

12.2.2   Consonants

STOPS and AFFRICATES
The realisation of plosives displays much variation. It is relatively common to find speakers from all socio-economic groups realising /t/ word-medially as a glottal plosive [ʔ], producing forms such as ['bɛʔïɹ, 'lɛʔïs, 'θïɹʔe, 'sɛɹʔïnle] *better, lettuce, thirty, certainly.* Among some speakers, especially those whose variety is closer to Scots than to ScE, /t/ may be realised as [ʔ] in initial position. It appears that this word-initial glottal usage only occurs with the infinitive marker *to* and temporal adverbs *today, tomorrow, tonight,* where the target syllable is unstressed. Thus we find forms such as ['tɹaeïn ʔe] *trying to,* [si jʌ̈ ʔʌ̈de] *see you today.*

All speakers will regularly realise word- and syllable-final /p, t, k/ as glottalised [ʔp, ʔt, ʔk], thus [ʌ̈ʔp, nɔʔt, ʃʉʔk, kʌm ʔpne, ïnʔtɹest, ɛʔksïɹsaez] *up, not, shook, company, interest, exercise.* The oral plosives may be unreleased. The same phenomenon affects the affricate /tʃ/. In final position both /t/ and /k/ (but not /p/) are regularly realised as a full glottal stop [ʔ], e.g. [ɹaʔ, nʌiʔ] *rat, night;* [teʔ, lʌiʔ] *take, like.* However, whereas /t/ can be realised as [ʔ] in any word-final consonant cluster, e.g. [donʔ, ʍïʔʃ], *don't, which,* [ʔ] for /k/ is restricted to word-final /kt/ clusters, e.g. [a̠ʔt] *act.*

In word-final position both voiced and voiceless plosives may be affricated and/or aspirated, e.g. [tʰeʔkˣʰ, fu̜dᶻʰ] *take, food*. Lenited versions of stops are also common, in which the active articulator fails to make full contact with the passive articulator. Thus we find realisations such as [lïvd̜] for *lived*.

Neither nasal release nor lateral release are automatic within the word, so pronunciations such as [ɹɔtⁿ] *rotten* and [lïtˡ] *little* are to be heard as well as [ɹɔtïn] and [lïtïl].

In utterance-final position speakers can also be heard on occasion to use ejective realisations of /p, t/ and /k/, e.g. [am gon tï ðï ʃɔpˀ] *I'm going to the shop*.

NASALS

/n/ is occasionally realised as a nasalisation of the preceding vowel, thus [dõʔ, ẍgẽst, a̱ʔsẽʔ] for *don't, against, accent*. As with stops, lenited variants are common, e.g. [dïn̜ïɹ] for *dinner*.

WH, X

The consonantal structure of EdinE is, in essence, similar to that of most other accents of English. The accent of the vast majority of EdinE speakers contains, however, two additional consonants compared with most other English accents: /ʍ, x/. Younger speakers at the Scots end of the continuum, however, may use neither /x/ nor /ʍ/ (thus [lɔk] rather than [lɔx] for *loch* and [welz] rather than [ʍelz] for *whales*).

Traditionally, the distribution of /w/ and /ʍ/ has been described in terms of orthography: /ʍ/ is said to be used where the spelling <wh> occurs, while /w/ is distributed where the spelling <w> occurs (Aitken 1984a: 101; Wells 1982: 408–9). However, the current situation is not as straightforward as this. A small group of words has been identified which, as it were, breaks the rule. Thus *whelk* is pronounced [wɛlk] and *weasel* is pronounced [ʍislʸ] (Wells 1982). Moreover, it would appear that there is a sound change in progress, in that younger speakers seem to be replacing /ʍ/ with /w/. First noticed among Glasgow speakers (Macafee 1983; see also Stuart-Smith this volume), it is also now apparent in Edinburgh (Chirrey in progress). Some EdinE speakers are consistent in maintaining /w/ and /ʍ/ as distinct phonemes, whereas other speakers are not predictable in their use of /w/ and /ʍ/. Rather, they regularly vary between /w/ and /ʍ/ for words that traditionally had /ʍ/. Therefore, the same speaker will pronounce *where* as [weɹ] on one occasion and as [ʍeɹ] on another. Furthermore, although the change in Glasgow was first noticed among younger speakers, and investigators such as Murray (1873) and Ellis (1889) did not remark upon it, the data collected for Chirrey (in progress) contain examples of speakers as old as 73 who use /w/ and /ʍ/ inconsistently. This suggests therefore that the change in fact has a considerable time-depth. (See also Lawson (1998) for an acoustic study of [x] and [ʍ] in the speech of Glasgow children.)

TH

/θ/ is very occasionally realised as [h] word-initially by older speakers and by younger speakers whose phonology follows a Scots rather than a ScE model. Thus *think* may be [hïŋʔk]. Older speakers and younger Scots speakers may retain the previously documented realisation of /θ/ before /r/ as [ɪ̥], thus *three* is [ɪ̥ɹi] (e.g. McAllister 1963: 57).

H

H-dropping is by no means widespread, but is possible in rapid colloquial speech in unstressed pronouns such as *he, her, him*.

R

A characteristic feature of EdinE, like other Scottish, as well as Irish, Canadian and most American accents of English, is that it remains rhotic. Thus /r/ is pronounced in word-initial, medial and final position (thus [ɹen, heɹe, heɹ] *rain, hairy, hair*).[3] Consequently, one also finds final consonant clusters which are not found in many EngE accents, e.g. /-rlz#/ *girls,* /-rm#/ *firm*. Epenthetic vowels are largely avoided in such clusters, especially by MC speakers.

The realisation of /r/ varies substantially. The most common realisation, found in all word positions, is the postalveolar approximant [ɹ]. With some speakers, it is apico-postalveolar and may be slightly or heavily retroflexed. In initial consonant clusters, the [ɹ] may show some transitional friction, e.g. [dɟɹɑg] for *drag*. The tap articulation [ɾ] is commonly found in intervocalic position, e.g. [hʌɾe] *hurry*, as well as in initial consonant clusters with plosives and occasionally with /θ/: [gɾet, kɾaʃ, bɾek, θrʉ] *great, crash, break, through*. Retroflex approximants are commonly found in word-final position and in postvocalic clusters: [fʌɭ, heɭd] *fur, heard*. On occasion, the preceding vowel may be somewhat /r/-coloured: [ke˞ɭb] *kerb*. Among older speakers, as well as among some younger speakers whose phonology is Scots rather than ScE, /r/ followed by /s/ or /z/ results in a retroflex realisation of both phones: [eɹ foɭʂ, kïɭʂte, jiɭʐ] *air force, Kirsty, years*.

The trill realisation [r] is very rare, and is more likely in the speech of older rather than younger speakers.[4] If it is used at all it will tend to be in word-initial stressed position, perhaps with an emphatic function, thus [ðï ˈolᵛd ˈrat] *the old rat*.

A recent structural change in Edinburgh (and perhaps wider afield in Scotland) is the occurrence of R in sites which are labelled 'intrusive' in non-rhotic varieties. Thus the phrase *idea of* may be pronounced [aediɹ ïv]. It may be misleading to use the label 'intrusive R' however, since the phonological process involved appears quite distinct from that which operates in non-rhotic varieties.[5] Unlike non-rhotic accents, in Edinburgh the process which gives rise to the surface [ɹ] is not automatic. Instead, the occurrence of [ɹ] in sites where it is not etymologically appropriate is restricted to a relatively small set of lexical items. It therefore probably reflects an underlying structural difference in these items, rather than a phonological rule of segment insertion or deletion. It remains to be investigated to what extent the set of affected items is idiosyncratic.

L

Characteristically /l/ is a voiced velarised lateral [lˠ], although the exact degree of velarisation may vary (Speitel 1969: 53; Catford 1977: 193; Wells 1982: 411–12; Aitken 1984a: 102). A palatalised lateral is possible in initial position and appears to correlate with a following front close or close-mid vowel, thus [lʲet] *late*. The place of articulation of /l/ would appear to be dental (Aitken 1984a: 102), although interdental as well as simultaneous dental and alveolar realisations have been reported.[6]

L-vocalisation is very widespread though little noted in EdinE, where the /l/ is realised as a close or close-mid back vowel. The vowel will be unrounded unless followed by a labialised consonant. Thus we find realisations such as: [koʊd] *cold*, [wɔɤz] *walls*, [ɔɔɹʷɔʔn] *all rotten*, and [hoʉ ɹʷʉf] *whole roof*. This realisation appears only in syllable-final position and is particularly common in consonant clusters.

12.2.3 Suprasegmental features

The accent of Edinburgh is characterised by an overwhelming tendency to favour intonation patterns which terminate with a mid- to low fall, even with questions. There will, of course, be peaks of pitch throughout the utterance, but the pitch will display a final fall:

You're ˌgoing to ˌhave to ↘read your story?

The use of a high rising tone with statements is not noticeable in EdinE at the present time.

Notes

1 Thanks to Jim Scobbie, Jane Stuart-Smith, Dominic Watt and Paul Foulkes for their helpful comments on drafts of this chapter.
2 A full account of the history of Scots and ScE is available elsewhere, for example Aitken (1979, 1981a, 1984a, b), Murison (1979) and Jones (1997). The general systemic, structural, distributional and phonetic characteristics of Scottish accents have been outlined by, among others, Abercrombie (1979) and Aitken (1984a, b). See also Stuart-Smith (this volume).
3 This would seem to be at odds with what one might expect to encounter in the light of Romaine's (1978) findings concerning variable rhoticity among Edinburgh schoolchildren.
4 In the six hours of speech recorded for the purposes of this study, [r] appeared once, in the speech of the oldest male informant.
5 Discussions of the phonological process which gives rise to intrusive R in non-rhotic accents are numerous. See, for example, D. Jones (1956); Gimson (1980); Wells (1982: 284–5); Donegan (1993); McMahon, Foulkes & Tollfree (1994); Foulkes (1997a, b).
6 A recent acoustic study of ScE /l/ realisations revealed that Scottish /l/ is in general dental (Chirrey in progress).

13

Standard English in Edinburgh and Glasgow: the Scottish Vowel Length Rule revealed

James M. Scobbie, Nigel Hewlett and Alice Turk

13.1 *Introduction*

13.1.1 A significant aspect of Scottish sound systems

There are two main reasons for the continuing interest in the synchronic Scottish Vowel Length Rule ('SVLR').[1] Firstly, the SVLR patterns of vowel duration are a key diagnostic of Scots and Scottish English (Aitken 1981b) and have serious ramifications for the analysis of Scottish vowel systems (e.g. Lass 1974; Anderson 1994). Secondly, the combination of morphological, phonological and phonetic aspects of the SVLR raises challenging theoretical questions about the interface between these modules (e.g. McMahon 1991; Carr 1992; Scobbie, Turk & Hewlett 1999), and constitutes a serious challenge for phonetic explanations of allophonic vowel duration (see Keating 1985). Despite the importance of the phenomenon, there is a great deal of confusion as to its operation. This is partly due to the obscurity of the most comprehensive instrumental study to date: Gordon McKenna's unpublished M.Litt. thesis (McKenna 1988). The other factor is that the instrumental phonetic studies of SVLR focus on middle-class Scottish English, while the bulk of non-instrumental work on the SVLR uses rural working-class Scots data. In this paper, we will review these instrumental results, and conclude that there is broad agreement that the Scottish Vowel Length Rule in MC and WC Scottish Standard English applies only to the three vowels /i/, /u/ and /ai/.

This conclusion is apparently at odds with the consensus view of the SVLR in Scots (Johnston 1997b), though it is compatible with individual Scots dialects, such as Berwickshire (Wettstein 1942). It also contradicts the conclusions of A. J. Aitken, whose highly influential paper (Aitken 1981b) addresses mainly Scots, but also, to an extent, Scottish Standard English. Our conclusions, based on firm experimental evidence, therefore have important ramifications for all the descriptive and theoretical work which uncritically applies Aitken's results to Scottish Standard English.

13.1.2 Vowel duration: an overview

Vowel **length** and vowel **duration**[2] in Scottish varieties of English and in modern vernacular Scots are governed by linguistic systems rather different from those applying in most other dialects of English. The two main distinguishing characteristics of extrinsically conditioned vowel duration (in word-final stressed syllables) are summarised as the parameters (1) and (2), and illustrated for the vowel /u/ in Table 13.1. The question of exactly which vowels alternate is addressed below.

(1) **Consonantal conditioning.** The typical English pattern of extrinsic vowel duration is that phonetically much shorter allophones of vowels are found before *voiceless* consonants as opposed to *voiced* ones. In Scottish varieties voiced stops condition short duration vowels,[3] as indeed do nasals and /l/. Only voiced fricatives (/v ð z ʒ/) and /r/ condition long duration.

(2) **Morphological conditioning.** Although Scottish varieties follow the typical English pattern of word-final stressed vowels in open syllables having greater duration than the same vowels in closed syllables,[4] in Scots and Scottish English, consonantal suffixes such as /d/ do not condition shorter vowels. So, while [ʉ] in the open syllable of *brew* is much longer than the comparable vowel in the closed syllable of *brood*, the past tense suffix /d/ in the form *brewed* does not condition a short duration [ʉ]. This gives rise to such famous oppositions as *brood* < *brewed*. These are cases of quasi-phonemic (marginal or derived) contrast (Harris 1995) arising from the interplay of extrinsic vowel duration and suffixation.

13.1.3 Overview

It is hard to give a theoretical account of the SVLR without facing up to the phonetic underpinnings of the phenomenon and the patterns of dialectal variation. Well-designed instrumental studies are essential: a phenomenon consisting

Table 13.1 Broad characterisations, for one representative vowel [ʉ], of the conditioning effects of various contexts

Dialect	Duration	Consonantal context					Morphological context	
		_n	_s	_z	_t	_d	_#	_#d
Scottish English	*longer*	—	—	bruise	—	—	brew	brewed
	shorter	spoon	Bruce	—	brute	brood	—	—
Anglo English	*longer*	spoon	—	bruise	—	brood	brew	brewed
	shorter	—	Bruce	—	brute	—	—	—

of subtle differences in vowel duration cannot be adequately addressed using only introspection and transcription. In this chapter, we focus mainly on the phonetics of the SVLR,[5] which forces us to concentrate on Scottish Standard English, since there are no relevant instrumental studies on Scots, so far as we are aware. The structure of the paper is as follows. In section 13.2, we introduce the dialectal background confronting all phonetic SVLR studies. Thus prepared, in section 13.3 we discuss Aitken's (1981b) original presentation of the rule. In section 13.4 we discuss the results of three instrumental studies into the SVLR system of Scottish Standard English (SSE) (McClure 1977; Agutter 1988; McKenna 1988), and give our own synthesis of their findings. We also make reference to our own ongoing work at Queen Margaret University College, Edinburgh and the University of Edinburgh under ESRC grant R000237135, 'The Scottish Vowel Length Rule: the phonetics, phonology and acquisition of a marginal contrast'. This work in progress includes, to date, the acoustic analysis of data collected from the 32 Glasgow speakers analysed in Stuart-Smith's chapter in the present volume (Scobbie, Turk & Hewlett 1999), and the acoustic analysis of child speech data from Edinburgh (Hewlett, Matthews & Scobbie 1999). In section 13.5 we highlight some important social differences between Edinburgh and Glasgow which we think lead to linguistic differences in MC varieties of SSE, before presenting a summary in section 13.6.

13.2   *The SVLR and the Scots–SSE continuum*

One crucial cause of variation in the SVLR is the relative influence on a speaker's output from Scots *vis-à-vis non*-Scottish accents (notably various varieties of Anglo-English). These influences are often said to form a continuum, linking Scots dialects to Scottish Standard English (Aitken 1979, 1981b; Abercrombie 1979; Macafee 1997). Unfortunately, these end-points are rather nebulous. Scots comprises a range of dialects, and SSE encompasses a range of accents. As Abercrombie and Aitken make clear, SSE may be replete with non-Scottish accent features to the extent that there may be little linguistically Scottish to it. The speech continuum is seen as linking 'varieties of Standard English, spoken *either with RP* or with more or less Scottish accents at one pole and non-standard Scottish dialects at the other pole . . . [The speech on this continuum] which most people in Scotland hear most often . . . in effect is English spoken in some Scottish accent and with an occasional distinctively Scots form or word sprinkled through it' (Aitken 1981a: 74–5, our emphasis). Abercrombie (1979) states that the most linguistically interesting sources of dialectal differentiation are due to differences in phonological inventory and structure. Yet, though they are easy to quantify linguistically, purely phonological differences between dialects are not necessarily very important impressionistically to listeners. Lexical incidence and phonetic variation are more important in this regard: segmental and suprasegmental phonetic production provides many features which are important as sociolinguistic variables (see Stuart-Smith this volume; Macafee 1997: §12.2).

We focus here on patterns of phonetic vowel duration, making use of the data at our disposal, which have been collected in large part from middle-class speakers of Scottish English. Some MC speakers have phonological systems closer to RP than others (Aitken 1981a; Abercrombie 1979; Macafee 1997) by the presence of RP-like contrasts: /a/–/ɑ/, /ɔ/–/ɒ/, /u/–/ʊ/. These additional tense/lax vowel contrasts and the attendant phonetic reorganisation interfere considerably with the SVLR. Therefore, in discussing the *Scottish* phonetic system of vowel duration, it is important to study one vowel system at a time, beginning with one which is representative of the situation as a whole. We also need to be careful to avoid confusion with Scots phonological systems, for example in the behaviour of /ɔ/, of which more below.

Our discussion, therefore, addresses a single phonological system, of nine monophthongs /i e a ɔ o u ɪ ɛ ʌ/ and three diphthongs /ai au ɔi/. In principle, such an inventory may be associated with Standard English or with Scots grammar and lexis, whether 'dense' or 'thin' (McClure 1979). There are two supporting reasons for considering this system. First, it is essentially what Abercrombie (1979) calls the **basic Scottish vowel system**, and he thinks it is reasonable to claim that 'it is the most *Scottish* of the vowel systems of Standard English in Scotland' (Abercrombie 1979: 74, emphasis in original).[6] Second, the speakers in McKenna's (1988) important study of the SVLR all use this system. **Scottish Standard English (SSE)** in this paper means Standard (or near-Standard) English spoken with this basic vowel system.

Because we are defining Scottish Standard English with *phonological* precision, we must accept that our definition is imprecise sociolinguistically. Specifically, we do not limit SSE to middle-class varieties, a definition which may appear to some to be prescriptively unrealistic. It *would* be possible to define SSE to be Standard English as spoken by a particular group of speakers, namely middle-class ones (though where? – in Edinburgh? – in Glasgow?). But 'Scottish Standard English' would then be an oxymoron: the more *standard* the morphology, syntax and lexicon of MC speakers, the less distinctively *Scottish* the accent tends to be (cf. Abercrombie 1979; Aitken 1979).

Another advantage of looking only at the basic vowel system is that social variation in the phonetics can be addressed much more easily. Although most instrumental studies to date have looked only at MC speakers, the Stuart-Smith/SVLR Project word-list data presented in section 13.4.3 includes 16 WC speakers who predominantly use the basic vowel system with different lexical incidence.

13.3   *Aitken's specification of the SVLR*

Aitken's work on the synchrony and diachrony of Scottish vowel duration and vowel length is wide-ranging and highly influential, to the extent that the SVLR is frequently called 'Aitken's Law', especially in its diachronic incarnation. In his major paper on the phenomenon, Aitken (1981b) brings diachronic and synchronic data to bear that relate more towards the Scots end of the spectrum. He does, however, include SSE in his presentation at various points, though his definition of the SVLR as it applies in the *basic* vowel system is not explicitly tabulated but has to be inferred.[7] Since the instrumental studies which we consider below use speakers of SSE, we will need to apply his results to the SSE basic vowel system, an operation that must be done with caution.

From Aitken (1981b), we need to draw up a candidate set of vowels *from the basic vowel set* that seem likely to undergo the SVLR in SSE. The set in (3) follows closely on Aitken's presentation. It excludes four vowels. Aitken characterises /ɪ/ and /ʌ/ as short in all cases, with which we concur. There is uncertainty about the status of /ɔi/.[8] He also excludes /ɔ/, which is invariably long in some dialects of Scots in a restricted class of L-dropping words such as *fall* and *fault*.

(3)   Candidates in SSE for the SVLR (preliminary version): /i e ɛ a o u ai au/.

This candidate set is unacceptable as it stands. First, in Scots, the word classes LOT, THOUGHT, CLOTH have /o/, so Scots /ɔ/ has an entirely different lexical incidence from SSE /ɔ/, a point of confusion which is usually overlooked (an exception being McKenna 1988: 78). In SSE, we would expect a fully general SVLR to apply to /ɔ/. Aitken includes /ɛ/ as one of the *alternating* SVLR vowels, but we agree with McMahon (1991) that it ought to be grouped with /ɪ/ and /ʌ/. The low vowel /a/ is said to alternate, but for many MC SSE speakers the morphological conditioning of /a/ is primarily qualitative (*bad* [bad] versus *baa'd* [bɑd]), so care needs to be taken here. However, even if we accept that there are some points of uncertainty in extrapolating Aitken's presentation to the basic Scottish vowel system (cf. Macafee 1983: 35), *most* vowels in SSE are potentially subject to the SVLR.

(4)   Candidate vowel set: /i e a ɔ o u ai au/, plus perhaps: /ɔi/.
(5)   Candidate environments: 'the long environments are: a following voiced fricative … /r/, or a morpheme boundary, all of these either final or followed by a consonant constituting a second morpheme' (Aitken 1981b: 135). In polysyllabic words, hiatus is likely to be a lengthening environment.

But it must not be assumed that (4) and (5) amount to a homogenous 'rule': that all alternating vowels are likely to be equally affected by all triggering environments (see section 13.1). Where Aitken considers variation in Scots and SSE, it is mentioned mainly with respect to the set of input vowels: 'in some (mainly Central Scots?) dialects the Rule seems to operate for all the specified vowels … and in all dialects for at least some of the specified vowels … Nearly all Scots dialects (and Scottish Standard English) agree in displaying fully long realisations of the affected vowels in these environments' (Aitken 1981b: 134–5). In fact, since Aitken (1981b) it has been generally accepted that the very *smallest* SVLR set would be /i u/ plus /ai/, though this seems to have been proposed only with respect to morphological conditioning (Wells 1982: 401; Carr 1992: 94).[9] As noted above, some Scots dialects have only this set (Wettstein 1942). If a larger set undergoes the rule, then /i u/ and /ai/ are often said to follow the rule more 'solidly' (Johnston 1997a: 67) or 'markedly' (Aitken 1981b: 137), whatever that means.

13.4   *Instrumental and experimental data*

Quantitative measurements of vowel duration are neither simple to make nor to interpret. One problem is that the speech sample is typically recorded in a studio, the subject reading aloud from a list. Thus the register is formal and reading-based. Nevertheless, the analysis of laboratory data relating to vowel duration is essential, since an experimental methodology is able to reveal gross perceptible patterns *and* covert patterns of variation. It also avoids a flaw common to all studies that make use of uncontrolled natural dialogues, one particularly problematic for duration-based phenomena: the wide range of conditioning factors (segmental, morphological and prosodic) that affect vowel duration to various degrees.

A second problem with acoustic analysis is the complex relationship between a transcription and a set of spectrographic measurements of the same raw speech data. The transcription of vowel length can make subtle use of many phonetic cues, but instrumental measurement is more mechanistic and is typically based on the segmentation of a waveform or spectrogram. Vowel segmentation criteria are extremely hard to justify and apply in certain cases, for example when an approximant flanks a vowel, or when devoicing of the vowel occurs (due to aspiration, pre-aspiration or glottalisation). McKenna (1988), measuring from waveform and spectrogram (with acoustic feedback), is the only study to give full details of segmentation criteria. They seem appropriate, and his data are well controlled. We conclude that McKenna's work provides the only authoritative raw data on SVLR to date. The other studies merit consideration, however. Firstly, they provide points of comparison; secondly, they are much more widely known; and thirdly, the significance of their results has not been generally understood.

13.4.1 Agutter's study (and McMahon's reanalysis)

Agutter (1988) is a comparative study of two RP speakers and four Edinburgh SSE speakers, all MC undergraduates at Edinburgh University, aged 18–23. Their phonological systems are not indicated. The materials were words in frame sentences, and one token of each word was elicited. Five vowels, /i ɪ ɔ ai au/, were examined in a range of environments. The limited materials were not controlled for onsets, leading to some pairs that are not properly comparable (e.g. *feed* versus *tee'd*), and judging from the materials and results, we do not consider the data to be particularly reliable. The study is important, however, and deserves careful scrutiny. Basing her hypotheses on Aitken (1981b), Agutter expected /i ai au/ to exhibit SVLR, /ı/ to be uniformly short and /ɔ/ uniformly long.[10] Although the paper does include the raw numerical data, Agutter bases her discussion on data *normalised* across speakers. She concludes that 'SVLR applies . . . [but not] that it characterises anything phonetically distinctive of Scots' (Agutter 1988: 129).

McMahon (1991) shows that Agutter's method of reducing speaker variation also reduces cross-dialectal variation. On a reanalysis, although *some* aspects of the Scottish and RP systems still display a common phonetic pattern, which McMahon calls **low level lengthening (LLL)**, other aspects (extra lengthening before voiced fricatives, /r/, pause and /#d/) are systematically distinctive and appear only in Scottish varieties. In RP, only LLL operates. As might be deduced from our presentation in section 13.1, we agree with the spirit of McMahon's subdivision of Aitken's conditioning environment, but not with her specific proposals about low level lengthening, which cross-cut our own division of consonantal and morphological environments. We do not regard the durational system of RP either as 'low level' or as being common to both varieties. Rather, Scottish varieties *and* RP have their own language-specific, partially phonetically motivated systems sitting on top of a more universally natural phonetic base. Indeed, the *small* difference in duration between *feet* and *feed* in Scottish varieties is more likely to be a genuinely 'low level' alternation, i.e. to be no more than a natural result of coarticulation between vowels and voiced/voiceless consonants. Elsewhere, vowel allophony in both dialects is much more systematised, each in its own way. As mentioned above, we have to leave almost untouched the morphophonological and phonological ramifications of the SVLR, and the reader should consult especially McMahon (1991) and Carr (1992) for relevant discussion. We focus here on the phonetic patterns.

McMahon (1991) offers a reanalysis of Agutter's raw data, but in fact her reanalysis partly obscures Agutter's results. Consequently, the patterns in Agutter's raw data have never received proper consideration. McMahon *pools* data for /ai/ and /i/ (both of which are assumed to alternate on the basis of Aitken 1981b), and /ɔ/ and /ı/ (both assumed to be non-alternating), to compensate for the impoverished data. But pooling data for these vowels is invalid. First, /ai/ is much longer than /i/ in raw duration. Second, /ai/, being a diphthong, is likely to have less flexibility than /i/ in its durational variation. Third, /ai/ has quality *and* quantity differences in its allophones (short [ʌi] and long [ae]), but /i/ has only quantitative differences, so again their durational properties are not comparable. Turning to /ı/ and /ɔ/: first, /ı/ is much shorter than /ɔ/ in raw duration. Second, /ı/ cannot occur in open syllables while /ɔ/ *is* able to. Assuming that this is due to a minimal word constraint, /ı/ must be monomoraic ('short') while /ɔ/ is bimoraic ('long'). Third, there are clearly observable differences in duration for /ɔ/ that simply don't apply to /ı/: for example, *lot < law*. If we simply present a graph of mean duration calculated from Agutter's raw data (Figure 13.1), the non-congruity of /ai/ and /i/, and /ɔ/ and /ɪ/ can be clearly seen. Additionally, unreliable as the data may be, clear patterns exist.

Most importantly, it emerges that Agutter's study disproved Aitken's (1981b: 133) explicit claim that the SVLR applies to /au/ in SSE, at least with respect to morphological conditioning, a fact that was submerged by Agutter's general conclusions about the SVLR. McMahon (1991: 42) is aware of this result, however, as is Johnston (1997b: 474). So Agutter's study provides an indication that Aitken's SVLR does not transfer in a simple fashion to SSE. Given the lack of further data, McMahon assumes that the SVLR does indeed apply otherwise just as Aitken's account would lead us to expect: it affects /ai/ and /i/ 'and also /u e o/ and perhaps /a ɔɪ/, although these were not tested by Agutter' (McMahon 1991: 44). We agree that neither /au/ nor /ɔ/ is subject to the SVLR in SSE, but conclude that this contradicts Aitken (1981b: 133) *in both cases*. The monomoraic /ɪ/ shows, unsurprisingly, a little durational allophony, but since /ɪ/ cannot undergo morphologically conditioned allophony, it is peripheral to this aspect of the SVLR system. So, in Agutter's study, quasi-phonemic contrast is demonstrated only for /i/ and /ai/.[11]

We do not have space to consider the phonological conditioning of duration, except to say that no uniform pattern before stops is evident cross-dialectally, and that voiced fricatives tend to lengthen /i au ɪ/ in SSE nearly twice as much as they do in RP. The diphthong /ai/ has similar relative increases in duration in both dialects at approximately 80% (cf. note 11), while /i/ in SSE is nearly 150% longer before a voiced fricative, compared to only 80% in RP.

13.4.2   McKenna's and McClure's studies

Gordon McKenna's unpublished M.Litt. thesis from the Department of Linguistics at Edinburgh University (McKenna 1988) is the most detailed investigation of the SVLR to date. It is explicitly aimed at illuminating the

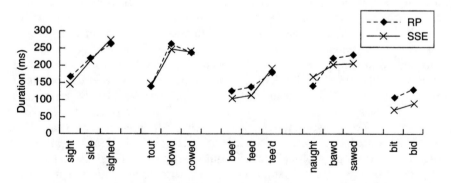

Fig. 13.1 Mean vowel duration before /t/, /d/ and /#d/, for RP (two speakers) and SSE (four speakers), from Agutter (1988)

phenomenon in Scottish Standard English. For comparison purposes we will also look at McClure (1977).[12] McKenna has four SSE subjects, all undergraduates at Edinburgh University, and all with a basic Scottish vowel system. Two are from Edinburgh, one is from Dundee and one is from Dunfermline. Means are calculated from eight tokens (four subjects, two repetitions of each word) spoken in a carrier phrase. We present only the most relevant data, and the reader should consult McKenna (1988) for the full findings. Figure 13.2 illustrates various effects, including intrinsic duration due to vowel height (which arises because lower vowels take longer to articulate) and extrinsic duration due to the manner and voicing of the following consonant. In general, vowels before a voiced consonant are longer than those before the voiceless congener – the general pattern for English and many other languages (Keating 1985). What appears to be specific to Scottish Standard English, however, is the durational behaviour of /i/ and /u/. In comparison with American English (House & Fairbanks 1953), we can see that the close vowels before /d/ and /s/ in particular are of a surprisingly small duration.

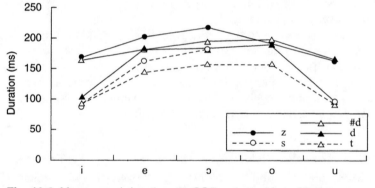

Fig. 13.2 Mean vowel durations in SSE, adapted from McKenna
(1988) (note that there are no data for /o/ + /s/)

Let us look first at consonantal conditioning. Figure 13.3a illustrates how the small duration of /i/ and /u/ before /s/ gives rise to a disproportionately large increase in relative duration before /z/. The non-high vowels are only about 20% longer before /z/. On the other hand, the high vowels have *less* of a differential in the stop environment, at only about 10%. Before /d/, the non-high vowels /e ɔ o/ are again roughly 20% longer. The non-high vowels in McKenna's study therefore have a small and relatively consistent lengthening effect before *all* voiced obstruents. McClure's data (Figure 13.3b) appear broadly compatible with these observations. In other varieties of English, 'the duration of a vowel preceding a voiced consonant is approximately [50%] greater than that of the same vowel preceding a voiceless consonant' (Lehiste 1996: 228). The peculiarly Scottish aspects of phonological conditioning are that differential vowel duration is large before fricatives, small before stops for /i/ and /u/, and uniformly small in both environments for the non-high vowels.

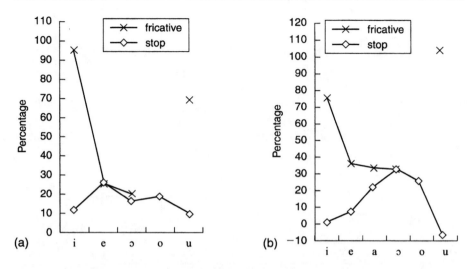

Figure 13.3 Consonantal conditioning of SVLR in SSE: increase in vowel duration in voiced context as a percentage of vowel duration in voiceless context. (a) Calculated from data in McKenna (1988); (b) Calculated from data in McClure (1977), as described in the text

Turning now to the morphological conditioning of vowel duration, Figure 13.4a illustrates McKenna's findings that in SSE only the high vowels /i/ and /u/ can convey quasi-phonemic contrast before /d/ and /#d/, because the non-high vowels /e ɔ o/ have the same duration before /d/ as they do before /#d/. This means that in SSE the following pairs rhyme: *raid/arrayed, odd/awed, road/rowed.*[13]

McKenna interprets McClure's (1977) findings as confirming his own results, and we can indeed see in Figure 13.4 that there is, as in Figure 13.3, a broad agreement between these studies. Indeed, McClure himself notes (p. 16) that /i/ and /u/ (and /ai/ to an extent) differ from the 'other' alternating vowels in being shorter in the short environments and having a more decisive break between shorter and longer allophones. Nevertheless, McClure concludes that his results give 'especially striking' evidence of a durational contrast between such pairs as *pod/pawed* and *toad/towed.* Compared to /i/ and /u/, Aitken found the differences in /e ɛ a ɔ ai/ and /au/ 'smaller, but still convincing' (Aitken 1981b: 136). We think, with McKenna, that the putative SVLR differences in /e a ɔ o/ etc. are an artefact of McClure's experimental procedure, due especially to the very slow speech rate. Figure 13.4b suggests that the ratio of /#z/ and /z/, with its consistently low value of around 25%, is also to be disregarded.

To summarise, McKenna's study clearly indicates that *only* /i u ai/ are subject to the SVLR. This is evident both in the consonantal and in the morphological condition. With the benefit of a reliable companion study, McClure (1977) in retrospect leads to the same conclusion.

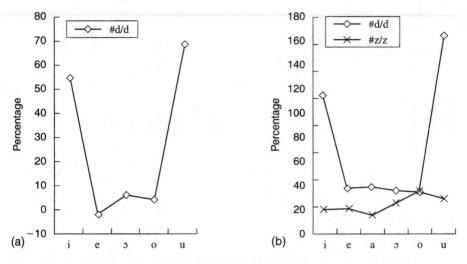

Fig. 13.4 Morphological conditioning of SVLR in SSE: relative vowel duration conditioned by /#d/ and /#z/ expressed as percentage increase, calculated relative to the duration in syllables closed by a tautomorphemic /d/ and /z/. (a) Calculated from data in McKenna (1988); (b) Calculated from data in McClure (1977)

13.4.3   The Scottish Vowel Length Rule Project

This project is ongoing, but results available at the time of going to press are worth a brief mention. Hewlett, Matthews & Scobbie (1999) report on an acquisition study of MC children aged 4–9 living in Corstorphine, Edinburgh, focused on the duration of /i/ and /u/ in the consonantal condition. Preliminary results indicate that the children have acquired the SVLR for /i/ and /u/ as follows. Before fricatives, voicing conditions about a 75% increase in vowel duration, but before stops the increase is only about 10%. The chances of acquiring this pattern robustly are reduced, however, in cases where the parents do not have Scottish accents themselves. The failure to acquire SVLR robustly does not imply that the child doesn't use the basic Scottish vowel system, however, indicating that the SVLR may be particularly susceptible to variation and influence from non-Scottish dialects.

Scobbie, Turk & Hewlett (1999) report on a study of the word-list component of the Glasgow data collected by Jane Stuart-Smith (this volume). It focuses on the morphological conditioning of the SVLR, looking at the vowels /ai i u o ɔ/. From the durational data, *all groups* (see Stuart-Smith this volume) have a statistically significant quasi-phonemic contrast in /i/, /u/ and /ai/ but not in /o/ or /ɔ/ (Table 13.2).

Spectral analysis reveals no qualitative differences in the monophthongs, other than, perhaps, in the young female WC group, who might be showing a fronted and slight lowered [i̞] in *agreed* relative to the high and slightly

Table 13.2   Mean vowel duration in ms (32 Glasgow speakers) and the increase in duration before heteromorphemic word-final /#d/ relative to tautomorphemic word-final /d/

Vowel	_d	_#d	% increase
i	123	205	66
u	117	199	70
ai	227	281	24
o	201	193	−4
ɔ	207	222	7

retracted [i̠] in *greed*. The allophones of /ai/ have *strong* qualitative differences, however, both in *side* and *sighed* and in a pre-fricative context (*ice* versus *eyes*). Before /d/ and /s/, the vowel begins and may end higher and a little fronter than before /#d/ and /#z/ respectively. This can be transcribed broadly as [ʌi] and [ae] respectively. The timing characteristics of the vowels are very different: in [ae] the back-central open or mid-open target is held stable and followed by an off-glide in the direction of [i], whereas in [ʌi], an on-glide coming apparently from the direction of [ɑ] approaches [i] and may be held stable there. Finally, consider how the SVLR conditioning cross-cuts the social variation in /ai/. We will exemplify this with the young female speakers' productions of *ice*/*spice* and *eyes*/*spies*. Spectrographic analysis confirms that the first target of the diphthongs is higher for WC than for MC speakers (Table 13.3). Less obviously, the MC speakers have a greater difference in duration (81%) than the WC speakers (53%).

Further analysis is under way of the distribution of /ai/ allophones in the first syllable of disyllabic trochees (*hydro, title, tidal, sidle, crisis, miser*, etc.) from the word-list. Preliminary results indicate that the choice of allophone before a voiceless fricative may be a sociolinguistic variable. In the word *crisis*, for example, older MC males prefer [ae] while older WC males prefer [ʌi]. Young WC and MC females show a great deal of variability, unlike the other groups. The spectral characteristics of the variants of /ai/ are similar to those of /ai/ in monosyllables, but there appear to be *no* durational generalisations relevant to defining the 'long' and 'short' allophones.

Table 13.3   Typical /ai/ allophones, young Glasgow females, word-list data

	_s	_#z
WC	ə̝ɪ	ʌ̞ë
MC	ɜ̝ɪ	ɐ̝ë

13.5   *The SVLR and SSE in Edinburgh and Glasgow*

As indicated above in section 13.2, Scottish Standard English as it is normally defined encompasses a range of phonological and phonetic systems. In the extreme case, a small but significant proportion of native Scottish MC speakers use phonological and phonetic systems which are near-RP. This is observable in the speech of, for example, some MPs and lawyers. Formal broadcast Scottish English is often nearer to RP than to either of the MC varieties tabulated in this volume (Stuart-Smith's 'Glasgow Standard' and Chirrey's 'Edinburgh English'). Based on informal observation we think there is a greater amount of near-RP speech amongst the Edinburgh middle class than there is in Glasgow, but until comparative data are collected, we cannot be sure how this affects the SVLR.

There are various contemporary and historical differences between the middle classes in these cities which would lead us to expect a greater influence of Anglo English on the Edinburgh middle class. The 1991 Census shows that Edinburgh has more middle-class residents, and more English residents. While Edinburgh has 38% of residents in social groups I, II and IIIN, Glasgow has only 22%. Edinburgh has 9.5% residents born in England (39,682) while Glasgow, Bearsden and Milngavie combined have only 3.5% (24,275).[14] These proportions are not unrelated, since 'most English families settling in Scotland are well educated and tend to be employed in high-status jobs': results from the ESRC Scottish Devolution Referendum Project (R000237374) indicate that in 1997, 23% of Scottish residents born in Scotland had a higher education qualification compared to 38% of Scottish residents who were born in England, and that similar results hold for occupation (Lindsay Paterson, personal communication). The record of births at the General Register Office for Scotland contains information about the social class and country of birth of the child's parents: these records show a similar correlation between middle-class occupation and an English birthplace. Looking just at a subset of children (about 75% of the MC total) who were born into a Scottish, English or mixed Scottish/English family with a 'professional' or 'executive' parent (social class codes 1 and 2) in 1997, we see that in Edinburgh, 23% (633/2,728) have at least one English parent, while in Glasgow, Bearsden and Milngavie, only 12% do. There is also a much higher proportion of children in Edinburgh who attend independent schools (Scottish Office, personal communication), as shown in Table 13.4. Taking these demographic trends together, we predict that MC SSE in Edinburgh will be further along the continuum towards RP as a result of the greater exposure of the Scottish MC to MC Anglo-English models.

The potential Anglo-English influence on Scottish students in higher education should also be considered, especially since McKenna's and Agutter's subjects were drawn from this pool. Edinburgh University hosts a much larger proportion of Anglo-English students than Glasgow University (Table 13.5) (EU website http://www.cpa.ed.ac.uk/facts/ 18/12/98; GU website http://www.gla.ac.uk/Otherdepts/IPS/FastFacts/studentn.htm 18/12/98). We do

Table 13.4 Numbers of school pupils in schools run by City of Edinburgh and Glasgow City Council and in independent schools in those areas

	Edinburgh City, Sept. 1997		Glasgow City, Sept. 1997	
	State	Independent	State	Independent
Primary	30,590	4,055 (12%)	49,439	2,509 (5%)
Secondary	18,714	6,136 (25%)	29,952	4,108 (12%)
Total	49,304	10,191 (17%)	79,391	6,617 (8%)

Table 13.5 Residency of students at Edinburgh University and Glasgow University

Home residence	EU students (full and part-time) 1997–98 (%)	GU students (full-time) 1996–97 (%)
Scotland	43	71
Rest of the UK	40	16

not know whether Agutter's (1988) MC Edinburgh speakers had the basic Scottish vowel system. McKenna (1988) used a questionnaire to make sure that his Edinburgh MC subjects had a basic Scottish system, meaning that we can be confident of his results providing a valid picture of MC SSE as *we* have defined it, in terms of the basic Scottish vowel system, making his results likely to be applicable in the Glasgow context too.

In conclusion, we think it likely that if Stuart-Smith's study were repeated in Edinburgh, more of the MC speakers would have non-Scottish contrasts supplementing Abercrombie's basic Scottish system than she found in Bearsden. There is great potential for interesting comparisons to be made between the MC varieties of Edinburgh and Glasgow, and between the speech of Scottish children at state and independent schools in each city. Casual observation in Edinburgh and Glasgow of pupils from independent schools indicates, for example, that RP-like non-rhoticity has a higher incidence in Edinburgh independent schools, which may indicate, in combination with Stuart-Smith's results, that rhoticity is retreating in more than one sociolinguistic group.

13.6   *Conclusions*

We have reviewed and reinterpreted the available instrumental experimental phonetic data on the SVLR. Most of the subjects investigated spoke Scottish Standard English with Abercrombie's (1979) basic Scottish vowel system, including all four subjects in McKenna (1988), our major source.

Morphologically conditioned quasi-phonemic contrasts in duration have been observed for the high bimoraic vowels /i/ and /u/, and the diphthong /ai/. The diphthongal contrast is less in degree, but is accompanied by strong qualitative cues. A contrast has been shown to be absent for /e ɔ o/ and /au/ (and /a/ in McClure's Ayrshire data), and it cannot be conditioned for /ɛ ɪ ʌ/. We can conclude on this basis that the morphological pattern of the SVLR affects only /i/, /u/ and /ai/ in Scottish Standard English. Little is known about the consonantal conditioning of vowel duration before non-alveolar consonants, but before alveolar stops and fricatives it is clear that high vowels pattern very differently from non-high vowels: /i/ and /u/ are particularly short before /t/, /d/ and /s/, but /ai/ shows less extreme durational variation. In polysyllabic words, indeed, the two qualitative variants of /ai/ may not differ in duration at all, only in quality.

Variation in the SVLR can reveal much of interest. Our ongoing analysis of /ai/ in the Glasgow data is beginning to reveal interesting preliminary results. The SVLR is susceptible to pressure from non-Scottish varieties, as shown in acquisition by Hewlett *et al.* (1999). Given the result, and the demographic situations in Glasgow and Edinburgh, child language acquisition in Scotland emerges as an area of important future research.

Our analysis runs counter to other accounts that imply or claim a much wider applicability for the SVLR. One of the implications of our analysis is that phonological analyses of the basic Scottish vowel system will have to be redrawn, with a much smaller role for the SVLR. Moreover, the literature leads us to expect that other Scottish systems will exhibit more general SVLR patterns, but clearly, given the history of research into this phenomenon, the status of the SVLR in other varieties must be regarded as less than settled. More instrumental phonetic research is urgently required.

Notes

1 We acknowledge the support of ESRC grant R000237135. Thanks are due to the editors for their encouragement. Thanks also to Jane Stuart-Smith, April McMahon, Gerry Docherty and Ben Matthews for discussion and comments, to Lindsay Paterson (University of Edinburgh) and Ian Brown (GROS) for their help with materials for section 13.5, and to our subjects and their families.
2 We attempt to avoid terminological and conceptual confusion as follows. The terms **long** and **short** imply a categorical phonological opposition of **length**. The terms **duration, durationally long** and **durationally short** imply relative amounts of real phonetic time, and the comparative adjectives **longer** and **shorter** also refer to phonetic duration.
3 More precisely, vowels before tautomorphemic voiced coda stops are only barely longer than the comparable vowels before cognate voiceless stops, suggesting that the residual, low level difference is irreducible.
4 Due to the interaction with segmental conditioning, vowels in closed syllables are markedly shorter only if the closing consonant is a stop, nasal, voiceless fricative or /l/. Syllables closed by voiced continuants seem to be comparable in duration to open syllables. The behaviour of closing clusters is unclear.
5 We concentrate on patterns of duration and have relatively little to say about phono

logical length. We will see that the basic Scottish vowel system has a reduced role for length as a contrastive phonological feature. There are only three unquestionably short vowels (i.e. monomoraic vowels that cannot appear in open syllables), namely /ɪ ɛ ʌ/ (KIT, DRESS, STRUT). We assume that the other vowels are bimoraic, i.e. long, though nothing hangs on that here. The status of length in Scottish varieties is controversial, a situation caused in large part by the complex phonetic-phonological-morphological systems governing vowel duration.

6 This system derives historically from the varieties of Scots spoken in the Central Lowlands encompassing Glasgow and Edinburgh.

7 Since our description of the SVLR in this paper concentrates on SSE and the basic system, we cannot devote the necessary space to consideration of specifically Scots vowels such as /ø/. Nor can we consider properly here the complex behaviour of /ai/, the SVLR-governed allophony of which ([ʌi ~ ae]) exists in Scots alongside a *contrast* between /ʌi/ and /ae/ (and /e/) in one lengthening environment: stressed open syllables with the cognate suffixed forms (e.g. [pʌi] *pay*, [pʌid] *paid*). The SVLR behaviour of Scots phonemes /ae/ and /ʌi/ is the same as for the single SSE phoneme /ai/ in all other environments. Even in the open syllable environment, Scots /ae/, in *pie*, for example, acts just like SSE /ai/. The single difference is that Scots-influenced speech also permits [ʌi] *with a different lexical incidence from SSE* /ae/ to appear. Interestingly, the behaviour of /ai/ in SSE in *polysyllabic* words is also suggestive of a phonemic split. See Aitken (1981b) who makes this point and Scobbie *et al.* (1999) for some acoustic data. Aitken should also be consulted for his discussion of morphophonological data, especially /ai/ again in plurals like /lʌivz/ *lives* rather than /laivz/ with a longer duration allophone.

8 In Scots, many (most?) CHOICE words in SVLR shortening environments (e.g. *join, oil, choice*) have /ʌi/ (see note 7). Aitken notes that /ɔi/ may be invariably long in some dialects of Scots, as [oe]. Our informal observations suggest that [oe] production (which can sound disyllabic in open syllables) appears mainly in SVLR long environments. Such SVLR-related patterning of lexical incidence echoes the distribution of /ae/ and /ʌi/.

9 Allophony of /ai/ permeates into the north of England, in rural (Kolb, Glauser, Elmer & Stamm 1979) and urban speech (J. Milroy 1995).

10 This is a mistaken reading of Aitken (1981b). See section 13.3 for discussion of /ɔ/. In SSE, LOT, CLOTH, THOUGHT *do* have /ɔ/ and it is observably not uniformly long. McMahon (1991) perpetuates Agutter's error.

11 Note that /ai/ is similar in duration in the 'short' *side* and 'long' *sighed* environments in both dialects, indicating the crucial importance of the *quality* difference between [ʌi] and [ae] in SSE.

12 The experimental materials are similar in both studies, and both consider MC SSE. McClure's (1977) study examines a single speaker, the author himself (Ayrshire), so it in turn needs to be examined in the context of McKenna's more reliable study. While McKenna (1988) is obscure, McClure's (1977) study is cited much more widely, e.g. in Wells (1982). Our presentation of McClure (1977) uses values which are the mean of his in-isolation mean (N = 2) and his sentential measurement (N = 1).

13 Presumably *rode* and *rowed* are homophonous, giving one less morphophonological alternation for the Lexical Phonologist to worry about (e.g. Carr 1992).

14 Bearsden and Milngavie are not and have not been part of the City of Glasgow Council.

14

(London)Derry: between Ulster and local speech – class, ethnicity and language change

Kevin McCafferty

14.1 *Brief history*

(London)Derry English (LDE), as a variety of Northern Ireland English (NIE), is a result of the mixing of Ulster-Scots and other varieties of English brought to the region during the seventeenth-century Plantation of Ulster and subsequent Irish Gaelic influence, as the Irish-speaking population shifted to English. Like the variety spoken in Belfast, LDE is probably best regarded as a variety of Mid-Ulster English. Geographically, (London)Derry is wedged between two of the areas identified as Ulster-Scots-speaking by Gregg (1972, 1985), and much of its population growth has been fed by the influx of workers from Donegal in the west and the surrounding areas of counties (London) Derry and Tyrone to the east and south.

In 1613 the government of James VI/I granted the region to the liveried companies of the City of London and ordered a fortified city to be built on the site of ancient monastic settlements by the River Foyle; the city was to be known as Londonderry in recognition of the connection with the City. However, the latter turned out to be reluctant colonists who never fully fulfilled the terms of their contract, which included clearing the area of native Irish and 'planting' it with loyal English and Scottish Protestant settlers. Some historical sources put the proportions of Scots to English in the mid-seventeenth century as high as 20:1 in the city (Simpson 1847: 54). By the 1830s the proportions of Scots, English and Irish were approximately 25:25:50 (Colby 1837: 191), and from then on the Irish (Catholic) proportion increased rapidly as the population grew and the city industrialised, albeit on a smaller scale than Belfast (Lacy 1990: 169; Thomas 1997b: 77). Currently, the Catholic:Protestant proportions are approximately 75:25 (DHSS 1991). Ethnic segregation of Catholics and Protestants (A. Robinson 1969; Bell 1987, 1990), reinforced by competition for jobs and other resources, has been a feature of the local scene since the early 1800s (Lacy 1990: 167–87). The city was one of the most sharply segregated urban areas in Northern Ireland in the late 1960s (Poole 1982) and the Troubles after 1969 led to the migration of about two-thirds of the city's Protestants from the west bank of the River Foyle to the east, making segregation today firmer than ever (Lacy 1990: 270).

14.1.1 Fieldwork

This chapter is based on material gathered by participant observation during a total of seven months of fieldwork conducted in 1994 and 1995. So far, 107 of the recorded interviews have been used for sociolinguistic analysis, but participant observation was also intended to provide data for an ethnography of aspects of interethnic relations in the city (e.g. McCafferty 1997: 177–233). The data used here are for 59 teenagers and 48 adults born 1921–40, these being the age groups for which there is full coverage in cells defined by ethnic group, social class and sex (the latter disregarded here).

The interviews took the form of unscripted informal conversations, sometimes in informants' own homes, but usually at community centres, youth clubs, etc., where I had been present several times before asking for interviews. Talk ranged over areas of informants' or mutual interests, usually arising out of previous contact or information supplied, such as the fact that a particular person would know a lot about, for example, the shirt industry that once dominated the local economy, the history of the workhouse, etc. This renders the data useless for analysis of style-shifting, so that this is a single-style study. However, the primary sociolinguistic issues are *whether* and *how* ethnicity and other social factors relate to variation and change, and whether they interact with one another. These can be approached in a single-style study for which everyone was taped in the same situation.

14.2 *Descriptive material*

14.2.1 Vowels

Like other varieties of Irish English (IE), North and South, LDE is rhotic, with /r/ a fairly weak approximant [ɹ], occasionally slightly retroflexed. The

Table 14.1 (London)Derry vowels – summary

KIT	ɪ > ë ~ ǽ	FLEECE	i	NEAR	i > iə
DRESS	ɛ	FACE	e ~ ɪ ~ iə	SQUARE	ɛ > ö
TRAP	a ~ æ	PALM	a ~ æ	START	a ~ æ
LOT	ɔ ~ ɒ	THOUGHT	ɔ ~ ɒ	NORTH	ɔ ~ ɒ > o
STRUT	ö	GOAT	o	FORCE	o
FOOT	ö ~ ʉ	GOOSE	ʉ	CURE	jø: ~ jy:
BATH	a ~ æ	PRICE	eɪ ~ ɛɪ > ɑe > ʌɪ ~ aɪ	happy	i
CLOTH	ɔ ~ ɒ > o	CHOICE	ɔɪ	letter	ə
NURSE	ö	MOUTH	əʉ ~ öy	horses	ə
				comma	ə

Scottish Vowel Length Rule applies (Aitken 1981b; Harris 1985; Scobbie, Hewlett & Turk this volume), so that phonemic vowel-length distinctions have been almost completely lost, but phonetic lengthening is activated before /v, ð, z, r/ and word-finally for all but the KIT and STRUT vowels, which are short in all environments. With the latter exceptions, LDE vowels are subject to SVLR conditioning.

KIT
[ï] is centred by most speakers in informal styles; [ɪ] in formal styles for some of the middle class. [ë ~ ǽ] occur only before [k].

DRESS, SQUARE
[ɛ] varies little in LDE – lowering to [æ], as in Belfast vernacular, does not occur (yet?). However, before /r/, SQUARE items are at present merging with NURSE, especially for the Protestant middle class, a merger spreading from the east of Northern Ireland (McCafferty 1997: 100–9; 1998b).

TRAP, BATH, PALM, START
[a]~[æ] (the latter before /p, t/) shows little variation in contemporary LDE: Belfast vernacular backing and raising of, e.g., *man* [mɔːn] does not occur (yet?); and Belfast fronting and raising of e.g. *bag* [bɛːg] (see e.g. J. Milroy 1981, 1992; L. Milroy 1987b) is found only among the oldest speakers.

LOT, CLOTH, THOUGHT, NORTH
[ɔ] may be realised as [ɒ] by older and working-class speakers. Before /r/ (NORTH), a merger in [o] (FORCE) is spreading from other parts of the North into LDE, led by middle-class Protestants (McCafferty 1997: 91–9; 1998b).

STRUT, FOOT, NURSE, GOOSE
[ɔ̈] in vernacular LDE, though FOOT may also be [ʉ] and GOOSE is always so. This feature shows subtle interaction with class and ethnicity (see below; McCafferty 1997: 157–76).

FLEECE, NEAR
[i] may have a centring glide [iə] before /r/, but shows little variation in LDE.

FACE
[e] is common, especially in formal styles; in more informal speech, among the working class, and for Catholics, [ɪ] is frequent, while a diphthongised variant [iə] is becoming more common among younger Protestants (McCafferty 1997: 111–30, 1998a, b).

GOAT, FORCE
[o] shows little variation, except in SVLR environments.

PRICE

[ei]~[ɛi] in informal vernacular speech; in SVLR environments, [ɑe] occurs. More formal pronunciations: [ʌi]~[ɑi].

CHOICE

[ɔi] shows little or no variation, though some speakers may have a more open first element.

MOUTH

[əʉ]: both elements of the diphthong may be rounded to [ɔ̈y]. Does not seem to be sensitive to social or stylistic variation. Belfast [a]~[ɑ] (J. Milroy 1981), though used by some speakers in pre-/r/ environments (making *tower* and *tar* homophones), are not widely used as part of a correcting or standardising strategy in LDE.

14.2.2 Consonants

P, T, K

/p, t, k/ have not been studied in detail, but glottal reinforcement occurs intervocalically and word-finally. Many speakers use glottal stops, but no comments can be made on the social significance of this. A voiced tap [ɾ] is the norm intervocalically and across word boundaries, e.g. *butter, latter, get off*.

K, G

Word-initial palatalisation of /k, g/ occurs in older LDE speech and among the working class, as reported also from Belfast (J. Milroy 1981), making e.g. *car* sound like [kjaɹ].

TH

Dropping of both voiced and voiceless interdental fricatives is frequent. This occurs variably in all environments, and is sensitive to social factors. For /ð/, in addition to elision (L. Milroy 1987b), replacement with a lateral approximant [l] is increasingly frequent, especially intervocalically in proximity to /r/ (typical items are *mother, father*, etc.), which would suggest that liquid assimilation has an effect. The [l] variant is most common among Catholics and the working class. For some speakers, [l] is also used word-initially in *the, these*, etc. (see below; also McCafferty 1997: 131–55). Besides dropping, /θ/ may also be lenited to [h] in initial and medial positions, e.g. *thanks, nothing*. This is most prevalent among the young, the working class, and males, but does not pattern ethnically. Southern British [v] and [f] for /ð/ and /θ/, respectively, occur only extremely infrequently among a small number of teenagers, and thus may be related to developmental factors, rather than any ongoing change.

X

The full velar fricative [x] is apparently becoming less common. Where pronounced at all, constriction is weak, more like [h], especially medially, as in

Banagher; word-finally [x] is retained, in particular by older speakers, while the young increasingly use [k] in e.g. *Enagh Lough.*

H

[h] is generally pronounced in LDE, as elsewhere in Ireland, north and south.

J

J-dropping does not occur in LDE.

R

/r/ is a weak alveolar approximant [ɹ], possibly with some retroflexion.

L

/l/ is generally clear, but is dark for some, especially in syllable-final positions. While this has social significance in Coleraine (Kingsmore 1995: 111–37), it has not been studied in LDE (or anywhere else in Northern Ireland). Vocalisation, a feature of Ulster-Scots (Gregg 1985), is very rare.

14.2.3   Prosody

High rising intonation occurs in declarative utterances. It is especially notice-able in the speech of the younger age groups. McElholm's (1986) experiment found rising intonation to be the unmarked norm in LDE; in fact, none of the utterances tested for that study occurred with purely falling intonation (see also Cruttenden 1995).

14.3   *Sociolinguistic issues*

The division between Catholic and Protestant in Northern Ireland has acknowledged ethnic nationalist, rather than religious, connotations (Jenkins 1986): Catholics identify overwhelmingly with the Irish Republic, while the preferred national allegiance of most Protestants is with Northern Ireland or the United Kingdom (Rose 1971; Moxon-Brown 1983, 1991; Gallagher 1995). It is also widely assumed that nationalist division, prejudice and segregation are strongest among the urban working class (Boserup & Iversen 1967; Boal & Poole 1972; Larsen 1973, 1982a, 1982b; Leyton 1975; Donnan & McFarlane 1983; Boal, Campbell & Livingstone 1985). My purpose here is to examine this supposed interaction between ethnicity and class in relation to change in Northern Ireland English (NIE) as spoken in (London)Derry (LDE). What are the sociolinguistic consequences of these ethnic nationalist identities and social segregation? To what extent do members of a Northern Ireland speech community orient themselves towards British, (Southern) Irish, common Ulster, or local speech forms? And how does class interact with the ethnic dimension?

14.3.1 Background

In a review of work on Irish English, Harris (1991: 46) notes that, while the study of Catholic/Protestant ethnicity is a neglected aspect of NIE studies, Unionists and Nationalists in peripheral areas of Northern Ireland do not share linguistic norms:

> The impression that strikes anyone who is familiar with the sociolinguistic situation in the North is that, for some nationalists, linguistic targets dictating the direction of standardisation appear to be defined at least in part by southern norms.

This accords well with Gunn's (1990, 1994) study of political speeches, which finds Nationalist and Unionist politicians appealing to their respective audiences by emphasising Southern Irish and Ulster-Scots features, respectively. While Harris is speaking of standardisation, we might expect the same orientations to affect the adoption of vernacular variants. However, to date most studies of NIE do not include explicit analysis of the ethnic factor (e.g. L. Milroy 1987b; J. Milroy 1992), or have used data that does not permit analysis along such lines (e.g. Douglas-Cowie 1978; Kingsmore 1983, 1995).

As regards social organisation, ethnic segregation in Northern Ireland is often acknowledged to be greater among the working class than the middle class. In relation to language variation, this might be expected to result in greater middle-class consensus and working-class divergence on either side of the ethnic divide. However, studies of NIE (J. & L. Milroy 1977; Douglas-Cowie 1978, Douglas 1979; J. Milroy, L. Milroy, Harris, Gunn, Pitts & Policansky 1982; Pitts 1982, 1985, 1989; Kingsmore 1983, 1995; Todd 1984, 1989) have tended not to be based on data that adequately cover more than one social class, so we have simply had no way of telling whether this is the case.

The current chapter reports from the first sociolinguistic survey in Northern Ireland to permit discussion of both social class and Protestant/Catholic ethnicity (McCafferty 1997), and interactions between the two. Results for several variables that are undergoing change in LDE do not confirm the above expectations: Protestants are not oriented towards British (vernacular) speech forms, nor are Catholics towards Southern Irish ones; and ethnolinguistic differentiation is not greatest in the working class.

14.3.2 (London)Derry and the survey

The population of (London)Derry (95,500 at the 1991 Census) is about 75% Catholic. As in many other places in Northern Ireland, there is a high degree of residential segregation – a comparative study of 26 towns, based on the 1971 Census data, found (London)Derry at that time one of the three most segregated urban areas in the country (Poole 1982). Since then, violence, intimidation or fear have led to some 60% of the Protestant population migrating across the River Foyle (Lacy 1990: 270), which cuts the city in two. West of the river, where most of the population lives, is today virtually exclusively Catholic, while east of the Foyle, where almost all the Protestant minority lives, the ethnic proportions are more even. While the details of the present pattern result from the mass migration of the years following the outbreak of hostilities in 1969, this is a reinforcement of historical patterns, rather than the outcome of recent violence: in a study carried out just before the start of the Troubles, Robinson (1969) charts very clear residential segregation in the city, and almost total activity segregation (Boal 1969) between adjoining Catholic and Protestant areas.

Evidence suggests that actual contact is rare in the lives of many in Northern Ireland, and both sides indulge in 'avoidance' strategies to lessen the risk of encountering someone of the other side and avoid giving offence (Larsen 1973, 1982a). One way of doing so is to steer clear of places where one might meet the other group. Avoidance means that, for Protestants in particular, much of the city is effectively out-of-bounds, including many leisure facilities and much of the city centre (located on the west bank of the Foyle). Consequently, they feel marginalised, deprived and discriminated against. Informants are precisely aware of the ethnic make-up of the city as a whole and their own neighbourhoods; some express a preference for living among their own sort. The city is clearly perceived as a divided place, although an ideal version seeks to present a harmonious, peaceful, undivided place (e.g. Burnside 1994b; also many of the informants cited in McCafferty 1997: chs 8 and 9).

14.3.3   Three LDE variables

The three variables studied here (summarised in Table 14.2) permit us to examine the spread of four linguistic changes that might be expected to correlate with class and ethnicity in different ways. The changes represent: a standardising innovation; two more recent vernacular innovations from the east; and a recent vernacular innovation peculiar to LDE:

(a) the gradual replacement of older [ʌ] with [ʉ] – a NIE standard form – which has been ongoing in the north of Ireland and Scotland for some time (Wells 1982: 196–9; Harris 1990b, 1996; Macafee 1994: 225; Kingsmore 1995);

(b) a widespread vernacular innovation originating in the east of Northern Ireland (Gregg 1958, 1959, 1964; Adams 1964b), which sees older [ɪ] replaced by [iə] in the FACE class, and both of these alternating with standard [e] (J. Milroy 1981: 73–8; J. Milroy *et al.* 1982; Kingsmore 1983: 299);

(c) (i) a vernacular innovation that appears to have originated in the east in the last hundred years, by which intervocalic [ð] is dropped, giving a Ø variant (J & L. Milroy 1977; Kingsmore 1983: 306; J. Milroy *et al.* 1982; L. Milroy 1987b), and

(c) (ii) a localised LDE vernacular innovation which realises the same inter-vocalic [ð] as a lateral [l] (McCafferty 1997: 131–55).

Table 14.2 Three LDE variables

Variable	Standard NIE	Older LDE	Newer LDE		Lexical set
			Ulster origin	Local origin	
(ʌ)	[ʉ]	[ʌ]			STRUT
(e)	[e]	[ɪ]	[iə]		FACE
(ð)	[ð]		Ø	[l]	TH

14.3.3.1 The (ʌ) variable

Variation between [ʉ] and [ʌ] occurs in a small number of words, most with initial labials – *pull, push, bull, full, would,* etc. (but see McConnell 1989, 1990, 1996; McCafferty 1997: 168). While [ʉ] seems to be gaining ground in NIE, the change is a gradual one, with items being transferred one at a time from the variable set to the class of words with categorical [ʉ] (see e.g. Harris 1986, 1990b, 1996). This is by now a well-known feature of urban NIE, having been investigated during the first Belfast survey (Maclaran 1976; J. & L. Milroy 1977; L. Milroy 1987b; J. Milroy 1992). From Belfast and Coleraine (Kingsmore 1983) there is evidence that older vernacular [ʌ] is dying out as [ʉ] spreads, with the latter reported as the only form used by the middle class in Belfast.

14.3.3.2 The (e) variable

The FACE vowel in NIE is subject to geographical and social variation. In LDE, standard [e] and vernacular [ɪ] vary with [iə], a Belfast vernacular variant (Adams 1964b: 3; J. Milroy 1981: 73–8) which is spreading at the expense of [ɪ], for instance to Coleraine (Kingsmore 1983: 300) and Articlave (Douglas 1975, 1979). A pointer to its social significance is that diphthongisation is more frequent in inner-city Belfast than in the slightly higher-status outer city (J. Milroy *et al.* 1982: 32–4). Social salience is indicated, too, in Belfast poet Michael Longley's (1994: 25) comments on [e] belonging to the middle-class accent of his home, while the diphthong characterised the working-class accents of the world beyond:

> [. . .] the accent, abrasive and raucous as a football rattle [. . .] I soon acquired in order to make myself less unacceptable. 'Len' us a mey-ek' – 'Lend me a make' (a ha'penny). At home I would try to remember to ask for 'a slice of cake' and not 'a slice of cey-ek' [. . .]. By the age of six or seven I was beginning to lead a double life, learning how to recreate myself twice daily.

And class differentiation within the Protestant community is suggested by Foster's (1994: 25) observation that members of the more populist, working-class oriented Democratic Unionist Party use [iə], while representatives of the more middle-class Ulster Unionist Party use [e].

14.3.3.3   The (ð) variable

The dropping of intervocalic (ð) in words like *mother* is by now well known from the Belfast projects (J. & L. Milroy 1977; J. Milroy *et al.* 1982). LDE has a third variant, a lateral approximant [l], which is common in medial positions (and is used by some word-initially). This lateral realisation has not been reported elsewhere in the sociolinguistic literature on NIE; however, a recent dialect grammar reports this phenomenon in Belfast and surrounding districts of north Down and south Antrim (P. Robinson 1997: 67).

The Belfast projects assume (ð)-dropping to be a stable marker of male sex (L. Milroy 1976: 12; L. Milroy 1987b: 128), informal style (J. & L. Milroy 1977: 6–7), and membership of the working class (J. Milroy 1992: 86). However, I interpret the absence of comment on TH-dropping in the pre-1970s literature as evidence of recent innovation. For instance, Patterson (1860), whose concern is to correct the provincialisms of Belfast, does not number TH-dropping among the features he deplores. Nor is this phenomenon mentioned by other early commentators (e.g. Staples 1898; Hart 1899), which suggests that it is a twentieth-century innovation. The apparent-time increase in dropping in Protestant East Belfast shows the younger men following the lead of the older men, but extending elision into formal as well as informal speech styles. This pattern is apparently spreading into Catholic West Belfast (J. & L. Milroy 1977: 6; McCafferty 1997: 131–4), and dropping has also been noted in Coleraine (Kingsmore 1983: 306).

LDE speakers participate in this development. However, LDE is also innovating at the local level, with the appearance of the [l] variant. The only published records of this innovation are McConnell's phrase-books (1989, 1990, 1996). It appears to be an even more recent innovation than TH-dropping. With this range of variation, (ð) has distinctive localised, regional (Northern Ireland), and 'universal' English variants.

Two further variants are worth considering briefly: the labiodental [v] realisation, common in south-eastern England, and reportedly spreading from there into other parts of Great Britain (Trudgill 1988: 42–4; Macafee 1994: 29; Docherty & Foulkes this volume; Williams & Kerswill this volume), and [d], which is widely used in the south of Ireland. These two might be expected to indicate sociopolitical orientation towards Britain or the Republic of Ireland along the lines suggested by Harris (1991) and Gunn (1990, 1994). However, they are so infrequent in the LDE material that they may be disregarded: of 1,846 tokens of (ð), there are only three [v] forms and a single [d] realisation. In other words, for this most obvious of variables at least, easily identifiable British and Southern Irish vernacular forms do not function as ethnic (or sociopolitical) markers in LDE. The question remains how local and more widespread Ulster forms of this and the other variables pattern.

14.3.4 Discussion

14.3.4.1 (ʌ) in LDE

LDE data for (ʌ) do not attest steady progress towards a Belfast middle-class standard. The vernacular variant is not a recessive relic feature, as in the larger city. It is, however, subject to slow change, as illustrated in Table 14.3 and Figures 14.1 and 14.2. In LDE variation appears to be gradually taking on the same stable profile across ethnic and class boundaries, rather than being a clear process of attrition by which the older [ʌ] form is disappearing.

Progress towards categorical use of [ʉ], as reported for the middle class in Belfast (Maclaran 1976: 45), seems to have been arrested. The (London)Derry middle class use no more than 60–65% [ʉ], retaining the [ʌ] about one third of the time, while their Belfast counterparts are reported as not having the latter variant at all. In fact, the teenage CM use only marginally more [ʉ] than the adults, while the teenage PM use *less* [ʉ] than their adult counterparts. On the other hand, the CW and PW show marked increases in their use of this form between the two age-groups. The change is still progressing, but only in the speech of the working class, who are gradually approximating to the (London)Derry middle class pattern. For this variable, ethnicity appears to be less important than class.

Table 14.3 (ʌ) by ethnicity and class

	Adults					Teenagers				
	[ʉ]	%	[ʌ]	%	Total	[ʉ]	%	[ʌ]	%	Total
PM	211	64	118	36	*329*	140	58	100	42	*240*
PW	105	28	265	72	*370*	93	40	140	60	*233*
CM	218	47	247	53	*465*	128	48	138	52	*266*
CW	172	26	502	74	*674*	182	34	359	66	*541*
Total	706	38	1,132	62	*1,838*	543	42	737	58	*1,280*

Key
PM – Protestant Middle class   CM – Catholic Middle class
PW – Protestant Working class   CW – Catholic Working class

Table 14.4 (ʌ): Goldvarb analysis of social factors

Adults				Teenagers			
Ethnicity		**Class**		**Ethnicity**		**Class**	
Overall tendency: 0.595				Overall tendency: 0.551			
Protestant	0.552	Middle	0.641	Protestant	0.543	Middle	0.581
Catholic	0.448	Working	0.359	Catholic	0.457	Working	0.419
Both factor groups significant				Both factor groups significant			
p < 0.001				*p* < 0.001			

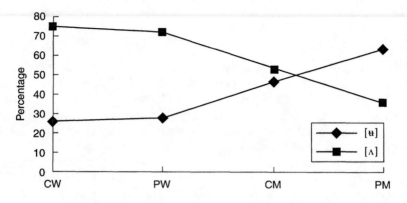

Fig. 14.1 (ʌ): adults by ethnicity and class sub-groups

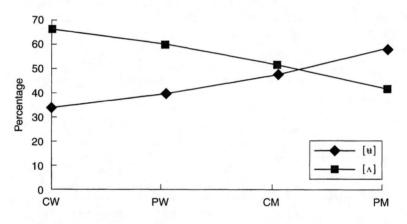

Fig. 14.2 (ʌ): teenagers by ethnicity and class sub-groups

Goldvarb (Rand & Sankoff 1988) analysis of LDE (ʌ) produces the results in Table 14.4. For both age groups, the ranking of the social factors is the same, while the decrease of the overall tendency, from 0.595 for adults to 0.551 for teenagers, indicates the stasis or minor regression already outlined. For both adults and teenagers, class is the most salient factor group, with the middle class weighted most favourably towards [ʉ]. In both age groups, Protestants are more likely to employ the innovative variant. Although class is the more important social dimension in relation to (ʌ) in LDE, ethnicity still plays a significant, if secondary, part.

This follows the general pattern of shift in NIE, with Belfast English forms diffusing outwards into other urban areas, being taken up first by Protestants and the middle class (Pitts 1982, 1989; McCafferty 1997, 1998a, b). But differentiation is very finely graded in relation to this change, which has been under way for a long time; it is mainly class-driven, with [ʉ] more of a middle-class marker than anything else. Nonetheless, there is nothing to suggest that the middle class in (London)Derry are moving in the direction of their class-fellows in Belfast; in fact, they still use [ʌ] up to 40–50% of the time. With middle-class LDE speakers apparently having reached their limit of [ʉ]-use, the change is driven by the working class, who have still to approach that limit. For the latter, [ʌ] can hardly be said to function as a working-class marker in the same way as it clearly does in Belfast.

Table 14.5 (e) vernacular usage by ethnicity, sex and class sub-groups

	N	[e]	%	[ɪ]	%	[iə]	%	Total
				Adults				
PM	10	364	76	31	7	81	17	476
PW	10	259	52	162	33	76	15	497
CM	12	489	83	93	16	6	1	588
CW	16	471	59	319	40	8	1	798
Total	48	1,583	67	605	26	171	7	2,359
				Teenagers				
	N	[e]	%	[ɪ]	%	[iə]	%	Total
PM	12	370	57	71	11	205	32	646
PW	14	259	43	142	23	203	34	604
CM	11	365	69	123	23	38	8	526
CW	22	707	63	397	36	7	1	1,111
Total	59	1,701	59	733	25	453	16	2,887

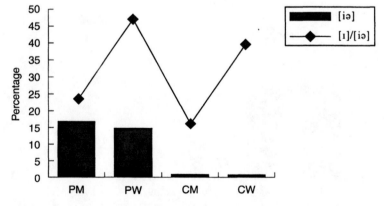

Fig. 14.3 (e) vernacular variants by ethnicity, sex and class (adults)

14.3.4.2   (e) in LDE

Data for (e) are displayed in Table 14.5 and Figures 14.3 and 14.4. Since change is taking place in the vernacular, the graphs show combined scores for the two vernacular variants (as a line graph) and percentages for the incoming diphthongs (columns).

Among adults (Figure 14.3), there emerges a very sharp pattern of differentiation by both ethnicity and class. The working class use at least twice as many vernacular variants as the middle class. But there is an ethnic gap, too: Catholics of both classes use less than 1% [iə], while it accounts for 15–17% of Protestant tokens, and for the PM this is the predominant vernacular form, being more than twice as frequent as [ɪ].

In Figure 14.4, although the general level of vernacular usage has increased across the board, the class difference in terms of combined vernacular scores is less marked, especially on the Catholic side. The teenage CW maintain [ɪ], using less than 1% diphthongs, while the CM use 8% [iə]. Nonetheless, Catholic teenagers of both classes use overwhelming proportions of [ɪ] as their vernacular variant. Protestants' preference for [iə], already established in the older PM, is even more pronounced in both classes among the younger age group. Thus, diphthongisation of (e) is primarily a Protestant phenomenon in LDE, although the middle class in both Catholic and Protestant sections of the population – the PM at a higher and CM at a much lower level – lead in adopting eastern [iə] variants.

Running Goldvarb twice to assess the weightings for these two factor groups – once for [e] versus both vernacular variants combined (Run 1), and once for older vernacular [ɪ] versus newer [iə] (Run 2) – gives the results presented in Table 14.6.

The apparent-time change is indicated by the increase in the overall tendencies for teenagers as opposed to adults. In the adult sample, membership of the

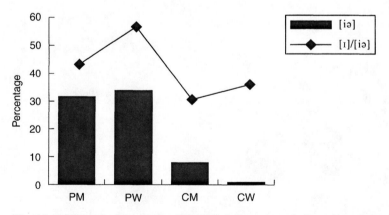

Fig. 14.4 (e) vernacular variants by ethnicity, sex and class (teenagers)

working class selects most strongly for use of the vernacular variants (Run 1), with Protestant ethnicity second. However, Protestant ethnic background is the factor that most strongly promotes adoption of diphthongs (Run 2), while class remains very highly significant in this respect, too. The change between the two age groups is underlined by the fact that, for teenagers, Protestant ethnic identity is the social factor that most strongly influences both the use of vernacular variants in general, and of [iə] diphthongs in particular. Nonetheless, class is also important in selecting vernacular variants, with the teenage working class weighted significantly in favour of the vernacular variants, and the middle class selecting strongly for [iə].

In short, ethnicity is the more important social factor affecting this vernacular change, but [iə] is a form that has entered from the east via the PM, and is still currently used for the most part by Protestants, although it appears to be

Table 14.6 (e): Goldvarb analysis of social factors

	Adults (N = 48)	
	Run 1[a]	Run 2[b]
Overall tendency:	0.309	0.158
Ethnicity		
Protestant	0.541	0.845
Catholic	0.459	0.155
Class		
Middle	0.358	0.702
Working	0.642	0.298

[a] Run 1: class significant at $p < 0.0001$, ethnicity at $p < 0.01$
[b] Run 2: both factor groups significant at $p < 0.0001$

	Teenagers (N = 59)	
	Run 1[a]	Run 2[b]
Overall tendency:	0.416	0.326
Ethnicity		
Protestant	0.586	0.833
Catholic	0.414	0.167
Class		
Middle	0.458	0.654
Working	0.542	0.346

[a] Run 1: ethnicity significant at $p < 0.0001$, class at $p < 0.05$
[b] Run 2: both factor groups significant at $p < 0.0001$

spreading across the ethnic barrier, as indicated by the CM's scores and Gold-varb ratings for the middle class in general. As a result of having [iə] in addition to [e] and [ɪ], Protestants in (London)Derry are shifting towards patterns typical of the rest of Northern Ireland, while Catholics maintain an older, increasingly more localised, pattern. The clear class differentiation on either side of the divide also works differently: among Catholics it is marked by use or non-use of diphthongs, while for Protestants, it is more a matter of differential levels of combined vernacular versus standard variants.

14.3.4.3   (ð) in LDE

Data for (ð) in LDE are displayed in Table 14.7 and Figures 14.5 and 14.6, which show overall combined vernacular scores as a line graph and scores for innovative vernacular [l] as columns.

Figure 14.5 reveals a striking difference between the adult middle and working classes in terms of overall vernacular scores, with both middle classes using only 6% vernacular variants, and not a single [l]. Meanwhile, the working class use some [l] tokens, making this an exclusively working-class variant, albeit one used at low levels of frequency. No definite ethnic pattern is apparent for this age group: use of the lateral approximant, though minimal for any group, serves more to reinforce class differentiation than anything else.

Table 14.7 medial (ð) by ethnicity and class sub-groups

	Adults						
	[ð]	%	ø	%	[l]	%	Total
PM	166	94	11	6	0	0	177
PW	72	52	56	41	10	7	138
CM	253	94	17	6	0	0	270
CW	291	64	152	33	14	3	457
Total	782	75	236	23	24	2	1,042

	Teenagers						
	[ð]	%	ø	%	[l]	%	Total
PM	144	85	26	15	0	0	170
PW	45	34	67	51	19	15	131
CM	58	35	79	47	31	18	168
CW	81	24	162	49	89	27	332
Total	328	41	334	42	139	17	801

Compared to the adult patterns, teenagers' distribution of (ð) variants (Figure 14.6) indicates apparent-time change: generally speaking, they are much more likely to drop ᴛʜ, and they use far more [l] than the older speakers. Variation in (ð) among teenagers is also affected by both ethnicity and class, but the pattern is very different from the adult one. Middle-class teenagers display clearer ethnic differentiation: the CM use in excess of four times as many non-standard variants as the PM, and even outscore the PW for [l]. As a result, sharp class differentiation remains on the Protestant side, with the combined vernacular score of the PW (66%) contrasting dramatically with the PM's 15%, and being further emphasised by the latter's non-use of [l]. Class differences on the Catholic side have levelled out: the CM and CW have similar patterns, though the latter use more of both vernacular variants. Meanwhile, the PW may be orienting itself towards Catholic usage, since the dominant and most numerous middle class locally is Catholic, and these both drop ᴛʜ to a high degree and use [l].

As a consequence of the PM's non-participation in the local innovation, they remain more like speakers elsewhere in Northern Ireland, but their usage diverges from that of others in (London)Derry. This also means that, in the younger age group, the sharpest class by ethnicity difference obtains between the two middle classes, who diverge markedly from one another, while there is little ethnolinguistic differentiation in the working class. Class and ethnicity obviously interact in (ð) variation, and the ethnic factor has come to play a more important part.

Table 14.8 summarises the Goldvarb analyses of (ð), testing first the use of the standard variant against the combined non-standard ones (Run 1), and then the use of the innovative local [l] against the more widespread NIE elision (Run 2).

Run 1 for adults shows class to be the most significant factor: working-class background is shown to heavily favour vernacular use. Ethnicity did not produce significant weightings on this run. In Run 2, class was a 'knockout' because no middle-class informants use [l] – Goldvarb refuses to analyse data containing

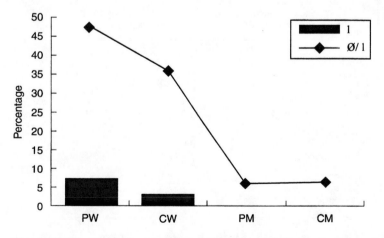

Fig. 14.5 (ð) vernacular variants by ethnicity and class sub-groups (adults)

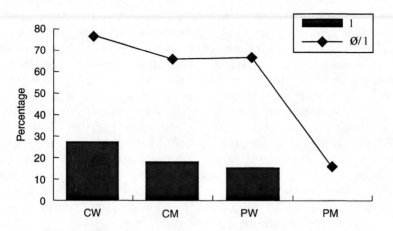

Fig. 14.6 (ð) vernacular variants by ethnicity and class sub-groups (teenagers)

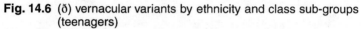

Table 14.8 (ð): Goldvarb analysis of social factors

	Adults	
	Run 1[a] [ð]~ ø/[l]	**Run 2**[b] ø~[l]
Overall tendency	0.180	0.092
Ethnicity		
Catholic	0.505	0.570
Protestant	0.495	0.430
Class		
Middle	0.248	0 K/O
Working	0.752	1.0 K/O

[a] Run 1: class significant at $p < 0.001$; ethnicity not significant
[b] Run 2: ethnicity not significant; class a 'knockout'

	Teenagers	
	Run 1[a] [ð]~ ø/[l]	**Run 2**[b] ø~[l]
Overall tendency	0.535	0.221
Ethnicity		
Catholic	0.673	0.608
Protestant	0.327	0.392
Class		
Middle	0.357	0.448
Working	0.643	0.552

[a]Run 1: both ethnicity and class significant at $p < 0.001$
[b]Run 2: ethnicity significant at $p < 0.001$; class at $p < 0.05$

factor groups which display no variation in use of a linguistic variable. On this test of the use of vernacular elision versus [l], the ethnic factor was not significant either, probably due to a combination of low frequency of [l] (approximants occurred only 24 times in the adult data) and similarities between group scores. For this age group, treatment of the (ð) variable is primarily conditioned by class membership.

Teenagers' weightings indicate the progress of the change between the two age groups in the increase of the overall tendencies. Here, ethnicity is the most significant factor, in relation to both use of the vernacular variants *vis-à-vis* the standard one (Run 1), and use of [l] as opposed to the more widespread TH-dropping (Run 2). Catholic ethnicity militates both for use of vernacular variants in general, and for use of the local innovative form. The weightings for social class are lower, but also significant, with membership of the working class weighted in favour of the two vernacular variants, and also in favour of the local one. However, class is significant at a lower level of confidence on Run 2.

In the development of (ð) variation in LDE, we are witnessing overlapping changes, with a new innovation occurring before an earlier one has fully run its course. The variable (ð) has undergone change in LDE, as in other varieties of NIE, in the twentieth century. To the general NIE development of TH-dropping has been added a localised [l] realisation. These changes have spread through the population of the city, at first as class-related developments, but patterns of (ð) variation have taken on more of an ethnic character, especially in the middle class.

For most adult informants, there are only two variants, standard [ð] and Ø (or TH-dropping), and the extent of dropping is related principally to class membership; realisation as [l] occurs only among the working class. Among teenagers, on the other hand, ethnicity has taken over from class as the most salient factor in relation to (ð) differentiation, although class remains significant to a lesser degree. Both elision and the [l] variant have become more prevalent in the speech of Catholics, with the working class leading by a small margin. The general ethnic differentiation pattern comes about in tandem with the class patterns: the Protestant working class use the lateral approximant as much as Catholics, so that ethnic difference is particularly marked in the middle class. Differentiation between the ethnic groups on this variable is primarily due to the non-participation of the PM in the [l] innovation, as well as their generally much more standard-like behaviour.

14.4 Conclusions

In the case of [ʉ] replacing [ʌ], a change that has been in progress for a very long time, we find very fine grading by ethnicity and class, with both social factors playing a role in relation to the change. As for the more recent changes in (e) and (ð), Protestants (a minority locally, but part of the majority in Northern Ireland as a whole) diverge from the Catholic population towards more widespread NIE patterns. On the other hand, Catholics (the local majority, but Northern Ireland minority) maintain local forms often regarded as rural and/or archaic, or lead in promoting local innovations. The Protestant divergence is most marked in the middle class, because the PM are early adopters of certain innovations from eastern parts, such as the [iə] variant, and do not participate in local innovations, such as the [l] variant of (ð). In contrast, the CM are slower to pick up eastern features, but adopt and use new local ones.

Results for these three linguistic variables provide qualified support for Harris's (1991) assertion that sociolinguistic perspectives on NIE must consider the possible consequences of speakers' sociopolitical orientations (towards Britain, Southern Ireland, or some notion of Ulster or Northern Ireland). However, it seems that (London)Derry Catholics and Protestants are not so much oriented respectively towards Southern Irish and British speech norms as towards local and more generalised NIE patterns. Whereas identifiably British and Southern Irish forms of, for instance, (ð) are rare in LDE, people from both ethnic communities use the vernacular forms of these variables present in local English, and their use has increased between the two age groups studied. There are, however, differences between the ethnic groups: Catholics, of whatever class, are more likely to use variants characteristic of LDE, whether these are local innovations or old established variants that are dying out in other parts of Northern Ireland; Protestants are apparently more willing to adopt innovations from the rest of the North, especially Belfast (and by definition more typical of Ulster Protestants in general), and are less likely to use localised forms, new or old.

15

Dublin English: current changes and their motivation

Raymond Hickey

15.1 *Introduction*

Among the varieties of urban English in the British Isles, that of Dublin enjoys a special position. There are several reasons for this. The most important is that, while geographically within these islands, the English-speaking sector of the Republic of Ireland does not look to England for a standard reference accent of English. In the south of Ireland the prestige form of English is that spoken in the capital, Dublin. Here the ceiling in terms of standardness is the speech of educated, weak-tie speakers on the south side of the city. For the southern Irish, Received Pronunciation is an extra-national norm not aspired to. Indeed, the emulation of anything like this accent of English is regarded as snobbish, slightly ridiculous and definitely un-Irish. The sociolinguistic significance of this fact is considerable and will be evident in the discussion of the vowel shift currently in progress in the capital. At present, the speech of Dublin is going through a major sound change which started in the early to mid-1980s and which has led to a considerable gap between strongly local forms of Dublin English (henceforth DE) and those of the more fashionable quarters of the city.[1] This change is the main subject of the present chapter.

The data for the present analysis have been collected since 1994 with particular attention paid since 1997 in a quantitative survey of speech among a selected group of informants. In essence, a series of commercial areas of Dublin were chosen as representative of lower-class, mainstream and fashionable shopping quarters of the city. The occurrence of key variables was examined using a surreptitious observation procedure similar to that employed by Labov (1966) in his early investigations of New York English. This method proved particularly suitable for the observation of vowel realisations among speakers from shops in socially different parts of Dublin, and corroborated findings made by the present author in other collections of data that the present-day changes are most often found among younger females on the lower range of the middle class. For reasons of space it is not possible to discuss the data collection techniques and results in detail. Suffice it to say here that the group designated as 'fashionable

Dublin English' speakers below is that for which there is ample quantitative support of their innovative role in current changes in Dublin English.

15.1.1   History

The English language in Dublin has been spoken since the late twelfth century when the first settlers came up from the south-east where they had landed around 1169. The first few centuries form the first period, which lasted up to around 1600 and which in its closing phase was characterised by considerable Gaelicisation outside the capital and within. Despite this resurgence of native culture and language, English never died out in the capital and there are some features of colloquial DE which can be traced to the first period.

The seventeenth century in Ireland marks the beginning of the second period and is characterised chiefly by the re-introduction of English on a large scale. This happened in the north of the country with a steady influx of immigrants from the Scottish Lowlands who came to form the base of the Ulster Protestant community. In the south, the new English settlers came as a result of plantations and land confiscations under Oliver Cromwell in the mid seventeenth century.

15.1.1.1   Documentation

The records of DE are slight and consist before 1600 mainly of municipal records which here and there betray the kind of English which must have been spoken in the city. For a historical background to present-day speech one must look to the elocutioner Thomas Sheridan (the father of the playwright) who in 1781 published *A Rhetorical Grammar of the English Language* with an appendix in which he commented on the English used by middle-class Dubliners, the 'gentlemen of Ireland' in his words, which he regarded as worthy of censure on his part. Sheridan's remarks are a valuable source of information on what Dublin English was like two centuries ago. Among the features he listed are the following (the phonetic values have been ascertained with reasonable certainty by interpreting his own system of transcription, which is decipherable and fairly consistent):

1. Middle English /ɛː/ was not raised to /iː/. The pronunciation [ɛː] can still be heard in Dublin in words like *tea, sea, please*. Of these, the first is still found as a caricature of a by-gone Irish pronunciation of English. Hogan (1927: 65) noted in his day that the non-raised vowel was rapidly receding. Today it is somewhat artificial; the pronunciation is also found in the north of the country, where equally it is a retention of an earlier value.
2. A pronunciation of English /ai/ from Middle English /iː/ as [ei] is found, though it is uncertain whether Sheridan means this or perhaps [əi], which would tally better with what is known from present-day DE.

When discussing consonants Sheridan remarks on 'the thickening [of] the sounds of *d* and *t* in certain situations'. Here he is probably referring to the realisation of dental fricatives as alveolar plosives as found in colloquial forms today. There is no hint in Sheridan of anything like a distinction between dental and alveolar plosive realisations, which is now an essential marker of local versus non-local speech.

(1)	Local Dublin		Non-local Dublin	
	thank, tank	[tæŋk]	*thank*	[t̪æŋk]
			tank	[tæŋk]

Already in Sheridan's days linguistic behaviour was apparently prevalent which aimed at dissociating middle-class speech from more local forms, as evidenced in the many instances of hypercorrection which he quotes: 'instead of *great* they [middle-class Dubliners – Sheridan's group of speakers, RH] say *greet*, for *occasion, occeesion, days dees*, &c.' (1781: 142).

15.1.1.2 *The supra-regional variety of English*

In the Republic of Ireland (that is, excluding the north which, because of its different demographical history, is linguistically quite separate from the rest of the country) there is something like a supra-regional standard, which is characterised by the speech of middle-class urbanites. This can be classified into different sub-varieties on the basis of features which are found in one and not the other. For instance, the urban speech of Cork may show a tendency to raise /ɛ/ before nasals, e.g. *pen* [pɪn], and that of Dublin may raise and lengthen /ɒ/ before voiceless fricatives, e.g. *lost* [lɔːst]. Despite this there is a core of common features which can be taken as characteristic of general middle-class speech of the south and it is these which the non-Irish use as clues for identifying an Irish accent, e.g. rhoticism (with a velarised [ɹˠ]), dental stops for dental fricatives, fricativisation of /t, d/ intervocalically and pre-pausally, monophthong equivalents of the RP diphthongs /ei/ and /əu/, clear /l/ in all positions, the retention of the contrast between /ʍ/ and /w/ and the lack of any significant distinction between phonemically long and short low vowels before voiced consonants (as in words of the PALM and DANCE lexical sets, for instance, both with [aː]), to mention just some of the more salient features.

15.1.2 Contemporary Dublin

Like any other modern city Dublin shows areas of high and low social prestige. The city lies at the mouth of the river Liffey in the centre of the east coast, and spreads along the shores of the horseshoe shape of Dublin bay. The suburbs, which have increased dramatically since the 1960s, reach down to Bray and beyond into Co. Wicklow in the south, to the west in the direction of Maynooth and to the north at least to Swords, the airport and beyond. The Dublin conurbation now encompasses about a third of the population of the Republic of Ireland.

Within Dublin there is a clear divide between the north and the south side of the city. The latter is regarded as more residentially desirable (with the exception of Howth and its surroundings on the peninsula which forms the north side of Dublin bay). Within the south there is a cline in prestige with the area around Ballsbridge and Donybrook enjoying highest status. This is the area of certain key complexes such as the Royal Dublin Society (an important exhibition and event centre in the capital) and the national television studios (RTE) and of the national university (University College Dublin) in Belfield. This entire area is known by its postal code, Dublin 4. Indeed this number has given the name to a sub-accent within DE known as the 'Dublin 4 accent'. The less prestigious parts of the city are known by their district names such as the Liberties in the centre of the city, immediately north of the river Liffey, and Ballymun, the only suburb in Ireland with high-rise flats and which is associated with adverse social conditions.

15.1.3   Varieties of Dublin English

Any discussion of English in Dublin necessitates a few basic divisions into types. For the present chapter a twofold division, with a further subdivision, is employed. The first group consists of those who use the inherited popular form of English in the capital. The term 'local' is intended to capture this and to emphasise that these speakers are those who show strongest identification with traditional conservative Dublin life, of which the popular accent is very much a part. The reverse of this is 'non-local' which refers to sections of the metropolitan population who do not wish a narrow, restrictive identification with popular Dublin culture. This group then subdivides into a larger, more general section which I label 'mainstream' and a currently smaller group which vigorously rejects a confining association with low-prestige Dublin. For want of a better term, this group is labelled 'fashionable'.

(2)   1. *local* Dublin English
        2. *non-local* Dublin English – (a) *mainstream* Dublin English
                                        (b) *fashionable* Dublin English

A central issue in contemporary DE is the set of vowel shifts which represent the most recent phonological innovation in Irish English. This is not surprising as Dublin is a typical location for language change, given the following features:

1. The city has expanded greatly in population since the 1960s. The increase in population has been due both to internal growth and to migration into the city from the rest of the country.
2. It has undergone an economic boom since the early 1980s, reflected in its position as an important financial centre and a location for many computer firms which run their European operations from Dublin.

The increase in wealth and international position has meant that many young people aspire to an urban sophistication which is divorced from strongly local

Dublin life. For this reason the developments in fashionable DE diverge from those in local DE, indeed can be interpreted as a reaction to it. This type of linguistic behaviour can be termed *local dissociation* as it is motivated by the desire of speakers to hive themselves off from vernacular forms of a variety spoken in their immediate surroundings (Hickey 1998, 1999). It is furthermore a clear instance of speaker-innovation leading to language change, much in the sense of James and Lesley Milroy (J. Milroy 1992: 169–72; 1999; L. & J. Milroy 1997).

15.2 *Descriptive material*

A common practice in discussing varieties of English is to avail of the lexical sets established by Wells (1982). This provides a framework for dealing with variation both within a single variety as well as across differing ones. For instance, the vowel in FACE is a diphthong in RP but a monophthong in Irish English, but there is a real sense in which one is concerned in each case with the same systemic entity: a long mid-front vowel. Furthermore, the notion of lexical set allows one to discuss variation among sets of varieties satisfactorily. With some speakers of Northern Irish English, for example, the word *pull* belongs to the STRUT lexical set rather than to the FOOT set. Recognising this alignment saves one from assertions like 'the realisation of /u/ is [ʌ] in *pull*', which is plainly inaccurate.

Wells' original set needs some modification when dealing with contemporary Dublin English because this variety contains realisations which are not necessarily of importance in forms of British English. In particular four extensions are required:

- MEAT is needed to refer to the reflexes of Middle English /ɛː/;
- GIRL is required alongside NURSE as there is a two-way distinction among short vowels before /r/;
- DANCE is necessary as words with /aːnC#/ have [ɑː] in RP but [aː] in Irish English, a sociolinguistically sensitive realisation; this item is not given by Wells as a representative of a lexical set in its own right but it is mentioned in his examples for the BATH lexical set (1982: xviii);
- PRIZE must be included here as it has /ai/ before a voiced consonant and hence a different realisation than does the diphthong in the PRICE lexical set.

For the discussion of consonants below a comparable technique has been used. Here small capitals are employed to refer to systemic units. Thus the difficulty of what symbol to use on a phonemic level is avoided. For instance, to speak of TH and DH circumvents the problem of whether to assign [ṭ, ḍ] to /θ, ð/ or /ṭ, ḍ/ respectively in the context of Southern Irish English.

Table 15.1 Dublin vowels – summary

	Local DE	Mainstream	Fashionable
KIT	ɪ	ɪ	ɪ
DRESS	ɛ	ɛ	ɛ
TRAP	æ	æ	æ
LOT	a	ɒ	ɔ
STRUT	ʊ	ʌ	ʌ
FOOT	ʊ	ʊ	ʊ
BATH	æː	aː	aː
DANCE	æː	aː	aː
NURSE	ʊː	əː	əː
GIRL	ɛː	əː	əː
FLEECE	ijə	iː	iː
FACE	ɛː	eː	eː
MEAT	iː	iː	iː
PALM	æː	aː	aː
THOUGHT	aː	ɒː	ɔː
GOAT	ʌo	ou	əu
GOOSE	uwə	uː	uː
PRICE	əjə	aɪ	aɪ
PRIZE	əjə	aɪ	ɑɪ
CHOICE	aɪ	ɒɪ	ɔɪ
MOUTH	ɛwə	æu	æu
NEAR	ɪɐ	iə	iə
SQUARE	ɛɐ	eə	əː
START	æː	ɑː	ɑː
NORTH	aː	ɒː	oː
FORCE	ʌo	oː	oː
CURE	jʊɐ	juə	juə
happY	i	i	i
lettER	ɐ	ə	ə
horsES	ə	ə	ə
commA	ə	ə	ə

15.2.1   Vowels

15.2.1.1   *Vowel breaking*

Long high vowels are realised as two syllables with a hiatus between the two when they occur in closed syllables. The hiatus element is [j] with front vowels and [w] with back vowels, as in (3).

(3)   a.   *clean*   [klijən]   but: *be*   [biː]
      b.   *fool*   [fuwəl]   *who* [huː]

The disyllabification of long high vowels extends to diphthongs which have a high ending point, as can be seen in the realisations in (4).

(4)   a.   *time*   [təjəm]   but: *fly*   [fləi]
      b.   *pound* [pɛwən]   *how* [hɛu]

If one recognises a cline within local DE then this disyllabification is definitely at the lower end. For instance, the front onset of the vowel in the MOUTH lexical set is quite common in colloquial, but not necessarily local varieties of DE. However, one does not have a hiatus [w] or the deletion of the post-sonorant nasal (with or without a glottal stop as trace).

15.2.1.2 *Variation and change in the vowel system*

For further details on vowel variants and ongoing changes, see the detailed discussion in sections 15.3 and 15.4 below.

15.2.2 Consonants

T, D

The clearest phonetic feature of Southern Irish English is the reduction of /t/ and /d/ to a fricative with identical characteristics of the stop, i.e. an apico-alveolar fricative in weak positions. This cannot be indicated in English orthography, of course, but vacillation between *t* and *th* for /t/ is found already in the *Kildare Poems* (probably early fourteenth century, Hickey 1993: 220ff.) which would suggest that it was a feature of English in Ireland in the first period.

The lenition of /t/ – phonetically $[t]^2$ – intervocalically or pre-pausally is not continued in non-local DE beyond the initial stage with the exception of one or two lexicalised items such as *Saturday* ['sæhə¹de]. However, it is precisely the extension beyond the apico-alveolar fricative which is characteristic of local DE. The sequence is usually as follows:

(5)		/t/	[t]	→	[h]	→	Ø
	a.	*motorway*	['mo:ţəwe]		['mo:həwe]		['mo:we]
	b.	*thought*	[ta:ţ]		[ta:h]		[ta:]

STOPS

Post-sonorant stop deletion is unique to DE. In other varieties in the Republic the tendency is not to delete the stop in this position but to retain it and, if voiced, to devoice it, e.g. *bend* [bɛnt]. The Dublin phenomenon is confined to positions after /n/ and /l/ and may involve a glottal stop as a reflex of the deleted stop, as in (6).

(6)	*pound* [pɛwən(ʔ)]	*belt* [bɛl(ʔ)]

NG

The realisation of the final nasal of the present participle is one of the most common variables in all varieties of English. In this respect DE is no exception with the low-prestige varieties preferring [n] over [ŋ].

TH, DH

It is safe to assume that the realisation of the first sound in the THOUGHT lexical set in local DE as an alveolar plosive [t] is not a recent phenomenon. Hogan

(1927: 71ff.) notes that it is found in seventeenth-century plays (assuming that *t*, *d* represent [t, d]) and furthermore in the Dublin City Records (from the first period, i.e. before the seventeenth century, see above) where the third person singular ending -*th* appears as -*t*. According to Hogan alveolar realisations are common in rural varieties in the south and south-west of Ireland. Here they are probably a contact phenomenon deriving ultimately from the realisation of non-palatal /t, d/ in Irish. Hogan (1927) incidentally also remarks on the dental stops which are found in present-day Irish English. The acoustic sensitivity of the Irish to the shift from dental to alveolar derives not least from the merger which results from it as indicated by such homophonic pairs as *thinker* and *tinker*, both [tɪŋkɐ] and *third* or *turd*, both [tʊːd] in DE.

H

H is never dropped in Irish English.

R

Local DE tends not to be rhotic or only weakly so; the loss of /r/ is clearest in unstressed word-final position, as pronunciations like [pʌotɐ] for *porter* testify. The allophony of vowels deriving from a former sequence of short vowel plus /r/ is quite complicated because of rounding which occurs after labials in this position and a general lengthening resulting from mora compensation on the loss of /r/. The labial rounding can be accompanied by retraction, giving a vowel continuum from low front rounded to back mid to high rounded.

(7)   a.   *circles*   [sɛːkl̩z]
       b.   *first*   [fʊːst] ~ [fœːst]

The speech of the middle classes in Dublin has one remarkable feature, and that is its rhoticism (Wells 1982: 418). /r/ may be realised as a retroflex [ɻ] (see further below). The fact that syllable-final /r/ should be maintained so consistently in educated DE is deserving of comment. If there were a tendency for this variety to approximate to more standard forms of (British) English then one would expect rhoticism to decline. However, this would create a similarity with local DE which would work against the aim of increasing the distance between low- and high-prestige varieties of English in the capital. In this respect Dublin is similar to New York. In both cities rhoticism is prestigious as lower-class speech tends to lack syllable-final /r/. But within the context of English in the British Isles the maintenance of rhoticism cannot be interpreted as a shift towards standardisation.

L

L is always clear in Irish English.

15.3   *The Dublin Vowel Shift*

In present-day Dublin the speakers of what is labelled here 'fashionable Dublin English' (see (2) above) are engaging in a shift of most long vowels and diphthongs which constitutes a divergent development away from local Dublin English. This shift centres around the /ai/ diphthong and the low back vowels and has led to a phonetic redistribution of values for these sounds, which are discussed in the following sections.

15.3.1   The variable (ai) in Irish English

The first point to note is that a conservative pronunciation of (ai) in Dublin is maintained in lower-class speech as [əɪ] (historically, also the middle-class realisation). The supra-regional variety of the south has for (ai) a diphthong which has a low mid or low front starting point, i.e., either [aɪ] or [æɪ]. What is significant here is that a non-central starting point is the commonest one for most varieties of Southern Irish English. If one now considers local DE one finds that its realisation for (ai) as [əɪ] is quite stigmatised in Dublin. One can maintain that the greater the phonetic separation of middle class DE from more local forms in the capital became, the more the corresponding forms of the lower social classes became stigmatised.

It is difficult to predict whether this distribution will remain typical for the Dublin Vowel Shift. It may very well be that it is only characteristic of an initial phase and that the shift will spread to all instances of (ai), masking the present

However, the matter does not end there. For middle-class Dubliners the [aɪ, æɪ] pronunciations sufficiently delimit them from local DE. But increasingly, a back starting-point is being used for this diphthong, i.e. in a word like *style* the pronunciation is not [staɪl] but rather [stɑɪl]. This retracted starting point is particularly noticeable before /r/ so that the name of the country is realised in fashionable DE as [ɑɪʴlənd] rather than [aɪʲlənd].

15.3.2   Distribution of the (ai) shift

The most noticeable aspect of the shift is that it does not apply to all possible inputs, as can be seen from the examples with (ai) in (8).

(8)   a.   *rice*   [raɪs]   *rise*   [rɑɪz]
       b.   *tight*   [taɪt̪]   *tide*   [tɑɪd̪]
       c.   *life*   [laɪf]   *lives*   [lɑɪvz]

The generalisation here is that retraction to [ɑɪ] only occurs before voiced segments. This makes phonetic sense: vowels before voiced consonants are phonetically longer, giving the tongue more time to travel the longer distance down and back for [ɑɪ] (see Hickey 1986 for a fuller discussion of the correlation of length with backness for low vowels).

It is difficult to predict whether this distribution will remain typical for the Dublin Vowel Shift. It may very well be that it is only characteristic of an initial phase and that the shift will spread to all instances of (ai), masking the present distribution. Or it may freeze at this stage, as has been the case with the similar phenomenon of Canadian Raising (Chambers 1973) which maintains a differential realisation of the vowels in the PRICE and MOUTH lexical sets before voiceless and voiced segments respectively.

15.3.3   General shift of low vowels

The vowel shift in DE is not confined to the realisation of (ai). Other vowels in the area of this diphthong are affected, particularly the diphthong in the CHOICE lexical set and the low and mid vowels in the LOT and THOUGHT sets which usually have a lower realisation than in Britain (or unrounded in the case of the LOT vowel).

(9)   a.   *boy*   /ɔɪ/   →   [bɒɪ]
       b.   *pot*   /ɒ/   →   [pɒt̞] ~ [pɑt̞]
       c.   *law*   /ɔː/   →   [lɒː]

These realisations show that the change has the characteristics of a chain shift, that is, it affects several segments by a process of retraction and raising in phonological vowel space.

15.3.4   Fashionable Dublin: how to avoid local features

The retraction of low vowels and the raising of back vowels is the most auditorily salient feature of fashionable DE and it is this which constitutes the core of the Dublin Vowel Shift. But other avoidance strategies are used to maximally differentiate fashionable forms from local forms of Dublin speech. The following list gives some indication of what is involved here:

(a) Local DE has a distinction between historic back and front short vowels before /r/, in the NURSE and GIRL lexical sets, [nuː(ɹ)s] and [gɛː(ɹ)l] respectively. But because the open front realisation is so typical of local DE, there is a migration in fashionable DE of historically front *long* vowels to the central rhotic type, as seen in words from the SQUARE lexical set such as *carefully* [ˈkəɫːfəli] and *daring* [dəːɹɪŋ]. This realisation has no precedent in the history of Irish English.

(b) Connected with the previous feature is the strict avoidance of schwa retraction before /r/ in NURSE words such as *third* [təɫːd], *purse* [pəɫːs], not [tuː(ɹ)d] and [puː(ɹ)s].

(c) The local back rounded vowel /ʊ/ in the STRUT lexical set is replaced by an unrounded front vowel which is almost /ɪ/, as in *Sunday* [sɪnde].

(d) A syllable-final retroflex /r/, [ɻ], is used which has the advantage of marking the /r/ even more clearly *vis-à-vis* the local forms of DE which, if at all, only have a weak syllable-final /r/.

From these considerations it is clear that the vowel shift is not simply an approximation to mainstream British pronunciations of English; after all, syllable-final

/r/, the lack of /ɑː/ in words of the DANCE lexical set and the differential retraction of /ai/ all point to the independence of Irish English from Britain. Furthermore, there is an imperviousness in Ireland to many sociolinguistic features of British urban speech, for instance the loss of initial H, T-glottaling or TH-fronting.

(10)   Summary of Dublin Vowel Shift

    (a)   retraction of diphthongs with a low or back starting point

        time   [taɪm] →   [tɑɪm]

        toy   [tɒɪ]   →   [tɔɪ], [toɪ]

    (b)   raising of low back vowels

        cot   [kɒt̪] →   [kɔt̪]

        caught [kɒːt̪] →   [kɔːt̪], [koːt̪]

		oɪ		oː
		↑		↑
Raising		ɔɪ	ɔ	ɔː
		↑	↑	↑
		ɒɪ	ɒ	ɒː
Retraction	aɪ	→	ɑɪ	

To understand the framework for vowel realisations such as those just mentioned it is appropriate at this point to juxtapose the vowel systems of the three main variety groups in DE organised as standard lexical sets. These are given in (11).

(11)			Local DE	Mainstream	Fashionable
	A	*long vowels*			
		FLEECE	[flijəs]	[fliːs]	[fliːs]
		FACE	[fɛːs]	[feːs]	[feːs]
		PALM	[pæːm]	[paːm]	[paːm]
		BATH	[bæːt]	[baːt̪]	[baːt̪]
		DANCE	[dæːns]	[daːns]	[daːns]
		THOUGHT	[taːh]	[t̪ɒːt̪]	[t̪ɔːt̪]
		GOAT	[gʌoh]	[gout̪]	[gəut̪]
		GOOSE	[guwəs]	[guːs]	[guːs]
	B	*diphthongs*			
		PRICE	[pɹəjəs]	[pɹaɪs]	[pɹaɪs]
		PRIZE	[pɹəjəz]	[pɹaɪz]	[pɹɑɪz]
		MOUTH	[mɛwət]	[mæut̪]	[mæut̪]
		CHOICE	[tʃaɪs]	[tʃɒɪs]	[tʃɔɪs]

		Local DE	Mainstream	Fashionable
C	*rhotacised vowels*			
	START	[staːʈ]	[stɑˀːʈ]	[stɑˡːʈ]
	NORTH	[naːt]	[nɒˀːʈ]	[noˡːʈ]
	FORCE	[fʌos]	[foˀːs]	[foˡːs]
	NURSE	[nuːs]	[nəˀːs]	[nəˡːs]
	GIRL	[geːl]	[gəˀːl]	[gəˡːl]
	NEAR	[nɪɐ]	[niəˀ]	[niəˡ]
	SQUARE	[skwɛɐ]	[skweəˀ]	[skwəˡ]
	CURE	[kjuɐ]	[kjuəˀ]	[kjuəˡ]
D	*short vowels*			
	KIT	[kɪh]	[kɪt]	[kɪʈ]
	DRESS	[d̪ɹes]	[dɹɛs]	[dɹɛs]
	TRAP	[ʈɹæp]	[tɹæp]	[tɹæp]
	LOT	[lah]	[lɒʈ]	[lɔʈ]
	STRUT	[stɹʊh]	[stɹʌʈ]	[stɹʌʈ]
	FOOT	[fʊh]	[fʊʈ]	[fʊʈ]
E	*unstressed vowels*			
	commA	[ˈkamə]	[ˈkɒmə]	[ˈkɔmə]
	lettER	[ˈlɛhɐ]	[ˈlɛʈəˀ]	[ˈlɛʈəˡ]
	happY	[ˈhæpi]	[ˈhæpi]	[ˈhæpi]
	horsES	[haːsəz]	[hɒˀːsəz]	[hoˡːsəz]

Notes

- not all speakers of local DE lack syllable-final /r/
- T-lenition can be manifested as [h], or [ʈ] in somewhat less casual speech
- the vowel deriving from historical /ər/ tends to be very open, hence the transcription as [ɐ]
- in the GOAT lexical set fashionable DE has a diphthong with an increasingly central starting point. Synchronically this is a coincidental similarity with RP arising in DE from the upward movement of the vowel in the THOUGHT set. The more this closes the greater the degree of diphthongisation found in GOAT words. From a historic point of view this motivation may be similar to that in RP.

15.4   *Discussion*

There is an essential premise for the current changes in DE, and that is that speakers are unconsciously aware of minute phonetic shifts which are taking place in the language around them and that they themselves can and do become the proponents of such changes. Speakers also recognise unconsciously the direction in which a change is moving and can thus force the change beyond the stage at which it is currently. For instance, if a speaker intuitively grasps that back vowels are being raised then he/she can actively participate in this process, e.g. by raising [ɑ] beyond [ɔ] to [o] in words of the LOT lexical set. In order to do this, of course, speakers must first of all realise that there exist gradations along a cline of pronunciations. Speakers are unconsciously aware of such a spectrum by exposure to variation in the community of which they are members and by noticing the relative frequency and the conditions of occurrence (situation, speaker group, etc.) of sets of pronunciations for given phonological segments. They build up an awareness of variation and change which is part and parcel of their knowledge of their native language. Without this assumption there is no principled and coherent way of explaining the origin and course of a shift like the current one. Assuming unconscious awareness accounts for the non-random nature of change; it sees speakers as aware of the direction in which their language is moving.

15.4.1 Pushing the vowel shift

Speakers of fashionable DE would seem to notice the trajectory on which the vowel shift is located, even though their own personal realisation of key vowels may not be at the most innovative end. Furthermore, this explains why young speakers are seen to push the vowel shift. The trajectory for the shift is unconsciously recognised by speakers and they can not only move within a degree of personal variation on this curve but they can also shift their range of realisations in the direction of innovation, in this case backwards and upwards, often beyond the current upper end of the trajectory.

(12) [ɒɪ] → [ɔɪ] → [oɪ] *boys* [boɪz]; *noise* [noɪz]

There would appear to be a certain awareness of this behaviour in contemporary DE, as a term has emerged in recent years for a kind of exaggerated accent which is putatively typical of one of the more prestigious areas of Dublin (the aforementioned 'Dublin 4 accent'). Speakers with this accent are recognised as having more extreme vowel values for the vowel shift and are often ridiculed by more mainstream speakers. However, with time, such extreme values may come to be regarded as possible realisations for other groups of speakers if the latter no longer regard the speech of a small minority as unduly exaggerated.

15.4.2 Downward percolation

A change rarely remains restricted to one layer in a society. For the Dublin Vowel Shift a phenomenon can be observed, albeit embryonically, among local varieties of DE. This is what I term *downward percolation*. It denotes the adoption of the shift by speakers who would not normally show it as they have come to realise that it is typical of more prestigious speech in the city, for instance in pronunciations like [staɪl], [taɪm], [maɪld], etc. If this happens on a broad scale, the ultimate fate of the shift is then uncertain. What has started as a feature unique to socially pretentious speakers in Dublin may well spread vertically in the city (as it is beginning to do regionally for many younger generation urbanites) and very gradually lose the significance it has at the moment as a delimiting factor *vis-à-vis* the lower classes in the capital.

15.4.3   Propagation of sound change

In current sociolinguistic discourse two models are considered valid scenarios for language change: these are the view ultimately propounded by the Neogrammarians and that known as lexical diffusion (Wang 1969; Chen & Wang 1975). The Neogrammarian view of a sound change implies that any possible input is affected, i.e. the change is phonetically gradual and lexically universal. In the present case this means that all instances of /ai/ are retracted. If this were the entire story then there would be no exceptions; the change would show *Ausnahmslosigkeit* 'exceptionlessness'. This is not always the case, however, as some potential input to a change shows phonetic resistance, which acts as a brake on the Neogrammarian advance. With reference to the Dublin Vowel Shift the cases of phonetic resistance are those where /ai/ occurs before a voiceless segment, which, because of its fortis quality, results in a somewhat shorter vowel preceding it so that the tongue has less time to move down and back to the position for [ɑɪ].

The lexical diffusion hypothesis essentially claims that a change starts with some words and spreads to others, encompassing the entire vocabulary of a language, given the important proviso that the change does not lose momentum, i.e. that it is carried through along the S-curve to 100%. With the lexical diffusion model, a question arises which is not of relevance with the Neogrammarian model: what words are affected and is there is any generalisation which can be made as to those which first undergo the change, that is, how does the change proceed through the lexicon?

15.4.4   Participants in and progress of sound change

There is a standard wisdom on the occurrence of Neogrammarian advance versus lexical diffusion: Labov (1981: 304) maintains that 'low-level output rules' typically show gradual change across the board (Neogrammarian advance) whereas 'changes across subsystems', e.g. long to short vowels, proceed by a process of lexical diffusion.

Now the current investigation of the Dublin Vowel Shift shows quite clearly that what I call **motivated participants** – fashionable Dubliners – display the Neogrammarian advance for the shift, whereas what I term **detached participants** – socially conscious urbanites from outside Dublin – exhibit lexical diffusion, although the change is still in its infancy and constitutes a case of Labov's 'low-level output rules'.

With the group of detached participants the first word to show the Dublin

Vowel Shift is *Ireland* and its derivative *Irish*. This is almost a test case, a key-word, for those speakers who are beginning to participate in the shift. The key-word view of lexical diffusion is closely linked to the notion of salience with certain words. Often the words are used as carrier forms for a characteristic pro-nunciation of a group; common items with this function are the keywords *Irish* and *Ireland*, the numerals *five* and *nine* along with various frequently occurring adjectives like *wild, mild, kind*; nouns like *time, mind, side*; verbs like *rise, drive, hide*, etc.

15.4.5 Types, tokens and lexical diffusion

The theory of lexical diffusion implies furthermore that not only does a certain change – a new vowel value – spread gradually through the lexicon of the vari-ety/language affected, but also that not all *tokens* of a given *type* (lexeme) exhibit the new pronunciation immediately. This is clear in the group of detached participants and, if the observations on the Dublin Vowel Shift are correct, it would seem that the older members of this group show the new pro-nunciation for given lexemes only for a percentage of tokens; e.g. the realisation [ɑɾʲlənd] rather than [aɾʲlənd] is found with only some tokens of the country's name. Any situation like this with co-variants occurring alternatively implies that there is external conditioning on their occurrence. The circumstances for the use of the retracted diphthong in Irish English is something which is cer-tainly sensitive to social factors in discourse settings.

The question arises from the observations made above as to why lexical dif-fusion is typical of detached participants. The answer lies in the lack of motiva-tion on their part. For urbanites outside Dublin there is no reason to use a different realisation of (ai) from that which they acquired natively, usually [aɪ]. Hence they do not grasp the motivation among their metropolitan counterparts actively involved in the shift. They adopt the shift as they are confronted with it in words with high salience (*Ireland* and *Irish*) and/or high statistical frequency (numerals, common adjectives, nouns, verbs, etc.).

Another issue which arises in this context is the length of time for which there are two types of propagation. The distinction in the course of a sound change – Neogrammarian advance or lexical diffusion – appears to hold most clearly while a shift is taking place. Furthermore, depending on such aspects as the quantitative relationship of motivated participants to detached participants the latter may be marginalised by the former and the shift takes place fully. Or the level of exposure may lead to detached participants adopting an ever-increasing number of words with the new pronunciation, and this may eventually lead to the demise for them of their old pronunciation as it does not survive anywhere in their lexicon. Both these situations would mask the stage of lexical diffusion and make the sound change appear to have proceeded by Neogrammarian advance.

15.4.6   Conclusion

It would seem fitting to conclude this overview of current Dublin English with a conjecture about the future. In linguistic terms the issue is called the **termination problem**. It really involves two questions, depending on linguistic model. The first is: when is a sound change, proceeding by lexical diffusion, complete? The answer is fairly simple: when there is no unconditional instance of the original sound value left and when further movement in vowel space does not appear to be happening; for example, the lowering of early modern English /u/ more or less terminated when the value [ä] (in southern British English) was reached by all words which participated in the shift.

The second question is: when is a change, which is taking place by Neogrammarian advance, complete? The answer here is that there is no termination point. There is simply a stage when speakers regard the change as having crossed a phonological threshold, i.e. when a pronunciation is assigned to one phoneme as opposed to another. This is particularly clear when phonemic contrast either arises or is lost.

But when the new pronunciation is moving towards a value not already present in the phonological system of the variety concerned – as is the case with the new [ɑɪ] of the Dublin Vowel Shift – then there is no given end-point.

It is too soon to say what will happen to the Dublin Vowel Shift. For its continuation the behaviour of key sectors of Dublin society is most important. Assuming that the unarticulated goal of these speakers is to evolve a form of speech phonetically distinct from that of local DE, then that goal is all but attained. The shift has created the new allophones [ɑɪ] for former [aɪ] (in the PRIZE lexical set), [ɔɪ] and [oɪ] for former [ɒɪ] (in the CHOICE lexical set), but there are no threatening mergers so that there is no system-internal pressure to continue on a shift cycle and to re-align phonemic oppositions.

15.5   *Epilogue – how do supra-regional varieties of language arise?*

The changes described here can be seen as characteristic of the genesis of non-local varieties of language in general. The Dublin Vowel Shift is clearly not motivated by any external influence on DE, such as that of southern British English, let alone American English. Furthermore, it is not internally motivated as is analogical change such as morphological regularisation (the discrete replacement of one form by another). The only remaining conclusion is that it is motivated by social factors within Dublin.

It is also not unreasonable to conclude that the Dublin Vowel Shift shows an incipient stage of a new supra-regional variety: the emergence of non-local forms in the speech of the metropolis could well, given the dominant social and economic position of the capital, lead to these forms becoming defining features of the supra-regional variety of English throughout the entire Republic of Ireland.

Notes

1 The only studies of Dublin English are Bertz (1975) and Bertz (1987), a derivative of the first study, neither of which contains any indication of a vowel shift.

2 The sound referred to here is an apico-alveolar fricative (similar to the realisation of /s/ in those languages without an /s/–/ʃ/ contrast such as Dutch, Finnish, Greek, Spanish, etc.). Note that it is quite distinct from the laminal-alveolar fricative [s] so that *kiss* [kɪs] and *kit* [kɪt̪] are *not* homophones in Southern Irish English. There is no symbol for this sound in the IPA. The present author uses a subscript caret to indicate the apical and open articulation, a convention introduced in Hickey (1984). See also the discussion by Pandeli, Eska, Ball & Rahilly (1997).

Appendix

Urban Voices: audio samples

A cassette tape and CD are available to accompany this book. The recordings contain samples of accents from 24 locations across the United Kingdom and Ireland. The first samples represent the locations featured in this book: Newcastle upon Tyne, Derby, Sheffield, Wirral, Sandwell, Norwich, Milton Keynes, Reading, Hull, South East London, Cardiff, Glasgow, Edinburgh, (London)Derry, and Dublin. We have included additional samples from Cork, Belfast, Stornoway, Wrexham, Bolton, Bradford, and Birmingham, as well as examples of 'Estuary English' and Received Pronunciation.

As many of the chapters in the book point out, there is often a wide degree of variation in accent even with a single community. This is particularly true with respect to different generations. In order to establish a degree of consistency across our samples we have therefore collected material from speakers in a narrow range (17 to 34). Each sample has two parts. The first part consists of around a minute and a half of unscripted speech. Most speakers discuss a range of personal interests and background details. In the second part the speakers read a 72-item word-list, designed to elicit examples of a wide range of vowels and consonants. The list begins with the keywords used in the descriptive portions of *Urban Voices*. The full list is as follows:

KIT	MEAT	START	OLD
DRESS	PALM	BIRTH	BRILLIANT
HEAD	THOUGHT	BERTH	FREEZE
NEVER	GOAT	NORTH	CLEAN
TRAP	GOAL	FORCE	THROAT
LOT	MORE	CURE	GLEAM
STRUT	GOOSE	HAPPY	TREACLE
ONE	GHOUL	LETTER	SING
FOOT	BOOK	HORSES	GOING
BATH	PRICE	COMMA	BEETLE
AFTER	PRIZE	FREE	THRONE
DANCE	FIRE	METER	BEAGLE
CLOTH	CHOICE	FATAL	ROLLS
NURSE	MOUTH	EIGHTY-EIGHT	NOTHING
GIRL	POWER	CARTER	WITH
FLEECE	NEAR	DAUGHTER	US
FACE	BEER	FREES	NEITHER
STAY	SQUARE	EITHER	TUESDAY

References

Abbreviations after each reference indicate the chapter(s) in which the work is cited. Chapters are abbreviated as follows:

C – Cardiff (Mees & Collins)
D – Dublin (Hickey)
DN – Derby & Newcastle (Docherty & Foulkes)
EC – Edinburgh (Chirrey)
EG – Edinburgh & Glasgow (Scobbie, Hewlett & Turk)
G – Glasgow (Stuart-Smith)
L – South East London (Tollfree)
LD – (London)Derry (McCafferty)
M – Milton Keynes, Reading & Hull (Williams & Kerswill)
N – Norwich (Trudgill)
NC – Newcastle (Watt & Milroy)
O – Overview (Foulkes & Docherty)
S – Sheffield (Stoddart, Upton & Widdowson)
SW – Sandwell (Mathisen)
W – West Wirral (Newbrook)

Abercrombie, D. (1954). A Scottish vowel. *Le Maître Phonétique*, juillet-décembre 1954. 23–4. **EC**

Abercrombie, D. (1967). *Elements of General Phonetics.* Edinburgh: Edinburgh University Press. **G**

Abercrombie, D. (1979). The accents of standard English in Scotland. In Aitken, A. J. & McArthur, T. (eds) pp. 65–84. **EC, EG, G**

Abercrombie, D., Fry, D. B., MacCarthy, P. A. D., Scott, N. C. & Trim, J. L. M. (eds) (1964). *In Honour of Daniel Jones.* London: Longman. **C**

Adams, G. B. (ed.)(1964a). *Ulster Dialects. An Introductory Symposium.* Cultra: Ulster Folk and Transport Museum. **LD**

Adams, G. B. (1964b). Introduction: Ulster dialects. In Adams, G. B. (ed.) pp. 1–4. **LD**

Agutter, A. (1988). The not-so-Scottish Vowel Length Rule. In Anderson, J. M. & MacLeod, N. (eds) pp. 120–32. **EG**

Aitken, A. J. (1979). Scottish speech: a historical view with special reference to the Standard English of Scotland. In Aitken, A. J. & McArthur, T. (eds) pp. 85–118. **EC, EG, G**

Aitken, A. J. (1981a). The good old Scots tongue: does Scots have an identity? In Haugen, E., McClure, J. D. & Thomson, D. (eds) pp. 72–90. **EC, EG**

Aitken, A. J. (1981b). The Scottish Vowel Length Rule. In Benskin, M. & Samuels, M. L. (eds) pp. 131–57. **EC, EG, LD**

Aitken, A. J. (1984a). Scottish accents and dialects. In Trudgill, P. J. (ed.) pp. 94–118. **EC**

Aitken, A. J. (1984b). Scots and English in Scotland. In Trudgill, P. J. (ed.) pp. 517–32. **EC**

Aitken, A. J. & McArthur, T. (eds) (1979). *Languages of Scotland*. Edinburgh: W. & R. Chambers. **EC, EG, G**

Anderson, J. M. (1994). Contrastivity and non-specification in a dependency phonology of English. *Studia Anglica Posnaniensia* **28**. 3–35. **EG**

Anderson, J. M. & Jones, C. (eds) (1974). *Historical Linguistics II. Theory and Description in Phonology*. Amsterdam: North-Holland. **DN, EG**

Anderson, J. M. & MacLeod, N. (eds) (1988). *Edinburgh Studies in the English Language*. Edinburgh: John Donald Publishers. **EG**

Anderson, P. M. (1975). The Dialect of Eaton-by-Tarporley, Cheshire: A Descriptive and Historical Grammar. Unpublished PhD dissertation (2 volumes), University of Leeds. **W**

Andrésen, B. S. (1968). *Pre-glottalization in English Standard Pronunciation*. Oslo: Norwegian Universities Press. **O**

Auer, P. & Hinskens, F. (1996). New and not so new developments in an old area. *Sociolinguistica* **10**. 1–30. **NC**

Barke, M. & Buswell, R. J. (eds) (1992). *Newcastle's Changing Map*. Newcastle upon Tyne: City Libraries & Arts. **NC**

Barry, M. V. (1958). The Phonology of the Living Dialect of Neston (Cheshire). Unpublished BA dissertation, University of Leeds. **W**

Beaken, M. A. (1971). A Study of Phonological Development in a Primary School Population of East London. Unpublished PhD dissertation, University of London. **L**

Beal, J. (1985). Lengthening of *a* in Tyneside English. In Eaton, R. *et al.* (eds) pp. 31–44. **NC**

Bell, D. (1987). Acts of Union: youth sub-culture and ethnic identity amongst Protestants in Northern Ireland. *British Journal of Sociology* **38**. 158–83. **LD**

Bell, D. (1990). *Acts of Union. Youth Culture and Sectarianism in Northern Ireland*. London: Macmillan. **LD**

Benskin, M. & Samuels, M. L. (eds) (1981). *So Meny People Longages and Tonges: Philological Essays in Scots and Mediaeval English Presented to Angus McIntosh*. Edinburgh: Middle English Dialect Project. **EC, EG, LD**

Bertelson, P. & de Gelder, B. (1991). The emergence of phonological awareness: comparative approaches. In Mattingly, I. G. & Studdert-Kennedy, M. (eds) pp. 393–412. **O**

Bertz, S. (1975). Der Dubliner Stadtdialekt. Teil I: Phonologie. Unpublished PhD dissertation, University of Freiburg. **D**

Bertz, S. (1987). Variation in Dublin English. *Teanga* **7**. 35–53. **D**

Binfield, C., Childs, R., Harman, R., Harper, R., Hey, D., Martin, D. & Tweedale, G. (eds) (1993). *The History of the City of Sheffield 1843–1993* (3 vols). Sheffield: Sheffield Academic Press. **S**

Bladon, R. A. & Al-Bamerni, A. (1976). Coarticulation resistance in English /l/. *Journal of Phonetics* **4**. 137–50. **L**

Boal, F. W. (1969). Territoriality on the Shankill–Falls divide in Belfast. *Irish Geography* **6**. 30–50. **LD**

Boal, F. W., Campbell, J. A. & Livingstone, D. N. (1985). *Protestants and Social Change in the Belfast Area: A Socio-geographic Study*. London: Economic and Social Research Council. **LD**

Boal, F. W. & Douglas, J. N. H. (eds) (1982). *Integration and Division: Geographical Perspectives on the Northern Ireland Problem*. London: Academic Press. **LD**

Boal, F. W. & Poole, M. A. (1972). Religious residential segregation in Belfast in mid-1969: a multi-level analysis. In Clarke, B. D. & Gleave, M. B. (eds) pp. 1–40. **LD**

Boserup, A. & Iversen, C. (1967). Rank analysis of a polarized community: a case study from Northern Ireland. *Peace Research Society International Papers* **8**. 59–76. **LD**

Bowyer, R. (1973). A Study of Social Accents in a South London Suburb. Unpublished MPhil dissertation, University of Leeds. **L**

Bradford Education (1996). *Manningham in Context*. Bradford Education Policy and Information Unit. **O**

Breivik, L. & Jahr, H. (eds) (1989). *Language Change: Contributions to the Study of its Causes*. Berlin: Mouton de Gruyter. **DN**

Britain, D. (1997a). Dialect contact, focusing and phonological rule complexity: the koineization of Fenland English. *University of Pennsylvania Working Papers in Linguistics* **4**(1). 141–70. **NC**

Britain, D. (1997b). Dialect contact and phonological reallocation: 'Canadian Raising' in the English Fens. *Language in Society* **26**. 15–46. **M**

Browman, C. P. & Goldstein, L. (1986). Towards an articulatory phonology. *Phonology Yearbook* **3**. 219–52. **L**

Browman, C. P. & Goldstein, L. (1989). Articulatory gestures as phonological units. *Phonology* **6**. 201–52. **L**

Browman, C. P. & Goldstein, L. (1990a). Gestural specification using dynamically-defined articulatory structures. *Journal of Phonetics* **18**. 299–320. **L**

Browman, C. P. & Goldstein, L. (1990b). Tiers in articulatory phonology, with some implications for casual speech. In Kingston, J. & Beckman, M. E. (eds) pp. 341–76. **L**

Browman, C. P. & Goldstein, L. (1991). Gestural structures: distinctiveness, phonological processes, and historical change. In Mattingly, I. G. & Studdert-Kennedy, M. (eds) pp. 313–38. **L**

Browman, C. P. & Goldstein, L. (1992a). Articulatory Phonology: an overview. *Phonetica* **49**. 155–80. **DN, L**

Browman, C. P. & Goldstein, L. (1992b). 'Targetless' schwa: an articulatory analysis. In Docherty, G. J. & Ladd, D. R. (eds) pp. 26–67. **L**

Brown, B., Strong, W. & Rencher, A. (1975). Acoustic determinants of perceptions of personality from speech. *International Journal of the Sociology of Language* **6**. 11–32. **G**

Brown, G. (1977). *Listening to Spoken English*. London: Longman. **C**

Burnside, S. (ed.) (1994a). *The Glow upon the Fringe: Literary Journeys Around Derry and the North West*. Londonderry: Verbal Arts Centre. **LD**

Burnside, S. (1994b). Within and without the magic circle: the literary heritages of Derry City. In Burnside, S. (ed.) pp. 1–29. **LD**

Butcher, A. (1982). Cardinal vowels and other problems. In Crystal, D. (ed.) pp. 50–72. **O**

Byrd, D. (1994). Relations of sex and dialect to reduction. *Speech Communication* **15**. 39–54. **DN**

Cameron, D. (1990). Demythologizing sociolinguistics: why language does not reflect society. In Joseph, J. E. & Taylor, T. J. (eds) pp. 79–93. **O**

Carr, P. (1992). Strict cyclicity, structure preservation and the Scottish Vowel-Length Rule. *Journal of Linguistics* **28**. 91–114. **EG**

Carr, P. (1993). *Phonology*. London: Macmillan. **L**

Carterette, E. C. & Friedman, M. P. (eds) (1976). *Handbook of Perception*, Vol. 7: *Language and Speech*. New York: Academic Press. **G**

Catford, J. C. (1977). *Fundamental Problems in Phonetics*. Edinburgh: Edinburgh University Press. **C, EC, G**

Chambers, J. K. (1973). Canadian raising. *Canadian Journal of Linguistics* **18**. 113–35. **D**

Chambers, J. K. (1989). Canadian raising: blocking, fronting, etc. *American Speech* **64**. 75–88. **SW**

Chambers, J. K. (1992). Dialect acquisition. *Language* **68**(4). 673–705. **M**

Chambers, J. K. (1993). Sociolinguistic dialectology. In Preston, D. (ed.) pp. 133–64. **SW**

Chambers, J. K. (1995). *Sociolinguistic Theory*. Oxford: Blackwell. **NC, O**

Chambers, J. K. & Trudgill, P. J. (1980). *Dialectology*. Cambridge: Cambridge University Press. **O, S, SW**

Champion, A. & Green, A. (1990). *The Spread of Prosperity and the North–South Divide: Local Economic Performance in Britain in the Late Eighties*. Gosforth and Kenilworth: Booming Towns. **M**

Charette, M. (1990). License to govern. *Phonology* 7. 233–54. **L**

Chen, M. & Wang, W. (1975). Sound change: actuation and implementation. *Language* **51**. 255–81. **D**

Cheshire, J. (ed.) (1991). *English Around the World: Sociolinguistic Perspectives*. Cambridge: Cambridge University Press. **LD**

Cheshire, J., Edwards, V. & Whittle, P. (1993). Urban British dialect grammar: the question of dialect levelling. In Milroy, J. & Milroy, L. (eds) pp. 54–96. **M**

Chirrey, D. A. (in progress). An Articulatory and Acoustic Phonetic Study of Selected Consonants in Accents of Scottish English. Unpublished PhD dissertation, University of Glasgow. **EC**

Chomsky, N. (1981). *Lectures on Government and Binding*. Dordrecht: Foris. **L**

Chomsky, N. (1982). *Some Concepts and Consequences of the Theory of Government and Binding*. Cambridge, MA: MIT Press. **L**

Clark, S., Elms, F. & Youssef, A. (1995). The third dialect of English: some Canadian evidence. *Language Variation and Change* 7. 209–28. **DN**

Clarke, B. D. & Gleave, M. B. (eds) (1972). *Social Patterns in Cities*. London: Institute of British Geographers. **LD**

Clarke, H. B. (ed.) (1997). *Irish Cities* (The Thomas Davis Lecture Series). Cork: Radio Telefís Éireann/The Mercier Press. **LD**

Clements, G. N. (1992). Phonological primes: features or gestures? *Phonetica* **49**. 181–93. **DN**

Cohen, A. P. (ed.) (1982). *Belonging. Identity and Social Organisation in British Rural Cultures*. Manchester: Manchester University Press. **LD**

Cohen, P. (1972). Subcultural conflict and working-class community. *Working Papers in Cultural Studies* **2**. Centre for Contemporary Cultural Studies, University of Birmingham. **M**

Colby, T. (1837). *Ordnance Survey Memoir of Londonderry*. Vol. 1: *Memoir of the City and North Western Liberties of Londonderry. Parish of Templemore*. Dublin: Hodges & Smith. (Facsimile edition, North West Books, Limavady, 1990.) **LD**

Collins, B. & Mees, I. M. (1988). The Cardiff accent: an atypical variety of Welsh English. *Dutch Working Papers in English Language and Linguistics* **5**. 1–20. **C**

Collins, B. & Mees, I. M. (1990). The phonetics of Cardiff English. In Coupland, N. & Thomas, A. (eds) pp. 87–103. **C**

Collins, B. & Mees, I. M. (1991). English through Welsh ears: the 1857 pronunciation dictionary of Robert Ioan Prys. In Tieken-Boon van Ostade, I. & Frankis, J. (eds) pp. 75–90. **C**

Collins, B. & Mees, I. M. (1996). Spreading everywhere? How recent a phenomenon is glottalisation in Received Pronunciation? *English World-Wide* **17**. 175–87. **C, O**

Connell, B. & Arvaniti, A. (eds) (1995). *Phonology and Phonetic Evidence. Papers in Laboratory Phonology IV*. Cambridge: Cambridge University Press. **DN, O**

Connolly, J. H. (1981). On the segmental phonology of a south Welsh accent of English. *Journal of the International Phonetic Association* **11**. 51–61. **C**

Connolly, J. H. (1990). Port Talbot English. In Coupland, N. & Thomas, A. (eds) pp. 121–9. **C**

Coupland, N. (1980). Style-shifting in a Cardiff work-setting. *Language in Society* **9**. 1–12. **C**

Coupland, N. (1988). *Dialect in Use: Sociolinguistic Variation in Cardiff English*. Cardiff: University of Wales Press. **C**

Coupland, N. & Thomas, A. (eds) (1990). *English in Wales: Diversity, Conflict and Change*. Clevedon: Multilingual Matters. **C**

Cross, D. F. W. (1990). *Counterurbanization in England and Wales*. Aldershot: Avebury. **NC**

Crothers, J. (1978). Typology and universals of vowel systems. In Greenberg, J. H. (ed.) pp. 93–152. **NC**

Crowley, T. (1991). *Proper English? Readings in Language, History and Cultural Identity.* London: Routledge. **L**

Cruttenden, A. (1995). Rises in English. In Windsor Lewis, J. (ed.) pp. 155–73. **DN, G, LD**

Cruttenden, A. (1997). *Intonation* (2nd edn). Cambridge: Cambridge University Press. **DN, M, NC, O**

Cruttenden, A. & Gimson, A. C. (1994). *Gimson's Pronunciation of English* (5th edn). London: Edward Arnold. **C**

Crystal, D. (ed.) (1982). *Linguistic Controversies*. London: Edward Arnold. **O**

Crystal, T. & House, A. (1988). Segmental durations in connected-speech signals: syllabic stress. *Journal of the Acoustic Society of America* **83**. 1574–85. **L**

Cutler, A. (1992). Psychology and the segment. In Docherty, G. J. & Ladd, D. R. (eds) pp. 290–5. **O**

Darby, J. (ed.) (1983). *Northern Ireland: The Background to the Conflict*. Belfast: Appletree Press. **LD**

Darlington, T. (1887). *The Folk-speech of South Cheshire*. London: Trübner & Co. (English Dialect Society). **W**

Davenport, M., Hansen, E. & Nielsen, H. F. (eds) (1983). *Proceedings of the Second International Conference on English Historical Linguistics. (Current Topics in English Historical Linguistics* **4**.) Odense: Odense University Press. **NC**

De Lyon, H. (1981). A Sociolinguistic Study of Aspects of the Liverpool Accent. Unpublished MPhil dissertation, University of Liverpool. **W**

DHSS (Department of Health and Social Security) (1991). *The Northern Ireland Census 1991. Religion Report*. Belfast: Registrar General Northern Ireland/HMSO. **LD**

Dixon, R. M. W. (1997). *The Rise and Fall of Languages*. Cambridge: Cambridge University Press. **O**

Dobson, S. (1987). *Larn Yersel' Geordie*. Rothbury: Butler Press. **NC**

Docherty, G. J. (forthcoming). Commentary on papers by Zawadeh; Silverman; Hayward & Watkins; and Tajima & Port. To appear in Local, J., Ogden, R. & Temple, R. (eds). **O**

Docherty, G. J., Foulkes, P., Milroy, J., Milroy, L. & Walshaw, D. (1997). Descriptive adequacy in phonology: a variationist perspective. *Journal of Linguistics* **33**. 275–310. **C, DN, G, NC, O, SW**

Docherty, G. J. & Ladd, D. R. (eds) (1992). *Papers in Laboratory Phonology II: Gesture, Segment, Prosody*. Cambridge: Cambridge University Press. **DN, L, O**

Donegan, P. (1993). On the phonetic basis of phonological change. In Jones, C. (ed.) pp. 98–130. **EC**

Donnan, H. G. & McFarlane, G. (1983). Informal social organisation. In Darby, J. (ed.) pp. 110–35. **LD**

Dorling, D. (1995). *A New Social Atlas of Britain*. New York: Wiley. **NC**

Dorling, D. & Atkins, D. (1995). *Population Density, Change and Concentration in Great Britain 1971, 1981 and 1991*. London: HMSO. **M**

Douglas, E. (1975). A sociolinguistic study of Articlave, Co. Londonderry – a preliminary report. *Ulster Folklife* **21**. 55–67. **LD**

Douglas, E. (1979). A Sociolinguistic Study of Articlave, Co. Londonderry. Unpublished DPhil dissertation, New University of Ulster, Coleraine. **LD**

Douglas-Cowie, E. (1978). Linguistic code-switching in a Northern Irish village: social interaction and social ambition. In Trudgill, P. J. (ed.) pp. 37–51. **C, LD**

Easson, G. J. (1998). The social and regional variation of two 'things' in England. Unpublished seminar paper, University of Toronto. **S**

Eaton, R., Fischer, O., Koopman, W. & van der Leek, F. (eds) (1985). *Papers from the 4th International Conference on English Historical Linguistics, Amsterdam.* Amsterdam: John Benjamins. **NC**

Eckert, P. (ed.) (1991). *New Ways of Analyzing Sound Change.* New York: Academic Press. **NC**

Eliasson, S. & Jahr, E. H. (eds) (1997). *Language and its Ecology: Essays in Memory of Einar Haugen.* Berlin: Mouton de Gruyter. **D**

Ellis, A. J. (1889). *On Early English Pronunciation. Part V: The Existing Phonology of English Dialects.* London: Trübner & Co. **EC, W**

Ellis, S. (1952/53) The Survey of English Dialects (SED), field notebook for Sheffield 11/12/1952, 2/1/1953; Fieldworker: S. Ellis. University of Leeds. **S**

Esling, J. H. (1978a). Voice Quality in Edinburgh: A Sociolinguistic and Phonetic Study. Unpublished PhD dissertation, University of Edinburgh. **G**

Esling, J. H. (1978b). The identification of features of voice quality in social groups. *Journal of the International Phonetic Association* 7. 18–23. **G**

Esling, J. H. & Dickson, B. C. (1985). Acoustical procedures for articulatory setting analysis in accent. In Warkentyne, H. J. (ed.) pp. 155–70. **G**

Faber, A. & Di Paolo, M. (1995). The discriminability of nearly merged sounds. *Language Variation and Change* 7. 35–78. **DN, NC**

Farrar, K. J., Grabe, E. & Nolan, F. J. (forthcoming). English intonation in the British Isles. To appear in *Leeds Studies in English.* **O**

Fasold, R. W. & Schiffrin, D. (eds) (1989). *Language Change and Variation.* Amsterdam: John Benjamins. **LD**

Fischer, J. L. (1958). Social influences on the choice of a linguistic variant. *Word* **14**. 47–56. **SW**

Fisiak, J. & Krygier, M. (eds) (1998). *English Historical Linguistics 1996.* Berlin: Mouton de Gruyter. **D**

Forby, R. (1830). *The Vocabulary of East Anglia.* London. **N**

Foster, J. W. (1994). A runagate tongue: or, English as we speak it in Ulster. *Causeway* **1**(2). 19–26. **LD**

Foulkes, P. (1997a). English [r]-sandhi – a sociolinguistic perspective. *Histoire, Epistémologie, Langage* **19**. 73–96. [Also in *Leeds Working Papers in Linguistics and Phonetics* **6**. 18–38. (1998)] **DN, EC, NC**

Foulkes, P. (1997b). Rule inversion in a British English dialect – a sociolinguistic investigation of [r]-sandhi in Newcastle upon Tyne. *University of Pennsylvania Working Papers in Linguistics* **4**(1). 259–70. **DN, EC, NC**

Foulkes, P. (1997c). Historical laboratory phonology: investigating /p/ > /f/ > /h/ changes. *Language and Speech* **40**. 249–76. **O**

Foulkes, P. & Docherty, G. J. (in press). Another chapter in the story of /r/: 'labiodental' variants in British English. To appear in *Journal of Sociolinguistics.* **DN, G, M, NC**

Fromkin, V. (ed.) (1985). *Phonetic Linguistics: Essays in Honor of Peter Ladefoged.* Orlando: Academic Press. **EG**

Fudge, E. (1977). Long and short [æ] in one Southern British speaker's English. *Journal of the International Phonetic Association* 7. 55–65. **C**

Gallagher, M. (1995). How many nations are there in Ireland? In O'Leary, B. & McGarry, J. (eds) pp. 715–39. **LD**

Garcia, O. & Otheguy, R. (eds) (1989). *English Across Cultures, Cultures Across English: A Reader in Cross-cultural Communication.* New York: Mouton de Gruyter. **LD**

Giddens, A. (1997). *Sociology* (3rd edn). Cambridge: Polity Press. **M, O**

Giles, H. (1970). Evaluative reactions to accents. *Educational Review* **22**. 211–27. **O**

Gimson, A. C. (1980). *An Introduction to the Pronunciation of English* (3rd edn). London: Edward Arnold. **EC**

Gordon, M. J. (1997). Urban Sound Change Beyond City Limits: The Spread of the Northern Cities Shift in Michigan. Unpublished PhD dissertation, University of Michigan. **NC**

Görlach, M. (ed.) (1985). *Focus on Scotland.* Amsterdam: John Benjamins. **EC, G**

Grabe, E., Nolan, F. J. & Farrar, K. J. (forthcoming). IViE – a comparative transcription system for intonational variation in English. To appear in *Proceedings of the International Conference on Spoken Language Processing,* Sydney, Australia, December 1998. **O**

Graddol, D., Swann, J. & Leith, D. (eds) (1996). *English: History, Diversity and Change.* London: Routledge. **M**

Greenberg, J. H. (ed.) (1978). *Universals of Human Language,* Vol. II: *Phonology.* Stanford: Stanford University Press. **NC**

Gregg, R. J. (1958). Notes on the phonology of a County Antrim Scotch-Irish dialect. *Orbis* **7**. 392–406. **LD**

Gregg, R. J. (1959). Notes on the phonology of a County Antrim Scotch-Irish dialect. Part II: Historical phonology (I). *Orbis* **8**. 400–24. **LD**

Gregg, R. J. (1964). Scotch-Irish urban speech in Ulster. In Adams, G. B. (ed.) pp. 163–92. **LD**

Gregg, R. J. (1972). The Scotch-Irish dialect boundaries in Ulster. In Wakelin, M. F. (ed.) pp. 109–39. **LD**

Gregg, R. J. (1985). *The Scotch-Irish Dialect Boundaries in the Province of Ulster.* Port Credit, Ontario: Canadian Federation for the Humanities. **LD**

Grice, M. & Barry, W. (1991). Problems of transcription and labelling in the specification of segmental and prosodic structure. *Proceedings of the XIIth International Congress of Phonetic Sciences* **5**. 66–9. Aix-en-Provence. **DN**

Gunn, B. (1990). The Politic Word. Unpublished DPhil dissertation, University of Ulster at Jordanstown. **LD**

Gunn, B. (1994). 'No surrender': existentialist sociolinguistics and politics in Northern Ireland. *Belfast Working Papers in Language and Linguistics* **12**. 98–133. **LD**

Guy, G., Feagin, C., Schiffrin, D. & Baugh, J. (eds) (1996). *Towards a Social Science of Language,* Vol. 1. Amsterdam/Philadelphia: John Benjamins. **M**

Haag, K. (1929/30). Sprachwandel im Lichte der Mundartgrenzen. *Teuthonista* **6**(1). 1–35. **NC**

Hamilton, F. E. I. (1991). A new geography of London's manufacturing. In Hoggart, K. & Green, D. R. (eds) pp. 51–78. **L**

Hardcastle, W. J. & Laver, J. (eds) (1997). *The Handbook of Phonetic Sciences.* Oxford: Blackwell. **DN, O**

Hardcastle, W. J. & Marchal, A. (eds) (1990). *Speech Production and Speech Modelling.* Amsterdam: Kluwer. **DN**

Harris, J. (1985). *Phonological Variation and Change: Studies in Hiberno-English.* Cambridge: Cambridge University Press. **DN, LD, O**

Harris, J. (1986). The lexicon in phonological variation. In Harris, J., Little, D. & Singleton, D. (eds) pp. 187–208. **LD**

Harris, J. (1990a). Segmental complexity and phonological government. *Phonology* **7**. 255–300. **L**

Harris, J. (1990b). More on Brogues and Creoles: what's been happening to English short *u*? *Irish University Review* **20**(1). 73–90. **LD**

Harris, J. (1991). Ireland. In Cheshire, J. (ed.) pp. 37–50. **LD**

Harris, J. (1995). *English Sound Structure.* Oxford: Blackwell. **EG**

Harris, J. (1996). On the trail of short *u*. *English World-Wide* **17**(1). 1–42. **LD**

Harris, J. & Kaye, J. (1990). A tale of two cities: London glottalling and New York City tapping. *The Linguistic Review* **7**. 251–74. **L**

Harris, J., Little, D. & Singleton, D. (eds) (1986). *Perspectives on the English Language in Ireland. Proceedings of the First Symposium on Hiberno-English Held at Trinity College*

Dublin, 16–17 September 1985. Dublin: Centre for Language and Communication Studies, Trinity College Dublin. **LD**

Hart, H. C. (1899). *Notes on the Ulster Dialect, Chiefly Donegal*. London: The Philological Society. **LD**

Haugen, E., McClure, J. D. & Thomson, D. (eds) (1981). *Minority Languages Today*. Edinburgh: Edinburgh University Press. **EC, EG**

Heath, C. D. (1980). *The Pronunciation of English in Cannock, Staffordshire*. Oxford: Blackwell (Philological Society). **SW, W**

Henton, C. & Bladon, A. (1985). Breathiness in a normal female speaker: inefficiency versus desirability. *Language and Communication* **5**. 221–7. **G**

Henton, C. & Bladon, A. (1988). Creak as a sociophonetic marker. In Hyman, L. & Li, C. (eds) pp. 3–29. **G**

Henton, C., Ladefoged, P. & Maddieson, I. (1992). Stops in the world's languages. *Phonetica* **49**. 65–101. **DN**

Heselwood, B. & McChrystal, L. (1998). The devoicing of Panjabi stop consonants by younger generation speakers in Bradford, England: an acoustic study. Unpublished seminar paper, Leeds Metropolitan University. **O**

Hewlett, N., Matthews, B. & Scobbie, J. M. (1999). Vowel duration in Scottish English speaking children. *Proceedings of the XIVth International Congress of Phonetic Sciences*. University of California, Berkeley. **EG**

Hey, D. (1993). Continuities and perceptions. In Binfield, C. *et al.* (eds), vol. 2, pp. 7–16. **S**

Hey, D. (1997). The local history of family names. *The Local Historian* **27**(4). Supplement. **S**

Hickey, R. (1984). Coronal segments in Irish English. *Journal of Linguistics* **20**. 233–51. **D**

Hickey, R. (1986). Length and frontness with low vowels in Irish English. *Studia Linguistica* **39**. 143–56. **D**

Hickey, R. (1993). The beginnings of Irish English. *Folia Linguistica Historica* **14**. 213–38. **D**

Hickey, R. (1998). The Dublin vowel shift and the historical perspective. In Fisiak, J. & Krygier, M. (eds) pp. 79–106. **D**

Hickey, R. (1999). Developments and change in Dublin English. In Jahr, E. H. (ed.) pp. 209–43. **D**

Hinskens, F., Van Hout, R. & Wetzels, W. L. (eds) (1997). *Variation, Change, and Phonological Theory*. Amsterdam: John Benjamins. **O**

Hoequist, C. & Nolan, F. J. (1991). On an application of phonological knowledge in automatic speech recognition. *Computer Speech and Language* **5**. 133–53. **O**

Hogan, J. J. (1927). *The English Language in Ireland*. Dublin: Educational Company of Ireland. **D**

Hoggart, K. & Green, D. R. (eds) (1991). *London: A New Metropolitan Geography*. London: Edward Arnold. **L**

Holmes, J. (1994). New Zealand flappers: an analysis of τ voicing in New Zealand English. *English World-Wide* **15**. 195–224. **C**

Holmes, J. (1995). Glottal stops in New Zealand English: an analysis of variants of word-final /t/. *Linguistics* **33**. 433–63. **DN, SW**

Holmes, J. N. (1986). Normalization and vowel perception. In Perkell, J. S. & Klatt, D. H. (eds) pp. 346–57. **DN**

Holst, T. & Nolan, F. J. (1995). The influence of syntactic structure on [s] to [ʃ] assimilation. In Connell, B. & Arvaniti, A. (eds) pp. 315–33. **O**

Honikman, B. (1964). Articulatory settings. In Abercrombie, D. *et al.* (eds) pp. 73–84. **C, G**

Horvath, B. (1985). *Variation in Australian English: The Sociolects of Sydney*. Cambridge: Cambridge University Press. **C**

Houck, C. L. (1966). A computerized statistical methodology for linguistic geography: a pilot study. *Folia Linguistica* **1**. 80–95. **S**

Houck, C. L. (1967). Methodology of an Urban Speech Survey. Unpublished MS, Institute of Dialect and Folk Life Studies, University of Leeds. **S**

House, A. S. & Fairbanks, G. (1953). The influence of consonant environment upon the secondary acoustical characteristics of vowels. *Journal of the Acoustical Society of America* **25**. 105–13. **EG**

Hudson, R. A. (1996). *Sociolinguistics*. Cambridge: Cambridge University Press. **SW**

Hughes, A. & Trudgill, P. J. (1996). *English Accents and Dialects: An Introduction to Social and Regional Varieties of British English* (3rd edn). London: Edward Arnold. **C, DN, L, NC**

Hulme, H. M. (1941). Derbyshire dialect in the seventeenth century. From the Bakewell Parish records. *Journal of the Derbyshire Archæological and Natural History Society* **62**. 88–103. **DN**

Hyman, L. & Li, C. (eds) (1988). *Language, Speech and Mind*. London: Routledge. **G**

IPD (1996). Press release, Institute of Personnel and Development, London. **O**

Jahr, E. H. (ed.) (1992). *Language Contact: Theoretical and Empirical Studies*. Berlin: Mouton de Gruyter. **M**

Jahr, E. H. (ed.) (1999). *Language Change: Advances in Historical Sociolinguistics*. Berlin: Mouton de Gruyter. **D**

Jenkins, R. (1986). Northern Ireland: in what sense religions in conflict? In Jenkins, R., Donnan, H. & McFarlane, G. (eds) pp. 1–21. **LD**

Jenkins, R., Donnan, H. & McFarlane, G. (eds) (1986). *The Sectarian Divide in Northern Ireland Today*. London: Royal Anthropological Institute of Great Britain and Ireland. **LD**

Johnson, K. & Mullenix, J. W. (eds) (1997). *Talker Variability in Speech Processing*. San Diego: Academic Press. **DN**

Johnston, P. A. (1983). Irregular style variation patterns in Edinburgh speech. *Scottish Language* **2**. 1–19. **EC, G**

Johnston, P. A. (1984). Variation in the Standard Scottish English of Morningside. *English World-Wide* **5**. 133–85. **EC**

Johnston, P. A. (1985). The rise and fall of the Morningside/Kelvinside accent. In Görlach, M. (ed.) pp. 37–56. **EC, G**

Johnston, P. A. (1997a). Older Scots phonology and its regional variation. In Jones, C. (ed.) pp. 47–111. **EG**

Johnston, P. A. (1997b). Regional variation. In Jones, C. (ed.) pp. 432–513. **EG, G**

Jones, C. (1989). *History of English Phonology*. London: Longman. **L**

Jones, C. (ed.) (1993). *Historical Linguistics: Problems and Perspectives*. London: Longman. **EC**

Jones, C. (ed.) (1997). *The Edinburgh History of the Scots Language*. Edinburgh: Edinburgh University Press. **EC, EG, G**

Jones, D. (1911). English: Tyneside dialect (Northumberland). *Le Maître Phonétique* **26**. 184. **NC**

Jones, D. (1950). *The Pronunciation of English*. Cambridge: Cambridge University Press. **C**

Jones, D. (1956). *An Outline of English Phonetics* (8th edn). Cambridge: Cambridge University Press. **C, EC**

Jones, D. (1967a). *The Phoneme: Its Nature and Use* (3rd edn). Cambridge: Heffer. **C**

Jones, D. (1967b). *The Pronunciation of English* (4th edn). Cambridge: Cambridge University Press. **DN**

Joseph, J. E. & Taylor, T. J. (eds) (1990). *Ideologies of Language*. London: Routledge. **O**

Kaye, J. (1990). 'Coda' licensing. *Phonology* **7**. 301–30. **L**

Kaye, J., Lowenstamm, J. & Vergnaud, J. -R. (1985). The internal structure of phonological elements: a theory of charm and government. *Phonology Yearbook* **2**. 305–28. **L**

Kaye, J., Lowenstamm, J. & Vergnaud, J. -R. (1990). Constituent structure and government in phonology. *Phonology* 7. 193–231. **L**

Keating, P. A. (1985). Universal phonetics and the organisation of grammars. In Fromkin, V. (ed.) pp. 115–32. **EG**

Keating, P. A. (ed.) (1994). *Phonological Structure and Phonetic Form. Papers in Laboratory Phonology III.* Cambridge: Cambridge University Press. **DN, M**

Keller, R. (1994). *On Language Change. The Invisible Hand in Language.* London: Routledge. **DN**

Kelly, J. & Local, J. (1989). *Doing Phonology: Observing, Recording, Interpreting.* Manchester: Manchester University Press. **O**

Kerswill, P. E. (1994a). *Dialects Converging: Rural Speech in Urban Norway.* Oxford: Clarendon Press. **M**

Kerswill, P. E. (1994b). Babel in Buckinghamshire? Pre-school children acquiring accent features in the New Town of Milton Keynes. In Melchers, G. & Johannessen, N. -L. (eds) pp. 64–84. **M**

Kerswill, P. E. (1996a) Milton Keynes and dialect levelling in south-eastern British English. In Graddol, D., Swann, J. & Leith, D. (eds) pp. 292–300. **M**

Kerswill, P. E. (1996b). Children, adolescents and language change. *Language Variation and Change* 8(2). 177–202. **M, NC**

Kerswill, P. E., Llamas, C. & Upton, C. (forthcoming). The First SuRE Moves: early steps towards a large dialect project. To appear in *Leeds Studies in English.* **O, S**

Kerswill, P. E. & Williams, A. (1997). Investigating social and linguistic identity in three British schools. In Kotsinas, U. -B., Stenström, A. -B. & Malin, A. -M. (eds) pp. 159–76. **M**

Kerswill, P. E. & Williams, A. (2000). Creating a new town koine: children and language change in Milton Keynes. *Language in Society* 29. **M**

Kerswill, P. E. & Wright, S. (1990). On the limits of auditory transcription: a socio-phonetic perspective. *Language Variation and Change* 2. 255–75. **DN, O**

Kingsmore, R. K. (1983). Coleraine Speech: Phonology and Sociolinguistics. Unpublished DPhil dissertation, New University of Ulster, Coleraine. **LD**

Kingsmore, R. K. (1995). *Ulster Scots Speech: A Sociolinguistic Study.* Tuscaloosa, Alabama: University of Alabama Press. **LD, SW**

Kingston, J. & Beckman, M. E. (eds) (1990). *Papers in Laboratory Phonology I. Between the Grammar and Physics of Speech.* Cambridge: Cambridge University Press. **DN, L**

Kiparsky, P. (1988). Phonological change. In Newmeyer, F. J. (ed.) pp. 363–416. **DN, O**

Kirk, J. M., Sanderson, S. & Widdowson, J. D. A. (eds) (1985). *Studies in Linguistic Geography: The Dialects of English in Britain and Ireland.* London: Croom Helm. **S, SW**

Kirkwood, H. (ed.) (1986). *Studies in Intonation.* (Occasional papers in linguistics and language learning 11.) Coleraine: University of Ulster. **LD**

Knowles, G. O. (1974). Scouse, the Urban Dialect of Liverpool. Unpublished PhD dissertation, University of Leeds. **G, W**

Knowles, G. O. (1978). The nature of phonological variables in Scouse. In Trudgill (ed.) pp. 80–90. **G, NC, SW, W**

Kolb, E., Glauser, B., Elmer, W. & Stamm, R. (1979). *Atlas of English Sounds.* Bern: Franke Verlag. **EG**

Kotsinas, U. -B., Stenström, A. -B. & Malin, A. -M. (eds) (1997). *Ungdomsspråk i Norden. Föredrag från ett Forskarsymposium [Youth Language in the Nordic Countries. Papers from a Research Symposium].* Series: MINS, No. 43. Stockholm: University of Stockholm, Department of Nordic Languages and Literature. **M**

Labov, W. (1963). The social motivation of a sound change. *Word* 19. 273–309. **NC**

Labov, W. (1966). *The Social Stratification of English in New York City.* Washington, DC: Center for Applied Linguistics. **C, D, S**

Labov, W. (1972). *Sociolinguistic Patterns.* Oxford: Blackwell. **SW**

Labov, W. (1981). Resolving the Neogrammarian controversy. *Language* 57. 267–308. **D**

Labov, W. (1986). Sources of inherent variation in the speech process. In Perkell, J. S. & Klatt, D. H. (eds) pp. 402–23. **DN**

Labov, W. (1990). The intersection of sex and social class in the course of linguistic change. *Language Variation and Change* **2**. 205–54. **NC, O, SW**

Labov, W. (1991). The three dialects of English. In Eckert, P. (ed.) pp. 1–44. **NC**

Labov, W. (1994). *Principles of Linguistic Change*. Vol. I: *Internal Factors*. Oxford: Blackwell. **C, DN, NC, O**

Labov, W., Yaeger, M. & Steiner, R. (1972). A quantitative study of sound change in progress. *Report on National Science Foundation Project no. GS-3287* (2 volumes). Philadelphia: US Regional Survey. **DN**

Lacy, B. (1990). *Siege City: The Story of Derry and Londonderry*. Belfast: Blackstaff Press. **LD**

Ladefoged, P. (1972). Phonetic prerequisites for a distinctive feature theory. In Valdmann, A. (ed.) pp. 273–85. **O**

Ladefoged, P. (1993). *A Course in Phonetics* (3rd edn). New York: Harcourt Brace Jovanovich. **DN**

Ladefoged, P. & Maddieson, I. (1996). *The Sounds of the World's Languages*. Oxford: Blackwell. **DN**

Larsen, S. S. (1973). [Kilbroney]. To Byer i Nord-Irland. Unpublished Magistergrad dissertation, University of Oslo. **LD**

Larsen, S. S. (1982a). The two sides of the house: identity and social organisation in Kilbroney, Northern Ireland. In Cohen, A. P. (ed.) pp. 131–64. **LD**

Larsen, S. S. (1982b). The glorious twelfth: a ritual expression of collective identity. In Cohen, A. P. (ed.) pp. 278–91. **LD**

Lass, N. J. (ed.) (1996). *Principles of Experimental Phonetics*. St Louis: Mosby. **EG**

Lass, R. (1974). Linguistic orthogenesis? Scots vowel quality and the English length conspiracy. In Anderson, J. M. & Jones, C. (eds) pp. 311–52. **EG**

Lass, R. (1983). Velar /r/ and the history of English. In Davenport, M., Hansen, E. & Nielsen, H. F. (eds) pp. 67–94. **NC**

Lass, R. (1989). System-shape and the eternal return: front rounded vowels in English. *Folia Linguistica Historica* **10**. 163–98. **NC, O**

Lass, R. (1990). A 'standard' South African vowel system. In Ramsaran, S. (ed.) pp. 272–85. **NC**

Laver, J. (1968). Voice quality and indexical information. *British Journal of Disorders of Communication* **3**. 43–54. [reprinted as Chapter 9 in Laver (1991)] **G**

Laver, J. (1976). Language and non-verbal communication. In Carterette, E. C. & Friedman, M. P. (eds) pp. 345–63. [reprinted as Chapter 8 in Laver (1991)] **G**

Laver, J. (1980). *The Phonetic Description of Voice Quality*. Cambridge: Cambridge University Press. **C, G**

Laver, J. (1991). *The Gift of Speech: Readings in the Analysis of Speech and Voice*. Edinburgh: Edinburgh University Press. **G**

Laver, J. (1994). *Principles of Phonetics*. Cambridge: Cambridge University Press. **G, O**

Laver, J. & Trudgill, P. J. (1979). Phonetic and linguistic markers in speech. In Scherer, K. R. & Giles, H. (eds) pp. 1–32. [reprinted as Chapter 14 in Laver (1991)] **G**

Laver, J., Wirz, S., Mackenzie, J. & Hiller, S. M. (1981). A perceptual protocol for the analysis of vocal profiles. *Edinburgh University Department of Linguistics Work in Progress* **14**. 139–55. [reprinted as Chapter 15 in Laver (1991)] **G**

Lawson, E. (1998). The 'Scottish' Consonants in the Speech of Glasgow Schoolchildren: A Sociophonetic Investigation. Vacation Scholarship Report to Carnegie Trust. **EC, G**

Lehiste, I. (1964). Acoustical characteristics of selected English consonants. *Indiana University Research Center in Anthropology, Folklore and Linguistics* **34**. 10–50. **L**

Lehiste, I. (1996). Suprasegmental features of speech. In Lass, N. J. (ed.) pp. 226–44. **EG**

Leith, D. (1983). *A Social History of English*. London: Routledge. **L**

Lenneberg, E. H. (1967). *Biological Foundations of Language*. New York: John Wiley & Sons. **M**

Le Page, R. B. (1980). Projection, focusing, diffusion, or, steps towards a sociolinguistic theory of language, illustrated from the Sociolinguistics Survey of Multilingual Communities. *York Papers in Linguistics* **9**. 9–32. **M**

Leyton, E. (1975). *The One Blood: Kinship and Class in an Irish Village*. St John's, Newfoundland: Memorial University of Newfoundland. **LD**

Liljencrants, J. & Lindblom, B. (1972). Numerical simulation of vowel quality systems: the role of perceptual contrast. *Language* **48**. 839–63. **NC**

Lindau, M. (1975). Features for vowels. *UCLA Working Papers in Phonetics* **30**. 1–155. **O**

Lindblom, B. (1963). Spectrographic study of vowel reduction. *Journal of the Acoustical Society of America* **35**. 1173–781. **DN**

Lindblom, B. (1986a). Phonetic universals in vowel systems. In Ohala, J. J. & Jaeger, J. J. (eds) pp. 13–44. **NC**

Lindblom, B. (1986b). On the origin and purpose of discreteness and invariance in sound patterns. In Perkell, J. S. & Klatt, D. H. (eds) pp. 493–510. **O**

Lindblom, B. (1990). Explaining phonetic variation: a sketch of the H&H theory. In Hardcastle, W. J. & Marchal, A. (eds) pp. 403–39. **DN, O**

Linell, P. (1979). *Psychological Reality in Phonology*. Cambridge: Cambridge University Press. **O**

Llamas, C. (1998). Language variation and innovation in Middlesbrough: a pilot study. *Leeds Working Papers in Linguistics and Phonetics* **6**. 98–115. **O**

Local, J. (1990). Some rhythm, resonance and quality variations in urban Tyneside speech. In Ramsaran, S. (ed.) pp. 286–92. **NC**

Local, J. K., Kelly, J. & Wells, W. H. G. (1986). Towards a phonology of conversation: turntaking in Tyneside. *Journal of Linguistics* **22**. 411–37. **DN, NC**

Local, J., Ogden, R. & Temple, R. (eds) (forthcoming). *Papers in Laboratory Phonology VI*. Cambridge: Cambridge University Press. **O**

Lodge, K. R. (1984). *Studies in the Phonology of Colloquial English*. London: Croom Helm. **SW**

Longley, M. (1994). *Tuppenny Stung: Autobiographical Chapters*. Belfast: Lagan Press. **LD**

Macafee, C. (1983). *Varieties of English around the World: Glasgow*. Amsterdam: John Benjamins. **EC, EG, G**

Macafee, C. (1994). *Traditional Dialect in the Modern World: A Glasgow Case Study*. Frankfurt am Main: Verlag Peter Lang. **G, LD**

Macafee, C. (1997). Ongoing change in Modern Scots: the social dimension. In Jones, C. (ed.) pp. 514–48. **EG**

McAllister, A. H. (1963). *A Year's Course in Speech Training*. London: University of London Press. **EC**

Macaulay, R. K. S. (1977). *Language, Social Class, and Education: A Glasgow Study*. Edinburgh: Edinburgh University Press. **DN, G, SW**

Macaulay, R. K. S. (1985). Linguistic maps: visual aid or abstract art? In Kirk, J. M., Sanderson, S. & Widdowson, J. D. A. (eds) pp. 172–86. **SW**

Macaulay, R. K. S. (1991). *Locating Dialect in Discourse: The Language of Honest Men and Bonnie Lasses in Ayr*. Oxford: Oxford University Press. **DN**

Macaulay, R. K. S. & Trevelyan, G. D. (1973). Language, Education and Employment in Glasgow. Final report to the SSRC. **G**

McCafferty, K. (1997). Open Minds, Barricaded Tongues: A Study of Ethnicity and Language Change in Derry/Londonderry, Northern Ireland. Unpublished Dr. art. dissertation, University of Tromsø. **LD**

McCafferty, K. (1998a). Barriers to change: Ethnic division and phonological innovation in Northern Hiberno-English. *English World-Wide* **19**(1). 7–35. **LD**

McCafferty, K. (1998b). Shared accents, divided speech community? Change in Northern Ireland English. *Language Variation and Change* 10(2). 97–121. **LD**

McClure, J. D. (1970). Some Features of Standard English as Spoken in South-West Scotland. Unpublished M Litt dissertation, University of Edinburgh. **EC**

McClure, J. D. (1977). Vowel duration in a Scottish accent. *Journal of the International Phonetic Association* 7. 10–16. **EG**

McClure, J. D. (1979). Scots: its range of uses. In Aitken, A. J. & McArthur, T. (eds) pp. 26–48. **EG**

McConnell, S. (1989). *Talk of the Town: A Derry Phrase Book.* Derry: Guildhall Press. **LD**

McConnell, S. (1990). *The Folly Up: Talk of the Town 2.* Derry: Guildhall Press. **LD**

McConnell, S. (1996). *The Wile Big Derry Phrase Book.* Derry: Guildhall Press. **LD**

McElholm, D. D. (1986). Intonation in Derry English. In Kirkwood, H. (ed.) pp. 1–58. **LD**

McKenna, G. E. (1988). Vowel Duration in the Standard English of Scotland. Unpublished M Litt dissertation, University of Edinburgh. **EG**

Mackenzie Beck, J. M. (1988). Organic Variation and Voice Quality. Unpublished PhD dissertation, University of Edinburgh. **G**

Maclaran, R. (1976). The variable (ʌ): a relic form with social correlates. *Belfast Working Papers in Language and Linguistics* 1. 45–68. **LD**

McMahon, A. M. S. (1991). Lexical phonology and sound change: the case of the Scottish Vowel Length Rule. *Journal of Linguistics* 27. 29–53. **EG**

McMahon, A. M. S. (1994). *Understanding Language Change.* Cambridge: Cambridge University Press. **DN**

McMahon, A. M. S., Foulkes, P. & Tollfree, L. F. (1994). Gestural representation and lexical phonology. *Phonology* 11. 277–316. **DN, EC, L, O**

MacNeilage, P. F. (ed.) (1983). *The Production of Speech.* New York: Springer-Verlag. **DN**

Mahoney, B., Dixon, J. & Cocks, R. (forthcoming). The effect of suspect accent and evidence on perceptions of their guilt and criminal behaviour. **O**

Marshall, G., Newby, H., Rose, D., & Vogler, C. (1988). *Social Class in Modern Britain.* London: Hutchinson. **M**

Mathisen, A. G. (1992). A Sociolinguistic Study of Sandwell English. Unpublished Cand. philol. dissertation, University of Oslo. **SW**

Mathisen, A. G. (forthcoming). Phonological Variation and Change Focusing on Teenage Speech. Unpublished Dr. art. dissertation, University of Oslo. **SW**

Mattingly, I. G. & Studdert-Kennedy, M. (eds) (1991). *Modularity and the Motor Theory of Speech Perception.* Hillsdale, NJ: Lawrence Erlbaum. **L, O**

Mayo, C. (1996). Prosodic Transcription of Glasgow English: An Evaluation Study of GlaToBI. Unpublished MSc dissertation, University of Edinburgh. **G**

Mees, I. M. (1977). Language and Social Class in Cardiff: A Survey of the Speech Habits of Schoolchildren. Unpublished Masters dissertation, University of Leiden. **C**

Mees, I. M. (1983). The Speech of Cardiff Schoolchildren: A Real Time Study. Unpublished Doctoral dissertation, University of Leiden. **C, SW**

Mees, I. M. (1987). Glottal stop as a prestigious feature in Cardiff English. *English World-Wide* 8. 25–39. **C, DN, SW**

Mees, I. M. (1990). Patterns of sociophonetic variation in the speech of Cardiff schoolchildren. In Coupland, N. & Thomas, A. (eds) pp. 87–103. **C, N**

Melchers, G. & Johannessen, N. -L. (eds) (1994). *Nonstandard Varieties of Language: Papers from the Stockholm Symposium.* Stockholm: Almqvist & Wiksell. **M, NC**

Milroy, J. (1981). *Regional Accents of English: Belfast.* Belfast: Blackstaff Press. **LD**

Milroy, J. (1992). *Linguistic Variation and Change.* Oxford: Blackwell. **D, DN, LD, N, NC, O**

Milroy, J. (1995). Investigating the Scottish Vowel Length Rule in a Northumbrian dialect. *Newcastle and Durham Working Papers in Linguistics* 3. 187–96. **EG, NC**

Milroy, J. (1996). A current change in British English: variation in (th) in Derby. *Newcastle and Durham Working Papers in Linguistics* 4. 213–22. **DN**

Milroy, J. (1999). Toward a speaker-based account of language change. In Jahr, E. H. (ed.) pp. 21–36. **D**

Milroy, J. & Harris, J. (1980). When is a merger not a merger? The MEAT/MATE problem in a present-day English vernacular. *English World-Wide* 1. 199–210. **NC**

Milroy, J. & Milroy, L. (1977). *Speech Community and Language Variety in Belfast.* Report to the Social Science Research Council, grant no. HR 3771. **LD**

Milroy, J. & Milroy, L. (1985a). *Authority in Language.* London: Routledge and Kegan Paul. **L, O**

Milroy, J. & Milroy, L. (1985b). Linguistic change, social network and speaker innovation. *Journal of Linguistics* 21. 339–84. **DN, NC, O, SW**

Milroy, J. & Milroy, L. (1993). Mechanisms of change in urban dialects: the role of class, social network and gender. *International Journal of Applied Linguistics* 3(1). 57–77. **M**

Milroy, J. & Milroy, L. (eds) (1993). *Real English: The Grammar of English Dialects in the British Isles.* London: Longman. **M, O**

Milroy, J., Milroy, L., Harris, J., Gunn, B., Pitts, A. & Policansky, L. (1982). *Sociolinguistic Variation and Linguistic Change in Belfast.* Report to the Social Science Research Council, grant no. HR 5777. **LD**

Milroy, J., Milroy, L. & Hartley, S. (1994). Local and supra-local change in British English: the case of glottalisation. *English World-Wide* 15. 1–33. **C, M, O, SW**

Milroy, J., Milroy, L., Hartley, S. & Walshaw, D. (1994). Glottal stops and Tyneside glottalization: competing patterns of variation and change in British English. *Language Variation and Change* 6. 327–57. **SW**

Milroy, L. (1976). Phonological correlates to community structure in Belfast. *Belfast Working Papers in Language and Linguistics* 1. 1–44. **LD**

Milroy, L. (1987a). *Observing and Analysing Natural Language.* Oxford: Blackwell. **O**

Milroy, L. (1987b). *Language and Social Networks* (2nd edn). Oxford: Blackwell. **LD, M, NC, O**

Milroy, L. (forthcoming). Histories of nations and contrasting language ideologies in Britain and the United States. To appear in Watts, R. & Bex, T. (eds). **NC**

Milroy, L. & Milroy, J. (1992). Social network and social class: toward an integrated sociolinguistic model. *Language in Society* 21. 1–26. **M**

Milroy, L. & Milroy, J. (1997). Exploring the social constraints on language change. In Eliasson, S. & Jahr, E. H. (eds) pp. 75–101. **D**

Milroy, L., Milroy, J. & Docherty, G. J. (1997). *Phonological Variation and Change in Contemporary Spoken British English.* Final Report to the UK Economic and Social Research Council, grant no. R000234892. **DN, NC**

MKDC (1990). *Milton Keynes Population Bulletin 1990.* Milton Keynes: Milton Keynes Development Corporation. **M**

Moxon-Brown, E. (1983). *Nation, Class and Creed in Northern Ireland.* Aldershot: Avebury. **LD**

Moxon-Brown, E. (1991). National identity in Northern Ireland. In Stringer, P. & Robinson, G. (eds) pp. 23–30. **LD**

Murison, D. (1979). The historical background. In Aitken, A. J. & McArthur, T. (eds) pp. 2–13. **EC**

Murray, J. A. H. (1873). *Dialect of the Southern Counties of Scotland.* London: Asher & Co. for the Philological Society. **EC**

Nagy, N. & Reynolds, B. (1997). Optimality Theory and variable word-final deletion in Faetar. *Language Variation and Change* 9(1). 37–55. **O**

Nathan, L., Wells, B. & Donlan, C. (1998). Children's comprehension of unfamiliar regional accents: a preliminary investigation. *Journal of Child Language* 25. 343–65. **O**

Newbrook, M. (1982). Sociolinguistic Reflexes of Dialect Interference in West Wirral. Unpublished PhD dissertation, University of Reading. **W**

Newbrook, M. (1986). *Sociolinguistic Reflexes of Dialect Interference in West Wirral.* Bern & Frankfurt am Main: Verlag Peter Lang. **DN, W**

Newbrook, M. (1987). Age-grading and change in progress. *University of East Anglia Papers in Linguistics* **27**. 27–44. **W**

Newmeyer, F. (ed.) (1988). *Linguistics: The Cambridge Survey,* Vol. 1. Cambridge: Cambridge University Press. **DN**

Nolan, F. J. (1983). *The Phonetic Bases of Speaker Recognition.* Cambridge: Cambridge University Press. **G**

Nolan, F. J. (1991). Forensic phonetics. *Journal of Linguistics* **27**. 483–93. **O**

Nolan, F. J. (1992). The descriptive role of segments: evidence from assimilation. In Docherty, G. J. & Ladd, D. R. (eds) pp. 261–80. **DN, O**

Nolan, F. J. (1995). The role of the jaw – active or passive? Comments on Lee. In Connell, B. & Arvaniti, A. (eds) pp. 361–7. **DN**

Nolan, F. J. (1997). Speaker recognition and forensic phonetics. In Hardcastle, W. J. & Laver, J. (eds) pp. 744–67. **O**

O'Connor, J. D. (1947). The phonetic system of a dialect of Newcastle upon Tyne. *Le Maître Phonétique* **87**. 6–8. **DN, NC**

O'Connor, J. D. (1973). *Phonetics.* Harmondsworth: Pelican. **DN**

O'Connor, J. D. & Arnold, G. F. (1973). *Intonation of Colloquial English* (2nd edn). London: Longman. **M**

OFSTED (1993). *Access and Achievement in Urban Education.* London: HMSO. **M**

Ohala, J. J. (1974). Experimental historical phonology. In Anderson, J. M. & Jones, C. (eds) pp. 353–89. **DN, O**

Ohala, J. J. (1983). The origin of sound patterns in vocal tract constraints. In MacNeilage, P. F. (ed.) pp. 189–216. **DN, O**

Ohala, J. J. (1989). Sound change is drawn from a pool of synchronic variation. In Breivik, L. & Jahr, H. (eds) pp. 173–98. **DN, O**

Ohala, J. J. (1992). The segment: primitive or derived? In Docherty, G. J. & Ladd, D. R. (eds) pp. 166–83. **O**

Ohala, J. J. & Jaeger, J. J. (eds) (1986). *Experimental Phonology.* Orlando: Academic Press. **NC**

O'Leary, B. & McGarry, J. (eds) (1995). *A State of Truce: Northern Ireland after Twenty-five Years of War.* (Special edition, *Ethnic and Racial Studies* **19**(4).) London: Routledge. **LD**

ONS/ESRC (1998). *ESRC Review of Government Social Classifications.* Swindon: Office for National Statistics/Economic and Social Research Council. **O**

Ortiz Lira, H. (1976). Some phonetic correlates of the rapid colloquial style. *Journal of the International Phonetic Association* **6**. 13–22. **C**

Orton, H. (1933). *The Phonology of a South Durham Dialect.* London: Kegan Paul, Trench & Trübner. **NC**

Orton, H. & Barry, M. V. (1969). *The Survey of English Dialects,* Vol. 2: *The West Midland Counties.* Leeds: Edward Arnold. **S, W**

Orton, H. & Halliday, W. J. (1963). *The Survey of English Dialects,* Vol. 1: *The Six Northern Counties and the Isle of Man.* Leeds: Edward Arnold. **M, S**

Orton, H., Sanderson, S. & Widdowson, J. (eds) (1978). *The Linguistic Atlas of England.* London: Croom Helm. **NC, S**

Orton, H. & Tilling, P. M. (1970). *The Survey of English Dialects,* Vol. 3: *The East Midland Counties and East Anglia.* Leeds: Edward Arnold. **M, S**

Orton, H. & Wakelin, M. F. (1967). *The Survey of English Dialects,* Vol. 4: *The Southern Counties.* Leeds: Edward Arnold. **M, S**

Påhlsson, C. (1972). *The Northumbrian Burr: A Sociolinguistic Study.* Lund: Gleerup. **NC**

Pandeli, H. (1993). The Articulation of Lingual Consonants: An EPG Study. Unpublished PhD dissertation, University of Cambridge. **O**

Pandeli, H., Eska, J. F., Ball, M. J. & Rahilly, J. (1997). Problems of phonetic transcription: the case of Hiberno-English slit-t. *Journal of the International Phonetic Association* **27**. 65–75. **D**

Patterson, D. (1860). *The Provincialisms of Belfast and the Surrounding Districts Pointed out and Corrected: To Which Is Added an Essay on the Mutual Improvement Societies.* Belfast: Alex Mayne. **LD**

Pegge, S. (1896). *Two Collections of Derbicisms.* London: English Dialect Society. **DN**

Perkell, J. S. & Klatt, D. H. (eds) (1986) *Invariance and Variability in Speech Processes.* Hillsdale, NJ: Lawrence Erlbaum Associates. **DN, O**

Peterson, G. E. & Lehiste, I. (1960). Duration of syllable nuclei in English. *Journal of the Acoustical Society of America* **32**. 693–703. **DN**

Pierrehumbert, J. & Talkin, D. (1992). Lenition of /h/ and glottal stop. In Docherty, G. J. & Ladd, D. R. (eds) pp. 90–119. **DN, L**

Pisoni, D. B. (1997). Some thoughts on 'normalization' in speech perception. In Johnson, K. & Mullenix, J. W. (eds) pp. 9–32. **DN, O**

Pittam, J. (1987). Discrimination of five voice qualities and prediction to perceptual ratings. *Phonetica* **44**. 38–49. **G**

Pitts, A. H. (1982). Urban Influence in Northern Irish English: A Comparison of Variation in Two Communities. Unpublished PhD dissertation, University of Michigan, Ann Arbor. **LD**

Pitts, A. H. (1985). Urban influence on phonological variation in a Northern Irish speech community. *English World-Wide* **6**. 59–85. **LD**

Pitts, A. H. (1989). Is urban influence varb-able? In Fasold, R. W. & Schiffrin, D. (eds) pp. 95–106. **LD**

Poole, M. A. (1982). Religious residential segregation in urban Northern Ireland. In Boal, F. W. & Douglas, J. N. H. (eds) pp. 281–308. **LD**

Preston, D. (ed.) (1993). *American Dialect Research.* Amsterdam: John Benjamins. **SW**

Ramsaran, S. (ed.) (1990). *Studies in the Pronunciation of English: A Commemorative Volume in Honour of A. C. Gimson.* London: Routledge. **NC**

Rand, D. & Sankoff, D. (1988). *Goldvarb: A Variable Rule Application for the Macintosh.* Montréal: Centre de recherches mathématiques, Université de Montréal. **LD**

Reid, E. (1978). Social and stylistic variation in the speech of children: some evidence from Edinburgh. In Trudgill, P. J. (ed.) pp. 158–71. **DN, SW**

Robinson, A. (1969). *Geographical Fieldwork in an Irish Border Area: Londonderry – Moville.* Lincoln: Bishop Grosseteste College of Education. **LD**

Robinson, P. (1997). *Ulster-Scots: A Grammar of the Traditional Written and Spoken Language.* Belfast: The Ullans Press. **LD**

Romaine, S. (1978). Postvocalic /r/ in Scottish English: sound change in progress? In Trudgill, P. J. (ed.) pp. 144–57. **EC, G**

Rose, R. (1971). *Governing Without Consensus: An Irish Perspective.* London: Faber & Faber. **LD**

Rosewarne, D. (1984). Estuary English. *Times Educational Supplement* **42**, 19 October. **C, O**

Rosewarne, D. (1994). Estuary English – tomorrow's RP? *English Today* **37**. 3–8. **O**

Ross, F., Stead, R. & Holderness, T. (1877). *A Glossary of Words used in Holderness in the East Riding of Yorkshire.* London: Trübner & Co. **M**

Rousselot, L'abbé (1891). *Les Modifications Phonétiques du Langage.* Paris: Welter. **DN**

Sabino, R. (1996). A peak at death: assessing continuity and change in an underdocumented language. *Language Variation and Change* **8**. 41–61. **DN**

Schaffer, F. (1972). *The New Town Story.* London: Paladin. **M**

Scherer, K. R. & Giles, H. (eds) (1979). *Social Markers in Speech.* Cambridge: Cambridge University Press. **G**

Schwartz, J. -L., Boë, L. -J., Vallée, N. & Abry, C. (1997). Major trends in vowel system inventories. *Journal of Phonetics* 25. 233–53. NC

Scobbie, J. M., Turk, A. E. & Hewlett, N. (1999). Morphemes, phonetics and lexical items: the case of the Scottish Vowel Length Rule. *Proceedings of the XIVth International Congress of Phonetic Sciences*. University of California, Berkeley. EG

Scollins, R. & Titford, J. (1976/77). *Ey Up Mi Duck! An Affectionate Look at the Speech, History and Folklore of Ilkeston, Derbyshire and the Erewash Valley* (3 volumes). Ilkeston: Scollins & Titford. DN

Sheridan, T. (1781). *A Rhetorical Grammar of the English Language Calculated Solely for the Purpose of Teaching Propriety of Pronunciation and Justness of Delivery, in that Tongue*. Dublin: Price. D

Siegel, J. (1985). Koines and koineization. *Language in Society* 14. 357–78. NC

Simpson, R. (1847). *The Annals of Derry, Showing the Rise and Progress of the Town from the Earliest Accounts on Record to the Plantation under King James I -1613. And Thence of the City of Londonderry to the Present Time*. Londonderry: Hempton. (Facsimile edition, North West Books, Limavady, 1987.) LD

Sivertsen, E. (1960). *Cockney Phonology*. Oslo: Oslo University Press. L

Smith, D. (1994). *North and South*. London: Penguin. M

Speitel, H. (1969). Some Studies in the Dialect of Midlothian. Unpublished PhD dissertation, University of Edinburgh. EC

Sproat, R. & Fujimura, O. (1993). Allophonic variation in English /l/ and its implications for phonetic implementation. *Journal of Phonetics* 21. 291–311. L

Staples, J. H. (1898). Notes on Ulster English dialect. *Transactions of the Philological Society*. 357–87. LD

Stevens, K. N. (1997). Articulatory–acoustic–auditory relationships. In Hardcastle, W. J. & Laver, J. (eds) pp. 462–506. DN

Stringer, P. & Robinson, G. (eds) (1991). *Social Attitudes in Northern Ireland*. Belfast: Blackstaff Press. LD

Stuart-Smith, J. (forthcoming). Glottals past and present: a study of т-glottalling in Glaswegian. To appear in *Leeds Studies in English*. G

Stuart-Smith, J. & Cortina-Borja, M. (1996). Tone-bearing consonants in British Panjabi. Poster paper presented at the Fifth Conference on Laboratory Phonology, Northwestern University, 6–8 July 1996. O

Stuart-Smith, J. & Früh, W. G. (in progress). *Voice Quality in Glaswegian*. G

Survey of Language and Folklore (SLF). Archive, University of Sheffield. S

Survey of Sheffield Usage (SSU). Archive, University of Sheffield. S

Tench, P. (1990). The pronunciation of English in Abercrave. In Coupland, N. & Thomas, A. (eds) pp. 130–41. C

Thelander, M. (ed.) (1996). *Samspel och Variation*. Uppsala: Uppsala Universitet. N

Thomas, A. (ed.) (1997a). *Issues and Methods in Dialectology*. Bangor: University of Wales Press. M

Thomas, A. (1997b). Derry – a spectacular maiden. In Clarke, H. B. (ed.) pp. 69–81. LD

Thomason, S. G. & Kaufman, T. (1988). *Language Contact, Creolization and Genetic Linguistics*. Berkeley: University of California Press. NC

Tieken-Boon van Ostade, I. & Frankis, J. (eds) (1991). *Language Usage and Description*. Amsterdam: Rodopi. C

Todd, G. (1987). *Todd's Geordie Words and Phrases: An Aid to Communication in Tyneside and Thereabouts*. Rothbury, Northumberland: Butler Press. NC

Todd, L. (1984). By their tongue divided: towards an analysis of speech communities in Northern Ireland. *English World-Wide* 5. 159–80. LD

Todd, L. (1989). Cultures in conflict: Varieties of English in Northern Ireland. In Garcia, O. & Otheguy, R. (eds) pp. 335–55. LD

Tollfree, L. F. (1996). Modelling Phonological Variation and Change: Evidence from English Consonants. Unpublished PhD dissertation, University of Cambridge. L

Torgersen, E. (1997). Some Phonological Innovations in Southeastern British English. Unpublished MA dissertation, University of Bergen. **M**

Trudgill, P. J. (1972). Sex, covert prestige and linguistic change in the urban British English of Norwich. *Language in Society* 1. 179–95. **N**

Trudgill, P. J. (1973). Linguistic change and diffusion: description and explanation in sociolinguistic dialect geography. *Language in Society* 3. 215–46. **N**

Trudgill, P. J. (1974). *The Sociolinguistic Differentiation of English in Norwich*. Cambridge: Cambridge University Press. **DN, G, N, S, SW, W**

Trudgill, P. J. (ed.) (1978). *Sociolinguistic Patterns in British English*. London: Edward Arnold. **C, DN, EC, LD, O, SW, W**

Trudgill, P. J. (ed.) (1984). Language in the British Isles. Cambridge: Cambridge University Press. **EC**

Trudgill, P. J. (1986). *Dialects in Contact*. Oxford: Blackwell. **M, N, NC, O**

Trudgill, P. J. (1988). Norwich revisited: recent linguistic changes in an English urban dialect. *English World-Wide* 9. 33–49. **DN, LD, N, O**

Trudgill, P. J. (1990). *The Dialects of England*. Oxford: Blackwell. **M, N, NC**

Trudgill, P. J. (1992). Dialect typology and social structure. In Jahr, E. H. (ed.) pp. 195–211. **M**

Trudgill, P. J. (1996a). Two hundred years of dedialectalisation: the East Anglian short vowel system. In Thelander, M. (ed.) pp. 469–78. **N**

Trudgill, P. J. (1996b). Dialect typology: isolation, social network and phonological structure. In Guy, G., Feagin, C., Schiffrin, D. & Baugh, J. (eds) pp. 3–21. **M**

Trudgill, P. J. (forthcoming). The great East Anglian merger mystery. **N**

Trudgill, P. J. & Foxcroft, T. (1978). On the sociolinguistics of vocalic mergers: transfer and approximation in East Anglia. In Trudgill, P. J. (ed.) pp. 69–79. **N**

Upton, C. & Llamas, C. (forthcoming). Two large-scale and long-term variation surveys: a retrospective and a plan. To appear in Conde-Silvestre, J.C. & Hernández-Campoy, J.M. (eds) *Cuadernos de Filologia Inglesa* 8. Departamento de Filologia Inglesa, Universidad de Murcia. **O, S**

Upton, C., Parry, D. & Widdowson, J. D. A. (1994). *Survey of English Dialects: The Dictionary and Grammar*. London: Routledge. **S**

Upton, C. & Widdowson, J. D. A. (1996). *An Atlas of English Dialects*. Oxford: Oxford University Press. **M**

Valdmann, A. (ed.) (1972). *Papers in Linguistics and Phonetics to the Memory of Pierre Delattre*. The Hague: Mouton. **O**

Viereck, W. (1966). *Phonematische Analyse des Dialekts von Gateshead upon Tyne/Co. Durham*. Hamburg: Cram, de Gruyter & Co. **NC**

Viereck, W. (1968). A diachronic-structural analysis of a northern English urban dialect. *Leeds Studies in English* 2. 65–79. **NC, O**

Wakelin, M. F. (ed.) (1972). *Patterns in the Folk Speech of the British Isles*. London: Athlone Press. **LD**

Walters, G. S. (1955). The Phonology of the Living Dialect of Hoylake, Cheshire. Unpublished BA dissertation, University of Leeds. **W**

Wang, W. (1969). Competing changes as a cause of residue. *Language* 45. 9–25. **D**

Wardhaugh, R. (1998). *An Introduction to Sociolinguistics* (3rd edn). Oxford: Blackwell. **O**

Warkentyne, H. J. (ed.) (1985). *Papers from the Fifth International Conference on Methods in Dialectology*. University of Victoria. **G**

Watt, D. J. L. (1996). Out of the frying pan into the fire: remerger of (ɜ) in Tyneside English? *Newcastle and Durham Working Papers in Linguistics* 4. 299–314. **NC**

Watt, D. J. L. (1998). Variation and Change in the Vowel System of Tyneside English. Unpublished PhD dissertation, University of Newcastle. **DN, NC, O**

Watt, D. J. L. & Tillotson, J. (1999). A spectrographic analysis of vowel fronting in Bradford English. *Leeds Working Papers in Linguistics and Phonetics* 7. **NC**.

Watts, R. & Bex, T. (eds) (forthcoming). *The Standard Language Question.* Oxford: Oxford University Press. **NC**

Wells, J. C. (1970). Local accents in England and Wales. *Journal of Linguistics* **6**. 231–52. **C**

Wells, J. C. (1973). *Jamaican Pronunciation in London.* Oxford: Blackwell. **O**

Wells, J. C. (1982). *Accents of English* (3 vols). Cambridge: Cambridge University Press. **C, D, DN, EC, EG, G, L, LD, M, N, NC, O, SW, W**

Wells, J. C. (1994). The Cockneyfication of R. P. ? In Melchers, G. & Johannessen, N. -L. (eds) pp. 198–205. **M, NC**

Wettstein, P. (1942). The Phonology of a Berwickshire Dialect. Unpublished PhD dissertation, University of Zürich. Zürich: Schüler S. A. Bienne. **EG**

Widdowson, J. D. A. (1992/93). From Hunter to Newspeak: dialect study in Sheffield, 1829–1984. *Lore and Language* **11**(2). 199–221. **S**

Williams, A. & Kerswill, P. (1997). Investigating dialect change in an English new town. In Thomas, A. (ed.) pp. 46–54. **M**

Williams, C. H. (1990). The anglicisation of Wales. In Coupland, N. & Thomas, A. (eds) pp. 19–47. **C**

Windsor Lewis, J. (1964). Glamorgan Spoken English. MS. **C**

Windsor Lewis, J. (1969). *A Guide to English Pronunciation.* Oslo: Universitetsforlaget. **C**

Windsor Lewis, J. (ed.) (1995). *Studies in General and English Phonetics: Essays in Honour of Professor J. D. O'Connor.* London: Routledge. **LD**

Wolfram, W. (1991). *Dialects and American English.* Englewood Cliffs, NJ: Prentice Hall. **NC**

Wrede, F. (1919). Zur Entwicklungsgeschichte der deutschen Mundartforschung. *Zeitschrift für deutsche Mundarten.* 3–18. **NC**

Wright, J. (1905). *The English Dialect Grammar.* Oxford: Henry Frowde. **DN, W**

Wright, P. (1975). *The Derbyshire Drawl – How it is Spoke.* Whitehaven: Dalesman Books. **DN**

Wright, S. (1986). The interaction of sociolinguistic and phonetically-conditioned CSPs in Cambridge English: auditory and electropalatographic evidence. *Cambridge Papers in Phonetics and Experimental Linguistics* **5**. **L**

Wright, S. (1989). The effects of speech style and speaking rate on /l/-vocalisation in local Cambridge English. *York Papers in Linguistics* **13**. 335–65. **L**

Yaeger-Dror, M. (1994). Phonetic evidence for sound change in Québec French. In Keating, P. A. (ed.) pp. 267–92. **M**

Yaeger-Dror, M. (1997). Contraction of negatives as evidence of variance in register-specific interactive rules. *Language Variation and Change* **9**. 1–36. **DN**

Index

Names

Subjects